THE

INFLUENCE OF SEA POWER

UPON THE

FRENCH REVOLUTION AND EMPIRE

1793–1812

BY

CAPTAIN A. T. MAHAN, D.C.L., LL.D.

UNITED STATES NAVY

IN TWO VOLUMES

VOL. II.

GREENWOOD PRESS, PUBLISHERS
NEW YORK

CONTENTS OF VOL. II.

CHAPTER XII.

EVENTS ON THE CONTINENT, 1798–1800.

DISORDERS OF FRANCE UNDER THE DIRECTORY. — DISASTROUS
WAR OF THE SECOND COALITION. — ESTABLISHMENT OF THE
CONSULATE. — BONAPARTE OVERTHROWS AUSTRIA AND FRAMES
AGAINST GREAT BRITAIN THE ARMED NEUTRALITY OF 1800. —
PEACE OF LUNÉVILLE WITH AUSTRIA.

CHAPTER XIII.

EVENTS OF 1801.

BRITISH EXPEDITION TO THE BALTIC. — BATTLE OF COPENHAGEN.
— BONAPARTE'S FUTILE ATTEMPTS TO CONTEST CONTROL OF
THE SEA. — HIS CONTINENTAL POLICY. — PRELIMINARIES OF
PEACE WITH GREAT BRITAIN, OCTOBER, 1801. — INFLUENCE
OF SEA POWER, SO FAR, ON THE COURSE OF THE REVOLUTION.

CHAPTER XIV.

OUTLINE OF EVENTS FROM THE SIGNATURE OF THE PRELIMINA
RIES TO THE RUPTURE OF THE PEACE OF AMIENS.

CHAPTER XV.

The Trafalgar Campaign to the Spanish Declaration of War. May, 1803—December, 1804.

Preparations for the Invasion of England. — The Great Flotilla. — Napoleon's Military and Naval Combinations, and British Naval Strategy. — Essential Unity of Napoleon's Purpose.—Causes of Spanish War.

CHAPTER XVI.

The Trafalgar Campaign — Concluded.
January — October, 1805.

Successive Modifications of Napoleon's Plan. — Narrative of Naval Movements. — Final Failure of Napoleon's Naval Combinations. — War with Austria, and Battle of Austerlitz. — Battle of Trafalgar. — Vital Change imposed upon Napoleon's Policy by the Result of the Naval Campaign.

CHAPTER XVII.

CHAPTER XVIII.

THE WARFARE AGAINST COMMERCE, 1806–1812.

THE BERLIN AND MILAN DECREES OF NAPOLEON, 1806 AND 1807.
— THE BRITISH ORDERS IN COUNCIL, 1807–1809. — ANALYSIS OF
THE POLICY OF THESE MEASURES OF THE TWO BELLIGERENTS.
— OUTLINE OF CONTEMPORARY LEADING EVENTS.

CHAPTER XIX.

SUMMARY. — THE FUNCTION OF SEA POWER AND THE POLICY OF
GREAT BRITAIN IN THE REVOLUTIONARY AND NAPOLEONIC
WARS.

NOTE. — The references to the "Correspondance de Napoléon" are to the quarto edition, in thirty-two volumes, published in Paris between 1858 and 1869.

INDEX

LIST OF ILLUSTRATIONS.

VOLUME II.

MAP AND BATTLE PLANS.

THE

INFLUENCE OF SEA POWER

UPON THE

FRENCH REVOLUTION AND EMPIRE.

CHAPTER XII.

EVENTS ON THE CONTINENT, 1798–1800.

DISORDERS OF FRANCE UNDER THE DIRECTORY.—DISASTROUS WAR OF THE SECOND COALITION.—ESTABLISHMENT OF THE CONSULATE.— BONAPARTE OVERTHROWS AUSTRIA AND FRAMES AGAINST GREAT BRITAIN THE ARMED NEUTRALITY OF 1800.— PEACE OF LUNÉVILLE WITH AUSTRIA.

WHILE Bonaparte was crossing the Syrian desert and chafing over the siege of Acre, the long gathering storm of war known as the Second Coalition had broken upon France. It had been preceded by a premature outburst of hostility on the part of the Two Sicilies, induced by the excitement consequent upon the battle of the Nile and fostered by Nelson;[1] who, however influenced, was largely responsible for the action of the court. Despite the advice of Austria to wait, a summons was sent to the French on the 22d of November, 1798, to evacuate the Papal States and Malta. A Neapolitan army of fifty thousand men marched upon Rome; and five thousand were carried by Nelson's ships to Leghorn with the idea of harassing the confidently-expected retreat of the enemy.[2]

---

[1] See, for instance, his letter to Lady Hamilton, Oct. 3, 1798 (Disp., vol. iii. p. 140), which is but one of many similar expressions in his correspondence.

[2] Nels. Disp., vol. iii. p. 177.

Leghorn was at once surrendered; but in the south the campaign ended in utter disaster. The French general Championnet, having but fifteen thousand men, evacuated Rome, which the Neapolitans consequently entered without opposition; but their field operations met with a series of humiliating reverses, due partly to bad generalship and partly to inexperience and the lack of mutual confidence often found among untried troops. The French re-entered Rome seventeen days after the campaign opened; and the king of Naples, who had made a triumphal entry into the city, hurried back to his capital, called upon the people to rise in defence of their homes against the invaders, and then fled with the royal family to Palermo, Nelson giving them and the Hamiltons passage on board his flagship. The peasantry and the populace flew to arms, in obedience to the king's proclamation and to their own feelings of hatred to the republicans. Under the guidance of the priests and monks, with hardy but undisciplined fury, they in the field harassed the advance of the French, and in the capital rose against the upper classes, who were suspected of secret intelligence with the enemy. Championnet, however, continued to advance; and on the 23d of January, 1799, Naples was stormed by his troops. After the occupation, a series of judicious concessions to the prejudices of the people induced their cheerful submission. The conquest was followed by the birth to the Batavian, Helvetian, Ligurian, Cisalpine, and Roman republics, of a little sister, named the Parthenopeian Republic, destined to a troubled existence as short as its name was long.

The Neapolitan declaration of war caused the ruin of the Piedmontese monarchy. The Directory, seeing that war with Austria was probable, decided to occupy all Piedmont. The king abdicated on the 9th of December, 1798; retiring to the island of Sardinia, which was left in his possession. Piedmont was soon after annexed to the French Republic.

On the 20th of February, 1799, having failed to receive

from the emperor the explanations demanded concerning the entrance of the Russian troops into his dominions, the Directory ordered its generals to advance. Jourdan was to command in Germany, Masséna in Switzerland, and Schérer in Italy. The armies of the republic, enfeebled by two years of peace and by the economies of a government always embarrassed for money and deficient in executive vigor, were everywhere inferior to those of the enemy ; and the plan of campaign, providing for several operations out of reach of mutual support, has been regarded by military critics as essentially vicious.

Jourdan crossed the Rhine at Strasburg on the first of March, advancing through the Black Forest upon the head waters of the Danube. On the 6th Masséna crossed the river above Lake Constance, and moved through the Alps toward the Tyrol, driving the Austrians before him on his right and.centre ; but on the left he entirely failed to carry the important position of Feldkirch, upon which would depend the communication between his left and the right of Jourdan, if the latter succeeded in pushing on as ordered. This, however, he was unable to do. After some severe partial encounters there was fought on March 25th, at Stokach, near the north-west extremity of Lake Constance, a pitched battle in which the French were defeated. Jourdan then saw that he had to do with largely superior forces and retreated upon the Rhine, which he recrossed above Strasburg on the 6th of April.

On the 26th of March, the day after the defeat of Jourdan at Stokach, Schérer in Italy attacked the Austrians, who were occupying the line of the Adige, rendered famous by Bonaparte in his great campaign of 1796. The events of that day were upon the whole favorable to the French ; but Schérer showed irresolution and consequent delay in improving such advantages as he had obtained. After a week of manœuvring the two armies met in battle on the 5th of April near Magnano, and after a long and bloody struggle the French were forced to give way. On the 6th, the day that Jourdan retreated across the Rhine, Schérer also fell back behind the Mincio. Not feeling secure there, although the Austrians did not pursue, he threw garrisons into the posts on that line, and on the 12th retired behind the Adda; sending word to Macdonald, Championnet's successor at Naples, to prepare to evacuate that kingdom and bring to northern Italy the thirty thousand men now so sorely needed.

Jourdan having offered his resignation after the battle of Stokach, the armies in Germany and in Switzerland were united under the command of Masséna; whose long front, extending from the Engadine, around the sources of the Inn, along the Rhine as low as Dusseldorf, was held by but one hundred thousand men, of whom two-thirds were in Switzerland. In the position which Switzerland occupies, thrust out to the eastward from the frontiers of France, having on the one flank the fields of Germany, on the other those of Italy, and approachable from both sides by many passes, the difficulties of defence are great;[1] and Masséna found himself menaced from both quarters, as well as in front, by enemies whose aggregate force was far superior to his own. Pressed along the line of the Rhine both above and below Lake Constance, he was compelled to retire upon works constructed by him around Zurich; being unable to prevent the junction of the enemy's forces, which approached from both directions. On the 4th of June the Austrians assaulted his lines; and, though the attack was repulsed, Masséna thought necessary to evacu-

---

[1] In an entirely open country, without natural obstacles, there are few or none of those strategic points, by occupying which in a central position an inferior force is able to multiply its action against the divided masses of the enemy. On the other hand, in a very broken country, such as Switzerland, the number of important strategic points, passes, heads of valleys, bridges, etc., are so multiplied, that either some must be left unoccupied, or the defenders lose, by dissemination, the advantage which concentration upon one or two controlling centres usually confers.

ate the place forty-eight hours later, falling back upon a position on the Albis mountains a few miles in his rear.

During the two months over which these contests between Masséna and his enemies were spread, the affairs of the French in Italy were growing daily more desperate. After the victory of Magnano the Austrians were joined, on the 24th of April, by twenty thousand Russians under Marshal Suwarrow, who became general-in-chief of the allied armies. On the 26th Schérer turned over his command to Moreau ; but, although the latter was an officer of very great capacity, the change was too late to avoid all the impending disasters. On the 27th the passage of the Adda was forced by the allies, and on the 29th they entered Milan ; the French retiring upon the Ticino, breaking down the bridges over the Po, and taking steps to secure their communications with Genoa. Pausing but a moment, they again retreated in two columns upon Turin and Alessandria ; Moreau drawing together near the latter place the bulk of his force, about twenty thousand men, and sending pressing invitations to Macdonald to hasten the northward march of the army of Naples. The new positions were taken the 7th of May, and it was not till the 5th that the Austro-Russians, delayed by the destruction of the bridges, could cross the Po. But the insurrection of the country in all directions was showing how little the submission of the people and the establishment of new republics were accompanied by any hearty fidelity to the French cause ; and on the 18th, leaving a garrison in Alessandria, Moreau retreated upon the Apennines. On the 6th of June his troops were distributed among the more important points on the crest of the range, from Pontremoli, above Spezia, to Loano, and all his convoys had safely crossed the mountains to the latter point. It was at this moment that he had an interview with Admiral Bruix, whose fleet had anchored in Vado Bay two days before.[1]

[1] See ante, vol. i. p. 313.

While events were thus passing in Upper Italy, Macdonald, in obedience to his orders, evacuated Naples on the 7th of May, at the moment when Moreau was taking his position on the Apennines and Bonaparte making his last fruitless assault upon Acre. Leaving garrisons at the principal strong places of the kingdom, he hurried north, and on the 25th entered Florence, where, though his junction with Moreau was far from being effected, he was for the first time in sure communication with him by courier. There were two routes that Macdonald might take, — either by the sea-shore, which was impracticable for artillery, or else, crossing the Apennines, he would find a better road in the plain south of the Po, through Modena and Parma, and by it might join the army of Italy under the walls of Tortona. The latter course was chosen, and after a delay too much prolonged the army of Naples set out on the 9th of June. All went well with it until the 17th, when, having passed Modena and Parma, routing the allied detachments which he encountered, Macdonald reached the Trebia. Here, however, he was met by Suwarrow, and after three days' desperate fighting was forced to retreat by the road he came, to his old positions on the other side of the mountains. On the same day the citadel of Turin capitulated to the allies. After pursuing Macdonald some distance, Suwarrow turned back to meet Moreau, and compelled him also to retire to his former posts. This disastrous attempt at a junction within the enemies' lines cost the French fifteen thousand men. It now became necessary for the army of Naples to get to Genoa at all costs by the Corniche road, and this it was able to do through the inactivity of the enemy, — due, so Jomini says, not to Suwarrow, but to the orders from Vienna. By the middle of July both armies were united under Moreau. As a result of the necessary abandonment of Naples by the French troops, the country fell at once into the power of the armed peasantry, except the garrisons left in a few strong places ; and these, by the help of the British navy, were also reduced by the 1st of August.

This striking practical illustration of the justness of Bonaparte's views, concerning the danger incurred by the French in Upper Italy through attempting to occupy Naples, was followed by further disasters. On the 21st of July the citadel of Alessandria capitulated ; and this loss was followed on the 30th by that of Mantua, which had caused Bonaparte so much delay and 'trouble in 1796. The latter success was somewhat dearly bought, inasmuch as the emperor of Germany had positively forbidden Suwarrow to make any further advance before Mantua fell.[1] Opportunity was thus given for the junction of Moreau and Macdonald, and for the reorganization of the latter's army, which the affairs of the Trebia and the subsequent precipitate retreat had left in a state of prostration and incoherence, from which it did not recover for a month. The delay would have been still more favorable to the French had Mantua resisted to the last moment; but it capitulated at a time when it could still have held out for several days, and Suwarrow was thus enabled to bring up the besieging corps to his support, unknown to the enemy.

Meanwhile Moreau had been relieved by Joubert, one of the most brilliant of the young generals who had fought under Bonaparte in Italy. The newcomer, reaching his headquarters on the 2d of August, at once determined upon the offensive, moved thereto by the wish to relieve Mantua, and also by the difficulty of feeding his army in the sterile mountains now that ruin had befallen the coastwise traffic of Genoa, by which supplies had before been maintained.[2] On the 10th of August the French advanced. On the 14th they were in position at Novi ; and there Joubert saw, but too late, that Suwarrow's army was far larger than he had

---

[1] It is said that the old marshal on receiving these orders cried: "This is the way armies are ruined."

[2] Jomini, Guerres de la Rév. Fran., livre xv. p. 124. Martin, Hist. de France depuis 1789, vol. iii. p. 50. It was just at this moment that Nelson sent a division to the Gulf of Genoa to co-operate with Suwarrow. (Nels. Disp., vol. iii. p. 431.)

expected, and that the rumor of Mantua's fall, which he had refused to credit, must be true. He intended to retreat; but the Russian marshal attacked the next morning, and after a fierce struggle, which the strength of their position enabled the French to prolong till night, they were driven from the field with heavy loss, four general officers and thirty-seven guns being captured. Joubert was killed early in the day; and Moreau, who had remained to aid him until familiar with all the details of his command, again took the temporary direction of the army by the agreement of the other generals. Immediately after the battle Suwarrow sent into the late Papal States a division which, co-operating with the Neapolitan royalists and the British navy, forced the French to evacuate the new Roman republic on the 27th of September, 1799.

At this moment of success new dispositions were taken by the allied governments, apparently through the initiative of Austria; which wished, by removing Suwarrow, to keep entire control of Italy in her own hands. This change of plan, made at so critical a moment, stopped the hitherto triumphant progress; and, by allowing time for Bonaparte to arrive and to act, turned victory into defeat. By it Suwarrow was to march across the Alps into Switzerland, and there take charge of the campaign against Masséna, having under him an army composed mainly of Russians. The Archduke Charles, now commanding in Switzerland, was to depart with the greater part of the Austrian contingent to the lower Rhine, where he would by his operations support the invasion of Holland then about to begin.

On the 13th of August,—the same day that Bruix entered Brest, carrying with him the Spanish fleet, and two days before the battle of Novi,—the expedition against Holland, composed of seventeen thousand Russians and thirty thousand British troops, sailed from England. Delayed first by light winds and then by heavy weather, the landing was not made till the 27th of the month. On the 31st the Archduke, taking with him thirty-six thousand Austrians, started for the lower Rhine, leaving General Hotze and the Russian Korsakoff to make head against Masséna until the arrival of Suwarrow. The latter, on the 11th of September, immediately after the surrender of Tortona, began his northward march.

At the moment the Archduke assumed his new command, the French on the lower Rhine, crossing at Mannheim, invested and bombarded Philipsburg; and their operations seemed so far serious as to draw him and a large part of his force in the same direction. This greatly diminished one of the difficulties confronting Masséna in the offensive movement he then had in contemplation. Hearing at the same time that Suwarrow had started from Italy, he made his principal attack from his left upon the Russians before Zurich on the 25th of September, the right wing of his long line advancing in concert against the Austrian position east of Lake Zurich upon its inlet, the Linth. Each effort was completely successful, and decisive; the enemy being in both directions driven back, and forced to recross the streams above and below the lake. Suwarrow, after a very painful march and hard fighting, reached his first appointed rendezvous at Mutten two days after the battle of Zurich had been lost; and the corps that were to have met him there, fearing their retreat would be cut off, had not awaited his arrival. The old marshal with great difficulty fought his way through the mountains to Ilanz, where at length he assembled his exhausted and shattered forces on the 9th of October, the day on which Bonaparte landed at Fréjus on his return from Egypt. By that time Switzerland was entirely cleared of Russians and Austrians. The river Rhine, both above and below Lake Constance, marked the dividing line between the belligerents.

The Anglo-Russian attack upon Holland had no better

fate. Landing upon the peninsula between the Zuyder Zee and the North Sea, the allies were for awhile successful; but their movements were cautious and slow, giving time for the local resistance to grow and for re-enforcements to come up. The remnants of the Dutch navy were surrendered and taken back to England; but the Duke of York, who had chief command of the allied troops, was compelled on the 18th of October to sign a convention, by which the invading force was permitted to retire unmolested by the first of December.

During the three remaining months of 1799 some further encounters took place in Germany and Italy. In the latter the result was a succession of disasters to the French, ending with the capitulation, on the 4th of December, of Coni, their last remaining stronghold in Piedmont, and the retreat of the army into the Riviera of Genoa. Corfu and the Ionian Islands having been reduced by the combined Russian and Turkish fleets in the previous March, and Ancona surrendered on the 10th of November, all Bonaparte's conquests in Italy and the Adriatic had been lost to France when the Directory fell. The brave soldiers of the army of Italy, destitute and starving, without food, without pay, without clothing or shoes, without even wood for camp-fires in the bitter winter nights on the slopes of the Apennines, deserted in crowds and made their way to the interior. In some regiments none but officers and non-commissioned officers were left. An epidemic born of want and exposure carried off men by hundreds. Championnet, overwhelmed by his misfortunes and by the sight of the misery surrounding him, fell ill and died. Bonaparte, now First Consul, sent Masséna to replace him.

In Germany nothing decisive occurred in the field; but in consequence of some disagreements of opinion between himself and the Archduke, Suwarrow declined further co-operation, and, alleging the absolute need of rest for his soldiers after their frightful exposure in Switzerland, marched them at the end of October into winter quarters in Bavaria. This closed the share of the Russians in the second coalition. The Czar, who had embarked in the war with the idea of restoring the rights of monarchs and the thrones that had been overturned, was dissatisfied both with the policy of Austria, which looked to her own pre-dominance in Italy, and with Great Britain. A twelve-month more was to see him at the head of a league of the northern states against the maritime claims of the great Sea Power, and completely won over to the friendship of Bonaparte by the military genius and wily flattery of the renowned captain.

During this disastrous year, in which France lost all Italy except the narrow strip of sea-coast about Genoa, and after months of desperate struggle had barely held her own in Switzerland, Germany, and Holland, the internal state of the country was deplorable. The Revolutionary govern-ment by the Committee of Public Safety had contrived, by the use of the extraordinary powers granted to it, to meet with greater or less success the demands of the passing hour ; although in so doing it was continually accumulat-ing embarrassments against a future day of reckoning. The Directory, deprived of the extraordinary powers of its predecessor, had succeeded to these embarrassments, and the day of reckoning had arrived. It has been seen how the reactionary spirit, which followed the rule of blood, had prevailed more and more until, in 1797, the political composition of the two Councils was so affected by it as to produce a strong conflict between them and the executive. This dead-lock had been overcome and harmony restored by the violent measures of September, 1797, by which two Directors and a number of members of the legislature had been forcibly expelled from their office. The parties, of two very different shades of opinion, to which the ejected members belonged, had not, however, ceased to exist. In 1798, in the yearly elections to replace one-third of the legislature, they again returned a body of representatives sufficient to put the Councils in opposition to the Directory; but this year the choice of the electors was baffled by a system of double returns. The sitting Councils, of the same political party as the Directory, pronounced upon these, taking care in so doing to insure that the majority in the new bodies should be the same as in the old. In May, 1799, however, the same circumstance again recurred. The fact is particularly interesting, as showing the opposition which was felt toward the government throughout the country.

This opposition was due to a cause which rarely fails to make governments unpopular. The Directory had been unsuccessful. It was called upon to pay the bills due to the public expectation of better things when once the war was over. This it was not able to do. Though peace had been made with the continent, there remained so many matters of doubt and contention that large armies had to be maintained. The expenses of the state went on, but the impoverished nation cried out against the heavy taxation laid to meet them; the revenues continually fell short of the expenditures, and the measures proposed by the ministers to remedy this evil excited vehement criticisms. The unpopularity of the government, arising from inefficient action, reacted upon and increased the weakness which was inherent in its cumbrous, many-headed form. Hence there resulted, from the debility of the head, an impotence which permeated all the links of the executive administration down to the lowest members.

In France itself the disorder and anarchy prevailing in the interior touched the verge of social dissolution.[1] Throughout the country, but especially in the south and west, prevailed brigandage on a large scale — partly political, partly of the ordinary highway type. There were

[1] The phrase is that of Thiers. Hist. de la Rév., vol. x. p. 353.

constant reports of diligences and mail-wagons stopped,[1] of public treasure plundered, of republican magistrates assassinated. Disorganization and robbery spread throughout the army, a natural result of small pay, irregularly received, and of the system of contributions, administered with little responsibility by the commanders of armies in the field. The attempt of the government to check and control this abuse was violently resented by generals, both of the better and the worse class; by the one as reflecting upon their character and injuring their position, by the other as depriving them of accustomed though unlawful gains. Two men of unblemished repute, Joubert and Championnet, came to a direct issue with the Directory upon this point. Joubert resigned the command of the army of Italy, in which Bernadotte from the same motive refused to replace him; while Championnet, in Naples, compelled the commissioner of the Directory to leave the kingdom. For this act, however, he was deprived and brought to a court-martial.

From the weakness pervading the administration and from the inadequate returns of the revenue, the government was driven to extraordinary measures and to the anticipation of its income. Greater and more onerous taxes were laid; and, as the product of these was not immediate, purchases had to be made at long and uncertain credit, and consequently were exorbitant in price while deficient in quantity and quality. From this arose much suffering among all government employés, but especially among the soldiers, who needed the first attention, and whose distress led them easily to side with their officers

---

[1] A curious evidence of the insecurity of the highways is afforded by an ordinance issued by Bonaparte a year after he became First Consul (Jan. 7, 1801), that no regular diligence should travel without carrying a corporal and four privates, with muskets and twenty rounds, and in addition, at night, two mounted gendarmes. If specie to the value of over 50,000 francs were carried, there must be four gendarmes by day and night. (Corr. de Nap., vol. vi. p. 697.)

against the administration. Contracts so made only staved off the evil day, at the price of increasing indebtedness for the state and of growing corruption among the contractor class and the officials dealing with them. Embarrassment and disorder consequently increased apace without any proportionate vigor in the external action of the government, and the effects were distributed among and keenly felt by all individuals, except the small number whose ability or whose corruptness enables them to grow rich when, and as, society becomes most distressed. The creditors of the nation, and especially the holders of bonds, could with difficulty obtain even partial payment. In the general distrust and perplexity individuals and communities took to hoarding both money and food, moved by the dangers of transit and by fear of the scarcity which they saw to be impending. This stagnation of internal circulation was accompanied by the entire destruction of maritime commerce, due to the pressure of the British navy and to the insane decree of Nivôse 29 (January 19, 1798).[1] Both concurred to paralyze the energies of the people, to foster indolence and penury, and by sheer want to induce a state of violence with which the executive was unable to cope.

When to this internal distress were added the military disasters just related, the outcry became loud and universal. All parties united against the Directors, who did not dare in 1799 to repeat the methods by which in the two previous years a majority had been obtained in the legislature. On the 18th of June the new Councils were able to force a change in the composition of the Directory, further enfeebling it through the personal weakness of the new members. These hastened to reverse many of the measures of their predecessors, but no change of policy could restore the lost prestige. The effect of these steps was only further to depress that branch of the government which, in so critical a moment and in so disordered a society, should overbear

[1] See *post,* Chapter XVII.

all others and save the state — not by discussion, but by action.

Such was the condition of affairs found by Bonaparte when he returned from Egypt. The revolution of Brumaire 18 (November 9, 1799) threw into his hands uncontrolled power. This he proceeded at once to use with the sagacity and vigor that rarely failed him in his early prime. The administration of the country was reconstituted on lines which sacrificed local independence, but invigorated the grasp of the central executive, and made its will felt in every corner of the land. Vexatious measures of the preceding government were repealed, and for them was substituted a policy of liberal conciliation, intended to rally all classes of Frenchmen to the support of the new rule. In the West and North, in La Vendée, Brittany, and Normandy, the insurrection once suppressed by Hoche had again raised its head against the Directory. To the insurgents Bonaparte offered reasonable inducements to submission, while asserting his firm determination to restore authority at any cost; and the rapid gathering of sixty thousand troops in the rebellious districts proved his resolution to use for that purpose a force so overwhelming, that the completion of its task would release it by the return of spring, to take the field against external foes. Before the end of February the risings were suppressed, and this time forever. Immediate steps were taken to put the finances on a sounder basis, and to repair the military disasters of the last twelvemonth. To the two principal armies, of the Rhine and of Italy, were sent respectively Moreau and Masséna, the two greatest generals of the republic after Bonaparte himself; and money advanced by Parisian bankers was forwarded to relieve the more pressing wants of the destitute soldiery.

At the same time that these means were used to recover France herself from the condition of debility into which she had fallen, the first consul made a move calculated either to gain for her the time she yet needed, or, in case it failed, to rally to his support all classes in the state. Departing from the usual diplomatic routine, he addressed a personal letter to the king of Great Britain and to the emperor of Germany, deploring the existing war, and expressing a wish that negotiations for peace might be opened. The reply from both sovereigns came through the ordinary channels of their respective ministries. Austria said civilly that she could not negotiate apart from her allies; and furthermore, that the war being only to preserve Europe from universal disorder, due to the unstable and aggressive character of the French governments since the Revolution, no stable peace could be made until there was some guarantee for a change of policy. This she could not yet recognize in the new administration, which owed its existence only to the violent overthrow of its predecessor. Great Britain took substantially the same ground. Peace was worse than worthless, if insecure; and experience had shown that no defence except that of steady and open hostility was availing, while the system which had prevailed in France remained the same. She could not recognize a change of system in the mere violent substitution of one set of rulers for another. Disavowing any claim to prescribe to France what should be her form of government, the British ministry nevertheless said distinctly that the best guarantee for a permanent change of policy would be the restoration of the Bourbons. This seemingly impolitic suggestion insured — what was very possibly its object — the continuance of the war until were realized the advantages that seemed about to accrue. Not only were the conditions at that time overwhelmingly in favor of the allies, but there was also every probability of the reduction of Egypt and Malta, and of further decisive successes in Italy. These, if obtained, would be so many cards strengthening their hands in the diplomatic game to be played in the negotiations for peace. Believing, as the British ministry of that day assuredly did, that a secure peace could only be based on the exhaustion, and not upon the moderation or good faith, of their enemy, it would have been the height of folly to concede time, or submit to that vacillation of purpose and relaxation of tension which their own people would certainly feel, if negotiations were opened.

Nor were these military and moral considerations the only ones affecting the decision of the government. Despite the immense burdens imposed by the war to support her own military expenditures and furnish the profuse subsidies paid to her allies, the power of the country to bear them was greatly increased. Thanks to the watery rampart which secured peace within her borders, Great Britain had now become the manufactory and warehouse of Europe. The commercial and maritime prostration of Holland and France, her two great rivals in trade and manufactures, had thrown into her hands these sources of their prosperity; and she, through the prodigious advances of the ten years' peace, was fully ready to profit by them. By the capture of their foreign possessions and the ruin of the splendid French colony in Haïti, she now controlled the chief regions whence were drawn the tropical products indispensable to Europeans. She monopolized their markets as well as the distribution of their produce. Jealously reserving to British merchant shipping the trade of her own and conquered colonies, she yet met the immense drain made by the navy upon her merchant seamen by relaxing the famous Navigation Laws; permitting her ships to be manned by foreigners, and foreign ships to engage in branches of her commerce closed to them in time of peace. But while thus encouraging neutrals to carry the surplus trade, whose rapid growth was outstripping the capacity of her own shipping, she rigorously denied their right to do as much for her enemies. These severe restrictions, which her uncontrolled sea-power enabled her to maintain, were re-enforced by suicidal edicts of the French government, retaliating upon the same unhappy neutrals the injury their weakness compelled them to accept from the mistress of the seas, — thus driving them from French shores, and losing a concurrence essential to French export and import. In this time of open war no flag was so safe from annoyance as the British, for none other was protected by a powerful navy. Neutrals sought its convoy against French depredations, and the navigation of the world was now swayed by this one great power, whom its necessities had not yet provoked to lay a yoke heavier than the oppressed could bear.

To this control of the carrying trade, and of so much of the agricultural production of the globe, was added a growing absorption of the manufactures of Europe, due to the long war paralyzing the peaceful energies of the continental peoples. In the great system of circulation and exchange, everything thus tended more and more to Great Britain; which was indicated as the natural centre for accumulation and distribution by its security, its accessibility, and its nearness to the continent on which were massed the largest body of consumers open to maritime commerce. Becoming thus the chief medium through which the business of the civilized world was carried on and its wants supplied, her capital grew apace; and was steadily applied, by the able hands in which it accumulated, to develop, by increased production and increased facilities of carriage, the powers of the country to supply demands that were continually increasing on both sides of the Atlantic. The foreign trade, export and import, which in 1792, the last year of peace, had amounted to £44,500,000, rose in 1797 to £50,000,000, and in 1800 to £73,700,000. Encouraged by these evident proofs of growing wealth, the ministry was able so to increase the revenue that its receipts, independent of extraordinary war taxes, far exceeded anything it had ever been before, "or," to use Pitt's words, "anything which the most sanguine hopes could have anticipated. If," he continued, " we compare this year of war with former years of peace, we shall in the produce of our revenue and in the extent of our commerce behold a spectacle at once paradoxical, inexplicable, and astonishing. We have increased our external and internal commerce to a greater pitch than ever it was before ; and we may look to the present as the proudest year that has ever occurred for this country." [1]

With such resources to sustain the armies of their allies, and certain of keeping a control of the sea unparalleled even in the history of Great Britain, the ministry looked hopefully forward to a year which should renew and complete the successes of 1799. They reckoned without Bonaparte, as Bonaparte in his turn reckoned again and again without Nelson.

Russia took no more part in the coalition ; but the forces of Germany, under the control of Austria and subsidized by Great Britain, either actually in the field or holding the fortified posts on which the operations depended, amounted to something over two hundred and fifty thousand men. Of these, one hundred and twenty-five thousand under Mélas were in Italy. The remainder under General Kray were in Germany, occupying the angle formed by the Rhine at Bâle, where, after flowing west from Lake Constance, it turns abruptly north for the remainder of its course. The plan of campaign was to stand on the defensive in Germany, holding in check the enemies there opposed to them, and in Italy to assume a vigorous offensive, so as to drive the French finally out of the country. That achieved, the idea was entertained of entering France at the extreme south, and possibly investing Toulon, supported by the British navy.

When Bonaparte first took charge, there remained to France only two hundred and fifty thousand soldiers, of whom at the opening of the campaign of 1800 there were in the field, opposed to the Austrians, but one hundred and

[1] Speech of February 18, 1801.

sixty-five thousand. One hundred thousand conscripts
were called for; but time would be needed to turn these
into soldiers, even with the advantage of the nucleus of
veterans around whom they would be gathered.. The equipment and provisioning both of the old and new levies also
required time and effort. Bonaparte's project was to assume the offensive in Germany, turning there the position
of the Austrians, and driving them northward from the
Rhine towards the head waters of the Danube. For this
great operation the army under Moreau was raised to an
equality with the enemy opposed to him. ⁻ Masséna in Italy
was directed to stand solely on the defensive, concentrating
around Genoa the bulk of the thirty-five or forty thousand
men which alone he had. While he held this position in
such force, the Austrians could scarcely advance into
France along the narrow coast road, leaving him in the
rear. When the expected success in Germany was won,
there was to be detached from that army, which should
then assume an attitude of observation, a corps twenty
thousand strong. This should cross Switzerland, entering
Italy by the St. Gothard Pass, and there joining a force of
forty thousand to be led by the First Consul in person
through the Pass of St. Bernard. This mass of sixty thousand men was to throw itself in rear of the Austrians,
forcing them to fight for their communications through
Lombardy, and hoping under the first general of the age to
win, over a less skilful opponent, such victories as had
illustrated the famous campaigns of 1796 and 1797.

Bonaparte's plan thus hinged upon the French occupation
of Switzerland, which, intervening as a great rampart between the Austrians in Germany and Italy, permitted him
to cover the movements against the former by the curtain
of the Rhine between Lake Constance and Bâle, and to use
safely and secretly the passes leading into the plains of
Lombardy and Piedmont. To this advantage of position
he conjoined, with inconceivable wiliness, an absolute

secrecy as to the very existence of the forty thousand, known as the Army of Reserve, which he himself was to lead. The orders constituting this force were given the utmost publicity. Its headquarters were established at Dijon, and one of Bonaparte's most trusted subordinates was sent to command it. An appeal was made to discharged soldiers to join its ranks; some material of war and some conscripts, with a corps of officers, were assembled. There preparations stopped—or went on so feebly in comparison with the glowing boasts of the French journals, that hostile spies were entirely deceived. The Army of Reserve became the joke of Europe, while the scattered detachments that were to compose it were assembling at points separated, yet chosen with Bonaparte's consummate skill to permit rapid concentration when the hour came. To insure perfect secrecy, the correspondence of these different bodies was with him alone, not through the Ministry of War.

The campaign was opened by the Austrians in Italy. Mélas, with seventy thousand men, attacked Masséna along the chain of the Apennines. Difficulties of subsistence had forced the latter to disseminate his troops between Genoa and Nice. Through this necessarily thin line the Austrians broke on the 5th of April, and after several days of strenuous resistance, furthered by the facilities for defence offered by that mountainous region, Masséna was driven into Genoa. The left wing of his army under Suchet was forced back toward Nice, where it took position on the Var. On the 18th of April Masséna was definitively shut up in Genoa with eighteen thousand men, and so short of provisions that it became a matter of the utmost urgency to relieve him.

On April 25 Moreau began his movements, of a somewhat complicated character, but resulting in his whole army being safely across the Rhine on the first of May. Eighty thousand French troops were then drawn up between Bâle and Lake Constance in an east and west direction, threat-

ening the left flank of the enemy, whose front was north
and south, and in position to attack both their line of retreat and the immense depots whose protection embarrassed all the movements of the Austrians. On the 3d of
May the latter were defeated at Engen, and their depot at
Stokach was captured. On the 5th they were again beaten
at Moesskirch, and on the 9th at Biberach, losing other
large deposits of stores. General Kray then retired upon
Ulm on the Danube, and the first act of Bonaparte's design
was accomplished. It had not corresponded with the lines
laid down by him, which were too adventurous to suit
Moreau, nor was the result equal to his expectations; but
the general strategic outcome was to check for the time
any movements of the enemy in Germany, and enable Moreau to send the force needed to co-operate with Bonaparte
in Italy. This started on the 13th of May, and was joined
on the way by some detachments in Switzerland; the
whole amounting to between fifteen and twenty thousand
men.[1]

On the 6th of May the first consul left Paris, having delayed to the last moment in order to keep up the illusions
of the Austrian commander-in-chief in Italy. The crossing
of the St. Bernard began on the 15th, and on the 20th the
whole army had passed. On the 26th it issued in the plains
of Piedmont; whence Bonaparte turned to the eastward, to
insure his great object of throwing his force across the
enemy's communications and taking from him all hope of
regaining them without a battle. On the first of June he
entered Milan.

Meanwhile Masséna's army, a prey to horrible famine,
prolonged in Genoa a resistance which greatly contributed
to the false position of the Austrians. Of these, twenty-
five thousand were before Nice, thirty thousand before
Genoa. Twenty thousand more had been lost by casualties
since the campaign opened. Unwilling to relinquish his

---

[1] Thiers, Cons. et Empire, vol. i., p. 532.

gains; Mélas waited too long to concentrate his scattered troops; and when at last he sent the necessary orders, Masséna was treating to evacuate Genoa. The Austrian officer on the spot, unwilling to lose the prize, postponed compliance until it was secured, — a delay fraught with serious results. On the 5th Genoa was given up, and the besiegers, leaving a garrison in the place, marched to join the commander-in-chief, who was gathering his forces around Alessandria. Meanwhile Bonaparte had crossed to the south side of the Po with half his army. On the 14th of June was fought the battle of Marengo. Anxious lest the foe might give him the slip, the first consul had spread his troops too widely; and the first events of the day were so far in favor of the Austrians that Mélas, who was seventy-six years old, left the field at two in the afternoon, certain of victory, to seek repose. An hour later the opportune arrival of General Desaix turned the scales, and Bonaparte remained conqueror on the ground, standing across the enemy's line of retreat. The following day Mélas signed a convention abandoning all northern Italy, as far as the Mincio, behind which the Austrians were to withdraw. All the fortified places were given up to France, including the hardly won Genoa. While awaiting the Emperor's answer to propositions of peace, sent by the First Consul, there was to be in Italy a suspension of arms, during which neither army should send detachments to Germany. On the 2d of July Bonaparte re-entered Paris in triumph, after an absence of less than two months.

Meantime Moreau, after learning the successful crossing of the St. Bernard, had resumed the offensive. Moving to the eastward, he crossed the Danube below Ulm with part of his force on the 19th of June, threatening Kray's communications with Bohemia. A partial encounter on that day left five thousand prisoners in the hands of the French, who maintained the position they had gained. The same night Kray evacuated Ulm, moving rapidly off by a road to the

northward and so effecting his escape. Moreau, unable to
intercept, followed for some distance and then stopped a
pursuit which promised small results. He was still ignorant of the battle of Marengo, of which the Austrians now
had news; and the latter, while concealing the victory, announced to him the suspension of arms, and suggested a
similar arrangement in Germany. Convinced that events
favorable to France lay behind this proposition, Moreau
would come to no agreement; but on the contrary decided
at once to secure for his victorious army the most advantageous conditions with which to enter upon negotiations.
Closely investing the important fortresses of Ulm and
Ingolstadt on the Danube, with part of his force, he recrossed the river with the remainder and advanced into
Bavaria. On the 28th of June he entered Munich; and
near there was signed on the 15th of July an armistice,
closely corresponding with that concluded by Bonaparte in
Italy just one month before. The two belligerents retired
behind appointed lines, not again to engage in hostilities
without twelve days' notice. During this suspension of
arms the blockaded Austrian fortresses should receive every
fortnight provisions proportioned to their consumption, so
that in case of renewed operations they would be in the same
condition as when the truce began. The two great French
armies were now encamped in the fertile plains of Italy and
Germany, living in quiet off districts external to France,
which was thus relieved of the larger part of their expense.

The effect of this short and brilliant campaign of unbrok-
en French successes was to dispose to peace both members
of the coalition. Neither, however, was yet reduced to
negotiate apart from its ally. On the very day the news of
Marengo was received at Vienna, but before the last reverses in Germany, Austria had renewed her engagements
with Great Britain, both powers stipulating not to treat
singly. The first consul, on the other hand, was distinctly
opposed to joint discussions, his constant policy in the cabi-

net as in the field being to separate his opponents. As
Austria's great need was to gain time, she sent to Paris an
envoy empowered to exchange views with the French government but to conclude nothing. The emperor also intimated his wish for a general pacification, and on the 9th
of August the British minister at Vienna notified to that
court the willingness of his own to enter into negotiations
for a general peace.

With this began an encounter of wits, in which Bonaparte
showed himself as astute at a bargain as he was wily in the
field. Austria, if not given too much time, was at his
mercy; but Great Britain held over him a like advantage in
her control of the sea, which was strangling the colonial
empire he passionately wished to restore. Haïti had escaped from all but nominal control; Martinique, the gem of
the Antilles, was in British hands; Malta and Egypt, the
trophies of his own enterprise, were slowly but surely expir-
ing. For these he too needed time; for with it there was
good prospect of soon playing a card which should reverse,
or at least seriously modify, the state of the game, by bringing Russia and the Baltic navies into the combination
against Great Britain. In this support, and in the extremity to which he might reduce Austria, lay his only chances
to check the great opponent of France; for, while almost
supreme on the Continent, he could not from the coast project his power beyond the range of a cannon's ball. His
correspondence throughout this period abounds with instructions and exhortations to fit out the fleets, to take the sea,
to relieve Malta and Egypt; to seize Sardinia by an expedition from Corsica, and Mahon by a squadron from Brest.
All fell fruitless before the exhaustion of French sea
power, as did also his plan for an extensive cruise on a
grand scale against British commerce in many quarters of
the world. "I see with regret," wrote he to the minister
of Marine, "that the armament of the fleet has been sacrificed to that of a great number of small vessels;" but in

truth there was nothing else to do. His ablest admirals failed to equip ships from which every resource was cut off by the omnipresent cruisers of the enemy. " We can never take Mahon," he writes to the court of Spain, in the full swing of his triumphs after Marengo ; " therefore make war on Portugal and take her provinces, so as to enter negotiations for peace with your hands as full as possible of equivalents."

The Czar Paul had joined the second coalition full of ardor against the French revolution and determined to restore the princes who had lost their thrones. He had been bitterly mortified by the reverses to his troops in 1799, and especially by the disaster to Suwarrow, for which he not unjustly blamed Austria. He was also dissatisfied to find in his allies less of zeal for unfortunate sovereigns than of desire to reduce the power of France, to whose system they attributed the misfortunes of Europe. Disappointment in his unbalanced mind turned soon to coolness and was rapidly passing to hostility. The transition was assisted, and a pretext for a breach with Great Britain afforded, by a fresh outbreak of the old dispute between her and the Baltic powers concerning the rights of neutrals. Denmark in 1799 adopted the policy of convoying her merchant vessels by ships of war, and claimed that a statement from the senior naval officer, that the cargoes contained nothing forbidden by the law of nations, exempted the convoy from the belligerent right of search. British statesmen denied that this conceded belligerent right could be nullified by any rule adopted by a neutral ; to which they were the more impelled as the Danes and themselves differed radically in the definition of contraband. Danish naval officers being instructed to resist the search of their convoys, two hostile encounters took place ; one in December, 1799, and the other in July, 1800. In the latter several were killed on both sides, and the Danish frigate was carried into the Downs. Seeing the threatening character of affairs, the British ministry took

immediate steps to bring them to an issue. An ambassador
was sent to Copenhagen supported by nine ships-of-the-line
and several bomb-vessels ; and on the 29th of August,
barely a month after the affray, a convention was signed
by which the general subject of searching ships under convoy was referred to future discussion, but Denmark consented to suspend her convoys until a definitive treaty was
made. The Danish frigate was at once released.

It will be observed that this collision occurred in the very
midst of the negotiations between Austria and France, to
which Great Britain claimed the right to be a party. The
whole vexed question of neutral and belligerent rights was
thus violently raised, at a moment most inauspicious to
the allies and most favorable to Bonaparte. The latter,
crowned with victory upon the Continent, found every neutral commercial state disposed to side with him in contesting positions considered by Great Britain to be vital to her
safety. It was for him to foster this disposition and combine the separate powers into one great effort, before which
the Mistress of the Seas should be compelled to recede and
submit. The occasion here arose, as it were spontaneously,
to realize what became the great dream of his life and ultimately led him to his ruin, — to unite the Continent against
the British Islands and, as he phrased it, " to conquer the
sea by the land." Circumstances, partly anterior to his
rise to power, and partly contrived by his sagacious policy
during the previous few months, particularly favored at
this moment such a league, for which the affair of the
Danish convoy supplied an impulse, and the prostration of
Great Britain's ally, Austria, an opportunity. Bonaparte
underestimated the vitality and influence of a state upon
which centred a far-reaching commercial system, and in
valuing naval power he did not appreciate that a mere mass
of ships had not the weight he himself was able to impart
to a mass of men. He never fully understood the maritime
problems with which from time to time he had to deal; but

he showed wonderful skill at this critical period in combining against his principal enemy an opposition, for which Prussia afforded the body and the hot temper of the Czar the animating soul.

Since 1795 Prussia had shut herself up to a rigorous neutrality, in which were embraced the North German states. Under this system, during the maritime war, the commerce of the larger part of the Continent poured in through these states — by the great German rivers, the Ems, the Weser, and the Elbe — and through the cities of Hamburg and Bremen. The tonnage clearing from Great Britain alone to North Germany increased from 120,000 in 1792 to 389,000 in 1800; a traffic of which Prussia took the lion's share. To these advantages of neutral territory it was desirable to join the utmost freedom for neutral navigation. Upon this Great Britain bore heavily; but so large a proportion of the trade was done through her, and the sea was so entirely under the power of her navy, that prudence had so far dictated acquiescence in her claims, even when not admitted. This was particularly the case while Russia, under Catherine II., and in the first years of her son, tacitly or openly supported Great Britain; and while Austria, though badly beaten in the field, remained unshaken in power. The weaker maritime countries, Sweden, Denmark, and the United States of America, were determined by similar motives. They groaned under the British exactions; but the expansion of their commerce outweighed the injuries received, and submission was less hurtful than resistance in arms. Russia herself, though not strictly a maritime state, was a large producer of articles which were mainly carried by British ships and for which England was the chief customer. The material interests of Russia, and especially of the powerful nobles, were therefore bound up with peace with Great Britain; but an absolute monarch could disregard this fact, at least for a time. The furious, impulsive temper of Paul I., if aroused, was quite capable of overleaping all prudential considerations, of using the colossal power of his empire to support the other states, and even of compelling them to act in concert with him.

Such were the discordant elements which Bonaparte had to reconcile into a common effort: on the one hand, the strong though short-sighted mercantile interests, which to retain great present advantages would favor submission rather than resistance to the exactions of Great Britain. These were represented by the development of carrying trade in the neutral Baltic states, by the enlarged commerce of Prussia and North Germany,— which through their neutrality in a maritime war had become the highway of intercourse between the Continent and the outer world,— and by the productions of Russia, which formed the revenue of her great proprietors, and found their way to market wholly by sea. Bound together by the close relations which commerce breeds between states, and by the dependence of each upon the capital and mercantile system of Great Britain, these interests constituted the prosperity of nations, and could by no rulers be lightly disregarded. On the other hand stood the dignity of neutral flags and their permanent interests, — always contrary to those of belligerents,— the ambition of Prussia and her jealousy of Austria, and finally the chivalrous, reckless, half insane Paul I., seeking now with all the bitterness of personal feeling to gratify his resentment against his late allies.

Bonaparte had already begun to work upon the Czar as well as upon the neutral powers. Closely observing the political horizon from his first accession to office, he had noted every condition capable of raising embarrassments to Great Britain, whom his unerring military insight had long before recognized [1] as the key to a military situation, in which his own object was the predominance of France,

1 See ante, p. 251.

not only on the Continent but throughout the world.
Sagacious a statesman as he was, and clearly as he recognized the power of moral and political motives, his ideal
of control was essentially forcible, based upon superior
armies and superior fleets; and consequently every political problem was by him viewed much as a campaign, in
which forces were to be moved, combined, and finally
massed upon the vital points of an enemy's position. The
power of Great Britain was sea power in its widest sense,
commercial and naval; against it, therefore, he aimed to
effect such a combination as would both destroy her commerce and cripple her navy. The impotence of France
and Spain, united, to injure the one or the other had been
clearly shown by repeated defeats, and by the failure of
the commerce-destroying so industriously carried on during seven years of war. Far from decaying or languishing, the commerce of Great Britain throve everywhere
with redoubled vigor, and her fleets rode triumphant in all
seas. There was, however, one quarter in which she had
not hitherto been disturbed, except by the quickly extinguished efforts of the Dutch navy; and just there, in the
Baltic and North Sea, was the point where, next to the
British islands and seas themselves, she was most vulnerable. There was concentrated a great part of her shipping; there was the market for the colonial produce stored
in her overflowing warehouses; there also were gathered
three navies, whose united masses — manned by hardy
seamen trained in a boisterous navigation and sheltered
in an enclosed sea of perilous access — might overweight
a force already strained to control the Mediterranean, to
blockade the hostile arsenals, and to protect the merchant
shipping which thronged over every ocean highway.

To close the north of Europe to British trade, and to
combine the Baltic navies against that of Great Britain,
became thenceforth the fixed ideas of Bonaparte's life.
To conciliate Denmark he released a number of Danish

ships, which had been arrested by the Directory for sub-
mitting to search by British cruisers. The extent of the
czar's alienation from his former allies not being at first
apparent, he next courted Prussia, the head of the North
German neutrality, in whose power it was to arrest British
trade both through her own territory and through Hamburg. Prussia was ambitious to play a leading part in
Europe. The five years spent by Austria, France, and
Great Britain in exhausting warfare, she had used to
consolidate her power and husband her resources. She
wished now to pose as a mediator, and looked for the
time when the prostration of the combatants and her own
restored strength would cause them to bend to her influence, and yield her points, through the simple exhibition of
her force. The advances and flatteries of the first consul
were graciously received, but the path Prussia had traced
for herself was to involve no risks — only gains; she
wished much, but would venture naught. It was a dangerous part to play, this waiting on opportunity, against
such a man as swayed the destinies of the Continent during the next twelve years. From it arose a hesitating,
selfish, and timid policy, fluctuating with every breath of
danger or hope of advantage, dishonoring the national
name, until it ended in Jena and the agonies of humiliation through which the country passed between that disaster and the overthrow of Napoleon. Such a spirit is prone
to side with a strong combination and to yield to a mas-
terful external impulse.

Under this Bonaparte next sought to bring her. "We
shall make nothing out of Prussia," he writes to Talleyrand on the first of June, 1800, on his way to Marengo;
and he adds, "If the news from Egypt [apparently the
defeat of the Turks by Kleber] is confirmed, it will become important to have some one in Russia. The Otto-
man Empire cannot exist much longer, and if Paul I.
turns his looks in that direction our interests become

common."[1] Bonaparte was at no pains to reconcile this view with an assurance made a month later to Turkey that "no anxiety need be felt about Egypt, which will be restored as soon as the Porte shall resume its former relations with France."[2] On the 4th of June he recommends general and flattering overtures to the czar, accompanied by special marks of consideration. The latter was fully prepared to be won by compliments from the man for whose military glory he had come to feel a profound enthusiasm. On the 4th of July Bonaparte's general advances took form in a definite proposal to surrender to Russian troops Malta, whose speedy loss by himself he saw to be inevitable; an offer calculated not only to charm the Czar, who delighted to fancy himself the head and protector of an ancient order of knights, but also to sow discord between him and Great Britain, if, as was probable, the latter declined to yield her prey to a friend who at a critical moment had forsaken her. The letter sketched by the first consul was carefully worded to quicken the ready vanity of its recipient. "Desiring to give a proof of personal consideration to the emperor of Russia and to distinguish him from the other enemies of the republic, who fight from a vile love of gain, the first consul wishes, if the garrison of Malta is constrained by famine to evacuate the place, to restore it to the hands of the czar as grand master of the order; and although the first consul is certain that Malta has provisions for several months,[3] he wishes his Majesty to inform him what conventions he would wish to make, and what measures to take, so that, if the case arise, his troops may enter that place."[4] This was shortly followed by the release of the Russian prisoners in France, in number between seven

---

[1] Corr. de Nap., vol. vi. p. 410.   [2] Ibid., vol. vi. p. 497.
[3] "Voyant bien," says M. Thiers, Bonaparte's panegyrist, "que Malta ne pouvait pas tenir longtemps." (Cons. et Emp., vol. ii. p. 92.)
[4] Corr. de Nap., vol. vi. p. 498.

and eight thousand, whom Bonaparte clad and dismissed
with their colors and their officers to return into Russia;
suggesting that, if the czar thought proper, he "might
demand of the English to release an equal number of
French prisoners; but if not, the first consul hoped he
would accept his troops as an especial mark of the esteem
felt for the brave Russian armies."[1]

Immediately after these transactions occurred the collision between British and Danish cruisers in the Channel,
and the entrance of the Baltic by the British fleet, to support its ambassador in his negotiation with Denmark.
Paul I. made of the latter a pretext for sequestrating all
British property in Russia, to be held as a guarantee
against the future action of Great Britain. This order,
dated August 29, 1800, was followed by another of September 10, announcing that "several political circumstances induced the emperor to think that a rupture of
friendship with England may ensue," and directing a concentration of Russian troops. The cloud blew over for a
moment, the sequestration being removed on the 22d of
September; but the fall of Malta, which had surrendered
on the 5th of the same month, brought matters to an issue.
The czar had gladly accepted Bonaparte's adroit advances
and designated a general to go to Paris, take command of
the released prisoners and with them repair to Malta.
The capitulation became known to him early in November; before which he had formally published his intention
to revive the Armed Neutrality of 1780 against the maritime claims of Great Britain. It being very doubtful
whether the latter would deliver the island after his unfriendly measures, a sequestration of British property was
again decreed. Some three hundred ships were seized,
their crews marched into the interior, and seals placed on
all warehouses containing British property; the czar declaring that the embargo should not be removed until the

[1] Corr. de Nap., vol. vi. p. 520.

acknowledgment of his rights to Malta, as grand master of the Order. The sequestrated property was to be held by an imperial commission and applied to pay debts due to Russian subjects by private Englishmen.

Affairs had now reached a stage where Prussia felt encouraged to move. The breach between Great Britain and Russia had opened wide, while the relations of the czar and first consul had become so friendly as to assure their concert. The armistice between Austria and France still continued, pending the decision whether the latter would negotiate with the emperor and Great Britain conjointly; but Bonaparte was a close as well as a hard bargainer. He would not admit the joint negotiation, nor postpone the renewal of hostilities beyond the 11th of September, except on condition of a maritime truce as favorable to France as he considered the land armistice to be to Austria. He proposed entire freedom of navigation to merchant vessels, the raising of the blockades of Brest, Cadiz, Toulon, and Flushing, and that Malta and Alexandria should be freely open to receive provisions by French or neutral vessels. The effect would be to allow the French dockyards to obtain naval stores, of which they were utterly destitute, and Malta and Egypt to receive undefined quantities of supplies and so prolong their resistance indefinitely. Great Britain was only willing to adopt for Egypt and Malta the literal terms of the armistice applied to the three Austrian fortresses blockaded by French troops. These were to receive every fortnight provisions proportioned to their consumption, and the British ministry offered to allow the same to Malta and Egypt. They also conceded free navigation, except in the articles of military and naval stores. Bonaparte refused. Austria's advantage in the armistice, he said, was not the mere retention of the fortresses, but the use she was making of her respite. Between these two extreme views no middle term could be found. In fact, great as were the results of Marengo, and of Moreau's more methodical advance into Germany, the material advantage of Great Britain over France still far exceeded that of France over Austria. The French had gained great successes, but they were now forcing the enemy back upon the centre of his power and they had not possession of his communications; whereas Great Britain had shut off, not merely Egypt and Malta, but France herself from all fruitful intercourse with the outer world. The negotiation for a maritime truce was broken off on the 9th of October. Meanwhile Bonaparte, declining to await its issue, had given notice that hostilities would be resumed between the 5th and 10th of September; and Austria, not yet ready, was fain to purchase a further delay by surrendering the blockaded places, Ulm, Ingolstadt, and Philipsburg. A convention to this effect was concluded, and the renewal of the war postponed for forty-five days dating from September 21st.

In such conditions Prussia saw one of those opportunities which, under Bonaparte's manipulation, so often misled her. The prostration of her German rival would be hastened, and the support of the first consul in the approaching apportionment of indemnities to German states secured, by joining the concert of the Baltic powers against Great Britain. Without this accession to the northern league the quarrel would be mainly naval, and its issue, before the disciplined valor of British seamen, scarcely doubtful. Prussia alone was so situated as to deal the direct and heavy blow at British commerce of closing its accustomed access to the Continent; and the injury thus inflicted so far exceeded any she herself could incidentally receive, as to make this course less hazardous than that of offending the czar and the French government. The political connection of Hanover with Great Britain was a further motive, giving Prussia the hope, so often dangled before her eyes by Bonaparte, of permanently annexing the German dominions of the British king. An occasion soon arose for showing her bias. In the latter part of October a British cruiser seized a Prussian merchantman trying to enter the Texel with a cargo of naval stores. The captor, through stress of weather, took his prize into Cuxhaven, a port at the mouth of the Elbe belonging to Hamburg, through which passed much of the British commerce with the Continent. Prussia demanded its release of the Hamburg senate, and upon refusal ordered two thousand troops to take possession of the port. The senate then bought the prize and delivered it to Prussia, and the British government also directed its restoration; a step of pure policy with which Fox taunted the ministry. It was, as he truly remarked, a concession of principle, dictated by the fact that Prussia, while capable of doing much harm to Great Britain, could not be reached by the British navy.

Whether it was wise to waive a point, in order to withhold an important member from the formidable combination of the North, may be argued; but the attempt met the usual fate of concessions attributed to weakness. The remonstrances of the British ambassador received the reply that the occupation, having been ordered, must be carried out; that the neutrality of Cuxhaven "being thus placed under the guarantee of the king will be more effectually out of the reach of all violation." Such reasoning indicated beyond doubt the stand Prussia was about to take; and her influence fixed the course of Denmark, which is said to have been averse from a step that threatened to stop her trade and would probably make her the first victim of Great Britain's resentment. On the 16th of December a treaty renewing the Armed Neutrality of 1780 was signed at St. Petersburg by Russia and Sweden, and received the prompt adherence of Denmark and Prussia. Its leading affirmations were that neutral ships were free to carry on the coasting and colonial trade of states

at war, that enemy's goods under the neutral flag were not
subject to seizure, and that blockades, to be respected,
must be supported by such a force of ships before the
port as to make the attempt to enter hazardous. A definition of contraband was adopted excluding naval stores
from that title; and the claim was affirmed that vessels
under convoy of a ship of war were not liable to the belligerent right of search. Each of these assertions contested one of the maritime claims upon which Great
Britain conceived her naval power, and consequently her
place among the nations, to depend; but the consenting
states bound themselves to maintain their positions by
force, if necessary.

Thus was successfully formed the combination of the
Northern powers against Great Britain, the first and most
willing of those effected by Bonaparte. By a singular
coincidence, which recalls the opportuneness of his departure from England in 1798 to check the yet undivined
expedition against Egypt,[1] Nelson, the man destined also
to strike this coalition to the ground, was during its formation slowly journeying from the Mediterranean, with
which his name and his glory both before and after are
most closely associated, to the North Sea; as though
again drawn by some mysterious influence, to be at hand
for unknown services which he alone could render. On
the 11th of July, a week after Bonaparte made his first
offer of Malta to the czar, Nelson left Leghorn for Trieste
and Vienna. He passed through Hamburg at the very
time that the affair of the Prussian prize was under discussion, and landed in England on the 6th of November.
Finding his health entirely restored by the land journey,
he applied for immediate service, and was assigned to
command a division of the Channel fleet under Lord St.
Vincent; but he did not go afloat until the 17th of January, 1801, when his flag was hoisted on board the "San

1 See vol. i. pp. 249, 256.

Josef," the three-decker he had captured at the battle of Cape St. Vincent. Meanwhile, however, it had been settled between the Admiralty and himself that if a fleet were sent into the Baltic, he should go as second in command to Sir Hyde Parker; and when in the very act of reporting to St. Vincent, the day before he joined the San Josef, a letter arrived from Parker announcing his appointment.

By this time Austria had received a final blow, which forced her to treat alone, and postponed for nearly five years her reappearance in the field. The emperor had sent an envoy to Lunéville, who was met by Joseph Bonaparte as the representative of France; but refusing to make peace apart from Great Britain, hostilities were resumed on the 28th of November. On the 3d of December Moreau won the great battle of Hohenlinden, and then advanced upon Vienna. On the 25th an armistice was signed at Steyer, within a hundred miles of the Austrian capital. Successes, less brilliant but decided, were obtained in Italy, resulting on the 16th of January, 1801, in an armistice between the armies there. At nearly the same moment with this last news the first consul received a letter from the czar, manifesting extremely friendly feelings towards France, while full of hatred towards England, and signifying his intention to send an ambassador to Paris. This filled Bonaparte with sanguine hopes, the expression of which shows how heavily sea power weighed in his estimation. "Peace with the emperor," he wrote to his brother at Lunéville, "is *nothing* in comparison with the alliance of the czar, which will *dominate England* and preserve Egypt for us;"[1] and he ordered him to prolong the negotiations until the arrival of the expected ambassador, that the engagements contracted with Germany might be made in concert with Russia. Upon a similar combined action he based extravagant expecta-

[1] Corr. de Nap., vol. vi. p. 738, Jan. 21, 1801.

.tions of naval results, dependent upon the impression, with which he so hardly parted, that one set of ships was equal to another.[1] A courier was at once dispatched to Spain to arrange expeditions against Ireland, against Brazil and the East Indies, to the Caribbean Sea for the recovery of the French and Spanish islands, and to the Mediterranean to regain Minorca. "In the embarrassment about to come upon England, threatened in the Archipelago by the Russians and in the northern seas by the combined Powers, it will be impossible for her long to keep a strong squadron in the Mediterranean."[2]

The Russian envoy not arriving, however, Joseph Bonaparte was instructed to bring matters to a conclusion; and on the 9th of February the Austrian minister at Lunéville, after a stubborn fight over the terms, signed a treaty of peace. The principal conditions were: 1. The definitive surrender of all German possessions west of the Rhine, so that the river became the frontier of France

---

[1] Contrast Bonaparte's reliance upon the aggregate numbers of Baltic navies with Nelson's professional opinion when about to fight them. "During the Council of War (March 31, 1801) certain difficulties were started by some of the members relative to each of the three Powers we should have to engage, either in succession or united, in those seas. The number of the Russians was in particular represented as formidable. Lord Nelson kept pacing the cabin, mortified at everything which savored either of alarm or irresolution. When the above remark was applied to the Swedes, he sharply observed, 'The more numerous the better;' and when to the Russians, he repeatedly said, 'So much the better; I wish they were twice as many, — the easier the victory, depend on it.' He alluded, as he afterwards explained in private, to the total want of tactique among the Northern fleets." (Col. Stewart's Narrative; Nelson's Dispatches, vol. iv. p. 301.)

James, who was a careful investigator, estimates the allied Russian, Swedish, and Danish navies in the Baltic at fifty-two sail, of which not over forty-one were in condition for service, instead of eighty-eight as represented by some writers. "It must have been a very happy combination of circumstances," he adds, "that could have assembled in one spot twenty-five of those forty-one; and against that twenty-five of three different nations, all mere novices in naval tactics, eighteen, or, with Nelson to command, fifteen British sail were more than a match." (Nav. Hist., vol. iii. p. 43; ed. 1878.)

[2] Corr. de Nap., vol. vi. p. 747. To Talleyrand, Jan. 27, 1801.

from Switzerland to Holland. 2. The cession of Belgium made at Campo Formio was confirmed. 3. In Italy, Austria herself was cónfined to the east bank of the Adige, and the princes of that house having principalities west of the river were dispossessed; their territories going to the Cisalpine Republic and to an infante of Spain, who was established in Tuscany with the title of King of Etruria. The Cisalpine and Etruria being dependent for their political existence upon France, the latter, through its control of their territory, interposed between Austria and Naples and shut off the British from access to Leghorn. 4. The eleventh article of the treaty guaranteed the independence of the Dutch, Swiss, Cisalpine and Ligurian republics. In its influence upon the future course of events this was the most important of all the stipulations. It gave to the political status of the Continent a definition, upon which Great Britain reckoned in her own treaty with France a few months later; and its virtual violation by Bonaparte became ultimately both the reason and the excuse for her refusal to fulfil the engagements about Malta, which led to the renewal of the war and so finally to the downfall of Napoleon. 5. The German Empire was pledged to give to the princes dispossessed on the west of the Rhine, and in Italy, an indemnity within the empire itself. By this Prussia, which was among the losers, reaped through Bonaparte's influence an abundant recompense for the support already given to his policy in the North. This success induced her to continue the same time-serving opportunism, until, when no longer necessary to France, she was thrown over with a rudeness that roused her to an isolated, and therefore speedily crushed resistance.

CHAPTER XIII.

EVENTS OF 1801.

BRITISH EXPEDITION TO THE BALTIC — BATTLE OF COPENHAGEN — BONAPARTE'S FUTILE ATTEMPTS TO CONTEST CONTROL OF THE SEA — HIS CONTINENTAL POLICY — PRELIMINARIES OF PEACE WITH GREAT BRITAIN, OCTOBER, 1801 — INFLUENCE OF SEA POWER SO FAR UPON THE COURSE OF THE REVOLUTION.

BY the peace of Lunéville Great Britain was left alone, and for the moment against all Europe. The ministry met the emergency with vigor and firmness, though possibly with too much reliance upon diplomacy and too little upon the military genius of the great seaman whose services were at their disposal. Upon the Continent nothing could be effected, all resistance to France had been crushed by the genius of Bonaparte; but time had to be gained for the expedition then under way against Egypt and destined to compel its evacuation by the French. The combination in the North also must be quickly dissolved, if the country were to treat on anything like equal terms.

An armed negotiation with the Baltic powers, similar to that employed with Denmark the preceding August, was therefore determined; and a fleet of eighteen sail-of-the-line with thirty-five smaller vessels was assembled at Yarmouth, on the east coast of England. Rapidity of movement was essential to secure the advantage from the ice, which, breaking up in the harbors less rapidly than in the open water, would delay the concentration of the hostile navies; and also to allow the Baltic powers the least possible time to prepare for hostilities which they had scarcely antici-

pated. Everything pointed to Nelson, the most energeti
and daring of British admirals, for the chief command of an
expedition in which so much depended upon the squadron,
numerically inferior to the aggregate of forces arrayed
against it, attacking separately each of the component parts
before their junction; but Nelson was still among the
junior flag-officers, and the rather erratic manner in which,
while in the central Mediterranean and under the influence
of Lady Hamilton, he had allowed his views of the political
situation to affect his actions even in questions of military
subordination, had probably excited in Earl Spencer, the
First Lord, by whom the officers were selected, a distrust of
his fitness for a charge requiring a certain delicacy of discretion as well as vigor of action. Whatever the reason,
withholding the chief command from him was unquestionably a mistake, — which would not have been made by St.
Vincent, who succeeded Spencer a few weeks later upon the
fall of the Pitt ministry. The conditions did not promise
a pacific solution when the expedition was planned, and the
prospect was even worse when it sailed. The instructions
given to Sir Hyde Parker allowed Denmark forty-eight
hours to accept Great Britain's terms and withdraw from
her engagements with the other Powers. Whether she
complied peaceably or not, after she was reduced to submission the division of the Russian fleet at Revel was to be
attacked, before the melting ice allowed it to join the main
body in Cronstadt; and Sweden was to be similarly dealt
with. Under such orders diplomacy had a minor part to play,
while in their directness and simplicity they were admirably suited to the fiery temper and prompt military action
which distinguished Nelson; and, but for the opportune
death of Paul I., Great Britain might have had reason to
regret that the opportunity to give Russia a severe reminder
of her sea power was allowed to slip through the lax grasp
of a sluggish admiral.

The fleet sailed from Yarmouth on the 12th of March,

1801; and on the 19th, although there had been some scattering in a heavy gale, nearly all were collected off the Skaw, the northern point of Jutland at the entrance of the Kattegat. The wind being north-west was fair for going to Copenhagen, and Nelson, if in command, would have advanced at once with the ambassador on board. "While the negotiation is going on," he said, "the Dane should see our flag waving every moment he lifted his head." As it was, the envoy went forward with a frigate alone and the fleet waited. On the 12th it was off Elsineur, where the envoy rejoined, Denmark having rejected the British terms.

This amounted to an acceptance of hostilities, and it only remained to the commander-in-chief to act at once; for the wind was favorable, an advantage which at any moment might be lost. On this day Nelson addressed Parker a letter, summing up in a luminous manner the features of the situation and the different methods of action. "Not a moment should be lost in attacking," he said; "we shall never be so good a match for them as at this moment." He next hinted, what he had probably already said, that the fleet ought to have been off Copenhagen, and not at Elsineur, when the negotiation failed. "Then you might instantly attack and there would be scarcely a doubt but the Danish fleet would be destroyed, and the capital made so hot that Denmark would listen to reason and its true interest." Since, however, the mistake of losing so much time had been made, he seeks to stir his superior to lose no more. "Almost the safety, certainly the honor, of England is more entrusted to you than ever yet fell to the lot of any British officer; . . . never did our country depend so much on the success of any fleet as of this."

Having thus shown the necessity for celerity, Nelson next discussed the plan of operations. Copenhagen is on the east side of the island of Zealand, fronting the coast of Sweden, from which it is separated by the passage called the Sound. On the west the island is divided from the other parts of Denmark by the Great Belt. The navigation of the latter being much the more difficult, the preparations of the Danes had been made on the side of the Sound, and chiefly about Copenhagen itself. For half a mile from the shore in front of the city, flats extend, and in the Sound itself at a distance of little over a mile, is a long shoal called the Middle Ground. Between these two bodies of shallow water is a channel, called the King's, through which a fleet of heavy ships could sail, and from whose northern end a deep pocket stretches toward Copenhagen, forming the harbor proper. The natural point of attack therefore appears to be at the north; and there the Danes had erected powerful works, rising on piles out of the shoal water off the harbor's mouth and known as the Three-Crown Batteries. Nelson, however, pointed out that not only was this head of the line exceedingly strong, but that the wind that was fair to attack would be foul to return; therefore a disabled ship would have no escape but by passing through the King's Channel. Doing so she would have to run the gantlet of a line of armed hulks, which the Danes had established as floating batteries along the inner edge of the channel — covering the front of Copenhagen — and would also be separated from her fleet. Nor was this difficulty, which may be called tactical, the only objection to a plan that he disparaged as "taking the bull by the horns." He remarked that so long as the British fleet remained in the Sound, without entering the Baltic, the way was left open for both the Swedes and the Russians, if released by the ice, to make a junction with the Danes. Consequently, he advised that a sufficiently strong force of the lighter ships-of-the-line should pass outside the Middle Ground, despite the difficulties of navigation, which were not insuperable, and come up in rear of the city. There they would interpose between the Danes and their allies, and be in position to assail the weaker part of the hostile order. He offered himself to lead this detachment.

BATTLE OF COPENHAGEN.

APRIL 2, 1801.

WIND ↖ S.S.E.

REFERENCES.

A. AGAMEMNON AT ANCHOR.
BB. BRITISH LINE OF BATTLE.
CC. BRITISH SHIPS AGROUND.
ff. BRITISH FRIGATES.

DD, DANISH LINE OF HULKS.
N, ANCHORAGE OF NELSON'S DIVISION, APRIL 1·2.·
P, ANCHORAGE OF BRITISH MAIN }
FLEET, UNDER SIR. H. PARKER .}

SHORE LINE

P ↓

½ MILE

FLATS

Five Fathom Line.

KING'S CHANNEL

WITHDRAWAL OF NELSON'S DIVISION AFTER BATTLE OF APRIL 2.

ADVANCE OF NELSON'S DIVISION, APRIL 1.

Five Fathom Line

Five Fathom Line

3¼ fathoms

HARBOR

Short Line

THREE CROWN BATTERY

D

5

B

MIDDLE GROUND (Shoal)

SALTHOLM FLAT

COPENHAGEN

FLATS

B

D.

B

DANISH BATTERIES

↓ N

This whole letter of March 24, 1801,[1] possesses peculiar interest; for it shows with a rare particularity, elicited by the need he felt of arousing and convincing his superior, Nelson's clear discernment of the decisive features òf a military situation. The fame of this great admiral has depended leşs upon his conduct of campaigns than upon the renowned victories he won in the actual collision of fleet with fleet; and even then has been mutilated by the obstinacy with which, despite the perfectly evident facts, men have persisted in seeing in them nothing but dash, — heart, not head.[2] Throughout his correspondence, it is true, there are frequent traces of the activity of his mental faculties and of the general accuracy of his military conclusions; but ordinarily it is from his actions that his reasonings and principles must be deduced. In the present case we have the views he held and the course he evidently would have pursued clearly formulated by himself; and it cannot but be a subject of regret that the naval world should have lost so fine an illustration as he would there have given of the principles and conduct of naval warfare. He concluded his letter with a suggestion worthy of Napo-

---

[1] Nelson's Letters and Dispatches, vol. iv. p. 295.

[2] While this work was going through the press, the author was gratified to find in the life of the late distinguished admiral Sir William Parker an anecdote of Nelson, which, as showing the military ideas of that great sea-officer, is worth a dozen of the "go straight at them" stories which pass current as embodying his precepts. "Throughout the month of October, 1804, Toulon was frequently reconnoitred, and the frigates 'Phoebe' and 'Amazon' were ordered to cruise together. Previous to their going away Lord Nelson gave to Captains Capel and Parker several injunctions, in case they should get an opportunity of attacking two of the French frigates, which now got under weigh more frequently. *The principal one was* that they should not each single out and attack an opponent, but 'that both should endeavor together to take *one frigate;* if successful, chase the other; but, if you do not take the second, still you have won a victory and your country will gain a frigate.' Then half laughing, and half snappishly, he said kindly to them as he wished them good-by, 'I daresay you consider yourselves a couple of fine fellows, and when you get away from me will do nothing of the sort, but think yourselves wiser than I am!'" ("The Last of Nelson's Captains," by Admiral Sir Augustus Phillimore, K. C. B., London, 1891, p. 122.)

leon himself, and which, if adopted, would have brought down the Baltic Confederacy with a crash that would have resounded throughout Europe. "Supposing us through the Belt with the wind first westerly, would it not be possible to go with the fleet, or detach ten ships of three and two decks, with one bomb and two fire-ships, to Revel, to destroy the Russian squadron at that place? I do not see the great risk of such a detachment, and with the remainder to attempt the business at Copenhagen. The measure may be thought bold, but I am of opinion the boldest are the safest; and our country demands a most vigorous exertion of her force, directed with judgment."

Committed as the Danes were to a stationary defence, this recommendation to strike at the soul of the confederacy evinced the clearest perception of the key to the situation, which Nelson himself summed up in the following words: "I look upon the Northern League to be like a tree, of which Paul was the trunk and Sweden and Denmark the branches. If I can get at the trunk and hew it down, the branches fall of course; but I may lop the branches and yet not be able to fell the tree, and my power must be weaker when its greatest strength is required" [1] — that is, the Russians should have been attacked before the fleet was weakened, as it inevitably must be, by the battle with the Danes. "If we could have cut up the Russian fleet," he said again, "that was my object." Whatever Denmark's wishes about fighting, she was by her continental possessions tied to the policy of Russia and Prussia, either of whom could overwhelm her by land. She dared not disregard them. The course of both depended upon the czar; for the temporizing policy of Prussia would at once embrace his withdrawal from the league as an excuse for doing the same. At Revel were twelve Russian ships-of-the-line, fully half their Baltic fleet,

[1] Nels. Disp., vol. iv. p. 355. See also a very emphatic statement of his views on the campaign, in a letter to Mr. Vansittart, p. 367.

whose destruction would have paralyzed the remainder
and the naval power of the empire. To persuade Parker
to such a step was, however, hopeless. "Our fleet would
never have acted against Russia and Sweden," wrote Nelson afterwards, "although Copenhagen would have been
burned; for Sir Hyde Parker was determined not to leave
Denmark hostile in his rear;"[1] a reason whose technical
accuracy under all the circumstances was nothing short
of pedantic, and illustrates the immense distance between
a good and accomplished officer, which Parker was, and a
genius whose comprehension of rules serves only to guide,
not to fetter, his judgment.

Although unable to rise equal to the great opportunity
indicated by Nelson, Sir Hyde Parker adopted his suggestion as to the method and direction of the principal attack
upon the defences of Copenhagen. For this, Nelson asked
ten ships-of-the-line and a number of smaller vessels, with
which he undertook to destroy the floating batteries covering the front of the city. These being reduced, the bomb
vessels could be placed so as to play with effect upon the
dock-yard, arsenals, and the town, in case further resistance was made.

The nights of the 30th and 31st of March were employed
sounding the channel. On the first of April the fleet
moved up to the north end of the Middle Ground, about
four miles from the city; and that afternoon Nelson's
division, to which Parker had assigned two ships-of-the-
line more than had been asked — or twelve altogether —
got under way, passed through the outer channel and anchored towards sundown off the south-east end of the
shoal, two miles from the head[2] of the Danish line.
Nelson announced his purpose to attack as soon as the
wind served; and the night was passed by him in arranging the order of battle. The enterprise was perilous, not

---

[1] Nelson's Disp., April 9, 1801, vol. iv. pp. 339 and 341.

[2] The Danes were moored with their heads to the southward.

on account of the force to be engaged, but because of the great difficulties of navigation. The pilots were mostly mates of merchantmen trading with the Baltic; and their experience in vessels of three or four hundred tons did not fit them for the charge of heavy battle-ships. They betrayed throughout great indecision, and their imperfect knowledge contributed to the principal mishaps of the day, as well as to a comparative incompleteness in the results of victory.

The next morning the wind came fair at south-south-east, and at eight A. M. the British captains were summoned to the flag-ship for their final instructions. The Danish line to be attacked extended in a north-west and south-east direction for somewhat over a mile. It was composed of hulks and floating batteries, eighteen to twenty in number and mounting 628 guns, of which about 375 would — fighting thus at anchor — be on the engaged side. The southern flank now to be assailed was partly supported by works on shore; but from the intervening shoal water these were too distant for thoroughly efficient fire. Being thus distinctly weaker than the northern extremity, which was covered by the Three-Crown Battery and a second line of heavy ships, this southern end was most properly chosen by the British as the point of their chief assault for tactical reasons, independently of the strategic advantage urged by Nelson in thus interposing between the enemy and his allies. At half-past nine signal was made to weigh. The ships were soon under sail; but the difficulties of pilotage, despite careful soundings made during the night by an experienced naval captain, were soon apparent. The "Agamemnon," of sixty-four guns, was unable to weather the point of the Middle Ground, and had to anchor out of range. She had no share in the battle. The "Bellona" and "Russell," seventy-fours, the fourth and fifth in the order, entered the Channel; but keeping too far to the eastward they ran ashore on its farther side — upon the Middle Ground. They were not out of action, but beyond the range of the most efficient gunnery under the conditions of that period. Nelson's flag-ship following them passed clear, as did the rest of the heavy ships; but the loss of these three out of the line prevented by so much its extension to the northward. The result was to expose that part of the British order to a weight of fire quite disproportioned to its strength. A body of frigates very gallantly undertook to fill the gap, which they could do but inadequately, and suffered heavy loss in attempting.

The battle was at its height at half-past eleven. There was then no more manœuvring, but the simple question of efficient gunnery and endurance. At about two P. M. a great part of the Danish line had ceased to fire, and the flag-ship "Dannebrog" was in flames. During the action the Danish crews were frequently re-enforced from the shore; and the new-comers in several cases, reaching the ships after they had struck, renewed the fight, either through ignorance or indifference to the fact. The land batteries also fired on boats trying to take possession. Nelson seized on this circumstance to bring the affair to a conclusion. He wrote a letter addressed "To the brothers of Englishmen, the Danes," and sent it under flag of truce to the Crown Prince, who was in the city. "Lord Nelson has directions to spare Denmark when no longer resisting; but if the firing is continued on the part of Denmark, Lord Nelson will be obliged to set on fire all the floating batteries he has taken, without having the power of saving the brave Danes who have defended them." The letter was sent on shore by a British officer who had served in the Russian navy and spoke Danish. The engagement continued until about three P. M., when the whole line of floating defences south-east of the Crown Batteries had either struck or been destroyed.

The fortifications were still unharmed, as were the ships

west of them covering the harbor proper; but their fire
was stopped by the bearer of a flag of truce who was
bringing to Nelson the reply of the Crown Prince. The
latter demanded the precise purport of the first message.
Nelson took a high hand. He had destroyed the part of
the enemy's line which he had attacked; but it was important now to withdraw his crippled ships, and with the
existing wind that could only be done by passing the
Crown Batteries. Had the three that ran aground been
in the line, it is permissible to believe that that work
would have been so far injured as to be practically harmless; but this was far from the case. The admiral in his
second letter politicly ignored this feature of the situation. He wrote, "Lord Nelson's object in sending on
shore a flag of truce is humanity;[1] he therefore *consents*
that hostilities shall cease till Lord Nelson can take his
prisoners out of the prizes, and he consents to land all the
wounded Danes and to burn or remove his prizes. Lord
Nelson, with humble duty to His Royal Highness, begs
leave to say that he will ever esteem it the greatest victory he ever gained, if this flag of truce may be the happy
forerunner of a lasting and happy union between my most
gracious Sovereign and His Majesty the King of Denmark." Having written the letter, he referred the bearer
for definite action to Sir Hyde Parker, who lay some four
miles off in the "London;" foreseeing that the long pull
there and back would give time for the leading ships,
which were much crippled, to clear the shoals, though
their course for so doing lay close under the Crown Batteries. Thus the exposed part of the British fleet was

---

[1] If Nelson had an *arrière pensée* in sending the flag, he never admitted
it, before or after, to friend or foe. "Many of my friends," he wrote a month
after the battle, "thought it a *ruse de guerre* and not quite justifiable. Very
few attribute it to the cause that I felt, and which I trust in God I shall retain
to the last moment, — *humanity*." He then enlarges upon the situation, and
says that the wounded Danes in the prizes were receiving half the shot fired
by the shore batteries. (Nels. Disp., vol. iv., p. 360.)

successfully removed from a dangerous position and rejoined Parker north of the Middle Ground. The advantage obtained by Nelson's presence of mind and promptness
in gaining this respite was shown by the difficulties attending the withdrawal. Three out of five ships-of-the-
line grounded, two of which remained fast for several
hours a mile from the batteries, but protected by the
truce.

The result of the battle of Copenhagen was to uncover
the front of the city and lay it, with its dockyards and
arsenals, open to bombardment. It was now safe to place
the bomb vessels in the King's Channel. It became a
question for Denmark to decide, whether fear of her powerful allies and zeal for the claims of neutrals should lead
her to undergo further punishment, or whether the suffering already endured and the danger still threatening were
excuse sufficient for abandoning the coalition. On the
other hand, Nelson, who was the brains as well as the
backbone of the British power in the North, cared little,
either now or before the battle, about the attitude of Denmark, except as it deterred Parker from advancing. Now,
as before, his one idea was to get at the Russian division
still locked in Revel by the ice. The negotiations were
carried on by him and resulted in an armistice for fourteen
teen weeks, after which hostilities could be resumed upon
fourteen days' notice. Thus was assured to Parker for
four months the entire immunity he desired for his communications. Fear of Russia long deterred the Danes
from this concession, which Nelson frankly told them he
must have, so as to be at liberty to act against the Russian
fleet and return to them; and he made it the indispensable requisite to sparing the city. During the discussions,
however, the Crown Prince received news of the czar's
death. Paul I. had been murdered by a body of conspira-
tors on the night of March 24. The Danish government
concealed the tidings; but the departure of the soul of the

confederacy relieved their worst fears and encouraged them to yield to Nelson's demands.

Denmark's part in the Armed Neutrality was suspended during the continuance of the armistice; but the British ministers showed as little appreciation of the military situation as did their commander-in-chief in the Baltic. "Upon a consideration of all the circumstances," they wrote to Nelson,[1] "His Majesty has thought fit to approve the armistice." Nelson was naturally and justly indignant at this absurdly inadequate understanding of the true nature of services, concerning whose military character a French naval critic has truly said that "they will always be in the eyes of seamen his fairest title to glory. He alone was capable of displaying such boldness and perseverance; he alone could confront the immense difficulties of that enterprise and overcome them."[2] But his conduct at Copenhagen, brilliant as was the display of energy, of daring and of endurance, was far from exhausting the merits of his Baltic campaign. He had lifted and carried on his shoulders the dead weight of his superior, he had clearly read the political as well as the military situation, and he never for one moment lost sight of the key to both. To bombard Copenhagen was to his mind a useless piece of vandalism, which would embitter a nation that ought to be conciliated, and destroy the only hold Great Britain still had over Denmark.[3] Except for the necessity of managing his lethargic and cautious commander-in-chief, we may believe he would never have contemplated it; but under the circumstances he used the threat as the one means by which he could extort truce from Denmark and induce Parker to move. With the latter to handle, the armistice slipped the knot of the

---

[1] April 20, 1801. Nels. Disp., vol. iv. p. 355, note.

[2] Jurien de la Gravière, Guerres Maritimes, vol. ii. p. 43, 1st edition.

[3] Having destroyed Copenhagen, we had done our worst, and not much nearer being friends. — *Nels. Disp.*, vol. iv. p. 361.

military difficulty; it was the one important point, alongside which every other fell into insignificance. "My object," he said, "was to get at Revel before the frost broke
up at Cronstadt, that the twelve sail-of-the-line might be
destroyed." Well might St. Vincent write, "Your Lord-
ship's whole conduct, from your first appointment to this
hour, is the subject of our constant admiration. It does
not become me to make comparisons; all agree there is
but one Nelson."

Meantime, while the British fleet had been dallying in
the approaches to the Baltic, important events had occurred, furthering the projects of Bonaparte in the North
and seriously complicating the position of Great Britain.
No formal declaration of war was at any time issued by
the latter country; but its government had not unjustly
regarded as an act of direct hostility the combination of
Denmark, Sweden, and Prussia, to support the czar in a
course first undertaken to assure his claim upon Malta,
and in furtherance of which he had seized as pledges three
hundred British merchant vessels with their crews.[1] As
an offset to the British interests thus foreclosed upon by
Russia, and to negotiate upon somewhat equal terms, the
government, on the 14th of January, 1801, ordered an embargo laid upon Russian, Danish, and Swedish vessels in
British ports, and the seizure of merchant ships of these
powers at sea. Of four hundred and fifty Swedish vessels
then abroad, two hundred were detained or brought into
British harbors. They were not, however, condemned as
prizes, but held inviolable to await the issue of the exist-

---

[1] The second embargo was laid on Nov. 7, 1800, for the sole purpose of
enforcing the surrender of Malta to Russia. (Annual Register, 1800; State
Papers, p. 253.) It antedated by six weeks the declaration of Armed Neutrality, by which the other powers, on the plea of neutral rights, agreed to
arm. (Ibid., p. 260.) In fact, the other powers urged upon Great Britain that
the Russian sequestration being on account of Malta, they had no share in it,
and so were not subjects for retaliation; ignoring that they had chosen that
moment to come to Russia's support.

ing difficulties. To the remonstrances of Sweden and Denmark, supported by Prussia, the British ministry replied definitely, on the 7th of March, that the embargo would not be revoked so long as the Powers affected " continued to form part of a confederacy which had for its object to impose by force on his Majesty a new system of maritime law, inconsistent with the dignity and independence of his crown, and the rights and interests of his people." [1] In consequence of this and of the entrance of the Sound by Parker's fleet, Prussia, on the 30th of March, and as a measure of retaliation, closed the mouths of the Elbe, the Weser, and the Ems — in other words, the ports of North Germany — against British commerce, and took possession of the German states belonging to the king of Great Britain. On the same day a corps of Danish troops occupied Hamburg, more certainly to stop British trade therewith.

Thus Bonaparte's conception was completely realized. There was not only a naval combination against Great Britain, but also an exclusion of her trade from one of its chief markets. The danger, however, was much less than it seemed. On the one hand, while the annoyances to neutral navigation were indisputable, the advantages it drew from the war were far greater; its interests really demanded peace, even at the price set by Great Britain. On the other hand, the more important claims of the great Sea Power, however judged by standards of natural right, had prescription on their side; and in the case of contraband, whatever may be thought of classifying naval stores as such, there was for it a colorable pretext in the fact that France then had no merchant shipping, except coasters; that naval stores entering her ports were almost certainly for ships of war; and that it was in part to the exclusion of such articles that Great Britain owed the maritime supremacy, which alone among armed forces had

[1] Annual Register, 1801 ; State Papers, p. 246.

successfully defied Bonaparte. In short, the interest of
the Northern states was to yield the points in dispute,
while that of Great Britain was not to yield; a truth not
only asserted by the ministry but conceded in the main
by the opposition. There needed therefore only to throw
a little weight into one scale, or to take a little from the
other, to turn the balance; while the coalition would dissolve entirely either upon decisive naval operations by
Great Britain, or upon the death of Paul I. The czar
was the only person embarked heart and soul in the Northern quarrel, because the only one deaf to the call of
clear interest. Herein is apparent the crying mistake of
intrusting the conduct of the naval campaign to another
than Nelson. The time placidly consumed by Parker in
deliberations and talking would have sufficed his lieuten-
ant to scour the Baltic, to destroy the Russians at Revel
as he did the Danish line at Copenhagen, and to convince
the neutral states of the hopelessness of the struggle.
Fortunately for Great Britain, the interests of Russian
proprietors, which were bound up with British commerce,
and hardly yielded eight years later to restrictions imposed by the popular Alexander I., rebelled against the
measures of a ruler whose insanity was no longer doubtful. The murder of Paul opened the way for peace.

Among the first measures of the new czar was the release of the British seamen imprisoned by his father.
This order was dated April 7. On the 12th the British
ships entered the Baltic,— much to the surprise of the
Northern Powers, who thought their heavy draught would
prevent. The three-deckers had to remove their guns to
pass some shoal ground ten miles above Copenhagen.
After an excursion to intercept a Swedish fleet said to be
at sea, Parker anchored his ships in Kioge Bay,— off the
coast of Zealand just within the entrance to the Baltic,—
and there awaited further instructions from home; the
Russian minister at Copenhagen having informed him

that the new czar would not go to war.[1] Nelson entirely disapproved of this inactive attitude. Russia might yield the conditions of Great Britain, but she would be more likely to do so if the British fleet lay off the harbor of Revel. This seems also to have been the view of the ministry. It received news of the battle of Copenhagen on April 15, and at about the same date learned the death of Paul I. Advantage was very properly taken of the latter to adopt a policy of conciliation. On the 17th orders were issued to Parker modifying his first instructions. If Alexander removed the embargo and released the seamen, all hostile movements were to be suspended. If not, a cessation of hostilities was tó be offered, if Russia were willing to treat; *but upon condition that, until these ships and men were released, the Revel division should not join that in Cronstadt, nor vice versâ.*[2] This presumed a position of the British fleet very different from Kioge Bay, over four hundred miles from Revel.

Four days later, orders were issued relieving Parker and leaving Nelson in command. Taken as this step was, only a week after the news of a victory, it can scarcely be construed otherwise than as an implied censure. To this view an expression of Nelson's lends color. "They are not Sir Hyde Parker's real friends who wish for an inquiry," he wrote to a confidential correspondent. "His friends in the fleet wish everything of this fleet to be forgot, for we all respect and love Sir Hyde; but the dearer his friends, the more uneasy they have been at his *idleness*, for that is the truth — no criminality."[3] The orders were received on May 5. Nelson's first signal was to hoist the boats aboard and prepare to weigh. "If Sir Hyde were gone," he wrote the 'same afternoon, "I would now be under sail." On the 7th the fleet left Kioge Bay and on the 12th appeared off Revel. The Russian division had

---

[1] Nels. Disp., vol. iv., pp. 349, 352.

[2] Ibid., p. 349; also see p. 379.   [3] Ibid., vol. iv. p. 416.

sailed three days before and was now safe under the guns
of Cronstadt. From Revel Nelson dispatched very com-
plimentary letters to the Russian minister of foreign
affairs, but received in reply the message that "the only
proof of the loyalty of his intentions that the czar could
accept was the prompt withdrawal of his fleet; and that
until then no negotiation could proceed." "I do not believe he would have written such a letter," said Nelson,
"if the Russian fleet had been in Revel;"[1] but the bird
was flown, and with a civil explanation he withdrew from
the port. He still remained in the Baltic, awaiting the
issue of the negotiations; but Russia meant peace, and on
the 17th of May the czar ordered the release of the embargoed British ships. On the 4th of June Great Britain
also released the Danes and Swedes detained in her ports.
Russia and Prussia had already agreed, on the 27th of
April, that hostile measures against England should
cease, Hamburg and Hanover be evacuated, and the free
navigation of the rivers restored.

On the 17th of June was signed at St. Petersburg a convention between Russia and Great Britain, settling the
points that had been in dispute. The question of Malta
was tacitly dropped. As regards neutral claims Russia
conceded that the neutral flag should not cover enemy's
goods; and while she obtained the formal admission that
articles of hostile origin which had become *bonâ fide* neutral
property were exempt from seizure, she yielded the very
important exception of colonial produce. This, no matter
who the owner, could not by a neutral be carried direct
from the colony to the mother country of a nation at war.[2]
Great Britain, on the other hand, conceded the right of
neutrals to carry on the coasting trade of a belligerent;

---

[1] Nels. Disp., vol. iv. p. 373.

[2] For the important bearings of this stipulation, which was made as an
additional and explanatory declaration to the main convention (Annual
Register, 1801; State Papers, p. 217), see *post*, Chapter XVI. It was a matter
in which Russia, not being a carrier, had no interest.

and that naval stores should not be classed as contraband
of war.   The latter was an important concession, the
former probably not, coasting trade being ordinarily done
by small craft especially adapted to the local conditions.
As regards searching merchant vessels under convoy of a
ship of war, Russia yielded the principle and Great Britain
accepted methods which would make the process less
offensive.   Privateers in such case could not search.   The
question was unimportant; for neutral merchant ships will
not lightly submit to the restraint and delays of convoy,
and so lose the chief advantage, that of speed, which they
have over belligerents.   When a neutral sees necessary to
convoy her merchantmen, the very fact shows relations
already strained.

Sweden and Denmark necessarily followed the course
of Russia and acceded to all the terms of the convention
between that court and Great Britain; Sweden on the 23d
of October, 1801, and Denmark on the 30th of the following March.   The claim to carry colonial produce to
Europe, thus abandoned, was of importance to them, though
not to Russia.   At the same time the Baltic states renewed
among themselves the engagements, which they had relinquished in their convention with Great Britain, that the
neutral flag should cover enemy's property on board and
that the convoy of a ship of war should exempt merchant
vessels from search.   These principles were in point of fact
modifications sought to be introduced into international
law, and not prescriptive rights, as commonly implied by
French historians [1] dealing with this question.   For this
reason both the United States and the Baltic powers, while
favoring the new rule, were little disposed to attempt by
arms to compel the surrender by Great Britain of a claim
sanctioned by long custom.

Thus had fallen resultless, as far as the objects of the
first consul were concerned, the vast combination against

[1] For instance, Thiers, H. Martin, and Lanfrey.

Great Britain which he had fostered in the North. During its short existence he had actively pursued in the south of Europe, against Naples and Portugal, other measures intended further to embarrass, isolate, and cripple the great Sea Power, and to facilitate throwing much needed supplies and re-enforcements into Egypt. " The ambassador of the republic," he wrote in February, 1801, " will make the Spanish ministry understand that we must at whatsoever cost become masters of the Mediterranean. . . . France will have fifteen ships-of-the-line in the Mediterranean before the equinox ; and, if Spain will join to them fifteen others, the English, who are about to have the ports of Lisbon, Sicily, and Naples closed to them, will not be able to keep thirty ships in the Mediterranean. That being so, I doubt not they will evacuate Mahon, being unable to remain in that sea." [1]

For the closure of the ports Bonaparte relied with good reason upon his armies; but in the concurrent expectation of uniting thirty French and Spanish ships he reckoned without his host, as he did also upon the Russian Black Sea fleet, and the numbers the British must keep in the Baltic and off Brest. After the armistice with Austria in Italy, a corps under Murat was pushed toward Naples; and on the same day that the treaty of Lunéville was concluded, February 9, a truce for thirty days was signed with the Two Sicilies. This was followed on the 28th of March by a definitive treaty of peace. Naples engaged to exclude from all her ports, including those of Sicily, the ships both of war and commerce belonging to Great Britain and Turkey ; while those of France and her allies, as well as of the Northern powers, should have free access. She also suffered some slight territorial loss ; but the most significant article was kept secret. The boot of Italy was to be occupied by a division of twelve or fifteen thousand French, whom Naples was to pay and support, and to whom

[1] Corr. de Nap. vol. vii. p. 25.

were to be delivered all the maritime fortresses south of the river Ofanto and east of the Bradano, including the ports of Taranto and Brindisi. "This occupation," wrote Bonaparte to his war-minister, "is only in order to facilitate the communications of the army of Egypt with France."[1] The Neapolitan ports became a refuge for French squadrons; while the army of occupation stood ready to embark, if any body of ships found their way to those shores. Unfortunately, the combined British and Turkish armies had already landed in Egypt, and had won the battle of Alexandria a week before the treaty with Naples was signed. As a speedy result the French in Egypt were divided; part being forced back upon Cairo and part shut up in Alexandria,—while the fleet of Admiral Keith cruised off the coast.

No French squadron succeeded in carrying to Egypt the desired re-enforcements, notwithstanding the numerous efforts made by the first consul. The failure arose from two causes: the penury of the French arsenals, and the difficulty of a large body of ships escaping together, or of several small bodies effecting a combination, in face of the watchfulness of the British. Both troubles were due mainly to the rigid and methodical system introduced by Earl St. Vincent; who, fortunately for Great Britain, assumed command of the Channel fleet at the same time that Bonaparte sought to impress upon the French navy a more sagacious direction and greater energy of action. His instructions to Admiral Bruix in February, 1800,[2] were to sail from Brest with over thirty French and Spanish sail-of-the-line, to drive the British blockaders from before the port, to relieve Malta, send a light squadron to Egypt,

---

[1] Corr. de Nap. vol. vii. p. 47.

[2] For full particulars of Bonaparte's views for the ships in Brest, which then contained the large body of Spaniards brought back by Bruix the previous August, see Corr. de Nap. vol. vi. pp. 181, 186. It must be remembered that there was then practically no French line-of-battle force in the Mediterranean.

and then bring his fleet to Toulon, where it would be favorably placed to control the Mediterranean. Delay ensuing, owing to lack of supplies and the unwillingness of the Spaniards, he wrote again at the end of March, " If the equinox passes without the British fleet dispersing, then, great as is our interest in raising the blockade of Malta and carrying help to Egypt, they must be abandoned ; " [1] and throughout the summer months he confined his action to the unremitting efforts, already noticed, to keep a stream of small vessels constantly moving towards Egypt.

After the autumn equinox Bonaparte again prepared for a grand naval operation. Admiral Ganteaume was detailed to sail from Brest with seven ships-of-the-line, carrying besides their crews four thousand troops and an immense amount of material. "Admiral Ganteaume," wrote he to Menou, commander-in-chief in Egypt, " brings to your army the succor we have not before been able to send. He will hand you this letter." The letter was dated October 29, 1800, but it never reached its destination. Ganteaume could not get out from Brest till nearly three months later, when, on January 23d, 1801, a terrible north-east gale drove off the British squadron and enabled him to put to sea. " A great imprudence," says Thiers, " but what could be done in presence of an enemy's fleet which incessantly blockaded Brest in all weathers, and only retired when cruising became impossible. It was necessary either never to go out, or to do so in a tempest which should remove the British squadron." The incident of the sortie, as well as Ganteaume's subsequent experiences, illustrates precisely the deterrent effect exercised by St. Vincent's blockades.[2] They could not prevent occasional escapes,

[1] Corr. de Nap., vol. vi. pp. 262, 263.

[2] The advantage of the close watch is also shown by the perplexity arising when an enemy's squadron did escape. In this case, seven ships-of-the-line were detached from the Channel fleet in chase of Ganteaume, but "owing to lack of information" they were sent to the West Indies instead of the Mediterranean. (James, vol. iii. p. 73.) The latter was sufficiently con-

but they did throw obstacles nearly insuperable in the way of combining and executing any of the major operations of war. Owing to the weather which had to be chosen for starting, the squadron was at once dispersed and underwent considerable damage.[1] It was not all reunited till a week later. On the 9th of February it passed Gibraltar; but news of its escape had already reached the British admiral Warren cruising off Cadiz, who followed quickly, entering Gibraltar only twenty-hours after the French went by. On the 13th of January Ganteaume captured a British frigate, from which he learned that the Mediterranean fleet under Lord Keith was then convoying an army of fifteen thousand British troops against Egypt. He expected that Warren also would soon be after him, and the injuries received in the gale weighed upon his mind. Considering all the circumstances, he decided to abandon Egypt and go to Toulon. Warren remained cruising in the Mediterranean watching for the French admiral, who twice again started for his destination. The first time he was obliged to return by a collision between two ships. The second, an outbreak of disease compelled him to send back three of the squadron. The other four reached the African coast some distance west of Alexandria, where they undertook to land the troops; but Keith's fleet appeared on the horizon, and, cutting their cables, they made a hasty retreat, without having effected their object.

Similar misfortune attended Bonaparte's attempt to collect an efficient force in Cadiz, where Spain had been induced or compelled to yield to him six ships-of-the-line, and where she herself had some vessels. To these he intended to send a large detachment from Rochefort under Admiral Bruix, who was to command the whole, when combined. To concentrations at any point, however, British squadrons

trolled by Keith with seven sail-of-the-line in the Levant, and Warren with five before Cadiz, to which he joined two more at Minorca.

[1] See *ante*, vol. i. p. 68, for particulars.

before the ports whence the divisions were to sail imposed
obstacles, which, even if occasionally evaded, were fatal to
the final great design. The advantage of the central position was consistently realized. On the other hand, where
a great number of ships happened to be together, as at
Brest in 1801, the want of supplies, caused by the same
close watch and by the seizure of naval stores as contraband, paralyzed their equipment. Finding himself baffled
at Brest for these reasons, the first consul appointed
Rochefort for the first concentration. When the second
was effected at Cadiz, Bruix was to hold himself ready for
further operations. If Egypt could not be directly assisted,
it might be indirectly by harassing the British communications. "Every day," wrote Bonaparte, "a hundred sails
pass the straits under weak convoy, to supply Malta and the
English fleet." If this route were flanked at Cadiz, by a
squadron like that of Bruix, much exertion would be needed
to protect it. But the concentration at Rochefort failed,
the ships from Brest could not get there, and the Rochefort
ships themselves never sailed.

Coincidently with this attempt, another effort was made
to strengthen the force at Cadiz.[1] The three vessels sent
back by Ganteaume, after his second sailing from Toulon,
were also ordered to proceed there, under command of Rear
Admiral Linois. Linois successfully reached the Straits of
Gibraltar, but there learned from a prize that seven British
ships were cruising off his destination. These had been
sent with Admiral Saumarez from the Channel fleet, to
replace Warren, when the admiralty learned the active
preparations making in Cadiz and the French ports. Not
venturing to proceed against so superior an enemy, Linois

---

[1] In the above the attempt has been merely to summarize the rapid succession of events, and the orders issuing from Bonaparte's intensely active
mind to meet the varying situations. Reference may be made by the student
to his correspondence, vol. vi. pp. 719, 729, 745; vol. vii. pp. 4, 24-26. 69-73,
125, 144, 164, 197, 198.

put into Gibraltar Bay, anchoring on the Spanish side under the guns of Algesiras. Word was speedily sent to Saumarez ; and on July 6, two days after Linois anchored, six British ships were seen rounding the west point of the bay. They attacked at once ; but the wind was baffling, they could not get their positions, and both flanks of the French line were supported by shore batteries, which were efficiently worked by soldiers landed from the squadron. The attack was repulsed, and one British seventy-four that grounded under a battery was forced to strike. Saumarez withdrew under Gibraltar and proceeded to refit ; the crews working all day and by watches at night to gain the opportunity to revenge their defeat. Linois sent to Cadiz for the help he needed, and on the 10th five Spanish ships-of-the-line and one French [1] from there anchored off Algesiras. On the 12th they got under way with Linois's three, and at the same time Saumarez with his six hauled out from Gibraltar. The allies retreated upon Cadiz, the British following. During the night the van of the pursuers brought the hostile rear to action, and a terrible scene ensued. A Spanish three-decker caught fire, and in the confusion was taken for an enemy by one of her own fleet of the same class. The two ships, of one hundred and twelve guns each and among the largest in the world, ran foul of each other and perished miserably in a common conflagration. The French " St. Antoine " was captured.

The incident of Saumarez's meeting with Linois has a particular value, because of the repulse and disaster to the British vessels on the first occasion. Unvarying success accounts, or seems to account, for itself ; but in this case the advantage of the squadron's position before Cadiz transpires through a failure on the battle-field. To that position was due, first, that Linois's detachment could not make its junction ; second, that it was attacked separately and very severely handled ; third, that in the retreat to Cadiz the

[1] This ship, the " St. Antoine," was one of those ceded to France by Spain.

three French ships were not in proper condition to engage, although one of them when brought to action made a very dogged resistance to, and escaped from, an inferior ship. Consequently, the six British that pursued had only six enemies instead of nine to encounter. After making allowance for the very superior quality of the British officers and crews over the Spanish, it is evident the distinguishing feature in these operations was that the British squadron brought the enemies' divisions to action separately. It was able to do so because it had been kept before the hostile port, interposing between them.

Saumarez had wrung success out of considerable difficulty. The failure of the wind greatly increased the disadvantage to his vessels, coming under sail into action with others already drawn up at anchor, and to whom the loss of spars for the moment meant little. These circumstances, added to the support of the French by land batteries and some gunboats, went far to neutralize tactically the superior numbers of the British. With all deductions, however, the fight at Algesiras was extremely creditable to Linois. He was a man not only distinguished for courage, but also of a cautious temper peculiarly fitted to secure every advantage offered by a defensive position. Despite his success there, the broad result was decisively in favor of his opponents. "Sir James Saumarez's action," wrote Lord St. Vincent, "has put us upon velvet." Seven British had worsted nine enemy's ships, as distinctly superior, for the most part, in individual force as they were in numbers. Not only had the Spaniards three of ninety guns and over, and one of eighty, but two of Linois's were of the latter class, of which Saumarez had but one. The difference between such and the seventy-fours was not only in number of pieces, but in weight also. The substantial issue, however, can be distinguished from the simple victory, and it was secured not only by superior efficiency but also by strategic disposition.

Brilliant as was Saumarez's achievement, which Nelson, then in England, warmly extolled in the House of Lords, the claim made by his biographer, that to these operations alone was wholly due the defeat of Bonaparte's plan, is exaggerated. It was arranged, he says, that when the junction was made, the Cadiz ships should proceed off Lisbon, sack that place, and destroy British merchantmen lying there; "then, being re-enforced by the Brest fleet, they were to pass the Straits of Gibraltar, steer direct for Alexandria, and there land such a body of troops as would raise the siege and drive the English out of Egypt. *This would certainly have succeeded* had the squadron under Linois not encountered that of Sir James, which led to the total defeat of their combined fleets and to the abandonment of the grand plan."[1] This might be allowed to stand as a harmless exhibition of a biographer's zeal, did it not tend to obscure the true lesson to be derived from this whole naval period, by attributing to a single encounter, however brilliant, results due to an extensive, well-conceived general system. Sir James Saumarez's operations were but an epitome of an action going on everywhere from the Baltic to Egypt. By this command of the sea the British fleets, after they had adopted the plan of close-watching the enemy's ports, held everywhere interior positions, which, by interposing between the hostile detachments, facilitated beating them in detail. For the most part this advantage of position resulted in quietly detaining the enemy in port, and so frustrating his combinations. It was Saumarez's good fortune to illustrate how it could also enable a compact body of highly disciplined ships to meet in rapid succession two parts of a force numerically very superior, and by the injuries inflicted on each neutralize the whole for a definite time. But, had he never seen Linois, Bonaparte's plan still required the junctions from Rochefort and Brest which were never effected.

[1] Ross's Life of Saumarez, vol. ii. p. 21.

By naval combinations and by holding the Neapolitan ports Bonaparte sought to preserve Egypt and force Great Britain to peace. "The question of maritime peace," he wrote to Ganteaume,[1] " hangs now upon the English expedition to Egypt." Portugal, the ancient ally of Great Britain, was designed to serve other purposes of his policy, — to furnish equivalents, with which to wrest from his chief enemy the conquests that the sea power of France and her allies could not touch. "Notify our minister at Madrid," wrote he to Talleyrand, September 30, 1800, "that the Spanish troops must be masters of Portugal before October 15. This is the only means by which we can have an equivalent for Malta, Mahon, and Trinidad. Besides, the danger of Portugal will be keenly felt in England, and will by so much quicken her disposition to peace."

A secret treaty ceding Louisiana to France, in return for Tuscany to the Spanish infante, had been signed the month before; and Spain at the same time undertook to bring Portugal to break with Great Britain. Solicitation proving ineffectual, Bonaparte in the spring again demanded the stronger measure of an armed occupation of the little kingdom; growing more urgent as it became evident that Egypt was slipping from his grasp. Spain finally agreed to invade Portugal, and accepted the co-operation of a French corps. The first consul purposed to occupy at least three of the Portuguese provinces; but he was outwitted by the adroitness of the Spanish government, unwillingly submissive to his pressure, and by the compliance of his brother Lucien, French minister to Madrid. Portugal made no efficient resistance; and the two peninsular courts quickly reached an agreement, by which the weaker closed her ports to Great Britain, paid twenty million francs to France, and ceded a small strip of territory to Spain.

Bonaparte was enraged at this treaty, which was rati-

[1] March 2, 1801. Corr. de Nap., vol. vii. p. 72.

fied without giving him a chance to interfere;[1] but in the summer of 1801 his diplomatic game reached a stage where further delay was impossible. He saw that the loss of Egypt was only a question of time; but so long as any French troops held out there it was a card in his hand, too valuable to risk for the trifling gain of a foothold in Portugal. "The English are not masters of Egypt," he writes boldly on the 23d of July to the French agent in London. "We have certain news that Alexandria can hold out a year, and Lord Hawkesbury knows that Egypt is in Alexandria;"[2] but four days later he sends the hopeless message to Murat, "There is no longer any question of embarking"[3] the troops about Taranto, sent there for the sole purpose of being nearer to Egypt.[4] He continues, in sharp contrast with his former expectation, "The station of the troops upon the Adriatic is intended to impose upon the Turks and the English, and to serve as material for compensation to the latter by evacuating those provinces." Both Naples and Portugal were too distant, too ex-centric, and thrust too far into contact with the British dominion of the sea to be profitably, or even safely, held by France in her condition of naval debility; a truth abundantly witnessed by the later events of Napoleon's reign, by the disastrous occupation of Portugal in 1807, by the reverses of Soult and Masséna in 1809 and 1811, and by the failure even to attempt the conquest of Sicily.

Russia and Prussia had grown less friendly since the death of Paul. Even their agreement that Hanover should be evacuated, disposed as they now were to please Great Britain, was to be postponed until "it was ascertained that a certain power would not occupy that country;"[5]

---

[1] The treaty was signed June 6, and ratified June 16. (Ann. Reg. 1801; State Papers, p. 351.) Bonaparte received his copy June 15. (Corr. de Nap., vol. vii. p. 215.)

[2] Corr. de Nap., vol. vii. p. 256.   [3] Ibid., p. 266.

[4] See ante, p. 60.   [5] Ann. Reg. 1801; State Papers, p. 257.

a stipulation which betrayed the distrust felt by both. Since then each had experienced evasions and rebuffs showing the unwillingness of the first consul to meet their wishes in his treatment of the smaller states; and they suspected, although they did not yet certainly know, the steps already taken to incorporate with France regions to whose independence they held.[1] Both were responding to the call of their interests, beneficially and vitally connected with the sea power of Great Britain, and threatened on the Continent by the encroaching course of the French ruler. Bonaparte felt that the attempt to make further gains in Europe, with which to traffic against those of Great Britain abroad, might arouse resistance in these great powers, not yet exhausted like Austria, and so indefinitely postpone the maritime peace essential to the revival of the French navy and the re-establishment of the colonial system; both at this time objects of prime importance in his eyes. Thus it was that, beginning the year 1801 without a single ally, in face of the triumphant march of the French armies and of a formidable maritime combination, the Sea Power of Great Britain had dispersed the Northern coalition, commanded the friendship of the great states, retained control of the Mediterranean,

---

[1] Paul I. had particularly held to the preservation of Naples and the restitution of Piedmont to the king of Sardinia. On April 12 the first consul heard of Paul's death, and the same day issued an order making Piedmont a military division of France. This was purposely antedated to April 2. (Corr. de Nap., vol. vii. p. 147.) Talleyrand was notified that this was a first, though tentative, step to incorporation. If the Prussian minister remonstrated, he was to, reply that France had not discussed the affairs of Italy with the king of Prussia. (Ibid., p. 153.) Alexander was civilly told that Paul's interest in the Italian princes was considered to be personal, not political. (Ibid., p. 169.) The Russian ambassador, however, a month later haughtily reminded Talleyrand that his mission depended upon the " kings of Sardinia and the Two Sicilies being again put in possession of the states which they possessed before the irruption of the French troops into Italy." (Ann. Reg., 1801 ; State Papers, pp. 340–342.) Liguria (Genoa) was also made a military division of France by order dated April 18. (Corr. de Nap., vol. vii. p. 162.)

reduced Egypt to submission, and forced even the invincible Bonaparte to wish a speedy cessation of hostilities.

The great aim of the first consul now was to bring
Great Britain to terms before news of the evacuation of
Alexandria could come to hand. Negotiations had been
slowly progressing for nearly six months; the first advances having been made on the 21st of March by the new
ministry which came into power upon Pitt's resignation.
Both parties being inclined to peace, the advantage necessarily belonged to the man who, untrammelled by associates in administration, held in absolute control the
direction of his country. The Addington ministry, ham-
pered by its own intrinsic weakness and by the eagerness
of the nation, necessarily yielded before the iron will of
one who was never more firm in outward bearing than in
the most critical moments. He threatened them with the
occupation of Hanover; he intimated great designs for
which troops were embarked at Rochefort, Brest, Toulon,
Cadiz, and ready to embark in Holland; he boasted that
Alexandria could hold out yet a year. Nevertheless, although the terms were incontestably more advantageous
to France than to Great Britain, the government of the
latter insisted upon and obtained one concession, that of
Trinidad, which Bonaparte at first withheld.[1] His eagerness to conclude was in truth as great as their own,
though better concealed. Finally, he sent on the 17th of
September an ultimatum, and added, "If preliminaries
are not signed by the 10th of Vendémiaire (October 2),
the negotiations will be broken." "You will appreciate
the importance of this clause," he wrote confidentially to
the French envoy, "when you reflect that Menou may possibly not be able to hold in Alexandria beyond the first of
Vendémiaire, that at this season the winds are fair to

---

[1] While refusing this in his instructions to the French negotiator, the latter was informed he might yield it, if necessary. (Corr. de Nap., vol. vii.,
pp. 255–258.) .

come from Egypt, and ships reach Italy and Trieste in very few days. Thus it is essential to push them to a finish before Vendémiaire 10;" that is, before they learn the fall of Alexandria. The question of terms, as he had said before, hinged on Egypt. The envoy, however, was furnished with a different but plausible reason. "Otto can give them to understand that from our inferiority at sea and our superiority on land the campaign begins for us in winter, and therefore I do not wish to remain longer in this stagnation."[1] Whatever motives influenced the British ministry, it is evident that Bonaparte was himself in a hurry for peace. The preliminaries were signed in London on the first of October, 1801.

The conditions are easily stated. Of all her conquests, Great Britain retained only the islands of Ceylon in the East Indies and Trinidad in the West. How great this concession, will be realized by enumerating the chief territories thus restored to their former owners. These were, in the Mediterranean, Elba, Malta, Minorca; in the West Indies, Tobago, Santa Lucia, Martinique, and the extensive Dutch possessions in Guiana; in Africa, the Cape of Good Hope; and in India, the French and Dutch stations in the peninsula. France consented to leave to Portugal her possessions entire, to withdraw her troops from the kingdom of Naples and the Roman territory, and to acknowledge the independence of the Republic of the Seven Islands. Under this name the former Venetian islands, Corfu and others — given to France by the treaty of Campo Formio — had, after their conquest in 1799 by the fleets of Russia and Turkey, been constituted into an independent state under the guarantee of those two powers. Their deliverance from France was considered an important security to the Turkish Empire. The capitulation of the French troops in Alexandria was not yet known in England; and the preliminaries merely stipu-

[1] Corr. de Nap., vol. vii. p. 323.

lated the return of Egypt to the Porte, whose dominions were to be preserved as they existed before the war. Malta, restored to the Knights of St. John, was to be freed from all French or British influence and placed under the guarantee of a third Power. Owing to the decay of the Order, the disposition of this important naval station, secretly coveted by both parties, was the most difficult matter to arrange satisfactorily. In the definitive treaty its status was sought to be secured by a cumbrous set of provisions, occupying one third of the entire text; and the final refusal of Great Britain to evacuate, until satisfaction was obtained for what she claimed to be violations of the spirit of the engagements between the two countries, became the test question upon which hinged the rupture of this short-lived peace.

As the first article of the preliminaries stipulated that upon their ratification hostilities in all parts of the world, by sea and land, should cease, they were regarded in both Great Britain and France as equivalent to a definitive treaty; the postponement of the latter being only to allow the negotiators time to settle the details of the intricate agreements, thus broadly outlined, without prolonging the sufferings of war. To France they could not but be acceptable. She regained much, and gave up nothing that she could have held without undue and often useless exertion. In Great Britain the general joy was marred by the severe, yet accurate, condemnation passed upon the terms by a body of exceptionally able men, drawn mainly from the ranks of the Pitt cabinet, although their leader gave his own approval. They pointed out, clearly and indisputably, that the disparity between the material gains of Great Britain and France was enormous, disproportionate to their relative advantages at the time of signature, and not to be reconciled with that security which had been the professed object of the struggle. They asserted with little exaggeration that the conditions were for France to hold what she had, and for Great Britain to recede to her possessions before the war. They predicted with fatal accuracy the speedy renewal of hostilities, under the disadvantage of having lost by the peace important positions not easy to be regained. The ministry had little to reply. To this or that item of criticism exception might be taken; but in the main their defence was that by the failure of their allies no hope remained of contesting the power of France on the Continent, and that Trinidad and Ceylon were very valuable acquisitions. Being insular, they were controlled by the nation ruling the sea, while, from their nearness to the mainlands of South America and of India, they were important as depots of trade, as well as for strategic reasons. The most assuring argument was put forward by the Minister of Foreign Affairs, who had negotiated the preliminaries. At the beginning of the war Great Britain had 135 ships-of-the-line and 133 frigates; at its close she had 202 of the former and 277 of the latter. France had begun with 80 of the line and 66 frigates, and ended with 39 and 35 respectively. However the first consul might exert himself, Lord Hawkesbury justly urged that the British might allow him many years labor and then be willing to chance a maritime war.[1]

Material advantages such as had thus been given up undoubtedly contribute to security. In surrendering as much as she did abroad, while France retained such extensive gains upon the Continent and acquired there such a preponderating influence, Great Britain, which had so large a stake in the European commonwealth, undoubtedly incurred a serious risk. The shortness of the peace, and the disquieting disputes which arose throughout it, sufficiently prove this. Nevertheless, could contemporaries accurately read the signs of their times, Englishmen of that day need not have been dissatisfied with the general results of the war. A long stage had been successfully

[1] Parliamentary History, vol. xxxvi. p. 47.

traversed towards the final solution of a great difficulty. In 1792 the spirit of propagating revolution by violence had taken possession of the French nation as a whole. As Napoleon has strikingly remarked, "It was part of the political religion of the France of that day to make war in the name of principles."[1] "The Montagnards and the Jacobins," says the republican historian Henri Martin, the bitter censurer of Bonaparte, "were resolved, like the Girondists, to propagate afar, by arms, the principles of the Revolution; and they hoped, by hurling a defiance at all kings, to put France in the impossibility of recoiling or stopping herself."[2] Such a design could be checked only by raising up against it a barrier of physical armed opposition. This had been effected and maintained chiefly by the Sea Power of Great Britain, the prime agent and moving spirit, directly through her navy, indirectly through the subsidies drawn from her commerce; and the latter had nearly doubled while carrying on this arduous and extensive war. In 1801 the aggressive tendencies of the French nation, as a whole, were exhausted. So far as they still survived, they were now embodied in and dependent upon a single man, in which shape they were at once more distinctly to be recognized and more odious. They were also less dangerous; because the power of one man, however eminent for genius, is far less for good or evil than the impulse of a great people.

The British statesmen of that day did not clearly distinguish this real nature of their gains, though they did intuitively discern the true character of the struggle in which they were engaged. As is not infrequent with intuitions, the reasoning by which they were supported was often faulty; but Pitt's formulation of the objects of Great Britain in the one word "security" was substantially correct. Security was her just and necessary aim, forced

[1] Commentaires de Napoléon, vol. iii. p. 377.
[2] Hist. de France depuis 1789, vol. i. p. 396.

upon her by the circumstances of the Revolution,— security not for herself alone, but for the community of states of which she was an important member. This was threatened with anarchy through the lawless spirit with which the French leaders proposed to force the spread of principles and methods, many of them good as well as many bad, but for whose healthful development were demanded both time and freedom of choice, which they in their impatience were unwilling to give. "Security," said Pitt in his speech upon the preliminaries, "was our great object; there were different means of accomplishing it, with better or worse prospects of success; and according to the different variations of policy occasioned by a change of circumstances, we still pursued our great object, Security. In order to obtain it we certainly did look for the subversion of that government founded upon revolutionary principles. . . . We have the satisfaction of knowing that we have survived the violence of the revolutionary fever, and we have seen the extent of its principles abated. We have seen Jacobinism deprived of its fascination; we have seen it stripped of the name and pretext of liberty; it has shown itself to be capable only of destroying, not of building, and that it must necessarily end in a military despotism."[1] Such, in truth, was the gain of the first war of Great Britain with the French Revolution. It was, however, but a stage in the progress; there remained still another, of warfare longer, more bitter, more furious,— a struggle for the mastery, whose end was not to be seen by the chief leaders of the one preceding it.

[1] Speech of Nov. 3, 1801.

CHAPTER XIV.

OUTLINE OF EVENTS FROM THE SIGNATURE OF THE PRELIMINARIES TO THE RUPTURE OF THE PEACE OF AMIENS.

OCTOBER, 1801. — MAY, 1803.

THE preliminaries of peace between Great Britain and France, signed on the first of October, 1801, were regarded by both parties, at least ostensibly, as settling their relative status and acquisitions. In their broad outlines no change would be worked by the definitive treaty, destined merely to regulate details whose adjustment would demand time and so prolong the distress of war. This expectation, that the basis of a durable peace had been reached, proved delusive. A series of unpleasant surprises awaited first one party and then the other, producing in Great Britain a feeling of insecurity, which gave point and added vigor to the declamations of those who from the first had scoffed at the idea of any peace proving permanent, if it rested upon the good faith of the French government and surrendered those material guarantees which alone, they asserted, could curb the ambition and enforce the respect of a man like Bonaparte. Bitter indeed must have been the unspoken thoughts of the ministry, as the revolving months brought with them an unceasing succession of events which justified their opponents' prophecies while proving themselves to be outwitted ; and which, by the increase given to French influence and power in Europe, necessitated the maintenance of large military establishments, and converted the peace from first to last into a condition of armed truce.

The day after the signature of the preliminaries news reached London[1] of the surrender of Alexandria, which completed the loss of Egypt by the French. It was believed that Bonaparte had, at the time of signing, possessed this information, which would have materially affected the footing upon which he was treating. However that was, he was undoubtedly assured of the issue,[2] and therefore precipitated a conclusion by which to France, and not to Great Britain, was attributed the gracious act of restoring its dominion to the Porte. Concealing the fact from the Turkish plenipotentiary in Paris, the French government on the 9th of October signed with him a treaty, by which it undertook to evacuate the province it no longer held. In return, Turkey conceded to France, her recent enemy, commercial privileges equal to those allowed Great Britain, to whose sea power alone she owed the recovery of Syria and Egypt. This bargain, concluded without the knowledge of the British ministry, was not made public until after the ratification of the preliminaries. At the same time became known a treaty with Portugal, signed at Madrid on the 29th of September. By the preliminaries with Great Britain, Portuguese territory was to remain intact; but by the treaty of Madrid so much of Brazil was added to French Guiana as to give the latter control of the northern outlet of the Amazon.

These events were surprises, and disagreeable surprises, to the British ministers. On the other hand, the existence of the secret treaty of March 21, 1801, by which Spain ceded to France the colony of Louisiana, was known to them,[3] though unavowed at the time of signing. While impressed with the importance of this transaction, following as it did the cession of the Spanish half of San Domingo, the ministry allowed the veil of mystery, with which

---

[1] Annual Register 1801, p. 280.

[2] See ante, p. 70.

[3] Am. State Papers, vol. ii. pp. 509, 511.

Bonaparte had been pleased to shroud it, to remain un-
lifted. The United States minister to London had procured
and forwarded to his government on the 20th of November
a copy of this treaty,[1] which so closely affected his fellow
countrymen; but it was not until January, 1802, that the
fact became generally known in England. Gloomy prophecies of French colonial aggrandizement were uttered by the
partisans of the Opposition, who pictured the hereditary
enemy of Great Britain planted by the Spanish treaty at
the mouth of the great river of North America, and by the
Portuguese at that of the artery of the southern continent;
while the vast and rich colonies of Spain, lying between
these two extremes, would be controlled by the supremacy
of France in the councils of the Peninsular courts. In a
generation which still retained the convictions of the eighteenth century on the subject of colonial expansion, these
predictions of evil struck heavily home,—enforced as they
were by the knowledge that full one fourth of the trade
which made the strength of Great Britain rested then upon
that Caribbean America, into which France was now
making a colossal intrusion. Faithful to the sagacious
principle by which he ever proportioned the extent of his
military preparation to the vastness of the end in view, the
expedition sent by Bonaparte to reassert in Haïti the long
dormant authority of the mother-country was calculated on
a scale which aroused intense alarm in London. On the
4th of December, 1801, only ten weeks after the preliminaries were signed, and long before the conclusion of the
definitive treaty, fifteen ships-of-the-line and six frigates
sailed from Brest for Haïti; and these were rapidly followed by other divisions, so that the whole force dispatched
much exceeded twenty ships-of-the-line, and carried over
twenty thousand troops. The number was none too great
for the arduous task, — indeed experience proved it to be
far from adequate to meet the waste due to climatic causes;

[1] Am. State Papers, vol. ii. p. 511.

but to Great Britain it was portentous. Distrusting Bonaparte's purposes, a large division of British ships was
ordered to re-enforce the squadron at Jamaica. Weary of
a nine-years war and expecting their discharge, the crews
of some of the vessels mutinied; and the execution of
several of these poor seamen was one of the first results of
Bonaparte's ill-fated attempt to restore the colonial system
of France.

The apprehensions shown concerning these distant undertakings partook more of panic than of reasonable fear.
They overlooked the long period that must pass between
possession and development, as well as the hopeless inferiority of France in that sea power upon which the tenure of
colonies must depend. They ignored the evident enormous
difficulties to be overcome, and were blind to the tottering condition of the Spanish colonial system, then rapidly approaching its fall. But if there was exaggeration in an anticipation
of danger, which the whole history of her maritime past
entitled Great Britain to reject with scorn, there was no
question that each month was revealing unexpected and
serious changes in the relative positions of the two powers,
which, if not wilfully concealed by France, had certainly
not been realized by the British ministers when the preliminaries were signed. Whether they had been cheated
or merely out-manœuvred, it became daily more plain that
the balance of power in Europe, of which Great Britain was
so important a factor, was no longer what it had been when
she made such heavy sacrifices of her maritime conquests
to secure the status of the Continent.

At the same time was unaccountably delayed the work
of the plenipotentiaries, who were to settle at Amiens the
terms of the definitive treaty. The British ambassador
left London on the first of November, and after some stop
in Paris reached Amiens on the first of December.' The
French and Dutch envoys arrived shortly after; but the
Spanish failed to appear, and on different pretexts nego-

tiations were spun out. That this was contrary to the
wishes of the British ministers scarcely admits of doubt.
They had already made every sacrifice they could afford;
and the position of a popular government, under the free
criticism of a people impatient for a settled condition of
affairs, and forced to temporizing expedients for carrying
on the state business during a period of uncertainty, was
too unpleasant to suggest bad faith on their part. While
this suspense still lasted, a startling event occurred,
greatly affecting the balance of power. The Cisalpine
Republic, whose independence was guaranteed by the treaty
of Lunéville, adopted toward the end of 1801 a new constitution, drawn up under the inspection of Bonaparte
himself. Delegates of the republic, to the number of
several hundred, were summoned to Lyon to confer with
the first consul on the permanent organization of their
state; and there, under his influence, as was alleged,
offered to him the presidency, with functions even more
extensive than those he enjoyed as ruler of France. The
offer was accepted by him on the 26th of January, 1802;
and thus the power of the Cisalpine, with its four million
inhabitants, was wielded by the same man who already
held that of the French republic. A few days later for
the name Cisalpine was substituted Italian,— a change
thought to indicate an aggressive attitude towards the
remaining states of Italy.

These proceedings at Lyon caused great alarm in England, and many persons before pacifically disposed now
wished to renew the war. The ministers nevertheless
ignored what had passed so publicly, and continued the
effort for peace, despite the delays and tergiversations of
which their envoy, Lord Cornwallis, bitterly complained;
but by the beginning of March, when negotiations had
lasted three months, their patience began to give way.
A number of ships were ordered into commission, and extensive naval preparations begun. At the same time an

ultimatum was sent forward, and Cornwallis instructed
to leave Amiens in eight days if it were not accepted.
The first consul had too much at stake on the seas to risk
a rupture,[1] when he had already gained so much by the
protraction of negotiations and by his astute diplomacy.
The definitive treaty was signed on the 25th of March,
1802. The terms did not materially differ from those of
the preliminaries, except in the article of Malta. The
boundary of French Guiana obtained from Portugal was
indeed pushed back off the Amazon, but no mention was
made of the now notorious cession of Louisiana.

The provisions touching the little island of Malta and
its dependencies, Gozo and Comino, were long and elaborate. The object of each country was to secure the exclusion of the other from a position so important for
controlling the Mediterranean and the approaches thereby
to Egypt and India. The Order of Knights was to be
restored, with the provision that no citizen either of Great
Britain or France was thereafter to be a member. The
independence and neutrality of the Order and of the island
were proclaimed. The British forces were to evacuate
within three months after the exchange of ratifications;
but this stipulation was qualified by the proviso that there
should then be on the spot a Grand Master to receive possession, and also two thousand Neapolitan troops which
the king of Naples was to be invited to send as a garrison. These were to remain for one year after its restitution to the Grand Master; or longer, if the Order had not
then provided the necessary force. Naples was thus
selected as guardian of the coveted position, because its
weakness could arouse no jealousy. The independence of
the islands was placed under the guarantee of Great
Britain, France, Austria, Spain, Russia, and Prussia;

[1] The slightest delay under these circumstances is very prejudicial, and
may be of great consequence to our squadrons and naval expeditions. — *Corr.
de Nap.,* March 11, 1802

the last four being also invited to accede to the long list of stipulations. The presence of a grand master and the guarantee of the four powers — whose acquiescence was not first obtained—were thus integral parts of the agreement; and upon their failure Great Britain afterwards justified the delays which left Malta still a pledge in her hands, when she demanded from France explanations and indemnities for subsequent actions, injurious, as she claimed, to her security and to her dignity.

By another clause of the treaty Great Britain consented to evacuate Porto Ferrajo, the principal port in Elba, which she had up to that time held by force of arms. It was then known that this was in effect to abandon the island to France, who had obtained its cession from Naples and Tuscany, formerly joint owners, by conventions first made known some time after the signature of the preliminaries. Elba was by its position fitted seriously to embarrass the trade of Great Britain with Northern Italy, under the restrictions laid wherever Bonaparte's power extended; but the most important feature of the transaction was the impression produced by the long concealment of treaties thus unexpectedly divulged. These sudden, unforeseen changes imparted an air of illusion to all existing conditions, and undermined the feeling of security essential to the permanent relations of states.

Despite the shocks caused by these various revelations, the treaty of Amiens was received in Great Britain with satisfaction, though not with the unmeasured demonstrations that followed the announcement of the preliminaries. In France the general joy was no less profound. "It was believed," writes M. Thiers, "that the true peace, the peace of the seas, was secured,— that peace which was the certain and necessary condition of peace on the Continent." The enthusiasm of the nation was poured out at the feet of the first consul, to whose genius for war and for diplomacy were not unjustly attributed the brilliant, as well

as apparently solid, results. Statesmen might murmur
that France had lost her colonial empire and failed to
hold Egypt and Malta, while Great Britain had extended
and consolidated her Indian empire by overthrowing the
Sultan of Mysore, the ancient ally of France and her own
most formidable foe in the peninsula; but the mass even
of intelligent Frenchmen stopped not to regard the wreck
of their sea power, of which those disastrous events were
but the sign. Facts so remote, and whose significance
was not immediately apparent, were lost to sight in the
glare of dazzling deeds wrought close at hand. All eyes
were held by the splendid succession of victories in Italy
and Germany, by the extension of the republic to her
natural limits at the Rhine and the Alps, by the restoration of internal order, and by the proudly dominant position accorded their ruler in the councils of the Continent.
To these was now added free access to the sea, wrung
by the same mighty hand — as was fondly believed — from
the weakening of the great Sea Power. At an extraordinary session of the Legislature, convoked to give legal
sanction to the treaties and measures of the government,
the Treaty of Amiens was presented last, as the crown-
ing work of the first consul; and it was used as the occasion for conferring upon him a striking mark of public
acknowledgment. After some hesitations, the question
was submitted to the nation whether his tenure of office
should be for life. The majority of votes cast were affirm-
ative; and on the 3d of August, 1802, the senate formally
presented to him a *senatus-consultum*, setting forth that
"the French people names, and the senate proclaims,
Napoleon Bonaparte consul for life."

Bonaparte had not waited for this exaltation to continue
his restless political activity, destined soon to make waste
paper of the Treaty of Amiens. Great Britain having
steadfastly refused to recognize the new states set up by
him in Italy, he argued she had forfeited all right to in-

terfere thenceforth in their concerns. From this he seems to have advanced to the position that she had no further claim to mingle in the affairs of the Continent at large. The consequent indifference shown by him to British sentiment and interests, in continental matters, was increased by his conviction that "in the existing state of Europe England cannot reasonably make war, alone, against us;"[1] an opinion whose open avowal in more offensive terms afterwards became the spark to kindle the final great conflagration.

The treaty of Lunéville had provided that the German princes, who by it lost territory on the west bank of the Rhine and in Italy, should receive compensation elsewhere in the German empire; and it was agreed that these indemnities should be made mainly at the expense of the ecclesiastical principalities, where, the tenure being for life only, least hardship would be involved. The difficulties attending these distributions, and the fixed animosity between Prussia and Austria, gave Bonaparte a fair pretext to intervene as mediator, and to guide the final settlement upon lines which should diminish the relative power and prestige of France's traditional enemy, Austria, and exalt her rivals. In doing this he adroitly obtained the imposing support of Russia, whose young sovereign readily accepted the flattering offer of joint intervention; the more so that the princes allied to his family might thus receive a disproportionate share of the spoils. Under Bonaparte's skilful handling, the acquisitions of Prussia were so far greater than those of Austria as to fulfil his prediction, that "the empire of Germany should be really divided into two empires, since its affairs will be arranged at two different centres."[2] After the settlement he boasted that "the affairs of Germany had been arranged entirely to the advantage of France and of

---

[1] Corr. de Nap., March 12, 1802, vol. vii. p. 522.
[2] Ibid., April 3, 1802, vol. vii. p. 543.

her allies."[1] Great Britain was not consulted; and her people, though silent, saw with displeasure the weakening of their ally and the aggrandizement of a state they held to be faithless as well as hostile. At the same time bad feeling was further excited by the peremptory demands of Bonaparte for the expulsion from England of certain French royalists, and for the repression of the freedom of the British press in its attacks upon himself. To these demands the British government declined to yield.

The reclamations of Bonaparte against the press, and his intervention in German affairs, preceded the proclamation of the consulate for life. It was followed at a short interval by the formal incorporation with France of Piedmont and Elba, by decree dated September 11, 1802. Piedmont had been organized as a French military department in April, 1801;[2] and Bonaparte had then secretly avowed the measure to be a first step to annexation. The significance of the present action was that it changed a condition which was *de facto* only, and presumably temporary, to one that was claimed to be *de jure* and permanent. As such, it was a distinct encroachment by France, much affecting the states of the Continent, and especially Austria, against whose Italian possessions Piedmont was meant to serve as a base of operations. The adjacent Republic of Liguria, as the Genoese territory was then styled, was also organized as a French military division,[3] and no security existed against similar action there,— most injurious to British commerce, and adding another to the transformation scenes passing before the eyes of Europe. Nor was the material gain to France alone considered; for, no compensation being given to the King of Sardinia for the loss of his most important state, this consummated injury was felt as a slight by both Great Britain

---

[1] Corr. de Nap., July 1, 1802, vol. vii. p. **641.**

[2] Ibid., April 13, 1801, vol. vii. p. 153.

[3] Ibid., April 18, 1801, vol. vii. p. 162.

and Russia, which had earnestly sought some reparation for him. For the time, however, no remonstrance was made by the ministry.

New offence was soon given, which, if not greater in degree, produced all the effect of cumulative grievance. The little canton of Valais, in south-western Switzerland, had in the spring of 1802 been forcibly detached from the confederation and proclaimed independent, in order to secure to the French the Simplon route passing through it to Italy; a measure which, wrote Bonaparte, "joined to the exclusive right of France to send her armies by that road, has changed the system of war to be adopted in Italy."[1] No further open step was then taken to control the affairs of Switzerland; but the French minister was instructed to support secretly the party in sympathy with the Revolution,[2] and an ominous sentence appeared in the message of the first consul to the Legislature, May 6, 1802, that "the counsels of the French government to the factions in Switzerland had so far been ineffective. It is still hoped that the voice of wisdom and moderation will command attention, and that the powers adjoining Helvetia will not be forced to intervene to stifle troubles whose continuance would threaten their own tranquillity."[3]

In Switzerland, perhaps more than in any other part of Europe, had been realized the purpose, announced by the National Convention in the celebrated decrees of November 19 and December 15, 1792, to propagate by force changes in the government of countries where the French armies could penetrate. Vast changes had indeed been made in Belgium, Holland, and Italy; but these when first invaded were in open war with France. The interference in Switzerland in 1798 had no characteristic of serious war, for no means of opposition existed in the in-

---

[1] Corr. de Nap., August 2, 1802, vol. vii. p. 696.

[2] Ibid., vol. vii. pp. 528, 544.

[3] Ibid., vol. vii. p. 578.

vaded cantons. It was an armed intervention, undertaken
by the Directory under the impulsion of Bonaparte, avowedly to support citizens of a foreign state "wishing to recover their liberty."[1] "As soon as the signal was given
by the entrance of the French armies in 1798 the rising
was prompt and general;"[2] and was followed by the
adoption of a highly centralized constitution, for which the
country was unprepared. From that time forward agitation was incessant. Two parties strove for the mastery;
the one favoring the new order, known as the Unitarians,
whose sympathies were with the French Revolution, the
other the Aristocratic, which sought to return towards the
former Constitution, and looked for countenance and support to the older governments of Europe. Between the
two there was a central party of more moderate opinions.

Having secured the Valais for France, Bonaparte in
August, 1802, withdrew the French troops till then maintained in Switzerland; a politic measure tending to show
Europe that he respected the independence of the country
guaranteed at Lunéville. The opposing parties soon came
to blows; and the nominal government of moderates,
which had obtained its authority by extra-constitutional
action,[3] found that it had on its side "neither the ardent
patriots, who wished absolute unity, nor the peaceable
masses sufficiently well disposed to the revolution, but
who knew it only by the horrors of war and the presence
of foreign troops."[4] The aristocratic party got the upper
hand and established itself in the capital, whence the government was driven. The latter appealed to Bonaparte
to intervene; and after a moment's refusal he decided to
do so. "I will not," he said, "deliver the formidable
bastions of the Alps to fifteen hundred mercenaries paid
by England." A French colonel was sent as special en-

[1] Decree of Nov. 19, 1792.
[2] Thiers, Cons. et Emp., livre xv. p. 38.
[3] Ibid., livre xv. pp. 50, 51.   [4] Ibid., xvi. p. 234.

voy bearing a proclamation, dated September 30, 1802, to command the oligarchic government to dissolve and all armed assemblies to disperse. To support this order, thirty thousand French soldiers, under General Ney, were massed on the frontiers and soon entered the country. Before this show of force all opposition in Switzerland at once ceased.

The emotion of Europe was profound; but of the great powers none save Great Britain spoke. What to Bonaparte was a step necessary to the supremacy of France, even though a violation of the treaty of Lunéville, was, in the eyes of Englishmen, not only among the ministry but among the most strenuous of the opposition, an oppressive interference with "the lawful efforts of a brave and generous people to recover their ancient laws and government, and to procure the re-establishment of a system which experience has demonstrated not only to be favorable to the maintenance of their domestic happiness, but to be perfectly consistent with the tranquillity and security of other powers." The British cabinet expressed an unwillingness to believe that there "would be any further attempt to control that independent nation in the exercise of its undoubted rights." [1]

Despite this avowed confidence, the ministry on the same day, October 10, that this vigorous remonstrance was penned, dispatched a special envoy with orders to station himself on the frontiers of Switzerland, ascertain the disposition of the people, and assure them that, if they were disposed to resist the French advance, Great Britain would furnish them pecuniary succors. The envoy was carefully to refrain from promoting resistance, if the Swiss did not spontaneously offer it; but if they did, he was to give them every facility to obtain arms and supplies. Being thus committed to a course which could

[1] Note Verbale. Remonstrance addressed to the French government (Ann. Reg. 1802; State Papers, p. 675.)

scarcely fail to lead to hostilities, the British ministry
next bethought itself to secure some conquests of the late
war, for whose restitution, in compliance with the treaty,
orders had already gone forward.   On the 17th of October
dispatches were sent to the West Indies, to Dutch Guiana,
and to the Cape of Good Hope, directing that the French
and Dutch colonies ordered to be restored should be retained until further instructions.

Upon receiving the British remonstrance, Bonaparte
broke into furious words mingled with threats.   On the
23d of October he dictated instructions to M. Otto, the
French minister in London, which are characterized even
by M. Thiers as truly extraordinary.   " He would not deliver the Alps to fifteen hundred mercenaries paid by
England.   If the British ministry, to support its parliamentary influence, should intimate that there was anything the first consul had not done, because he was
prevented from doing it, that instant he would do it."
He scouted the danger to France from maritime war, and
said plainly that, if it arose, the coasts of Europe from
Hanover to Taranto would be occupied by French troops
and closed to British commerce.   "Liguria, Lombardy,
Switzerland and Holland would be converted into French
provinces, realizing the Empire of the Gauls."   Great
Britain herself was threatened with invasion by a hundred
thousand soldiers; and if, to avert the danger, she succeeded in arousing another continental war, "it would be
England that forced us to conquer Europe.   The first
consul was but thirty-three.   He had as yet destroyed
only states of the second order.   Who knows how long it
would take him, if forced thereto, to change again the
face of Europe and revive the Empire of the West?"   The
minister was directed to state to the British government
that the policy of France towards England was "the whole
treaty of Amiens; nothing but the treaty of Amiens."   A
week later the same phrase was repeated in the Moniteur.

the official journal, in an article which expressly denied
Great Britain's right to appeal to the treaty of Lunéville,
because she had refused to recognize the new states constituted by it.   M. Otto wisely withheld the provoking
language of the dispatch, but necessarily communicated
the demand for the whole treaty of Amiens and the refusal of aught not therein found.   To this the British
minister of foreign affairs replied with the pregnant
words, "The state of the Continent when the treaty of
Amiens was signed, and nothing but that state."   The
two declarations created a dead-lock, unless one party
would recede.

Despite these explicit formulas both governments were
somewhat in the dark as to the extent of the dangers.
The British ministry had not heard all that Bonaparte
said, and he was ignorant of the orders sent to retain the
captured colonies.   Meanwhile, Swiss opposition having
failed, the British envoy to them was recalled; and on
the 15th of November new instructions were sent to the
Cape of Good Hope and the West Indies, revoking those
of the previous month to stop the restitutions.   It remained, however, a question whether the second vessel
would overtake the first.   If she did not, the action of the
British ministry would transpire in an offensive way.
Accordingly, when Parliament met on the 23d of November, the king's speech took the color of this perplexity,
alluding somewhat enigmatically to the necessity of watching the European situation and providing for security as
well as for peace.   The debates which followed were
tinged with the same hue of uncertainty.   The ministry
could only say that its policy was to preserve peace, if
possible; but that, in view of recent events, it must call
upon the House and the country to entertain a spirit of
watchfulness.[1]

The Swiss affair was the turning-point in the relations

---

[1] Lord Hawkesbury's speech; Parl. Hist., vol. xxxvi. p. 971.

of the two countries. The first consul's vigilance had
been lulled by the seeming easy acquiescence of the British ministry in previous encroachments, and the readiness
with which, notwithstanding these, they had surrendered
their conquests and continued to fulfil the terms of the
treaty. , Their present action not only exasperated, but
aroused him. The remonstrance ended in words; but,
like the little trickle which betrays the fissure in a dam,
it betokened danger and gave warning that the waters of
strife were ready to burst through the untempered barrier
put together to restrain them, and again pour their desolating flood over Europe. Bonaparte began to look carefully
at the existing situation, and found that the British troops
had not yet quitted Egypt nor surrendered Malta to the
Order of St. John. Representations were made on both
these subjects, and the British government was pressed to
evacuate Malta.[1]

The ministry, however, were also alive to the gravity of
the situation, increased as it was by the orders, not yet
known, to stop the restitutions. To abandon Egypt to
Turkey they had no objection; and to the French ambassador's demand replied, on November 30, that the failure
to do so had resulted from a misunderstanding on the part
of the British commander-in-chief, to whom explicit instructions were now sent. Regarding Malta, their feeling
was very different. Honestly intending to carry out the
treaty; they had admitted the Neapolitan garrison to the
island, though not yet to the fortifications; and their ambassadors to the Great Powers had been early directed to
ask their guarantee for the independence of the Order.
The French government did not instruct its representatives to do the same. Whether this was due, as Thiers
says, to the negligence of Talleyrand, or whether the first
consul preferred not to be troubled by the resistance of
other powers in case he again seized the island, the fail-

[1] Parl. Hist., vol. xxxvi. p. 1380.

ure of France to join in the application caused Russia and
Prussia to defer their answer to the British ambassadors.
The joint request was not made to Prussia until September, nor to the czar until November 3.   By this time the
Swiss incident had come and gone, leaving behind it the
state of tension already described.   Not till the 25th of
the month did the czar reply; and then, before giving his
acquiescence, he required in the organization of the island
changes seriously affecting the object of the treaty, which
aimed to base its independence upon its own people as
well as upon guarantees.   At Amiens it had been agreed
that the Order should be open to native Maltese, by whom
also at least half the government offices should be filled.
Half the garrison likewise was to be composed of natives.
To these provisions the czar excepted.   All such points of
interior organization were to be left to the decision of the
legal government of the Order;[1] i. e., of the Order as before constituted.

The record of the ministry in the matter of Malta was
so clear that it could well afford to protract discussion on
the points raised by Russia.   No cession made by the
treaty had been more generally lamented by Englishmen,
keenly sensitive to all that affected their position in the
Mediterranean or threatened the approaches to India.   In
case the peace which was its sole achievement failed, the
ministry could save from the wreck of its hopes no more
welcome prize with which to meet a disappointed people.
Other valid objections to restoration were not wanting.
No Grand Master had yet accepted.   Spain, notoriously
under Bonaparte's influence, had suppressed the revenues
of the Order within her limits.   Similar action had followed elsewhere, and it was argued that the income of
the Order would not suffice to maintain the defence of the
island, nor consequently its independence.   But, while
thus keeping its hold on Malta by diplomatic pleas, the

[1] Annual Register, 1803, p. 681.

ministry took broader ground in its discussions with France. Its envoy there was replaced by an ambassador of the highest rank, Lord Whitworth; who was instructed to affirm explicitly Great Britain's right to interfere in continental affairs, whenever in her judgment required by her own interests, or those of Europe in general. He was also to point out the various encroachments which had added to the influence and power of France, and to intimate that these changes in the conditions since the treaty had been concluded entitled Great Britain to compensations. The annexation of Piedmont, the renunciation of the Grand Duke of Parma in favor of France, the invasion of Switzerland, were specifically named as making a most material alteration in the state of engagements since the conclusion of the definitive treaty. Attention was also called to the fact that although, by a convention signed in August, 1801, French troops were to remain in Holland only until the conclusion of peace between Great Britain and France, they had not yet been withdrawn, thus violating the independence of the Batavian republic guaranteed at Lunéville. The ambassador was warned, however, not to commit the government to any specific determinations, and especially on the subject of Malta.[1]

The ministers, therefore, were still undecided. They had climbed upon the fence, but were prepared to get down again on the side whence they had started, if a fair opportunity were given. Unfortunately for the interests of peace, Bonaparte, in the madness of his strength, either exaggerating the weakness of the ministry or underestimating the impulsion it could receive from popular feeling, proceeded deliberately to arouse the spirit which he was never again able to lay. On the 30th of January, 1803, was published in the "Moniteur" Colonel Sébastiani's famous report of his mission to the Levant.

---

[1] Secret Instructions to Lord Whitworth; Yonge's Life of Lord Liverpool, vol. i. p. 93.

Sébastiani 'had been dispatched in a frigate the previous September, to visit Tripoli, Egypt, Syria, and the Ionian islands, and ascertain the political and military conditions. His report was in the main a fulsome narrative of the reverence in which the first consul was said to be held by the Eastern peoples; but, upon the very detailed account of the indifference to military preparations, followed the startling statement that "six thousand French troops would now suffice to conquer Egypt." The Ionian islands were also pronounced ready to declare themselves French at the first opportunity. Finally, General Stuart, commanding the British troops in Alexandria, was accused of seeking to compass Sébastiani's murder by sending to the Pasha a copy of a general order issued by Bonaparte when in Egypt.

The exasperation such a paper would excite in Great Britain was so obvious, that its publication has been attributed to the deliberate design to provoke a maritime war; under cover of which the first consul could, without open humiliation, abandon the enterprise against Haïti.[1] The first and general success of the French troops in that colony had been followed by a frightful pestilence of yellow fever; after which the negroes in every quarter again rose and defied the weakened bands of their enemies. On the 8th of January the "Moniteur" published the death of Leclerc, the commander-in-chief, with an account of the ravages of the disease. It was indeed painfully apparent that the colony could not be regained, and utilized, without an expenditure of life impossible to afford;[2] but the fever itself was an excuse even more potent than the British navy for abandoning the attempt without military dishonor. To penetrate the real motives of a spirit so subtle and unscrupulous as Bonaparte's is hopeless; nor can de-

---

[1] Adams, Hist. of the United States, 1801–1817, vol. ii. pp. 13–21.

[2] The San Domingo expedition cost the lives of over twenty-five thousand French soldiers.

pendence be placed upon the statements of his brothers
Lucien and Joseph, who are the sole authorities for the
purpose thus alleged for the publication. There seems
little cause to seek another reason than the same truculent
arrogance manifested in his instructions to Otto of October 23, and the success which his past experience had
taught him to expect from bluster. The secret mission to
Prussia of his confidential aid, Duroc, six weeks later,
clearly indicates that the result had disappointed him and
that he did not want war,—at least as yet.[1] Duroc was
instructed to see the king personally and say that, if war
broke out, French troops would occupy Hanover, a step
known to be particularly obnoxious to Prussia, who wished
herself to absorb it. Her repugnance was to be used as a
lever, to induce intervention with Great Britain to evacuate Malta.[2]

Bonaparte in truth was less interested in the West than
in the East, whose vast populations, vivid history, and
fabled riches struck his imagination far more forcibly
than the unpeopled wildernesses of America. Access to
the East, as to the West, was perforce by water, and so
controlled by the power that ruled the sea; but the way
by the Levant was shorter, evasion therefore easier.
Malta, Taranto, the Ionian islands, the Morea were gate-
ways to the East. The last three, as practically conti-

[1] The British ambassador in Paris reached the same conclusion from the
instructions sent by Talleyrand to the French envoy in London. "It appears
from this note that this government is not desirous to proceed to extremities;
that is to say, it is not prepared to do so." (March 18; Parl. Hist., vol. xxxvi.
p. 1315.) The United States minister in Paris also wrote, March 24, "Here
there is an earnest and sincere desire to avoid war, as well in the government
as the people." (Am. State Papers, ii. 549.)

[2] Instructions to Duroc, March 12, 1803; Corr. de Nap., vol. viii. pp. 307–
311. It is noteworthy that these instructions were issued the same day that
was received in Paris information of the king's message to Parliament of
March 8, that "in consequence of military preparations in the ports of France
and Holland he had adopted additional measures of precaution." Two days
later the militia was called out.

nental,[1] he considered to be within his own grasp; the
first alone could be readily and securely held by the
Power of the Seas.   From it therefore he sought to hasten
her.   On the 27th of January Talleyrand, "with great
solemnity and by express order of the first consul," required of Lord Whitworth to inform him what were his
Majesty's intentions regarding the evacuation of Malta.
No reply was given, except a promise to report the conversation.[2]   On the 30th was issued Sébastiani's report,
whose scarcely veiled threats against British interests in
the East might perhaps induce a weak government to
propitiate the first consul by compliance.

If so meant, the attempt was miscalculated.   The
British ministry replied that, despite his just claim for
compensation, the king would have withdrawn his force
from Malta, when the clauses of the treaty affecting it
were fulfilled; but that, in view of Sébastiani's report,
he would not do so until substantial security was provided
against the purposes therein revealed.   From that time
forward letters and interviews followed in rapid succession, the British ministry gradually stiffening in its attitude concerning the island.   On the 20th of February
Bonaparte gave a fresh provocation which deeply stirred
the British people, although no notice was taken of it by
the ministry.   In a message sent that day to the legislature, he declared the certainty of continental peace; but
concerning Great Britain he continued: "Two parties
there strive for power.   One has made peace and wishes
to keep it; the other has sworn implacable hatred to
France. . . . Whatever the success of intrigue in London,
it will not drag other nations into new leagues, and this
government says with just pride: ' England, alone, cannot to-day contend against France.'"

On March 8 the British government sent a message to

---

1 Corr. de Nap., vol. viii. p. 308.
2 Parl. Hist., vol. xxxvi. p. 1293.

Parliament, that, in consequence of military preparations
going on in the ports of France and Holland, the king
judged expedient to adopt additional measures of precaution for the security of his dominions.   It is fair to say
that these preparations were not on a scale by themselves
to warrant the proposed action; which was asserted by
critics of the ministry to be due to information of transactions at the Cape of Good Hope.   This had already been
delivered to the Dutch authorities when the orders coun-
termanding the restitution arrived; but the British commander had adroitly repossessed himself of the works.
This news reached London early in March; and the proposed armaments were thought to be precautions rather
against Bonaparte's action, when he too heard it, than
against the existing movements in French or Dutch
ports.

From this time forward Great Britain rather than
France was aggressive.   Receiving no explanation upon
the grievances advanced, Lord Whitworth was on the 4th
of April instructed to say that, if the French government
continued to evade discussion about compensations due
for its aggressions on the Continent and satisfaction for
Sébastiani's report, and yet demanded the evacuation of
Malta, he should declare that relations of amity could not
continue to exist, and that he must leave Paris within a
certain time.   If they were willing to discuss, he was instructed to propose the cession of Malta in perpetuity to
Great Britain and the evacuation of Holland and Switzerland by French troops; in return for which Great Britain
would confirm Elba to France and acknowledge the kingdom of Etruria.   If a satisfactory arrangement were made
in Italy for the king of Sardinia, she would further ac-
-knowledge the Italian and Ligurian republics.   The first
consul replied that he would sooner see the British on the
heights of Montmartre than in the possession of Malta.
Some futile efforts were made to find a middle term; but

the ministry having insisted, as its ultimatum, upon occupying the island for at least ten years, the ambassador demanded his passports and left Paris on the 12th of May. On the 16th Great Britain declared war against France. The following day Admiral Cornwallis sailed from Plymouth with ten ships-of-the-line, and two days later appeared off Brest, resuming the watch of that port. On the afternoon of the 18th Nelson hoisted his flag on board the "Victory" at Portsmouth, and on the 20th sailed for the Mediterranean, there to take the chief command.

Thus again, after a brief intermission, began the strife between Great Britain and France, destined during its twelve years' course to involve successively all the powers of Europe, from Portugal to Russia, from Turkey to Sweden. On the land, state after state went down before the great soldier who wielded the armies of France and the auxiliary legions of subject countries, added to her standards by his policy. Victory after victory graced his eagles, city after city and province after province were embodied in his empire, peace after peace was wrested from the conquered; but one enemy remained ever erect, unsubdued, defiant; and on the ocean there was neither peace nor truce, until the day when he himself fell under the hosts of foes, aroused by his vain attempt to overthrow, through their sufferings, the power that rested upon the seas.

The debates in the House of Commons revealed an agreement of sentiment unparalleled in the former war. Differences of opinion there were. A very few thought that hostilities might even yet be averted, while others argued bitterly that, had Bonaparte's first encroachments been resisted, the nation might have been spared, if not war, at least humiliation. But, while both groups condemned the administration, the one for precipitation, the other for pusillanimous and protracted submission, both agreed that just occasion for war had been given. As usual, opposition took the form of an amendment to the address, which, while carefully excluding any approval of the ministry, still "assured his Majesty of our firm determination to co-operate with his Majesty in calling forth the resources of the United Kingdom for the vigorous prosecution of the war in which we are involved." The proposer, Mr. Grey — one of the most strenuous opponents of the former war — was careful to say that, though he objected to some points of the late negotiation, he acknowledged the necessity of resisting the spirit of encroachment shown by France. Even for this very qualified disapproval of a ministry in whose capacity none had confidence, there could in this grave crisis be found only 67 votes, against 398 who preferred not to weaken, by an apparent discord, the unanimous voice. Having regard to the reasons for their dissent urged by the various speakers, the result disposes forever of the vain assertion that Great Britain feared to meet France alone. The solemn decision was not taken blindfold nor in haste. The exorbitant power of Bonaparte, the impossibility of allies, the burden that must be borne, were all quoted and faced; and Mr. Pitt, who then spoke for the first time in many months, while fully supporting the war, warned the members in his stately periods of the arduous struggle before them. "In giving their assurances he trusted that other gentlemen felt impressed with the same sense which he did of the awful importance of the engagement into which they were preparing to enter ; and that they considered those assurances, not as formal words of ceremony or custom, but as a solemn and deliberate pledge, on behalf of themselves and of the nation whom they represented, — knowing and feeling to their full extent the real difficulties and dangers of their situation, and being prepared to meet those difficulties and dangers with every exertion and every sacrifice which the unexampled circumstances of the times rendered indispensable for the public safety. . . . The scale of our exertions could not be measured by those of former times, or confined within the limits even of the great, and till then unexampled, efforts of the last war. "[1]

In the same speech Pitt correctly and explicitly indicated the two methods by which France might seek to subdue Great Britain. "If they indulge themselves in any expectation of success in the present contest, it is built chiefly on the supposition (1) that they can either break the spirit and shake the determination of the country by harassing us with perpetual apprehension of descent upon our coasts, or (2) that they can impair our resources and undermine our credit, by the effects of an expensive and protracted contest." Not to one only, but to both of these means did Bonaparte resort, on a scale proportioned to his comprehensive genius and his mighty resources. For the invasion of England preparations were at once begun, so extensive and so thorough as to indicate not a mere threat, but a fixed purpose ; and at the same time measures were taken to close to Great Britain the markets of the Continent, as well as to harass her commerce by the ordinary operations of maritime war. Trafalgar marked the term when all thought of invasion disappeared, and was succeeded by the vast combinations of the Continental System, itself but an expansion of the former measures of exclusion. Framed to impair the resources and sap the credit of Great Britain, this stupendous fabric, upheld, not by the cohesion of its parts, but by the dextrous balancing of an ever watchful policy, overtaxed the skill and strength of its designer, and crushed him in its fall.

[1] Speech of May 23, 1803,

CHAPTER XV.

PREPARATIONS FOR THE INVASION OF ENGLAND. — THE GREAT
FLOTILLA. — NAPOLEON'S MILITARY AND NAVAL COMBINATIONS
AND BRITISH NAVAL STRATEGY. — ESSENTIAL UNITY OF NAPO-
LEON'S PURPOSE.—CAUSES OF SPANISH WAR.

ALTHOUGH Great Britain and France had each, up to
the last moment, hoped to retain peace upon its own
terms, preparations for war had gone on rapidly ever since
the king's message of March 8. Immediately upon issuing
this, couriers were dispatched to the various sea-ports, with
orders to impress seamen for the numerous ships hastily
ordered into commission. Some details have come down
giving a vivid presentment of that lawless proceeding
known as a " hot press," at this period when it was on the
point of disappearing. " About 7 P. M. yesterday," says
the Plymouth report of March 10, " the town was alarmed
with the marching of several bodies of Royal Marines in
parties of twelve or fourteen each, with their officers and a
naval officer, armed. So secret were the orders kept that
they did not know the nature of the service on which they
were going, until they boarded the tier of colliers at the
new quay, and other gangs the ships at Catwater, the Pool
and the gin-shops. A great number of prime seamen were
taken out and sent on board the admiral's ship. In other
parts of the town, and in all the receiving and gin-shops at
Dock, several hundreds of seamen and landsmen were
picked up. By returns this morning it appears that

upwards of four hundred useful hands were pressed last night. One gang entered the Dock theatre and cleared the whole gallery except the women." Parties of seamen and marines were placed across all roads leading out of the towns, to intercept fugitives. In Portsmouth the colliers were stripped so clean of men that they could not put to sea; while frigates and smaller vessels swept the Channel and other sea-approaches to the kingdom, stopping all merchant ships, and taking from them a part of their crews. The whole flotilla of trawl-boats fishing off the Eddystone, forty in number, were searched, and two hands taken from each. Six East India ships, wind-bound off Plymouth on their outward voyage, were boarded by armed boats and robbed of three hundred seamen, till then unaware that a rupture with France was near.[1]

Bonaparte on his side had been no less active, although he sought by the secrecy of his movements to avert alarm and postpone, if possible, the war which for his aims was premature. Orders were given that re-enforcements for the colonies should go forward rapidly, ere peace was broken. No ships-of-the-line or frigates should henceforth go with them; and those already abroad were for the most part at once recalled. Troops were concentrated on the coasts of Holland and Flanders; and the flat-boats built in the last war with a view to invading England were assembled quietly in the Scheldt and the Channel ports. Plans were studied for the harassment of British commerce. On the 9th of April was commanded the armament of the shores, from the Scheldt westward to the Somme, a distance of one hundred and twenty miles, which afterwards became, to use Marmont's vivid expression, " a coast of iron and bronze." A few days later Elba and all the coasts and islands of France were ordered fortified; and the first consul's aides-de-camp sped north and east and west, to see and report the state of preparation in all quarters.

[1] Naval Chronicle, vol. ix. pp. 243, 247, 329, 330, 332, 491.

One affair of great importance still remained to arrange. The smaller French islands in the East and West Indies could be held in subjection by a moderate number of troops, who could also resist for a considerable time any attempt of the British, unless on a very large scale. This was not the case with Haïti or Louisiana. In the former the French, reduced by the fever, were now shut up in a few sea-ports; communication between· which, being only by water, must cease when the maritime war broke out. Between the blacks within and the British without, the loss of the island was therefore certain. Louisiana had not yet been occupied. Whatever its unknown possibilities, the immediate value to France of this possession, so lately regained, was as a source of supplies to Haïti, dependent for many essentials upon the American continent. With the fall of the island the colony on the mainland became useless. Its cession by Spain to France had at once aroused the jealousy, with which, from colonial days, the people of the United States have viewed any political interference by European nations on the American continent, even when involving only a transfer from one power to another. In the dire straits of the Revolution, when the need of help from abroad was so great, they had been careful to insert in the Treaty of Alliance with France an express stipulation, that she would not acquire for herself any of the possessions of Great Britain on the mainland; having then in view Canada and the Floridas. This feeling was intensified when, as now, the change of ownership was from a weak and inert state like Spain to one so powerful as France, with the reputation for aggressiveness that was fast gathering around the name of Bonaparte.

The fear and anger of the American people increased with the reserve shown by the French government, in replying to the questions of their minister in Paris, who asked repeatedly, but in vain, for assurances as to the navigation of the Mississippi; and the excitement reached a climax when in November, 1802, news was received that the Spanish authorities in New Orleans had refused to American citizens the right of deposit, conceded by the treaty of 1795 with Spain. This was naturally attributed to Bonaparte's influence, and the inhabitants of the upper Mississippi valley were ready to resort to arms to enforce their rights.

Such was the threatening state of affairs in America, while war with Great Britain was fast drawing on. Bonaparte was not the man to recede before a mere menace of hostilities in the distant wilderness of Louisiana; but it was plain that, in case of rupture with Great Britain, any possessions of France on the Gulf of Mexico were sure to fall either to her or to the Americans, if he incurred the enmity of the latter. It was then believed in Washington that France had also acquired from Spain the Floridas, which contained naval ports essential to the defence of Louisiana. On the 12th of April, 1803, arrived in Paris Mr. Monroe, sent by Jefferson as envoy extraordinary, to treat, in conjunction with the regular minister to France, for the cession of the Floridas and of the island of New Orleans to the United States; the object of the latter being to secure the Mississippi down to its mouth as their western boundary. Monroe's arrival was most opportune. Lord Whitworth had five days before communicated the message of the British cabinet that, unless the French government was prepared to enter into the required explanations, relations of amity could not exist, and at the same time the London papers were discussing a proposition to raise fifty thousand men to take New Orleans.[1] Three days later, April 10, the first consul decided to sell Louisiana;[2] and Monroe upon his arrival had only to settle the terms of the bargain, which did not indeed realize the precise object of his mission, but which gave to his country control of the west bank of the Mississippi throughout its course, and of both banks from its mouth nearly to Baton Rouge, a distance of

[1] Am. State Papers, vol. ii. p. 553.   [2] Ibid.

over two hundred miles. The treaty, signed April 30, 1803, gave to the United States "the whole of Louisiana as Spain had possessed it," for the sum of eighty million francs. Thus the fear of Great Britain's sea power was the determining factor [1] to sweep the vast region known as Louisiana, stretching from the Gulf toward Canada, and from the Mississippi toward Mexico, with ill-defined boundaries in either direction, into the hands of the United States, and started the latter on that course of expansion to the westward which has brought her to the shores of the Pacific.

Having thus relinquished a position he could not defend, and, as far as in him lay, secured the French possessions beyond the sea, Bonaparte could now give his whole attention to the plans for subjugating the British Islands which had long been ripening in his fertile brain.

It was from the first evident that Great Britain, having in the three kingdoms but fifteen million inhabitants, could not invade the territory of France with its population of over twenty-five millions. This was the more true because the demands of her navy, of her great mercantile shipping, and of a manufacturing and industrial system not only vast but complex, so that interference with parts would seriously derange the whole, left for recruiting the British armies a fraction, insignificant when compared with the resources in men of France; where capital and manufactures, commerce and shipping, had disappeared, leaving only an agricultural peasantry, upon which the conscription could freely draw without materially increasing the poverty of the country, or deranging a social system essentially simple.

This seeming inability to injure France gave rise to the sarcastic remark, that it was hardly worth while for a

---

[1] In case of war, it was the purpose of the British government to send an expedition to occupy New Orleans, as it did afterwards in 1814. (Am. State papers, vol. ii. pp. 551, 557.)

country to go to war in order to show that it could put itself in a good posture for defence. This, however, was a very superficial view of the matter. Great Britain's avowed reason for war was the necessity — forced upon a reluctant ministry and conceded by a bitter opposition — of resisting encroachments by a neighboring state. Of these, on the Continent, part had already occurred and were, for the time at least, irremediable ; but there had also been clearly revealed the purpose of continuing similar encroachments, in regions whose tenure by an enemy would seriously compromise her colonial empire. To prevent this, Great Britain, by declaring war, regained her belligerent rights, and so resumed at once that control of the sea which needed only them to complete. She pushed her sway up to every point of her enemy's long coast-line ; and following the strategy of the previous war, under the administration of the veteran seaman who had imparted to it such vigor, she prevented her enemy from combining any great operation, by which her world-wide dominion could be shaken or vital injury be inflicted at any point. The British squadrons, hugging the French coasts and blocking the French arsenals, were the first line of the defence, covering British interests from the Baltic to Egypt, the British colonies in the four quarters of the globe, and the British merchantmen which whitened every sea.

This was the defensive gain in a war whose motive was essentially defensive. Offensively Great Britain, by the suddenness with which she forced the issue, dealt a blow whose weight none understood better than Bonaparte. That he meant war eventually is most probable. His instructions to Decaen, Captain-General of the French East Indies, dated January 15, 1803, speak of the possibility of war by September, 1804 ; but how little the bravado of Sébastiani's report indicated a wish for an immediate rupture, is shown by the secret message sent to Andréossy in London, on the very day Whitworth left Paris. Despite the

bluster about his willingness to see Great Britain on Montmartre rather than in Malta, he then wrote : " Direct General Andréossy that when he is assured the accompanying
note has been communicated to the English government, he
cause it to be understood through Citizen Schimmelpenninck
or by any other indirect means, that if England absolutely
rejects the proposition of giving Malta to one of the guaran-
teeing powers, we would not here be averse from accepting
that England should retain Malta for ten years, and France
should occupy the peninsula of Otranto. *It is important, if*
this proposition has no chance of success, that no communica-
tion be made leaving any trace ; and that we here may always
be able to *deny that this government could have adhered to*
this proposition." [1] Bonaparte understood perfectly that
Great Britain, by forcing his hand, had struck down the
French navy before it had begun to rise. " Peace," he said,
" is necessary to restore a navy, — peace to fill our arsenals
empty of material, and peace because then only the one
drill-ground for fleets, the sea, is open." " Ships, colonies,
commerce," the wants he avowed later at Ulm, were swept
away by the same blow. How distressed the finances of
France, how devoid of credit, none knew better than he,
who then, as throughout his rule, was engaged in keeping
up the quotations by government manipulation ; and the
chief of all sources of wealth, maritime commerce, was
crushed by the sea power of Great Britain, which thenceforth coiled closely and with ever tightening compression
round the coasts of France.

Bonaparte could not indeed realize the full extent of the
injury that would be done. Impatient of obstacles, he
refused to see that the construction of the flotilla to invade
England would devour the scanty material for ship-
building, occupy all the workmen, and so stop the growth
of the real navy. Even when built, the ever-recurring

---

[1] Napoleon to Talleyrand; Corr. de Nap., May 13, 1803.

demand for repairs drained the dockyards of mechanics.[1] Nor could he foresee how completely Great Britain, by reviving the Rule of 1756 in all its rigor, and by replying to each blow from the land by one yet heavier from the sea, would cut off the resources of France and destroy her as a fortress falls by blockade. Unsparing ridicule has been heaped upon Pitt for predicting the break-down of the French Revolution, in its aggressive military character, by financial distress; but in fact Pitt, though he underestimated the time necessary and did not look for the vast system of spoliation which supplied the lack of regular income, was a true prophet. The republic had already devoured an immense capital;[2] and when the conquering spirit it ever displayed reached its natural culmination in Bonaparte, the constantly recurring need of money drove him on from violence to violence till it ended in his ruin. This penury was caused directly by the maritime war, which shut France off from commerce beyond the seas; and indirectly by the general prostration of business in Europe and consequent poverty of consumers, due to their isolation from the sea, enforced by Bonaparte as the only means of wearing out Great Britain.

In 1798, when the Peace of Campo Formio had left France face to face with Great Britain alone, the question of invading the latter had naturally arisen; but Bonaparte easily convinced himself and the Directory that the attempt was impossible with any naval force that could at that time be raised. He then pointed out that there were two other principal ways of injuring the enemy: one by occupying Hanover and Hamburg, through which British trade entered the Continent; the other by seizing Egypt as a base of operations against India. These two were somewhat of the nature of a flank attack; and the former being in the

---

[1] Thiers, Consulat et Empire, livre xx. p. 182.

[2] The French republic had devoured under the form of assignats an immense amount of national property. — THIERS: *Cons. et Emp.*, livre xvii. p. 377.

then state of the Continent inexpedient,— for both Hamburg
and Hanover were included in the North German neutrality
under the guarantee of Prussia, while Austria was by no
means so reduced as in 1803,— the expedition against Egypt
was determined. Whatever personal motives may then
have influenced Bonaparte, that undertaking, from the
military point of view and in the then condition of the
Mediterranean, was well conceived ; and, while allowing
for a large amount of good luck, the measure of success
achieved must be ascribed to the completeness and secrecy
of his preparations, as the final failure must to the sea
power of Great Britain.

In 1803 Bonaparte found himself no longer a simple
general, under a weak and jealous government upon whose
co-operation he could not certainly depend, but an absolute
ruler wielding all the resources of France. He resolved
therefore to strike straight at the vital centre of the British
power, by a direct invasion of the British Islands. The
very greatness of the peril in crossing the Channel, and in
leaving it between him and his base, was not without a
certain charm for his adventurous temper ; but, while
willing to take many a risk for so great an end, he left to
chance nothing for which he himself could provide. The
plan for the invasion was marked by the comprehensiveness
of view and the minute attention to detail which distinguished his campaigns ; and the preparations were on a
scale of entire adequacy, which he never failed to observe
when the power to do so was in his hands.

For these in their grandeur, however, time was needed ;
but the first consul was ready to move at once, as far as
was possible to land forces, upon the two flanks of the
British position. On the 26th of May a corps under
General Mortier entered Hanover ; while a few days later
another corps, under General St. Cyr, passed through the
Papal States into the kingdom of Naples, and resumed
possession of the peninsula of Otranto with the ports of

Brindisi and Taranto. From the latter the Ionian islands, the Morea, and Egypt, were all threatened; and the position kept alive, as in the deep strategy of Napoleon it was meant to do, the anxiety of Nelson concerning those points and the Levant generally. Upon this distraction of the greatest British admiral, justified as it was by the enemy's undoubted purposes in the eastern Mediterranean, depended a decisive part of Bonaparte's combination against Great Britain.

In Hanover British trade was struck. This German electorate of George III. bordered on both the Elbe and the Weser, in the lower part of their course; by occupying it France controlled the two great rivers and excluded from them all British goods. The act was censured as infringing the neutrality of Germany. Bonaparte justified it by the hostile character of the elector as king of Great Britain; but no such plea could be advanced for the occupation of Cuxhaven, the port of Hamburg, which lay on the Elbe outside Hanover. Triple offence was given to Prussia. Her ambition to figure as the guardian of North German neutrality was affronted, her particular wish to control Hanover slighted, and her trade most injuriously affected. To the exclusion of British goods Great Britain replied by blockading the mouths of the rivers, suffering no ships to pass where her own were not allowed, and holding Germany responsible for permitting a breach of its neutrality injurious to herself. The commerce of Hamburg and Bremen was thus stopped; and as they were the brokers who received and distributed the manufactures of Prussia, the blow was felt throughout the kingdom. The distress among the workmen was so wide-spread that the king had to come to their relief, and many wealthy men lost half their incomes. In addition to the advantages of position obtained in Hanover and Naples, Napoleon threw on these two neutral states the charge of supporting the corps quartered on them, amounting to some thirty thousand men in Hanover and half that number in Naples. Holland, against which as the ally of France[1] Great Britain also declared war, had to maintain a somewhat larger force. By such expedients Bonaparte eased his own finances at the expense of neutral or dependent countries ; but he was not therefore more beloved.

To invade Great Britain there had first to be concentrated round a chosen point the great armies required to insure success, and the very large number of vessels needed to transport them. Other corps, more or less numerous, destined to further the principal movement by diversions in different directions, distracting the enemy's attention, might embark at distant ports and sail independently of the main body; but for the latter it was necessary to start together and land simultaneously, in mass, at a given point of the English coast. To this principal effort Bonaparte destined one hundred and thirty thousand men; of whom one hundred thousand should form the first line and embark at the same hour from four different ports, which lay within a length of twenty miles on the Channel coast. The other thirty thousand constituted the reserve, and were to sail shortly after the first.

To carry any such force at once, in ordinary sea-going vessels of that day, was impracticable. The requisite number could not be had, and there was no French Channel port where they could safely lie. Even were these difficulties overcome, and the troops embarked together, the mere process of getting under way would entail endless delays, the vessels dependent upon sail could not keep together, and the only conditions of wind under which they could move at all would expose them to be scattered and

---

[1] "Holland," says Thiers, "would have wished to remain neutral ; but the first consul had taken a resolution, *whose justice cannot be denied*, to make every maritime nation aid in our strife against Great Britain." (Cons. et Emp., livre xvii. p. 383.)

destroyed by the British navy, which would have the same power of motion, and to which Bonaparte could oppose no equal force. The very gathering of so many helpless sailing transports would betray the place where the French navy must concentrate, and where therefore the hostile ships would assemble at the first indication of a combined movement. Finally, such transports must anchor at some distance from the British coast and the troops land from them in boats, an additional operation both troublesome and dangerous.

For these reasons the crossing must be made in vessels not dependent upon sail alone, but capable of being moved by oars. They must therefore be small and of very light draught, which would allow them to shelter in the shallow French harbors and be beached upon reaching the English coast, so that the troops could land directly from them. It was possible that a number of such vessels once started, and favored by fog or calm, might pass unseen, or even in defiance of the enemy's ships-of-war, lying helpless to attack through want of wind. It was upon this possibility that Bonaparte sought to fix the attention of the British government. As the occupation of Taranto and the movements in Italy were designed to divert Nelson's attention to the Levant, so the ostentatious preparation of the great flotilla to pass unsupported was meant to conceal the real purpose of supporting it. To concentrate the apprehensions of the British authorities upon the flotilla, to draw their eyes away from the naval ports in which lay the French squadrons, and then to unite the latter in the Channel, controlling it for a measurable time by a great fleet, was the grand combination by which Bonaparte hoped to insure the triumphant crossing of the army and the conquest of England. He kept it, however, in his own breast; a profound secret only gradually revealed to the very few men intrusted with its execution.

To create and organize the flotilla and the army of in-

vasion was the first task.   Preparations so extensive and
rapid demanded all the resources of France.   To build at
the same time the thousand and more of boats, each of
which should carry from sixty to a hundred soldiers, besides from two to four heavy cannon for its own defence,
overpassed the powers of any single port.   Far in the interior of France, on the banks of the numerous streams
running toward the Channel and the Bay of Biscay, as
well as in all the little coast harbors themselves, hosts of
men were busily working.   The North Sea and Holland
were also required to furnish their quota.   At the same
time measures were taken to facilitate their passage in
safety to the point of concentration, which was fixed at
Boulogne, and to harbor them commodiously upon arrival.   They could from their light draught run close
along shore, and from their construction be beached without harm.   Within easy gunshot of the coast, therefore,
lay the road they followed in their passages, which were
commonly made in bodies of thirty to sixty, and from
port to port, till the journey's end.   To support the movements, sea-coast batteries were established at short intervals; under which, if hard pressed, they could take
refuge.   In addition there were organized in each maritime district batteries of field artillery, which stood ready
to drive at once to the scene of action in case the enemy
attacked.   " One field-gun to every league of coast is the
least allowance," wrote Bonaparte.   In the early months
of the war great importance was attached by the British
to harassing these voyages and impeding the concentration, but the attempt was soon abandoned.   The boats, if
endangered, anchored under the nearest guns, infantry
and horse-artillery summoned by the coast-telegraph hurried to the scene, and the enemy's vessels soon found the
combined resistance too strong.   Ordinarily, indeed, the
coastwise movement of a division of the flotilla was a concerted operation, in which all the arms, afloat and ashore,

assisted. In extreme cases the vessels were beached, and British seamen fought hand to hand with French soldiers for possession; rarely, however, with success. "The cause of our flotilla not having succeeded in destroying the gun-vessels of the enemy," wrote Lord St. Vincent, "did not arise from their draught of water, but from the powerful batteries on the coast." The concentration, though accom plished less swiftly than Bonaparte's eagerness demanded, was little impeded by the British.

The port of Boulogne, near the eastern end of the English Channel, lies on a strip of coast which runs due south from the Straits of Dover to the mouth of the Somme, a distance of about fifty miles. It is a tidal harbor, the mouth of a little river called the Liane, on the north side of which the town is built. In it even boats of small draught then lay aground at low water; and its capacity at high water was limited. Extensive excavations were therefore ordered to be made by the soldiers encamped in the neighborhood, who received extra wages for the work. When finished, the port presented a double basin; the outer, oblong, bordering the river bed on either side of the channel, which was left clear; the inner of semi-circular form, dug out of the flats opposite the town and connected with the former by a narrow passage. Both were lined with quays, alongside which the vessels of the flotilla lay in tiers, sometimes nine deep; and in July, 1805, when the hour for the last and greatest of Napoleon's naval combinations was at hand, and Trafalgar itself in the near distance, Boulogne sheltered over a thousand gun-boats and transports ready to carry forty thousand men to the shores of England. North and south, not only the neighborhood of the harbor but the whole coast bristled with cannon; and opposite the entrance rose a powerful work, built upon piles, to protect the vessels when going out and also when anchored outside. For here was one of the great difficulties of the undertaking. So many boats

could not pass out through the narrow channel during one
high water. Two tides at the least, that is, twenty-four
hours, were needed, granting the most perfect organization
and most accurate movement. Half of the flotilla therefore
must lie outside for some hours; and it was not to be expected that the British cruisers would allow so critical a
moment to pass unimproved, unless deterred by the protection which the foresight of Bonaparte had provided.

North of Boulogne and within five miles of it were two
other much smaller harbors, likewise tidal, called Vimereux and Ambleteuse; and to the south, twelve miles distant, a third, named Étaples. Though insignificant, the
impossibility of enlarging Boulogne to hold the whole
flotilla compelled Bonaparte to develop these, and they
together held some seven hundred more gun-vessels and
transports. From the three, sixty-two thousand soldiers
were to embark; and from each of the four ports a due
proportion of field artillery, ammunition and other supplies were to go forward. Some six thousand horses were
also to be transported; but the greater part of the cavalry
took only their saddles and bridles, looking to find mounts
in the enemy's country. In the North Sea ports, Calais,
Dunkirk, and Ostend, the flotilla numbered four hundred,
the troops twenty-seven thousand, the horses twenty-five
hundred. These formed the reserve, to follow the main
body closely, but apart from it. In the end they also
were moved to the Boulogne coast, and their boats, after
some sharp fighting with British cruisers, joined the main
flotilla in the four Channel ports.

To handle such a mass of men upon the battle-field is a
faculty to which few generals, after years of experience,
attain. To effect the passage of a broad river with an
army of that size, before a watchful enemy of equal force,
is a delicate operation. To cross an arm of the sea nearly
forty miles wide — for such was the distance separating
Boulogne and its sister ports from the intended place of

landing, between Dover and Hastings — in the face of a foe whose control of the sea was for the most part undisputed, was an undertaking so bold that men still doubt whether Napoleon meant it; but he assuredly did. For success he looked to the perfect organization and drill of the army and the flotilla, which by practice in embarking and moving should be able to seize, without an hour's delay, the favorable moment he hoped to provide by the great naval combination concealed in his brain. This combination, modified and expanded as the months rolled by, but remaining essentially the same, was the germ whence sprang the intricate and stirring events recorded in this and the following chapters, — events obscured to most men by the dazzling lustre of Trafalgar.

[Between the penning and the publishing of this very positive assertion of the author's convictions, he has met renewed expressions of doubts as to Napoleon's purpose, based upon his words to Metternich in 1810,[1] as well as upon the opinions of persons more or less closely connected with the emperor. As regards the incident recorded by Metternich — it is not merely an easy way of overcoming a difficulty, but the statement of a simple fact, to say that no reliance can be placed upon any avowal of Napoleon's as to his intentions, unless corroborated by circumstances. That the position at Boulogne was well chosen for turning his arms against Austria at a moment's notice, is very true; but it is likewise true that, barring the power of the British navy, it was equally favorable to an invasion of England. What then does this amount to, but that the great captain, as always in his career, met a strategic exigency arising from the existence of two dangers in divergent directions, by taking a central position, whence he could readily turn his arms against either before the other came up?

The considerations that to the author possess irresisti-

1 Metternich's Memoirs, vol. i. p. 48, note.

ble force are: (1) that Napoleon actually did undertake
the almost equally hazardous expedition to Egypt; (2)
that he saw, with his clear intuition, that, if he did not
accept the risk of being destroyed with his army in crossing the Channel, Great Britain would in the end overwhelm him by her sea power, and that therefore, extreme
as was the danger of destruction in one case, it was less
than in the other alternative, — an argument further developed in the later portions of this work. (3) Inscrutable as
are the real purposes of so subtle a spirit, the author holds
with Thiers and Lanfrey, that it is impossible to rise
from the perusal of Napoleon's correspondence during
these thirty months, without the conviction that so sustained a deception as it would contain — on the supposition that the invasion was not intended — would be
impossible even to him. It may also be remarked that
the Memoirs of Marmont and Ney, who commanded corps
in the Army of Invasion, betray no doubt of a purpose which
the first explicitly asserts; nor does the life of Marshal
Davout, another corps commander, record any such impression on his part.[1]]

Meanwhile that period of waiting from May, 1803, to
August, 1805, when the tangled net of naval and military
movements began to unravel, was a striking and wonderful pause in the world's history. On the heights above
Boulogne, and along the narrow strip of beach from Étaples to Vimereux, were encamped one hundred and thirty
thousand of the most brilliant soldiery of all time, the
soldiers who had fought in Germany, Italy, and Egypt,
soldiers who were yet to win, from Austria, Ulm and
Austerlitz, and from Prussia, Auerstadt and Jena, to
hold their own, though barely, at Eylau against the army
of Russia, and to overthrow it also, a few months later,
on the bloody field of Friedland. Growing daily more
vigorous in the bracing sea air and the hardy life laid out

[1] Chénier's Vie du Maréchal Davout, Paris, 1866.

for them, they could on fine days, as they practised the
varied manœuvres which were to perfect the vast host in
embarking and disembarking with order and rapidity, see
the white cliffs fringing the only country that to the last
defied their arms.   Far away, Cornwallis off Brest, Collingwood off Rochefort, Pellew off Ferrol, were battling
the wild gales of the Bay of Biscay, in that tremendous
and sustained vigilance which reached its utmost tension
in the years preceding Trafalgar, concerning which Collingwood wrote that admirals need to be made of iron,
but which was forced upon them by the unquestionable
and imminent danger of the country.   Farther distant
still, severed apparently from all connection with the
busy scene at Boulogne, Nelson before Toulon was wearing away the last two years of his glorious but suffering
life, fighting the fierce north-westers of the Gulf of Lyon
and questioning, questioning continually with feverish
anxiety, whether Napoleon's object was Egypt again or
Great Britain really.   They were dull, weary, eventless
months, those months of watching and waiting of the
big ships before the French arsenals.   Purposeless they
surely seemed to many, but they saved England.   The
world has never seen a more impressive demonstration of
the influence of sea power upon its history.   Those far
distant, storm-beaten ships, upon which the Grand Army
never looked, stood between it and the dominion of the
world.   Holding the interior positions they did, before —
and therefore between — the chief dockyards and detachments of the French navy, the latter could unite only by
a concurrence of successful evasions, of which the failure
of any one nullified the result.   Linked together as the
various British fleets were by chains of smaller vessels,
chance alone could secure Bonaparte's great combination,
which depended upon the covert concentration of several
detachments upon a point practically within the enemy's
lines.   Thus, while bodily present before Brest, Roche-

fort, and Toulon, strategically the British squadrons lay
in the Straits of Dover barring the way against the Army
of Invasion.

The Straits themselves, of course, were not without
their own special protection. Both they and their approaches, in the broadest sense of the term, from the
Texel to the Channel Islands, were patrolled by numerous
frigates and smaller vessels, from one hundred to a hundred and fifty in all. These not only watched diligently
all that happened in the hostile harbors and sought to
impede the movements of the flat-boats, but also kept
touch with and maintained communication between the
detachments of ships-of-the-line. Of the latter, five off
the Texel watched the Dutch navy, while others were anchored off points of the English coast with reference to
probable movements of the enemy. Lord St. Vincent,
whose ideas on naval strategy were clear and sound,
though he did not use the technical terms of the art, dis-
cerned and provided against the very purpose entertained
by Bonaparte, of a concentration before Boulogne by ships
drawn from the Atlantic and Mediterranean. The best
security, the most advantageous strategic positions, were
doubtless those before the enemy's ports; and never in the
history of blockades has there been excelled, if ever
equalled, the close locking of Brest by Admiral Cornwallis, both winter and summer, between the outbreak of
war and the battle of Trafalgar. It excited not only
the admiration but the wonder of contemporaries.[1] In
case, however, the French at Brest got out, so the prime
minister of the day informed the speaker of the House,
Cornwallis's rendezvous was off the Lizard (due north
of Brest), so as to go for *Ireland, or follow the French up
Channel,* if they took either direction. *Should the French
run for the Downs,* the five sail-of-the-line at Spithead

[1] See Naval Chronicle, vol. x. pp. 508, 510; vol. xi. p. 81. Nelson's Dispatches, vol. v. p. 438.

would also follow them; and Lord Keith (in the Downs) would in addition to his six, and six block ships, have also the North Sea fleet at his command.[1] Thus provision was made, in case of danger, for the outlying detachments to fall back on the strategic centre, gradually accumulating strength, till they formed a body of from twenty-five to thirty heavy and disciplined ships-of-the-line, sufficient to meet all probable contingencies.

Hence, neither the Admiralty nor British naval officers in general shared the fears of the country concerning the peril from the flotilla. "Our first defence," wrote Nelson in 1801, "is close to the enemy's ports; and the Admiralty have taken such precautions, by having such a respectable force under my orders, that I venture to express a well-grounded hope that the enemy would be annihilated before they get ten miles from their own shores."[2] "As to the possibility of the enemy being able in a narrow sea to pass through our blockading and protecting squadron," said Pellew, "with all the secrecy and dexterity and by those hidden means that some worthy people expect, I really, from anything I have seen in the course of my professional experience, am not much disposed to concur in it."[3] Napoleon also understood that his gun-boats could not at sea contend against heavy ships with any founded hope of success. "A discussion was started in the camp," says Marmont, "as to the possibility of fighting ships of war with flat boats, armed with 24- and 36-pounders, and as to whether, with a flotilla of several thousands, a squadron might be attacked. It was sought to establish the belief in a possible success; . . . but, notwithstanding the confidence with which Bonaparte supported this view, he never shared it for a moment."[4] He

---

[1] Pellew's Life of Lord Sidmouth, vol. ii. p. 237.
[2] Nelson's Dispatches, vol. iv. p. 452.
[3] Parl. Debates, March 15, 1804.
[4] Mémoires du Duc de Raguse, vol. ii. p. 212.

could not, without belying every military conviction he ever held. Lord St. Vincent therefore steadily refused to countenance the creation of a large force of similar vessels on the plea of meeting them upon their own terms. "Our great reliance," he wrote, "is on the vigilance and activity of our cruisers at sea, any reduction in the number of which, by applying them to guard our ports, inlets, and beaches, would in my judgment tend to our destruction." He knew also that gunboats, if built, could only be manned, as the French flotilla was, by crippling the crews of the cruising ships; for, extensive as were Great Britain's maritime resources, they were taxed beyond their power by the exhausting demands of her navy and merchant shipping.

It is true there existed an enrolled organization called the Sea Fencibles, composed of men whose pursuits were about the water on the coasts and rivers of the United Kingdom; men who in the last war had been exempted from impressment, because of the obligation they took to turn out for the protection of the country when threatened with invasion. When, however, invasion did threaten in 1801, not even the stirring appeals of Nelson, to whom was then entrusted the defence system, could bring them forward; although he assured them their services were absolutely required, at the moment, and on board the coast-defence vessels. Out of a total of 2600 in four districts immediately menaced, only 385 were willing to enter into training or go afloat. The others could not leave their occupations without loss, and prayed that they might be held excused.[1] When the French were actually on the sea, coming, they professed their readiness to fly on board; so, wrote Nelson, we must "trust to our ships being manned at the last moment by this (almost) scrambling manner." In the present war, therefore, St. Vincent resisted the re-establishment of the corps until the impress

[1] Nelson's Disp. and Letters, vol. iv pp. 444–447.

had manned the ships first commissioned, and even then yielded only to the pressure in the cabinet. "It was an item in the estimates," he said with rough humor, "of no other use than to calm the fears of the old ladies, both in and out." It was upon his former system of close watching the enemy's ports that he relied for the mastery of the Channel, without which Bonaparte's flotilla dared not leave the French coast. "This boat business," as Nelson had said, "may be a part of a great plan of invasion; it can never be the only one." [1] The event did not deceive them.

In one very important particular, however, St. Vincent had seriously imperilled the success of his general policy. Feeling deeply the corruption prevailing in the dockyard and contract systems of that day, as soon as he came to the head of the Admiralty he entered upon a struggle with them, in which he showed both the singleness of purpose and the harshness of his character. Peace, by reducing the dependence of the country upon its naval establishments, favored his designs of reform; and he was consequently unwilling to recognize the signs of renewing strife, or to postpone changes which, however desirable, must inevitably introduce friction and delay under the press of war. Hence, in the second year of this war, Great Britain had in commission ten fewer line-of-battle-ships than at the same period of the former. "Many old and useful officers and a vast number of artificers had been discharged from the king's dockyards; the customary supplies of timber and other important articles of naval stores had been omitted to be kept up; and some articles, including a large portion of hemp, had actually been sold out of the service. A deficiency of workmen and of materials produced, of course, a suspension in the routine of dockyard business. New ships could not be built; nor could old ones be repaired. Many of the ships

[1] Nelson's Disp., vol. iv. p. 500.

in commission, too, having been merely patched up, were scarcely in a state to keep the sea." [1] On this point St. Vincent was vulnerable to the attack made upon his administration by Pitt in March, 1804; but as regarded Pitt's main criticism, the refusal to expend money and seamen upon gunboats, he was entirely right, and his view of the question was that of a statesman and of a man of correct military instincts. [2] Nor, after his experience with the Sea Fencibles, can he be blamed for not sharing Pitt's emotion over "a number of gallant and good old men, coming forward with the zeal and spirit of lads swearing allegiance to the king," &c. [3]

These ill-timed changes affected most injuriously that very station — the Mediterranean — upon which hinged Bonaparte's projected combination. Out of the insufficient numbers, the heaviest squadrons and most seaworthy ships were naturally and properly massed upon the Channel and Biscay coasts. "I know," said Sir Edward Pellew, speaking of his personal experience in command of a squadron of six of the line off Ferrol, "I know and can assert with confidence that our navy was never better found, that it was never better supplied and that our men were never better fed or better clothed;" [4] and the condition of the ships was proved not only by the tenacity with which Pellew and his chief, Cornwallis, kept their stations, but by the fact that in the furious winter gales little damage was received. But at the same time Nelson was complaining bitterly that his ships were not seaworthy, that they were shamefully equipped, and destitute of the most necessary stores; while St. Vincent was writing to him, "We can send you neither ships nor men, and with the resources of your mind, you will do without

---

[1] James, Nav. Hist., vol. iii. p. 212 (ed. 1878).

[2] See Cobbett's Reg., vol. v. pp. 442, 443, for some very sensible remarks on Pitt's attack, written by Cobbett himself.

[3] Stanhope's Pitt, vol. iv. p. 94.

[4] Parl Debates, 1804, p. 892.

them very well." [1]   "Bravo, my lord!" said Nelson, ironically; "but," he wrote a month later, "I do not believe Lord St. Vincent would have kept the sea with such ships;" [2] and again, naming seven out of the ten under his command, "These are certainly among the very finest ships in our service, the best commanded and the very best manned, yet I wish them safe in England and that I had ships not half so well manned in their room; for it is not a store-ship a week that would keep them in repair." [3]

Such weakness interfered seriously with the close watch of Toulon, in face of the furious weather for which the Gulf of Lyon is noted; yet, from the strategic conditions of the Mediterranean, in no station was it more important to get the earliest news of an enemy's sailing and to keep constant touch with him. With the Straits of Gibraltar at one end, involving in case of escape several different possibilities, and with Egypt fifteen hundred miles away at the other, the most sagacious admiral might be misled as to the destination of a French squadron, if once lost to sight. Upon this difficulty Bonaparte framed his combination. In his first purpose the Toulon fleet was to be raised to ten sail-of-the-line, and at the fitting moment was to sail with a north-west wind, steering a course which, if seen by any British lookout, would indicate an intention of going eastward. To strengthen this presumption, General St. Cyr at Taranto was ordered to raise batteries to shelter a fleet of ten sail, and to prepare half a million rations; while the Minister of War was instructed that an extraordinary operation in that direction was contemplated about the 20th of November. [4] Simultaneously, twenty ships-of-the-line carrying twenty thousand troops were to be ready in Brest for a descent upon Ireland, and

---

[1] Nels. Disp., vol. v. p. 283.   [2] Ibid., p. 306.

[3] Ibid., p. 174. The following references also show conditions of Nelson's ships: vol. v. pp. 179, 211, 306, 307, 319, 334; vol. vi. pp. 38, 84, 99, 100, 103, 134, 158.

[4] Corr. de Nap., vol. viii. p. 657.

to be maintained in a state of readiness for instant sailing. This would conduce to keep Cornwallis close to Brest and away from the approaches to the Channel. The Toulon fleet, after losing sight of the British, was to haul up for the Straits, be joined off Cadiz or Lisbon by a squadron from Rochefort, raising its force to fifteen or sixteen sail-of-the-line, and thence, passing midway between Ushant and the Scilly islands, come about the middle of February off Boulogne; were the first consul expected then to be ready for crossing with his one hundred and thirty thousand men.

For the Toulon fleet, as the pivot on which all turned, Bonaparte selected his boldest admiral, Latouche Tréville, and fixed the middle of January, 1804, as the time of sailing. All the French authorities were scrupulously deceived, except the admiral himself, the Minister of Marine, and the maritime prefect at Toulon, Ganteaume, who had divined the secret.[1] The orders to the latter, ostentatiously confidential to deceive the office clerks, announced Martinique as the real destination, but enjoined him to tell the general commanding the troops that the squadron was going to the Morea, touching at Taranto. At the same time staff-officers were sent to notify St. Cyr that re-enforcements, which would raise his force to thirty thousand men, were coming not only from Toulon but from other ports; and troops throughout northern Italy began to move toward the seaboard.

It is not wonderful that Nelson was misled by such an elaborate scheme of deception. To this day men doubt whether Bonaparte seriously meant to invade England, and naval men then realized too keenly the dangers of the undertaking not to suspect a feint in it. Under all the conditions of the problem, Egypt and the Straits were equally probable solutions, and Egypt was not the only possible objective east of Toulon. Sicily and Sardinia, the Ionian

[1] Corr de Nap., vol. ix. p. 168.

Islands and the Morea, were coveted by Bonaparte; both as forwarding his control of the Mediterranean and as measurable advances towards Egypt and the Levant, traditional objects of French ambition.   Nelson also suspected a secret understanding between France and Russia to divide the Turkish Empire;[1] a suspicion justified in the past by Bonaparte's actions and to be vindicated in the future by the agreements of Tilsit.   The perplexities of the British admiral were therefore simply the inevitable uncertainties of the defence, the part assumed perforce by the British Empire at large in this war.   He had to provide against widely divergent contingencies; and the question is not how far he guessed[2] the inscrutable purposes of Bonaparte, but how well he took measures for meeting either fortune.

Let it, however, be remarked in passing, that the great merit of St. Vincent's strategy was that it minimized the evil resulting from a single admiral's mis-step.   To the success of the French scheme it was necessary that, not only one but, all their detached efforts should succeed. The strength of the British strategy lay not in hermetically sealing any one port, but in effectually preventing a great combination from all the ports.   It was essential to Bonaparte not merely that his scattered squadrons should, one at one time and another at another, escape to sea, but that they should do so at periods so ordered, and by routes so determined, as to insure a rapid concentration at a particular point.   Against this the British provided by the old and sound usage of interior positions and lines. This advantage Bonaparte recognized, and sought to overthrow by inducing them to diverging operations — toward the Levant on one flank, toward Ireland on the other.   Both diverted from Boulogne.

[1] Nels. Disp., vol v. pp. 115, 136.

[2] "It is at best but a guess," to use his own words, "and the world attaches wisdom to him that guesses right." (Nels. Disp., vol. vi. p. 193.)

To return to Nelson. During the first six months of his command he believed that the Toulon fleet was bound out of the Mediterranean;[1] and indeed, despite Bonaparte's wiles and the opinions of most of his own friends, he continually reverted to that conviction up to the final escape of Villeneuve. He could not, however, on the ground of his own intuitions resist the facts reported to him. On December 12, 1803, he writes: "Who shall say where they are bound? My opinion is, certainly, out of the Mediterranean."[2] Again, January 16, 1804: "It is difficult to say what may be the destination of the Toulon fleet, Egypt or Ireland.. I rather lean to the latter."[3] A week later, January 23, the effect of Bonaparte's feints begins to show: "Information just received leads me to believe the French fleet is about to put to sea bound to the eastward toward Naples and Sicily."[4] February 10: "The French have thirty thousand men ready to embark from Marseilles and Nice, and I am led to believe the Ferrol ships will push for the Mediterranean. Egypt is Bonaparte's object."[5]

Against either contingency his course is perfectly clear, — never to lose touch of the Toulon fleet. "My eyes are constantly fixed on Toulon,"[6] he says. "I will not lose sight of the Toulon fleet."[7] "It is of the utmost importance," he writes to his lookout frigates, "that the enemy's squadron in Toulon should be most strictly watched, and that I should be made acquainted with their sailing and route with all dispatch."[8] But here the inadequacy of St. Vincent's navy told heavily; and to that, not to Nelson, must be attributed the missteps of the later campaign. "My crazy fleet," he writes. "If I am to watch the French I must be at sea,

[1] See Nels. Disp., vol. v. pp. 179, 185, 247, 309, 374.
[2] Nels. Disp., vol. v. p. 309.   [3] Ibid., p. 374.   [4] Ibid., p. 388.
[5] Ibid., pp. 405, 411.   [6] Ibid., p. 498.   [7] Ibid., p. 411.
[8] Ibid., p. 300.

and if at sea must have bad weather; and if the ships are not fit to stand bad weather they are useless."[1] "I know no way of watching the enemy but to be at sea," he tells St. Vincent himself, "and therefore good ships are necessary." Under such conditions, with "terrible weather," in winter, not four fine days in six weeks, and even in summer having a hard gale every week,[2] it was impossible to keep his rickety ships close up against Toulon, as Cornwallis kept against Brest. "I make it a rule not to contend with the north-westers," he said. "Going off large or furling all sail we escape damage by the constant care of the captains;" and he not unjustly claimed equal credit with Cornwallis, in that with such a fleet, to which nothing was sent, he kept the sea ten consecutive months, "not a ship refitted in any way, except what was done at sea."[3]

Though desirable for the battle-ships themselves to be near Toulon, it would have been possible, in so narrow a sea, to dispense with that by taking a central position, and keeping touch with the enemy by numerous frigates; but here also the deficiencies of the navy interfered. Among the Maddalena Islands, at the north end of Sardinia, was found an admirable central anchorage, well sheltered, and having eastern and western exits by which it could be left at a moment's notice in all winds. Here the fleet could safely lie, ready for instant action, within striking distance of any route taken by the enemy, and sure to be found by lookout ships bringing tidings. Thither, therefore, as the direction most favorable for intercepting the French,[4] Nelson went in January, 1804, when informed they were about to sail; but he wrote: "I am kept in great distress for frigates and smaller vessels at this critical moment. I want ten more than I have, in order to watch that the French should not escape me."[5] This but

---

[1] Nels. Disp., vol. v. p. 306.   [2] Ibid., pp. 253, 254.
[3] Ibid., p. 438.   [4] Ibid., p. 388.   [5] Ibid., p. 395.

summed up the constant worry of those anxious two
years,[1] as it does also the results of recent experience in
the annual manœuvres of European navies. Under such
circumstances all depends upon the position taken by the
main body and the number of scouts it can throw out.
Properly, these should move in couples; one of which can
carry information, while its consort keeps touch of the
enemy till it meets another of the lookouts scattered on
their different radii of action.

The situation of Nelson in the Mediterranean, the character of his anxieties, and the condition of his ships have
been given in some detail, because upon the opposing
Mediterranean fleets turns the chief strategic interest of
the intended invasion of England and of the campaign
which issued in Trafalgar. Lord St. Vincent left office
with the Addington Ministry in May, 1804, and under
the energetic rule of his successor, who threw his administrative system to the winds, the condition of Nelson's
fleet was somewhat bettered; but the change came too
late to remedy it altogether.

Various events meanwhile concurred to postpone the
execution of Bonaparte's project and so to prolong the
watch of the British admiral. The Boulogne flotilla itself was not as forward as had been expected; but the
drain made by it upon the French arsenals, for workmen
and materials, was a greater cause of delay, by retarding
the equipment of the ships meant to cover the crossing.
In December only seven of the line were ready in Toulon.[2] In the spring of 1804, the first consul's attention
was absorbed by the royalist plot, which led to the arrest
of Pichegru and Moreau, to the seizure of the Duc d'Enghien on German soil and to his execution at Vincennes in
March. This last event had diplomatic consequences, in
the attitude taken by Russia and Prussia, which still far-

---

[1] See Nels. Disp., vol. v. pp. 145, 162, 413; vol. vi. pp. 84, 328, 329.
[2] Corr. de. Nap., vol. ix. p. 226.

ther engrossed him; and the invasion of Great Britain was thus by successive delays put off to the summer of 1804. On May 25, Napoleon, who had assumed the imperial title on the 18th of that month, writes to Latouche [1] that on the ocean side all was prepared, that the project was only postponed, not abandoned, and asks if he will be ready by July. July 2 he writes again,[2] anticipating his sailing from Toulon by the first of August, instructs him to pick up at Cadiz one French ship-of-the-line which had taken refuge there, thence to go to Rochefort, and finally to reach Boulogne, according to the first plan, by passing through the Channel; or, if necessary, by going north of the British islands. In all passages from port to port he was to keep far out to sea to avoid detection. "Let us," he adds, "be masters of the Strait for six hours and we shall be masters of the world." On the 2d of August, however, Napoleon postpones the invasion for some weeks, because some divisions of the flotilla had not yet joined; and on the 20th of that month Latouche Tréville died.

This loss was serious, as there was not among the surviving French admirals any who had shown himself fit for so important a task, except perhaps Bruix. He, being already definitely associated with the flotilla, could not well be displaced; and his health, moreover, was very bad, so that he also died the following March. Of two others who might possibly prove equal to high command, Rosily and Villeneuve, Napoleon, after some hesitation and with much mistrust, chose the latter. "All naval expeditions undertaken since I have been at the head of the government," said he, "have always failed, because the admirals see double, and have learned — where, I do not know — *that war can be made without running risks.*" [3] From this simple and undeniable standpoint no choice more unfortunate than Villeneuve could have been made.

[1] Corr. de Nap., vol. ix. p. 475.
[2] Ibid., p. 513.   [3] Ibid., Sept. 12, 1804.

Accomplished, brave, and skilful, he saw the defects of the French navy with a clearness which absolutely sapped his power to take risks. Although capable of the utmost self-devotion, he was unable to devote his command as the forlorn hope upon which might follow a great achievement.

Doubting Villeneuve's resolution, Napoleon now changed the details of his combination; giving to the Toulon fleet the inferior rôle of a diversion, instead of the great part of covering the flotilla at the chief centre of strategic action. The Brest fleet, during the life of Latouche Tréville, had been destined to tie Cornwallis to the French coast by the passive service of a mere demonstration. It was now given the principal part. Its admiral, Ganteaume, had in 1801 been blamed for not relieving Egypt; but Napoleon still felt for him the partiality of close personal association, and knew him to be an able officer. In the new plan, therefore, the Irish expedition passed definitively from a demonstration to a resolve. To it were assigned eighteen thousand troops under Marshal Augereau. Embarking them, Ganteaume should sail with a fleet of twenty ships-of-the-line, pass far out into the Atlantic to baffle pursuit, and then head for the north of Ireland as though coming from Newfoundland. Having landed the soldiers, for which only thirty-six hours were allowed, the fleet should sail for the straits of Dover, either by the English Channel or by the north of Scotland, according to the winds. Arriving near its destination two courses were open, the choice between which would again depend on the wind. Either the Grand Army at Boulogne would cross at once to England, or a corps of twenty-five thousand assembled in Holland under General Marmont, would sail under Ganteaume's convoy for Ireland. "With only eighteen thousand men in Ireland," wrote Napoleon, "we would run great risks; but whether they be increased to forty thousand, or I myself be in

England and eighteen thousand in Ireland, the gain of the war will be ours."[1]

The Toulon and Rochefort squadrons were to favor these operations by a powerful diversion. They were to sail separately for the West Indies, the former numbering twelve of the line and the latter five. Upon reaching the Atlantic two of the Toulon ships were to be directed against St. Helena, which they were to seize and then cruise in its neighborhood for three months against British commerce. The rest of the division, carrying four thousand troops, was to retake Dutch Guiana and re-enforce San Domingo,[2] if possible. The Rochefort division, lately commanded by Villeneuve, but now by Missiessy, was to seize the islands Santa Lucia and Dominica, re-enforce Martinique and Guadaloupe and then join Villeneuve. Thus combined, all would return to Europe, appear before Ferrol, releasing five French ships which were there blockaded, and finally anchor at Rochefort. "Thus attacked simultaneously in Asia, Africa, and America," wrote Napoleon, "the English, long accustomed not to suffer from the war, will by these successive shocks to their commerce feel the evidence of their weakness. I think that the sailing of these twenty ships-of-the-line will oblige them to dispatch over thirty in pursuit."[3] Villeneuve was to sail by October 12, and Missiessy before November 1. The Irish expedition should await the departure of the others, but it was hoped might get away before November 23.

This second combination was more vast, more complicated and therefore much more difficult than the first. It is interesting chiefly as indicating the transition in the emperor's mind, from the comparatively simple scheme laid down for Latouche Tréville to the grandiose concep-

---

[1] Corr. de Nap., vol. ix. p. 700, Sept. 29, 1804.
[2] The former Spanish part of the island was still in the hands of France.
[3] Corr. de Nap. Sept. 27 and 29, 1804.

tion which ended in Trafalgar and claimed Villeneuve as its victim. The course of events, mightier than the wills of sovereigns, now intervened to change again Napoleon's purpose and restore to the Toulon fleet the central part in the great drama. In December, 1804, formal war broke out between Great Britain and Spain.

Spain since 1796 had been in defensive and offensive alliance with France. By the treaty of San Ildefonso, then signed, she had bound herself to furnish, upon the simple demand of the French government, fifteen ships-of-the-line to re-enforce the French navy, as well as a specified body of troops. Holland also had entered into a similar covenant "forever" against Great Britain. At the outbreak of hostilities, therefore, Bonaparte found on either flank a maritime state formally obliged to aid him, whatever its present wish. Holland, a small flat country near at hand, was easily dominated by his army. It was rich, had a valid government and energetic people; and its position admirably seconded his schemes against Great Britain. It therefore suited him to have the Batavian republic join in the war. Spain, on the contrary, being extensive and rugged, was with difficulty controlled by an armed force, as Napoleon afterwards learned to his cost. It was remote from the centre of his power and from the intended operations; while effective military support could not be had from its government, feeble to disorganization, nor from its people, indolent and jealous of foreigners. One thing only was left to Spain of her former greatness,— the silver poured into her treasury from her colonies.

Bonaparte therefore decided to allow the neutrality of Spain, and to relinquish the stipulated aid in kind, upon condition of receiving an equivalent in money. This he fixed at six million francs per month, or about fourteen million dollars annually. Spain protested earnestly against the amount, but the first consul was inexorable.

He required also that all levies of troops should cease, any land forces sent into the provinces adjoining France, since - September, 1801, should be withdrawn, and the Spanish navy reorganized. Further, he demanded that five French ships-of-the-line then in Ferrol, where they had taken refuge from the British navy in July, 1803, when returning from Haïti, should be by Spain repaired and got ready for sea. "Spain," said Bonaparte, "has three alternatives: 1, she may declare war against England; 2, she may pay the specified subsidy; 3, war will be declared by France against Spain." [1]

When war began, the British minister at Madrid was instructed to ask if Spain intended to furnish France the ships promised by the treaty. If the answer was yes, he was to express no opinion, but say that any excess over the stipulations would be regarded as a declaration of war. Later, when it became known that Spain had signed a convention [2] stipulating the payment of subsidies to France, the ministry took the ground that this was a just cause of war, whenever Great Britain chose so to consider it; though for the time she might pass it over. " You will explain distinctly," ran the ambassador's instructions, dated November 24, 1803, " that his Majesty can only be induced to abstain from immediate hostilities in consequence of such a measure, upon the consideration that it is a temporary expedient, . . . and that his Majesty must be at liberty to consider a perseverance in the system of furnishing succors to France as, at any future period, when circumstances may render it necessary, a just cause of war." [3] " I am expressly enjoined to declare," wrote the British ambassador, in making this communication, " that such payments are a war subsidy, a succor the most efficacious, the best

[1] For Bonaparte's attitude toward Spain, see two letters to Talleyrand, Aug. 14 and 16, 1803; Corr. de Nap. vol. viii. pp. 580–585.

[2] Signed Oct. 19, 1803. (Combate Naval de Trafalgar, by D. Jose de Couto, p. 79.)

[3] Parl. Debates, 1805, vol. iii. p. 70.

adapted to the wants and situation of the enemy, the most prejudicial to the interests of his Britannic Majesty's sub-jects, and the most dangerous to his dominions; in fine, more than equivalent to every other species of aggression."[1] Repeated inquiries failed to draw from the Spanish gov-ernment any official statement of the terms of its bargain, either as to the amount of the subsidy, the period during which it should continue, or other conditions of the agree-ment.[2] Such communication the French ambassador posi-tively over-ruled.[3]

Warning was therefore early given[4] that a condition essential to postponement of action by Great Britain was the suspension of all further arming in Spanish ports. This was repeated in the most formal terms, and as an ultimatum, a few weeks later, on the 18th of February, 1804. "I am ordered to declare to you that the system of forbearance on the part of England absolutely depends on the cessation of every naval armament, and I am expressly forbidden to prolong my residence here, if unfortunately this condition should be rejected."[5] It was alleged and was incontrovertibly true, that, while Spain was so evi-dently under Bonaparte's influence, armaments in her ports as effectively necessitated watching, and so as greatly added to Great Britain's burdens, as if war actually existed.[6] Another complaint was that prizes made by French priva-teers were, by process of law, condemned and sold in Spanish ports.[7] The same was doubtless allowed to Great Britain; but in the strict blockade of the ports of France the latter here derived a great benefit, while upon her enemy was simply imposed an additional burden in scour-ing all the Spanish coast, as though actually at war, in order to recapture inward-bound prizes. Once condemned,

---

[1] Parl. Debates, 1805, vol. iii. p. 72. [2] Ibid., p. 372.
[3] Ibid., p. 81.
[4] Jan. 24, 1804. Ibid., p. 85. [5] Ibid., p. 89.
[6] Ibid [7] Ibid., pp. 85, 89.

the prize goods found their way to the French ports by Spanish coasters. Independent of the difficulty of identifying the property, the small size of these neutral carriers made seizure inexpedient; for the costs of condemnation were greater than the value of the prize.[1] The Spanish government claimed that the condemnation and sale of prize goods in their ports was simply an act of authorized commerce, free from all hostility.[2] Americans who recall the cruises of the Alabama and her fellows will be disposed to think that, whatever the technical accuracy of the plea, neutrality benevolent to an enemy's cruisers constitutes a just cause of war, whenever policy so advises.

The relations between the two countries continued in this strained and critical condition during the greater part of 1804. Bonaparte insisted that the Spanish dockyards should repair the French ships in Ferrol and Cadiz, — which was indeed one of the conditions of the convention of October 19, 1803, concealed from Great Britain, — and should permit seamen to pass by land from one port of Spain to another, and from France through Spain, to complete their crews. He consented indeed that they should go in small bodies of thirty or forty, but the vigilance of the British officials could not be deceived. The relations between France and Spain at this time were not inaptly described in the letter of Napoleon to the king, announcing his assumption of the imperial dignity. He styled him therein "ally and confederate." In June, 1804, an aide-de-camp of the emperor visited Ferrol and Madrid, charged to ascertain the condition of the ships and demand their completion.[3] The British minister could obtain no explanation of this mission, which naturally aroused his atten-

---

[1] For some account of the advantages to French privateers arising from this use of Spanish ports, with interesting particulars, see Naval Chronicle, vol. xiii. p. 76. In March, 1804, Spain prohibited the sale of prizes in her ports.

[2] Parl. Debates, 1805, vol. iii. p. 86.

[3] Corr. de Nap. vol. ix. p. 482.

tion.[1] Spain in truth was no longer a free agent. On the
3d of July, Napoleon ordered his Minister of Marine to
send to Ferrol the men still needed to man the ships there;
and on the 19th of the month [2] the British admiral Cochrane, then blockading the port, remonstrated with the
governor of Galicia upon this procedure as hostile to
Great Britain. On the 3d of September, and again on the
11th, Cochrane wrote to his government that Spanish ships
in Ferrol were fitting for sea, that three first-rates were
expected from Cadiz, and that no doubt remained that the
French, Spanish, and Dutch ships in the port were to act
together. He had consequently found necessary to concentrate his force.[3] Immediately upon receiving this information, the British ministry notified the Spanish government
that orders had been sent to their admiral off Ferrol to
prevent any Spanish ships of war from entering or leaving
that port. The ambassador at Madrid was directed to
require that the armaments should be discontinued, and
placed upon the same footing as before the war. He was
also to demand a clear explanation of the relations existing
between France and Spain. Unless satisfactory replies
were given, he was ordered to quit Madrid.

At the same time the ministry took a more questionable
step. Orders were sent to Cornwallis, to Cochrane, to
Nelson, and to the naval officer off Cadiz to detain and
send to England all Spanish treasure-ships; the intention being to keep them as a pledge until satisfactory
arrangements with Spain were made. In consequence of
this, on the 5th of October, four British frigates stopped,
near Cadiz, four Spanish vessels, of the same class but
of inferior armament. The disparity of force was not
great enough to justify the Spanish commodore in yielding; and an action followed in which one of his frigates
blew up. The other three surrendered and were taken to

[1] Parl Debates, 1805, vol. iii. p. 93.
[2] Ibid., p. 122.   [3] Ibid., pp. 95, 122.

England.   Curiously enough, the news of this transaction had not reached Madrid when the British representative, on the 10th of November, left the city.   The final discussions between him and the Spanish government went on in complete ignorance of so decisive an event; but as he could get no explanation of the agreements between France and Spain, he persisted in demanding his passports.   On the 12th of December, 1804, Spain declared war.

That Great Britain had just cause for war can scarcely be denied.   She now for the first time came into contact with Napoleon's claim that it was, not merely the interest, but the bounden duty of every maritime state to join his attempt to crush her.[1]   Upon this principle he justified his policy of coercing all into such hostilities, and formulated at a later day the maxim, "There are no neutrals."   The subsidy paid by Spain, calculated on British rates of expenditure, was annually worth to France fifteen ships-of-the-line and two hundred thousand troops;[2] but against Napoleon's further extension of his principle, by suddenly calling into activity the Spanish navy, Great Britain's only safeguard was to insist upon the latter's remaining unarmed.   The Spanish government, having promised not to arm, suddenly and without explanation began to equip vessels in Ferrol,— an act which, coinciding with the passage of French seamen through Spain to that place, fairly excited alarm and justified the orders not to allow Spanish ships to enter or leave the port.

The seizure of the treasure-ships is less easily excused, though the obloquy attending it has been unduly heightened by the tragical explosion.   Its best palliation lies in Great Britain's previous experience that, in the commercial decadence and poverty of Spain, the treasures of the colonies were a determining factor in negotiations.

---

[1] Thiers, Cons. et Emp. livre xvii. pp. 383, 384.
[2] Pitt's Speech of February 11, 1805.

While they were on the sea, Spain temporized; when they arrived, she stiffened. The purpose was to retain them as a pledge, to be restored in case of a peaceable issue; as Swedish merchantmen were embargoed in 1801, and released when the Armed Neutrality dissolved. A Spanish naval historian, while censuring other acts of Great Britain, says: "The mere detention of the division from America, carrying specie which might be used in behalf of French preparations, could have been overlooked as an able and not very illegal means of bettering the prospects of the English reclamations, in consequence of the scanty satisfaction they obtained from our Court;" and again: "If all the circumstances are impartially weighed, . . . we shall see that all the charges made against England for the seizure of the frigates may be reduced simply to want of proper foresight in the strength of the force detailed to effect it." [1] The action, nevertheless, was precipitate, and extenuated by no urgent political necessity. Nelson, who certainly was not averse to strong measures, directed his captains to disobey the order, which he at first thought came only from Cornwallis; for, he said, "I am clearly of the opinion that Spain has no wish to go to war with England." [2]

[1] D. José de Couto, Combate Naval de Trafalgar (Madrid, 1851), pp. 83, 89.

[2] Nels. Disp., vol. vi. p. 240. This letter was not sent, Nelson soon after receiving the Admiralty's order.

CHAPTER XVI.

THE TRAFALGAR CAMPAIGN — CONCLUDED.

JANUARY — OCTOBER. 1805.

SUCCESSIVE MODIFICATIONS OF NAPOLEON'S PLAN. — NARRATIVE
OF NAVAL MOVEMENTS. — FINAL FAILURE OF NAPOLEON'S
NAVAL COMBINATIONS. — WAR WITH AUSTRIA, AND BATTLE
OF AUSTERLITZ. — BATTLE OF TRAFALGAR. — VITAL CHANGE
IMPOSED UPON NAPOLEON'S POLICY BY THE RESULT OF THE
NAVAL CAMPAIGN.

THE Spanish declaration of war was followed by a
new treaty of alliance with France, signed in Paris
on the 5th of January, 1805, and confirmed on the 18th of
the month at Madrid. Spain undertook to furnish, by
March 21, to the common cause, at least twenty-five ships-
of-the-line and eleven frigates; but the military direction
of the whole allied effort was entrusted to Napoleon.

This accession of Spain could not become immediately
operative, owing to the backward state of her armaments
caused by the previous demands of Great Britain. The
emperor therefore adhered for the time to his existing
plans, formulated on the 27th and 29th of September.
These proving abortive, he next framed, upon lines equal
both in boldness and scope to those of the Marengo and
Austerlitz campaigns, the immense combination which
resulted in Trafalgar.

The events of the ten following months, therefore, have
an interest wholly unique, as the development of the only
great naval campaign ever planned by this foremost captain of modern times. From his opponents, also, upon

whom was thrown the harder task of the defensive, was
elicited an exhibition of insight, combination, prompti-
tude, and decision, which showed them to be, on their
own element, not unworthy to match with the great emperor. For Napoleon was at this disadvantage, — he could
not fully realize the conditions of the sea. Accustomed
by forethought and sheer will to trample obstacles under
foot, remembering the midwinter passage of the Splugen
made by Macdonald at his command, and the extraordinary impediments overcome by himself in crossing the
Saint Bernard, he could not believe that the difficulties of
the sea could not be vanquished by unskilled men handling the ponderous machines entrusted to them, when confronted by a skilful enemy. To quote an able French
writer: "But one thing was wanting to the victor of Austerlitz, — *le sentiment exact des difficultés de la marine.*" [1]

With steam, possibly, this inequality of skill might have
been so reduced as to enable the generalship of Napoleon,
having also the advantage of the initiative, to turn the
scale. With sailing ships it was not so; and in following the story of Trafalgar it must be remembered that
the naval superiority of Great Britain lay not in the number of her ships, but in the wisdom, energy, and tenacity
of her admirals and seamen. At best her numbers were
but equal to those arrayed against her. The real contest
was between the naval combinations of Napoleon and the
insight of British officers, avoiding or remedying the
ex-centric movements he untiringly sought to impress
upon their forces.

In December detailed instructions for executing the
plan of September 29 were issued to Admirals Villeneuve
and Missiessy. [2] The latter, after leaving Rochefort, was
to steer between the Azores and Canaries, so as to avoid the
British squadrons off the Biscay coast of Spain, go direct

---

[1] Jurien de la Gravière, Revue des Deux Mondes, Oct. 1887, p. 611.
[2] Correspondance de Napoléon, vol x. pp. 79–97.

to Martinique, take the British islands Santa Lucia and Dominica, and upon Villeneuve's arrival place himself under his command. In pursuance of these orders Missiessy escaped from Rochefort on January 11. He was seen next day by a lookout vessel belonging to the blockading squadron; but the latter, for whatever reason, was off its post, and Missiessy reached Martinique safely on the 20th of February. On the 24th of that month six British ships-of-the-line, under Rear-Admiral Cochrane, sailed in pursuit from before Ferrol; where their place was taken by a detachment of equal force drawn from before Brest.

Villeneuve's orders were to go from Toulon direct to Cayenne, recapture the former Dutch colonies of Guiana, form a junction with Missiessy, re-enforce San Domingo, and start on his return for Europe not later than sixty days after reaching South America. With the combined squadrons he was to appear off Ferrol, release the French ships there blockaded, and bring the whole force, amounting to twenty of the line, to Rochefort. "The result of your cruise," wrote Napoleon to him, "will be to secure our colonies against any attack, and to retake the four Dutch colonies on the Continent, as well as such other British islands as may appear open to the force under your command." Six thousand troops were embarked on board his squadron for the operations on shore. Both he and Missiessy were expressly forbidden to land their crews for that purpose ; a decision of the great emperor worthy to be remembered in these days.

Villeneuve was ready to sail early in January, but his first need was to elude the watchfulness of Nelson. The British admiral was known to move from point to point in his command, between the Maddalena Islands and Cape San Sebastian on the Spanish coast, while he kept before Toulon lookout ships always informed of his whereabouts. Villeneuve therefore thought indispensable to start with a breeze strong enough to carry him a hundred miles the first night. For a fortnight the wind hung at north-east and south-east — fair but very light; but on the 17th of January it shifted to north-west, with signs of an approaching gale. The next morning Villeneuve sent a division to drive off the enemy's lookouts; and when these disappeared the squadron sailed, numbering ten of the line and seven frigates. Nelson with eleven ships-of-the-line was at the moment at anchor in Maddalena Bay.

Following Napoleon's plan for deceiving the British admiral, the French squadron steered for the south end of Sardinia, as though bound eastward. During the night it was dogged by the enemy's frigates, which had retired no further than was necessary to avoid capture. At ten o'clock they were close by; and at two in the morning, satisfied as to the French course, they parted company and hastened to Nelson, — the wind then blowing a whole gale from the north-west. Twelve hours later they were seen from the flag-ship with the signal flying that the enemy was at sea, and in two hours more the British fleet was under way. Unable to beat out by the western entrance in the teeth of the storm, it ran in single column through the narrow eastern pass as night fell, — Nelson's ship leading, the others steering by the poop lanterns of the vessel next ahead. When clear of the port the fleet hauled up to the southward, and during the night, which was unsettled and squally, kept along the east coast of Sardinia. The frigate "Seahorse" was sent ahead to pass round the south end of the island and get touch again of the enemy.

During the night the wind changed to south-south-west, and blew heavily throughout the 21st. On the forenoon of the 22d the fleet, still struggling against a heavy southwesterly gale, was fifty miles east of the south end of Sardinia. There it was rejoined by the "Seahorse," which the day before had caught sight of a French frigate standing in toward Cagliari, but had not seen the main body. Not till the 26th did Nelson reach Cagliari, where to his relief he found the French had not been. Nothing even was known of their movements; but the same day the frigate "Phœbe" joined from the westward with news that a French eighty-gun ship, partially dismasted, had put in to Ajaccio. The British fleet then stretched across to Palermo, where it arrived on the 28th. Having now fairly covered the approaches from the westward to Sardinia, Sicily, and Naples, Nelson reasoned that one of two things must have happened: either the French, despite the southerly gale, had succeeded in going east between Sicily and Africa, or they had put back disabled. In the latter case he could not now overtake them; in the former, he must follow.[1] Accordingly, after sending scouts to scour the seas, and three frigates to resume the watch off Toulon, he shaped his course along the north side of Sicily, and on the 30th of January passed through the straits of Messina on his way to Egypt.

Villeneuve had in fact returned to Toulon. On the first night an eighty-four-gun ship and three frigates separated, and the former put in dismasted to Ajaccio, as Nelson had learned. The following day and in the night, when the wind shifted to south-west, three more ships-of-the-line were crippled. Forced to the eastward by the gale, and aware that two enemy's frigates had marked his course, the admiral feared that he should meet the British at a disadvantage and determined to retreat.

Thus prematurely ended the first movement in Napoleon's naval combination for the invasion of England. The Rochefort squadron had escaped only to become a big detachment, wholly out of reach of support or recall. The Toulon fleet, forced to await a heavy wind in order to effect the evasion by which alone the combination could be formed, was through the inexperience of its seamen

_____
[1] Nelson's Dispatches, vol. vi. p. 333.

crippled by the very advantage it had secured. In truth, however, had it gone on, it would almost infallibly have been driven by the south-west gale into the very spot, between Sardinia and Sicily, where Nelson went to seek it, and which was ransacked by his lookouts.[1] Neither Villeneuve nor Nelson doubted the result of such meeting.[2]

The other factor in this combination, the Brest fleet and army corps of twenty thousand men, had been held in readiness to act, dependent upon the successful evasion of the two others. "I calculate," Napoleon had said, "that the sailing of twenty ships from Rochefort and Toulon will force the enemy to send thirty in pursuit;"[3] a diversion that would very materially increase the chances for the Brest armament. For a moment he spoke of sending to India this powerful body, strongly re-enforced from the French and Spanish ships in Ferrol.[4] This was, however, but a passing thought, rejected by his sound military instinct as an ex-centric movement, disseminating his force and weakening the purposed attack upon the heart of the British power. Three months later, when he began to fear failure for the latter attempt, he recurred to the East India project in terms which show why he at first laid it aside. "In case, through any event whatsoever, our expedition have not full success, and I cannot compass *the greatest of all ends, which will cause all the rest to fall*,[5] I think we must calculate the operation in India for September."[6] India in truth was to the imagination of Napoleon what Egypt was to Nelson,— an object which

---

[1] After writing these words the author noted Nelson's opinion to the same effect: "Had they not been crippled, nothing could have hindered our meeting them on January 21, off the south end of Sardinia." (Dispatches, vol. vi. p. 354.)

[2] For Villeneuve's opinion see Chevalier's Hist. de la Mar. Fran. sous l'Empire, p. 134; for Nelson's, Disp. vol. vi. pp. 334, 339.

[3] Corr. de Nap., vol. ix. p. 701.   [4] Ibid., Jan. 16, 1805.

[5] Compare with Nelson's views on attacking Russian fleet, *ante,* p. 46.

[6] Corr. de Nap., April 29, 1805, vol. x. p. 443.

colored all his ideas and constantly misled him. As was shrewdly said by an American citizen to the British government, in this very month of January, 1805, "The French in general believe that the fountains of British wealth are in India and China. They never appeared to me to understand that the most abundant source is in her agriculture, her manufactures, and the foreign demand."[1] This impression Napoleon fully shared, and it greatly affected his judgment during the coming campaign.

The return of Villeneuve and the delay necessary to repair his ships, concurring with the expected re-enforcements from Spain, wholly changed the details of Napoleon's plan. In essence it remained the same from first to last; but the large number of ships now soon to be at his command appealed powerfully to his love for great masses and wide combinations. Now, also, Villeneuve could not reach the West Indies before the sickly season.

The contemplated conquests in America, which had formed so important a part of the first plan, were therefore laid aside, and so was also the Irish expedition by Ganteaume's fleet. The concentration of naval forces in the West Indies or at some point exterior to France became now the great aim; and the sally of the various detachments, before intended to favor the crossing of the flotilla by a diversion, was now to be the direct means of covering it, by bringing them to the English Channel and before Boulogne. The operations were to begin in March; and urgent orders were sent to Spain to have the contingents in her several ports ready to move at a moment's notice.

The situations of the squadrons in March, when the

---

[1] Letter to Pitt by Robert Francis; Castlereagh's Memoirs, vol. v. p. 444. The whole letter is most suggestive, not to say prophetic. From internal indications it is extremely probable that the writer of these letters, signed Robert Francis, was Robert Fulton, though the fact is not mentioned in any of his biographies.

great Trafalgar campaign opened, need to be stated. On the extreme right, in the Texel, were nine ships-of-the-line with a due proportion of lighter vessels; and some eighty transports lay ready to embark Marmont's army corps of twenty-five thousand men.[1] The Boulogne flotilla was assembled; the few detachments still absent being so near at hand that their junction could be confidently expected before the appearance of the covering fleet. The army, one hundred and thirty thousand strong, was by frequent practice able to embark in two hours.[2] Two tides were needed for all the boats to clear the ports; but as word of the fleet's approach would precede its arrival, they could haul out betimes and lie in the open sea, under the batteries, ready to start. In Brest, Ganteaume had twenty-one ships-of-the-line. The Rochefort squadron was now in the West Indies with Missiessy; but two more ships were ready in that port and one in Lorient. In Ferrol were five French and ten Spanish; of the latter it was expected that six or eight could sail in March. In Cadiz the treaty called for twelve or fifteen to be ready at the same time, but only six were then actually able to move. There was also in Cadiz one French ship. In Cartagena were six Spaniards, which, however, took no part in the campaign. At Toulon Villeneuve would have eleven ships. All these were ships-of-the-line. The total available at the opening of the campaign was therefore sixty-seven; but it will be observed that they were disseminated in detachments, and that the strategic problem was, first, to unite them in the face of an enemy that controlled the communications, and, next, to bring them to the strategic centre.

As in 1796, the declaration of Spain in 1805 added immensely to the anxieties of Great Britain. Lord Melville, who succeeded St. Vincent as First Lord in May, 1804,

---

[1] Mémoires du Duc de Raguse, vol. ii. p. 261.

[2] Thiers, Cons. et Emp., vol. v. p. 413.

had at once contracted for several ships-of-the-line to be built in private yards;[1] but these were not yet ready. A somewhat singular expedient was then adopted to utilize worn-out vessels, twelve of which were in February, 1805, cased with two-inch oak plank, and with some additional bracing sent to sea. It is said some of these bore a part in the battle of Trafalgar.[2]

The disposition and strength of the British detachments varied with the movements of the enemy and with the increasing strength of their own navy. Lord Keith, in the Downs with eleven small ships-of-the-line, watched the Texel and the Straits of Dover. The Channel fleet under Cornwallis held Brest under lock and key, with a force varying from eleven, when the year began, to twenty or twenty-four in the following April. This was the centre of the great British naval line. Off Rochefort no squadron was kept after Missiessy's escape. In March that event had simply transferred to the West Indies five French and six British ships. Off Ferrol eight ships were watching the combined fifteen in the port. In October, when the Spanish war was threatening, a division of six was sent to blockade Cadiz. Nelson's command, which had before extended to Cape Finisterre, was now confined to Gibraltar as its western limit, and the Cadiz portion assigned to Sir John Orde,— a step particularly invidious to Nelson, depriving him of the most lucrative part of his station, in favor of one who was not only his senior, with power to annoy him, but reputed to be his personal enemy. Nelson had within the Straits twelve of the line, several of which, however, were in bad condition; and one, kept permanently at Naples for political reasons, was useless to him. Two others were on their way to join, but did not arrive before the campaign opened. It may be added that there were in India from eight to ten ships-of-the-line, and in

---

[1] Barrow's Autobiography, p. 263.
[2] Ibid. Nav. Chron., vol. xiii. p. 328.

the West Indies four, which Cochrane's arrival would raise to ten.[1]

On the 2d of March Napoleon issued specific orders for the campaign to Villeneuve and Ganteaume. The latter, who was to command-in-chief after the junction, was directed to sail at the first moment possible with his twenty-one ships, carrying besides their crews thirty-six hundred troops. He was to go first to Ferrol, destroy or drive off the blockading squadron, and be joined by the French and Spanish ships there ready; thence by the shortest route to Martinique, where he was to be met by Villeneuve and, it was hoped, by Missiessy also. If Villeneuve did not at once appear, he was to be awaited at least thirty days. When united, the whole force, amounting to over forty of the line, would, to avoid detection, steer for the Channel by an unusual route and proceed direct to Boulogne, where the emperor expected it between June 10 and July 10. If by Villeneuve's not coming, or other cause, Ganteaume found himself with less than twenty-five ships, he was to go to Ferrol; where it would be the emperor's care to assemble a re-enforcement. He might, however, even with so small a number, move straight on Boulogne if he thought advisable.[2]

Villeneuve's orders were to sail at the earliest date for Cadiz, where he was not to enter but be joined outside by the ships then ready. From Cadiz he was to go to Martinique, and there wait forty days for Ganteaume. If the latter did not then appear he was to call at San Domingo, land some troops and thence go to the Bay of Santiago in the Canary Islands,[3] where he would cruise twenty days. This provided a second rendezvous where Ganteaume could

---

[1] The above account depends mainly upon the "Naval Chronicle" for April 15, 1805; vol. xiii. pp. 365–367, — checked by James and other sources.

[2] Corr. de Nap., vol. x. p. 227.

[3] So in the orders, Corr. de Nap., vol. x. p. 232. At a later date this rendezvous is spoken of by Napoleon as in the Cape de Verde. (Corr. de Nap., vol. xi. p. 50.) A singular confusion in such important orders.

join, if unexpectedly delayed in Brest. The emperor, like all French rulers, did not wish to risk his fleet in battle with nearly equal forces. Whatever the result, his combinations would suffer. "I prefer," said he, "the rendezvous at Martinique to any other; but I also prefer Santiago to a junction before Brest, by raising the blockade, in order to avoid fighting of any kind."[1] When Ganteaume, at a most critical instant, only six days before Villeneuve got away, reported that he was ready, — that there were but fifteen British ships in the offing and success was sure, — Napoleon replied: "A naval victory now would lead to nothing. Have but one aim, — to fulfil your mission. Sail without fighting."[2] So to the old delusion of ulterior objects was sacrificed the one chance for compassing the junction essential to success. By April 1 the British fleet off Brest was increased to twenty-one sail.

Meanwhile Nelson had returned from his fruitless search at Alexandria, and on the 13th of March again appeared off Toulon. Thence he went to Cape San Sebastian, showing his ships off Barcelona to convince the enemy he was fixed on the coast of Spain; reasoning that if they thought him to the westward they would more readily start for Egypt, which he still believed to be their aim. He had by his communications with Alexandria learned the distracted state of that country since the destruction of the Mameluke power and its restoration to the Turks, and reported that the French could easily hold it, if they once effected a lodgment.[3] From Cape San Sebastian the fleet next went to the Gulf of Palmas, a convenient roadstead in the south of Sardinia, to fill with provisions from transports lately arrived. It anchored there on the 26th of March, but was again at sea when, at 8 A. M. of April 4, being then twenty miles west of the Gulf, a frigate

[1] Corr. de Nap., vol. x. p. 447.   [2] Ibid., 324.
[3] Nels. Disp., vol. vi. pp. 338–341.

brought word of the second sailing of the Toulon fleet.
When last seen, in the evening of March 31, it was sixty
miles south of Toulon, steering south with a north-west
wind. One of the pair of lookouts was then sent to
Nelson; and the other, losing sight of the enemy during
the night, joined him a few hours after the first. The
only clue she could give was that, having herself steered
south-west with a wind from west-north-west, the enemy
had probably kept on south or borne away to the eastward.
Nelson, therefore, took the fleet midway between Sardinia
and the African coast, scattering lookout ships along the
line between these two points.[1] He was thus centrally
placed to cover everything east of Sardinia, and with means
of speedy information if the French attempted to pass,
at any point, the line occupied by him.

Villeneuve had indeed headed as reported by the British
frigates, swayed by Nelson's ruse in appearing off Barcelona.[2] Believing the enemy off Cape San Sebastian, he
meant to go east of the Balearic Islands. The next day,
April 1, a neutral ship informed him that it had seen the
British fleet south of Sardinia. The wind fortunately
hauling to the eastward, Villeneuve changed his course to
pass north of the Balearics; and on the 6th of April, when
Nelson was watching for him between Sardinia and Africa,
he appeared off Cartagena. The Spanish division there
declined to join him, having no instructions from its government; and the French fleet, continuing at once with a
fresh easterly wind, passed Gibraltar on the 8th. On the
9th it reached Cadiz, driving away Orde's squadron.
Following his orders strictly, Villeneuve anchored outside the port; and was there at once joined by the French
seventy-four "l'Aigle," and six Spanish ships. During
the night the combined force of eighteen of the line sailed
for Martinique, where it anchored May 14, after a passage

---

[1] Nelson's Dispatches, vol. vi. p. 397.
[2] Chevalier, Mar. Fran. sous l'Empire, p. 142.

of thirty-four days.   Some Spanish ships separated the day after sailing; but, having sealed instructions giving the rendezvous, they arrived only two days later than the main body.

This sortie of Villeneuve had so far been exceptionally happy.   By a mere accident he had learned Nelson's position, while that admiral was misled by what seems to have been bad management on the part of his carefully placed lookouts.   Nelson was not prone to blame subordinates, but he apparently felt he had not been well served in this case.   Not till April 16, when Villeneuve was already six days on his way from Cadiz, did he learn from a passing ship that nine days before the French were seen off Cape de Gata, on the coast of Spain, steering westward with an east wind, evidently bound to the Atlantic.   To this piece of great good luck Villeneuve's fortune added another.   While he carried an east wind with him till clear of the Straits, Nelson, from the 4th of April to the 19th, had a succession of strong westerly gales.   "We have been nine days coming two hundred miles," he wrote.   "For a whole month we have had nothing like a Levanter except for the French fleet." [1]   Not till May 6, after a resolute struggle of over three weeks against contrary fortune, did he anchor his fleet in Gibraltar Bay. Five days later he was on his way to the West Indies. But while the escape from Toulon showed the impossibility of securing every naval detachment of the enemy, the events elsewhere happening proved the extreme difficulty of so timing the evasions as to effect a great combination. While Villeneuve with eighteen ships was hastening to the West Indies, Missiessy,[2] with five others, having very imperfectly fulfilled his mission to annoy the enemy's islands, was speeding back to Rochefort, where orders at

[1] Nelson's Dispatches, vol. vi. pp. 410, 411, 415.
[2] See *ante*, p. 142. Missiessy sailed from the West Indies in the same week that Villeneuve sailed for them.

once to retrace his steps were waiting. At the same time
Ganteaume with his twenty-one was hopelessly locked in
Brest. Amid all the difficulties of their task, the British
fleets, sticking close to the French arsenals, not only tempered their efficiency for war to the utmost toughness, but
reaped also the advantages inseparable from interior
positions.

The better to divert attention from his real designs,
Napoleon took the time appointed for his squadrons' sailing to visit Italy. Leaving Paris April 1, and journeying
leisurely, he was in Alessandria on the first of May and
in Milan on the 10th. There he remained a month, and
was on the 26th crowned king of the late Italian Republic. His stay in Italy was prolonged to July. It is probably to this carefully timed absence that we owe the full
and invaluable record of his hopes and fears, of the naval
combinations which chased each other through his tireless
mind, of the calculations and surmises — true or false,
but always ingenious — which are contained in his almost
daily letters to the Minister of Marine.

Prominent among his preoccupations were the detention of Ganteaume, — who, "hermetically blockaded and
thwarted by constant calms,"[1] could not get away, — and
the whereabouts of Nelson, who disappeared from his sight
as entirely, and from his knowledge far more completely,
than Villeneuve did from the British ken. "In God's
name! hurry my Brest squadron away, that it may have
time to join Villeneuve. Nelson has been again deceived
and gone to Egypt. Villeneuve was out of sight on the
10th of April. Send him word that Nelson is seeking
him in Egypt; I have sent the same news to Ganteaume
by a courier. God grant, however, that he may not find
him in Brest."[2] On the 15th of April Ganteaume did
make an attempt. The British fleet had been driven off

<hr />

[1] Corr. de Nap., April 13, 1805, vol. x. p. 390.
[2] Ibid, April 20 and 23.

by a gale on the 11th, but reappeared on the 13th. On the afternoon of the 14th word was brought to Admiral Gardner, who had temporarily relieved Cornwallis, that the French were getting under way. The next day they came out; but the enemy now numbered twenty-four sail to their twenty-one, and after a demonstration they retired within the port.

As the advancing season gave less and less hope of the blockade relaxing, Napoleon formed a new combination. Two ships-of-the-line, now nearly ready at Rochefort, should sail under Rear-Admiral Magon, carrying modified instructions to Villeneuve. The latter was now commanded to wait thirty-five days after Magon's arrival, and then, if Ganteaume had not appeared, return direct to Ferrol, discarding the alternative rendezvous of Santiago. At Ferrol he would find fifteen French and Spanish ships, making with his own and Magon's a total of thirty-five. With these he was to appear before Brest, where Ganteaume would join him, and with the combined force of fifty-six of the line at once enter the Channel. Magon sailed with these orders early in May, and on June 4 reached Villeneuve just in time to insure the direction given by the latter to his fleet upon its return. To facilitate the junction at Brest very heavy batteries were thrown up, covering the anchorage outside the Goulet; and there, in May, Ganteaume took up his position, covered by one hundred and fifty guns on shore.

It will be recognized that the emperor's plan, while retaining its essential features, had now undergone a most important modification, due to the closeness of the British blockade of Brest. A combination of his squadrons still remained the key-stone of the fabric; but the tenacity with which the largest of his detachments was held in check had forced him to accept — what he had re jected as least advantageous — a concentration in the Bay of Biscay, the great hive where swarmed the British navy.

It became therefore more than ever desirable to divert as many as possible of the enemy's cruisers from those waters; an object which now continuously occupied Napoleon's mind and curiously tinged his calculations with the color of his hopes. In defiance of statistics, he thought the East Indies, as has before been said, the first of British interests. He sought therefore to raise alarms about India, and persisted in believing that every division sailing from England was bound there. "Cochrane," he writes on April 13, "was before Lisbon on March 4. He must first have gone to the Cape de Verde, thence to Madeira, and if he gets no information he will go to India. That is what any admiral of sense would do in his case." [1] On the 10th of May, when Cochrane had been over a month in the West Indies, he reiterates this opinion, and at the same time conjectures that five thousand troops which sailed from England on the 15th of April with most secret orders were gone to the Cape of Good Hope. "Fears of Villeneuve's meeting this expedition will force them to send more ships to India." [2] On the 31st of May he guesses that eight ships-of-the-line, which sailed ten days before under Collingwood, were bound to India, [3] and a week later repeats the surmise emphatically: "The responsibility of the ministers is so great they cannot but send him to the East Indies." [4] On the 9th of June he writes: "Everything leads me to believe the English sent fifteen ships to the East Indies, when they learned that Cochrane reached Barbadoes a fortnight after Missiessy sailed; and in that case it is quite possible Nelson has been sent to America." [5] This opinion is repeated on the 13th and 14th; and on the 28th, as the veil was about to fall from his eyes, he sums up the acute reasoning which, starting from a false premise, had so misled him: "It is difficult to believe that without any news the English have

[1] Corr. de Nap., vol. x. p. 394.   [2] Ibid., p. 490.
[3] Ibid., p. 571.   [4] Ibid. p. 616.   [5] Ibid., p. 624.

sent seventeen ships-of-the-line (i. e. Nelson and Collingwood combined) to the West Indies, when Nelson, joining
his ten to Cochrane's six, and three at Jamaica, would
have nineteen — superior to our squadron; while Collingwood going to the East Indies with eight and finding
there nine, in all seventeen, also superior to us — it is
difficult, I say, to believe that the enemy, with the chance
of being everywhere superior, should blindly abandon the
East Indies." [1]

Some French writers, [2] as well as some English, have
disparaged the insight of Nelson, comparing him unfavor-
ably with Napoleon, and basing their estimate largely upon
his error in esteeming Egypt the aim of the French.   In
view of the foregoing extracts, and of other miscalcula-
tions made by the emperor during this remarkable campaign — which will appear farther on — it must be admitted
that when in the dark, without good information, both were
forced to inferences, more or less acute, but which, resting on no solid data, rose, as Nelson said, little above
guesses.   So also Collingwood has been credited with
completely unravelling Napoleon's plan, and his penetration has been exalted above Nelson's because, *after* the
latter's return from chasing Villeneuve to the West Indies,
he wrote that the flight there was to take off the British
naval force; overlooking his conjecture, two lines before,
that (not England, but) "Ireland is the real mark and butt
of all these operations."   Rather might each adopt for
himself Napoleon's own words, "I have so often in my life
been mistaken that I no longer blush for it." [3]   When his
frigates lost sight of Villeneuve, on the night of March 31,
Nelson went neither east nor west; he concentrated his force
to cover what he thought the most likely objects of the
enemy, and awaited information as to his movements.   "I

[1] Corr. de Nap., vol. x. p. 708.

[2] For example, Thiers, Cons. et Emp., liv. xx. p. 178 ; Jurien de la Gravière,
Guerres Maritimes, vol. ii. p. 224 (first edition).

[3] Corr. de Nap., vol. xi. p. 162.

shall neither go to the eastward of Sicily nor to the westward of Sardinia until I know something positive."[1] It
can be confidently said that under like conditions Napoleon
would have done the same.

The fault of Napoleon's calculations was in over-esti-
mating both the importance and the danger of India, and
also in not allowing for the insight and information of the
British government. He himself laid down, with his peculiarly sound judgment, the lines it ought to follow: "If
I had been in the British Admiralty, I would have sent a
light squadron to the East and West Indies, and formed
a strong fleet of twenty of the line which I would not have
dispatched until I knew Villeneuve's destination."[2] This
was just what the Admiralty did. A light squadron was
on its way to India, and eight ships were ordered to the
West Indies under Collingwood; but that able officer,
finding Nelson had started, contented himself with sending two to re-enforce him, and took up his own position
with six before Cadiz, thus blocking the junction of the
Cartagena ships. The strong body of twenty was kept
before Brest, much to Napoleon's annoyance. "If England realizes the serious game she is playing, she ought
to raise the blockade of Brest."[3] But here, as with regard
to the Indian expeditions, Napoleon's thought was fathered
by his wish. To weaken the Brest blockade, as he confessed a little later, was the great point for France.[4]

Nothing in fact is more noteworthy, nor more creditable,
than the intelligence and steadiness with which the British naval authorities resisted Napoleon's efforts to lead
them into ex-centric movements. This was partly due to

---

[1] Nels. Disp., vol. vi. p. 401. In a former work ("The Influence of Sea
Power upon History," p. 23), the author casually spoke of this as a false step,
into which Nelson had been misled. A closer study has convinced him that
the British admiral did quite right.

[2] Corr. de Nap., vol. x. p. 624. Compare this with Nelson's remark, just
quoted.

[3] Corr. de Nap., vol. x. p. 624.   [4] Ibid., June 22, 1805, p. 686.

an accurate judgment of the worth of the enemy's detached squadrons, partly to an intuitive sense of the
supreme importance of the Biscay positions, and partly to
information much more accurate than Napoleon imagined,
or than he himself received in naval transactions. "Those
boasted English," jeered he, when he thought them ignorant of Villeneuve's second sailing, "who claim to know
of everything, who have agents everywhere, couriers booted
and spurred everywhere, knew nothing of it."[1] Yet,
by a singular coincidence, on the very day, April 25, that
they were supposed thus deceived, the Admiralty were
hurrying letters to Nelson and to the West Indies with
the important tidings. "You reason," wrote he to Decrès, "as if the enemy were in the secret."[2] This is just
what they were,—not as to all details, but as to the main
features of his plans. While the emperor was wildly
reckoning on imaginary squadrons hastening to India, and
guessing where Nelson was, both the latter and his government knew where Villeneuve had gone, and the British
admiral was already in the West Indies. About the beginning of May it was known in England not only that
the Toulon fleet had sailed, but whither it was bound;[3]
and about the first of June, despite the cautions about
secrecy imposed by Bonaparte, the British were informed
by a prisoner that "the combined fleet, of sixty sail-of-the-
line, will fight our fleet (balayer la Manche), while the
large frigates will come up channel to convoy the flotilla
over. The troops are impatiently awaiting the appearance
of the ships to set them free."[4]

The Admiralty therefore understood as well as did
Napoleon that the crucial necessity in their dispositions

[1] Nap. to Decrès, May 10, 1805.
[2] Corr. de Nap., June 9, p. 624.
[3] Annual Register, 1805, p. 225 ; Naval Chronicle, vol. xiii. p. 399.
[4] Naval Chronicle, vol. xiii. p. 484. The expression "balayer la Manche"
—sweep the Channel—is far stronger than the Chronicle's translation, which
is preserved in the quotation.

was to prevent the combination of the enemy's squadrons, and that the chief scene of operations would be the Bay of Biscay and the approaches to the Channel. They contented themselves, consequently, with strengthening the force there, and keeping before Cadiz alone a detachment under Collingwood, lest a concentration in that port should compel them to weaken the Biscay squadrons. At the time Villeneuve sailed, an expedition of five thousand troops, whose destination was kept profoundly secret, was ready to start for the Mediterranean. This re-enforcement secured the naval bases of Gibraltar and Malta, and the Mediterranean otherwise was abandoned to frigates, supported by two or three ships-of-the-line. Herein also the practice of the Admiralty agreed with the precept of Napoleon. "The Mediterranean," wrote he on June 7 to his Minister of Marine, "is now nothing. I would rather see there two of Villeneuve's ships than forty;" and he added the pregnant counsel, which was exemplified by the British action, "It seems to me your purpose is *not exclusive enough* for a great operation. You must correct this fault, for that is the art of great successes and of great operations."

The secret expedition was met by Nelson just as he started for the West Indies. During his heavy beat down the Mediterranean he too, as carefully as Napoleon, had been studying the field on which he was to act; but while the one planned with all the freedom and certainty of an offensive, which, disposing of large means, moves upon a known object, the other, though in a restricted sphere, underwent the embarrassments of the defensive, ignorant where the blow was to. fall. ⋅ One clear light, however, shone step by step on his path, — wherever the French fleet was gone there should he go also.

The west wind which delayed his progress brought swiftly to him, on April 19, a vessel [1] from Gibraltar, with

[1] Apparently a prize. (Nels. Disp., vol. vi. p. 410.)

word that, two hours after Villeneuve passed the Straits, a frigate had started for England with the news, and that the French and Spaniards had sailed together from Cadiz. From this circumstance he reasoned, accurately, that the destination was the British Islands; [1] but he did not penetrate the deep design of a concentration in the West Indies. He therefore sent the frigate "Amazon" ahead of the fleet to Lisbon, to gather news and rejoin him off Cape St. Vincent; and by her he wrote the Admiralty, and also to the admirals off Brest and in Ireland, that he should take position fifty leagues west of the Scilly Islands, and thence steer slowly toward them. To any person who will plot this position on a map it will be apparent that, with winds prevailing from the westward, he would there be, as he said, equally well situated to reach Brest or Ireland; in short, in an excellent strategic position known to the authorities at home.

Stopping but four hours at Gibraltar on May 6, on the 9th he was off Cape St. Vincent, and there received news that the combined squadrons, to the number of eighteen of the line, had gone to the West Indies. His concern was great, for he fully understood the value of those islands. He had served there, knew them intimately, and had married there. Not a year before he had written, "If our islands should fall, England would be so clamorous for peace that we should humble ourselves." [2]   Still, with all his anxiety, he kept his head. The convoy of troops was close at hand, he must provide for its safety. On the 11th of May it arrived, Nelson's fleet being then under way. To the two ships-of-the-line guarding it he added a third, the "Royal Sovereign," whose bad sailing delayed him; and to this circumstance it was owing that that ship, newly coppered, bore Collingwood's flag far in advance of either British column into the fire at Trafalgar. Three hours after the convoy's junction, at 7 P.M. of May

[1] Nels. Disp., vol. vi. p. 411.   [2] Ibid., Sept. 6, 1804.

11, Nelson with ten ships was on his way to the West Indies, to seek eighteen which had thirty-one days' start.

On the 4th of June the British fleet, having gained eight days on the allies, anchored at Barbadoes, where it found Cochrane with two sail-of-the-line. The same day Magon with his two joined Villeneuve. In the three weeks the latter had now been in Martinique he had accomplished nothing but the capture of Diamond Rock, a small islet detached from the main island, which the British held and from which they annoyed the coasters. A frigate outstripping Magon had brought pressing orders to make conquests in the British possessions, during the thirty-five days of waiting for Ganteaume. In consequence, when Magon joined, the fleet was under way, standing north to clear the islands before making the stretch to the southward, and to windward, to reach Barbadoes; which Villeneuve had selected as his first point of attack.

On the 4th of June, therefore, the two hostile fleets were but a hundred miles apart, the distance separating Barbadoes from Martinique. Most singularly, at the very moment Villeneuve started north to return upon Barbadoes, false news, too plausible to be slighted, induced Nelson to go south. Positive information was sent by the officer commanding at Santa Lucia that the allies had been seen from there, May 29, steering south. Nelson anchored at Barbadoes at 5 P. M. June 4, embarked two thousand troops during the night, and at 10 A. M. next day made sail for the southward. On the 6th he passed Tobago, which was reported safe, and on the 7th anchored off Trinidad; where to the astonishment of every one nothing had been heard of the enemy. Cursing the news which had forced him to disregard his own judgment, when only a hundred miles of fair wind severed him from his prey, Nelson turned upon his tracks and steered for Martinique, tortured with fears for Jamaica and every exposed British possession.

On the 8th of June, when Nelson left Trinidad, the combined fleets were nearly four hundred miles from him, off the west side of Antigua. Here they captured fourteen merchant ships which had imprudently left port, and by them were informed that Nelson with fourteen ships (instead of ten) had reached Barbadoes. To these fourteen, Villeneuve, whose information was poor, added five as the force of Cochrane, making nineteen to his eighteen. Supposing therefore the enemy to be superior, not only in quality, which he conceded, but in numbers also, he decided, in view of so unexpected an event as the arrival on the scene of the greatest British admiral, to return at once to Europe. In this he doubtless met the wishes of Napoleon. "I think," said the latter, ere he knew the fact, "that the arrival of Nelson may lead Villeneuve to return to Europe;"[1] and he argued, still seeing things as he wished,— certainly not as a seaman would,— "When Nelson learns Villeneuve has left the Windward Islands, he will go to Jamaica,"[2] a thousand miles to leeward. "So far from being infallible like the Pope," wrote Nelson at the same moment, "I believe my opinions to be very fallible, and therefore I may be mistaken that the enemy's fleet is gone to Europe; but I cannot bring myself to think otherwise."[3] Then, having given his reasons, he seems to dive into Napoleon's mind and read his thoughts. "The enemy will not give me credit for quitting the West Indies for this month to come."[4]

Villeneuve also doubtless hoped to shake off his pursuer by his sudden change of purpose. Transferring troops necessary to garrison the French islands to four frigates, he directed the latter to land them at Guadaloupe and rejoin him off the Azores,— a mistaken rendezvous, which materially lengthened his backward voyage. The combined fleet then made sail on the 9th of June to the northward,

---

[1] Corr. de Nap., June 28, 1805, vol. x. p. 708.   [2] Ibid., p. 705.
[3] Nels. Disp., vol. vi. p. 457.   [4] Ibid., p. 45

to reach the westerly winds that favor the passage to Europe.

Three days later Nelson also was off Antigua, and convinced himself that the allies were bound back to Europe. With the tireless energy that brooked no rest when once resolve was formed, the night was passed transferring the troops which but one week before he had embarked at Barbadoes. But not even a night's delay was allowed in sending news to Europe. At 8 P. M. he hurried off the brig "Curieux" with dispatches to the Admiralty, which the captain, Bettesworth, was to deliver in person; a momentous action, and one fraught with decisive consequences to the campaign, although somewhat marred by an over-cautious admiral. On the 13th, at noon, the fleet itself, accompanied by one of Cochrane's two ships, the "Spartiate," sailed for the Straits of Gibraltar; but Nelson, uncertain as to the enemy's destination, also sent word to the officer commanding off Ferrol,[1] lest he might be taken unawares.

Although Villeneuve's decision to return was fortunate and characterized by the extraordinary good luck which upon the whole had so far attended him, it is evident that he ran the chance of crossing Ganteaume on the Atlantic, as he himself had been crossed by Missiessy. Napoleon had taken precautions to insure both his waiting long enough, and also his return in case Ganteaume could not get away by a certain time; but not having foreseen, nor until June 28[2] even known, Nelson's pursuit of Villeneuve, he could not anticipate the course of the latter in such a contingency, nor combine with it the action of the Brest fleet.

Ganteaume, however, was not able to elude Lord Gardner, and on the 8th of May the emperor, having received in Italy the news of Magon's sailing, gave his final deci-

[1] Nels. Disp., vol. vi. p. 459.
[2] On this date is the first intimation of Nelson's sailing as known to Napoleon. June 27, he writes, "I do not clearly see where Nelson has been." (Corr. de Nap., vol. x. p. 701.)

sion. If before midnight of May 20 an opportunity offered, the Brest fleet should start; but from daybreak of the 21st, had it every chance in the world, it should stand fast. A frigate was to be kept ready to sail the instant the latter condition took effect, carrying to Villeneuve orders for his action upon reaching Ferrol. This frigate did sail May 21, but of course did not find the admiral in the West Indies. Duplicate instructions were sent to Ferrol.

Villeneuve was by them informed that he would in Ferrol find ready for sea five French and nine Spanish ships, which, with those already under his orders, would make a force of thirty-four sail-of-the-line. In the roads off Rochefort would be five more. At Brest twenty-one ships were lying outside the Goulet, under the protection of one hundred and fifty cannon, ready to get under way at a moment's notice. The great point was to concentrate these three masses, or as much of them as possible, off Boulogne. Three courses were open to him. If the squadron at Ferrol could not leave the port when he appeared, on account of head winds, he should order it to join him at Rochefort and go there at once himself. Thence with forty ships he should proceed off Brest, join Ganteaume, and at once enter the Channel. If, however, the wind was fair for leaving Ferrol, that is, southerly, he would see in that a reason for hastening to Brest, without stopping for the Rochefort squadron; the more so as every delay would increase the British force before Brest. Thirdly, he might possibly, as he drew toward Ushant, find the winds so fair as to give the hope of getting to Boulogne with his thirty-five ships three or four days before the enemy's fleet at Brest could follow. If so, it was left to his discretion to embrace so favorable an opportunity.   To these three courses Napoleon added a fourth as a possible alternative. After rallying the Ferrol ships he might pass north of the British Islands, join the Dutch squadron of the Texel with Marmont's corps there embarked, and with these appear off Boulogne. The emperor, however, looked upon this rather as a last resort. A great concentration in the Bay of Biscay was the one aim he now favored.

To facilitate this he busied himself much with the question of diverting the enemy from that great centre of his operations. This it was that made him so ready to believe that each squadron that sailed was gone to the East Indies. If so, it was well removed from the Bay of Biscay. For this he sought to get the Cartagena ships to Toulon or to Cadiz. "If we can draw six English ships before each port," he writes, "that will be a fine diversion for us; and if I can get the Cartagena ships in Toulon I will threaten Egypt in so many ways that they will be obliged to keep there an imposing force. They will believe Villeneuve gone to the East Indies in concerted operation with the Toulon squadron." [1] For this he purposes to send Missiessy to Cadiz. In Rochefort that admiral will occupy a British detachment, but on the spot where the emperor does not wish it; at Cadiz it will be remote from the scene. But later on he says, "Perhaps the enemy, who are now thoroughly frightened, will not be led away; in that case I shall have dispersed my force uselessly." [2] Therefore he concludes to keep him at Rochefort, where, if blockaded, he reduces the force either off Ferrol or off Brest. If not blockaded, he is to go to sea, take a wide sweep in the Atlantic, and appear off Ireland. The English will then doubtless detach ships to seek him; but he will again disappear and take position near Cape Finisterre, where he will be likely to meet Villeneuve returning.[3] Finally, for the same reason, toward the end of June he tries to create alarm about the Texel. Marmont is directed to make demonstrations and even to embark his troops, while part of the emperor's guard is moved to Utrecht. "This will

---

[1] Corr. de Nap., vol. x. April 23 and May 4, 1805, pp. 420, 465.
[2] Ibid., May 24, p. 544.   [3] Ibid., May 29, pp. 563, 624.

lead the enemy to weaken his fleet before Brest, which is the great point." [1]

All these movements were sound and wise; but the emperor made the mistake of underestimating his enemy. "We have not to do," he said, "with a far-sighted, but with a very proud government. What we are doing is so simple that a government the least foresighted would not have made war. For an instant they have feared for London; soon they will be sending squadrons to the two Indies." [2]

The British government and the British Admiralty doubtless made blunders; but barring the one great mistake, for which the previous administration of St. Vincent was responsible, of allowing the material of the navy to fall below the necessities of the moment, the Trafalgar campaign was in its leading outlines well and adequately conceived, and in its execution, as event succeeded event, ably and even brilliantly directed. Adequate detachments were placed before each of the enemy's minor arsenals, while the fleet before Brest constituted the great central body upon which the several divisions might, and when necessity arose, actually did fall back. Sudden disaster, or being beaten in detail, thus became almost impossible. In the home ports was maintained a well-proportioned reserve, large enough to replace ships disabled or repairing, but not so large as seriously to weaken the force at sea. As a rule the Admiralty successfully shunned the ex-centric movements to which Napoleon would divert them, and clung steadfastly to that close watch which St. Vincent had perfected, and which unquestionably embodied the soundest strategic principles. Missiessy returned to Rochefort on the 26th of May and was promptly blocked by a body of five or six ships. As the force in Ferrol increased, by the preparation of ships for sea, the opposing squadron of six or seven was raised to ten, under Rear-

[1] Corr. de Nap., vol. x. June 22, p. 686.   [2] Ibid., p. 545.

Admiral Calder. Before Brest were from twenty to twenty-five, to whose command Admiral Cornwallis returned early in July, after a three months' sick leave. Collingwood with half a dozen was before Cadiz, where he effectually prevented a concentration, which, by its distance from the scene of action, would have seriously embarrassed the British navy. Such was the situation when Villeneuve and Nelson, in June and July, were re-crossing the Atlantic, heading the one for Ferrol, the other for the Straits; and when the crisis, to which all the previous movements had been leading, was approaching its culmination.

When Nelson started back for Europe, although convinced the French were thither bound, he had no absolute certainty of the fact.[1] For his decision he relied upon his own judgment. In dispatching the "Curieux" the night before he himself sailed, he directed her captain to steer a certain course, by following which he believed he would fall in with the allied fleet.[2] Accordingly the "Curieux" did, on the 19th of June, sight the enemy in latitude 33° 12' north and longitude 58° west, nine hundred miles north-north-east from Antigua, standing north-north-west. The same day Nelson himself learned from an American schooner that a fleet of about twenty-two large ships of war had been seen by it on the 15th, three hundred and fifty miles south of the position in which Bettesworth saw it four days later.

Bettesworth fully understood the importance of the knowledge thus gained. The precise destination of the enemy did not certainly appear, but there could be no doubt that he was returning to Europe. With that intelligence, and the information concerning Nelson's purposes,

[1] See, for his reasoning, letter of June 16, three days after leaving Antigua; and also, for his uncertainty after reaching Europe, July 18. (Nels. Disp., vol. vi. pp. 457, 473.)
[2] Naval Chronicle, vol. xiv. p. 64.

it was urgent to reach England speedily.   Carrying a
press of sail, the "Curieux" anchored at Plymouth on the
7th of July.   The captain posted at once to London, arriv
ing the evening of the 8th, at eleven.   The head of the
Admiralty at that time was Lord Barham, an aged naval
officer, who had been unexpectedly called to the office two
months before, in consequence of the impeachment of
Lord Melville, the successor to St. Vincent.   It was fortunate for Great Britain that the direction of naval operations at so critical a moment was in the hands of a man, who,
though over eighty and long a stranger to active service,
understood intuitively, and without need of explanation,
the various conditions of weather and service likely to
affect the movements of the scattered detachments, British
and hostile, upon whose rapid combinations so much now
depended.

Barham having gone to bed, Bettesworth's dispatches
were not given him till early next morning.   As soon as
he got them he exclaimed angrily at the loss of so many
precious hours; and, without waiting to dress, at once dictated orders with which, by 9 A. M. of the 9th, Admiralty
messengers were hurrying to Plymouth and Portsmouth.
Cornwallis was directed to raise the blockade at Rochefort, sending the five ships composing it to Sir Robert
Calder, then watching off Ferrol with ten; and the latter
was ordered, with the fifteen ships thus united under his
command, to cruise one hundr ' miles west of Cape Finisterre, to intercept Villeneuve and forestall his junction
with the Ferrol squadron.   With Nelson returning toward
Cadiz, where he would find Collingwood, and with Cornwallis off Brest, this disposition completed the arrangements necessary to thwart the primary combinations of
the emperor, unknown to, but shrewdly surmised by, his
opponents.   It realized for Ferrol that which Napoleon
had indicated as the proper course for the British fleet off
Brest, in case it received intelligence of Villeneuve's

approach there, — to meet the enemy so far at sea as to prevent the squadron in port from joining in the intended battle.[1]

Fair winds favoring the quick, Cornwallis received his orders on the 11th; and on the 15th, eight days after the "Curieux" anchored in Plymouth, the Rochefort ships joined Calder. The latter proceeded at once to the post assigned him, where on the 19th he received through Lisbon the tidings of Villeneuve's return sent by Nelson from the West Indies. The same day Nelson himself, having outstripped the combined fleets, anchored in Gibraltar. On the 22d the sudden lifting of a dense fog revealed to each other the hostile squadrons of Calder and Villeneuve; the British fifteen sail-of-the-line, the allies twenty. The numbers of the latter were an unpleasant surprise to Calder, the "Curieux" having reported them as only seventeen.[2]

It is difficult to praise too highly the prompt and decisive step taken by Lord Barham, when so suddenly confronted with the dilemma of either raising the blockade of Rochefort and Ferrol, or permitting Villeneuve to proceed unmolested to his destination, whatever that might be. To act instantly and rightly in so distressing a perplexity — to be able to make so unhesitating a sacrifice of advantages long and rightly cherished, in order to strike at once one of the two converging detachments of an enemy — shows generalship of a high order. It may be compared to Bonaparte's famous abandonment of the siege of Mantua in 1796, to throw himself upon the Austrian armies descending from the Tyrol. In the hands of a more resolute or more capable admiral than Calder, the campaign would probably have been settled off Finisterre. Notice has been taken of Barham's good luck, in that the brilliant period of Trafalgar fell within his nine months' tenure of office;[3] but Great Britain might better be con-

---

[1] Napoleon to Decrès, July 18, 1805.   [2] Naval Chronicle, vol. xiv. p. 64
[3] Barrow's Autobiography, pp. 276–290.

gratulated that so clear-headed a man held the reins at so critical a moment.

The length of Villeneuve's passage, which so happily concurred to assure the success of Barham's masterly move, was due not only to the inferior seamanship of the allies, but also to the mistaken rendezvous off the Azores,[1] — assigned by the French admiral when leaving the West Indies. The westerly gales, which prevail in the North Atlantic, blow during the summer from the south of west, west of the Azores, and from the north of west when east of them. A fleet bound for a European port north of the islands — as Ferrol is — should therefore so use the southwest winds as to cross their meridian well to the northward. Nelson himself sighted one of the group, though his destination was in a lower latitude. In consequence of his mistake, Villeneuve was by the north-west winds forced down on the coast of Portugal, where he met the north-easters prevalent at that season, against which he was struggling when encountered by Calder. This delay was therefore caused, not by bad luck, but by bad management.

Napoleon himself was entirely misled by Barham's measures, whose rapidity he himself could not have surpassed. He had left Turin on the 8th of July, and, travelling incessantly, reached Fontainebleau on the evening of the 11th. About the 20th he appears to have received the news brought ten days before by the "Curieux," and at the same time that of the Rochefort blockade being raised.[2] Not till the 27th did he learn that the British squadron off Ferrol had also disappeared, after being joined by the Rochefort ships. "The 'Curieux' only reached England on the 9th," he wrote to Decrès; "*the Admiralty could not decide the movements of its squadrons in twenty-four hours*, yet the Rochefort division disap-

---

[1] See *ante*, p. 162.

[2] Napoleon to Berthier, Decrès, and Ganteaume, July 20, 1805.

peared on the 12th. On the 15th it joined that off Ferrol, and the same day, or at latest the next, these fourteen ships departed by orders given *prior to* the arrival of the 'Curieux.' What news had the English before the arrival of that brig? That the French were at Martinique; that Nelson had then but nine ships. What should they have done? I should not be surprised if they have sent another squadron to strengthen Nelson, . . . and that it is these fourteen ships from before Ferrol they have sent to America." [1]

On the 2d of August the emperor set out for Boulogne, and there on the 8th received news of Villeneuve's action with Calder and of his subsequent entry into Ferrol. The fleets had fought on the afternoon of July 22, and two Spanish ships-of-the-line had been taken. Night-fall and fog parted the combatants; the obscurity being so great that the allies did not know their loss till next day. One of the British ships lost a foretopmast, and others suffered somewhat in their spars; but these mishaps, though pleaded in Calder's defence, do not seem to have been the chief reasons that deterred him from dogging the enemy till he had brought him again to action. He was preoccupied with the care of the prizes, a secondary matter, and with the thought of what would happen in case the Ferrol and Rochefort squadrons sailed. "I could not hope to succeed without receiving great damage; I had no friendly port to go to, and had the Ferrol and Rochefort squadrons come out, I must have fallen an easy prey. They might have gone to Ireland. Had I been defeated it is impossible to say what the consequences might have been." [2] In short, the British admiral had fallen into the error against which Napoleon used to caution his generals. He had "made to himself a pic-

---

[1] Napoleon to Decrès, July 27, 1805.

[2] Calder's Defence, Naval Chronicle, vol. xv. p. 167. The words quoted, frequently repeated in different terms, embody the spirit of the whole paper.

ture," and allowed the impression produced by it to blind him to the fact (if indeed he ever saw it) that he had before him the largest and most important of the several detachments of the enemy, that it was imperatively necessary not to permit it to escape unharmed, and that at no future day could he be sure of bringing his own squadron into play with such decisive effect. The wisdom of engaging at any particular moment was a tactical question, to be determined by the circumstances at the time; but the duty of keeping touch with the enemy, so as to use promptly any opportunity offered, was a strategic question, the answer to which admits of no doubt whatever. On the evening of the 24th the wind was fair to carry him to the enemy, but he parted from them. During the night it blew fresh; and on the morning of the 25th, says a French authority, the fleet was without order, several vessels had lost sails, and others sustained injuries to their spars.[1] Calder, however, was not on hand.

It is related of Nelson that, on his return voyage from the West Indies, he used to say to his captains, speaking of the fleet which Calder allowed to escape, "If we meet them we shall find them not less than eighteen, I rather think twenty, sail-of-the-line, and therefore do not be surprised if I should not fall on them immediately; *we won't part without a battle.* I will let them alone till we approach the shores of Europe, *or they give me an advantage too tempting to be resisted.*"[2] And again, after reaching England, he found on the 23d of August great anxiety prevailing about Calder, who with eighteen ships was then again cruising for Villeneuve, supposed to have been reenforced to twenty-eight by the Ferrol squadron. "I am no conjuror," he wrote, "but this I ventured without any

[1] Chevalier, Mar. Fran. sous l'Emp., p. 171. Couto (Combate de Trafalgar, p. 107) gives a very serious account of the injuries suffered by the four remaining Spanish ships.

[2] Nelson's Disp., vol. vi p. 457.

fear, that if Calder got fairly alongside their twenty-eight sail, by the time the enemy had beat our fleet soundly, they would do us no harm this year."[1] These two utterances of this consummate warrior sufficiently show how Calder should have viewed his opportunity in July.

Villeneuve had no more wish to renew the action than had Calder. Less even than that admiral could he rise to the height of risking a detachment in order to secure the success of a great design. In the eighteen ships left to him were over twelve hundred men so ill that it was necessary to put them ashore. Constrained by the winds, he put into Vigo on the 28th of July. Calder, on the other hand, having seen his prizes so far north as to insure their safety, returned off Cape Finisterre where he hoped to meet Nelson. Not finding him, he on the 29th resumed the blockade of Ferrol. On the 31st Villeneuve, leaving three of his worst vessels in Vigo, sailed for Ferrol with fifteen ships, of which two only were Spaniards. The fleet, having a strong south-west gale, kept close along shore to avoid meeting Calder; but the latter, having been blown off by the storm, was not in sight when Villeneuve reached the harbor's mouth. The allied ships were entering with a fair wind, when the French admiral received dispatches forbidding him to anchor in Ferrol. If, from injuries received in battle, or losses from any causes whatever, he was unable to carry out the plan of entering the Channel, the emperor preferred that, after rallying the Ferrol and Rochefort squadrons, he should go to Cadiz; but, the Brest fleet being ready and the other preparations complete, he hoped everything from the skill, zeal, and courage of Villeneuve. "Make us masters of the Straits of Dover," he implored, "be it but for four or five days."[2] Napoleon leaned on a broken reed. Forbidden

[1] Nelson's Disp., vol. vii. p. 16.
[2] Corr. de Napoléon, July 16, 1805

to enter Ferrol, Villeneuve took his ships into the adjacent harbor of Coruña,[1] where he anchored August 1.

Thus was effected the junction which Calder had been expected to prevent. His absence on the particular day may have been unavoidable; but, if so, it does but emphasize his fault in losing sight of the allies on the 24th of July, when he had a fair wind. Twenty-nine French and Spanish ships were now concentrated at Ferrol. The popular outcry was so great that he felt compelled to ask an enquiry. The Admiralty having, by a movement both judiciously and promptly ordered, secured a meeting with the enemy's force so far from Ferrol as to deprive it of the support of the ships there, was justly incensed at the failure to reap the full advantage. It therefore ordered a court-martial. The trial was held the following December; and the admiral, while expressly cleared of either cowardice or disaffection, was adjudged not to have done his utmost to renew the engagement and to take or destroy every ship of the enemy. His conduct was pronounced highly censurable, and he was sentenced to be severely reprimanded.

This was after Trafalgar. The immediate result of the junction in Ferrol was the abandonment of the blockade there. On the 2d of August Calder sent five ships to resume the watch off Rochefort, whence the French squadron had meantime escaped. Not till August 9 did he know of Villeneuve's entrance into Ferrol. Having with him then but nine ships, he fell back upon the main body before Brest, which he joined on the 14th, — Cornwallis then having under him seventeen ships, which Calder's junction raised to twenty-six.

The next day, August 15, Nelson also joined the fleet. On the 25th of July, a week after reaching Gibraltar, he had received the "Curieux's" news. Obeying his constant

[1] The harbors of Ferrol, Coruña, and a third called Betanzos, are inlets having a common entrance from the sea.

rule to seek the French, he at once started north with the eleven ships which had accompanied him from the West Indies, — intending to go either to Ferrol, Brest, or Ireland, according to the tidings which might reach him on the way. After communicating with Cornwallis, he continued on to England with his own ship, the "Victory," and one other whose condition required immediate repairs. On the 18th he landed in Portsmouth, after an absence of over two years.

Cornwallis had now under his command a concentrated force of thirty-four or thirty-five sail-of-the-line, all admirably seasoned and disciplined. The allies had in Brest twenty-one, in Ferrol twenty-nine; two great bodies, neither of which, however, was equal in number, nor still less in quality, to his. Adrift somewhere on the sea were the five French ships from Rochefort. For more than five months these vessels, which sailed on the 17th of July, five days after the blockading ships had left to join Calder, ranged the seas without meeting an equal British division, — a circumstance which earned for them from the French the name of "the Invisible Squadron." But, while thus fortunately unseen by the enemy, Napoleon found it equally impossible to bring them within the scope of his combinations;[1] and it may be doubted whether commerce-destroying to the sum of two million dollars compensated for the loss of so important a military factor.

The ships in Cadiz being blocked by Collingwood, and those in Cartagena remaining always inert, the naval situation was now comparatively simple. Cornwallis was superior to either of the enemy's detachments, and he held an interior position. In case Villeneuve approached, it was scarcely possible that the two hostile squadrons, dependent upon the wind, which if fair for one would be foul to the other, could unite before he had effectually crushed one of them. It ought to be equally improbable,

---

[1] See Napoleon's letters to Decrès, Allemand, and others, July 26, 1805.

with proper lookouts, that Villeneuve could elude the British fleet and gain so far the start of it as to cover the Straits of Dover during the time required by Napoleon. In his concentrated force and his interior position Cornwallis controlled the issue, — barring of course those accidents which cannot be foreseen, and which at times derange the best-laid plans.

Such was the situation when, on August 17, Cornwallis was informed that Villeneuve had put to sea with, it was said, twenty-seven or twenty-eight ships-of-the-line. He at once detached toward Ferrol Sir Robert Calder with eighteen sail, keeping with himself sixteen. This division of his fleet, which is condemned by the simplest and most generally admitted principles of warfare, transferred to Villeneuve all the advantage of central position and superior force, and was stigmatized by Napoleon as a "glaring blunder." "What a chance," he wrote, upon hearing it when all was over, "has Villeneuve missed. He might, by coming upon Brest from a wide sweep to sea, have played hide and seek with Calder and fallen upon Cornwallis; or else, with his thirty ships have beaten Calder's twenty and gained a decided preponderance."[1] This censure of both admirals was just.

While the British squadrons were concentrating in the Bay of Biscay, and the happy insight and diligence of Nelson were bringing the Mediterranean ships to the critical centre of action, Napoleon, from the heights overlooking Boulogne, was eagerly awaiting news from Villeneuve, and at the same time anxiously watching the signs of the times on the Continent, where the sky was already dark with a gathering storm. The encroachments which led to the second war with Great Britain, in 1803, had excited no less distrust among the continental powers, who were indeed more immediately and disastrously affected by them; but none had then dared to move. The violation

[1] Napoleon to Decrès, August 29.

of German neutrality in 1804, by the seizure of the Duc
d'Enghien on the soil of Baden, had caused a general
indignation; which, on the part of Russia and Austria,
was quickened into a desire to act by his execution, regarded by most as a judicial murder. Prussia shared the
anger and fears of the other powers, but not enough to
decide her vacillating government.

In this state of things the fall of the Addington ministry, and the consequent vigor imparted to the foreign
policy of Great Britain by Pitt's second accession to
power, led naturally to another coalition; the centre of
which, as ever, was found in London. The czar having
remonstrated vigorously, both with Napoleon and the
German Diet, upon the seizure of the Duc d'Enghien, a
bitter correspondence had followed, causing the rupture
of diplomatic relations between France and Russia in
August, 1804. For similar reasons, and at the same time,
the French embassy to Sweden was recalled. Austria
still temporized, though her actions excited Napoleon's
suspicions.

Early in 1805 the czar sent special envoys to London,
to treat concerning certain vast schemes for the reorganization of Europe in the interests of general peace. The
particular object was not reached; but on the 11th of
April a treaty between Great Britain and Russia was
signed, the two agreeing to promote a league among the
powers to stop further encroachments by Napoleon. Six
weeks later the emperor was crowned King of Italy, and
in June Genoa was annexed to France. This last act,
contemplated by Napoleon for many years,[1] determined
Austria's accession to the treaty. By her signature, given
August 9,[2] the third coalition was formed. Sweden be-

---

[1] Napoleon to Talleyrand, Dec. 18, 1799. "Frame your reply to Genoa in
such terms as to leave us free to incorporate the Ligurian Republic with
France, within a few months."

[2] Stanhope's Pitt, vol. iv. p. 318.

came a party to it at the same time, and Great Britain undertook to pay subsidies to all the members.

The preparations of Austria, ever deliberate, could not escape Napoleon's watchful eye. "All my news from Italy is warlike," he writes, "and indeed Austria no longer observes any concealment." [1] Yet, trusting to his enemy's slowness and his own readiness, he did not lose hope. The position was precisely analogous to those military situations in which he had so often snatched success from overwhelming numbers, by rapidly throwing himself on one enemy before the other could join. He might even yet deal his long cherished blow to Great Britain, under which, if successful, Austria also would at once succumb. On August 13, two days after learning of Villeneuve's entry into Coruña, he instructs Talleyrand to notify the emperor that the troops assembled in the Tyrol *must* be withdrawn to Bohemia, leaving him free to carry on his war with England undisturbed, or by November he will be in Vienna. [2] Urgent messages are the same day sent to Villeneuve to hasten and fulfil his mission, for time was pressing; threatened by Austria and Great Britain, a blow must speedily be struck. He is no longer ordered to refrain from fighting. On the contrary, if superior to the British, counting two Spanish ships equal to one French, he is to attack at all hazards. [3] "If with thirty ships my admirals fear to attack twenty-four British, we may as well give up all hope of a navy." [4]

On the 23d of August the emperor announces to Talleyrand his final and momentous decision: "My squadron sailed August 14 from Ferrol with thirty-four ships; [5] it had no enemy in sight. If it follows my instructions,

---

[1] Napoleon to Talleyrand, July 31, 1805.   [2] Ibid., August 13.

[3] Napoleon to Villeneuve, August 13.

[4] Napoleon to Decrès, August 14.

[5] Twenty-nine only of the line.

joins the Brest squadron and enters the Channel, there is still time; I am master of England. If, on the contrary, my admirals hesitate, manœuvre badly, and do not fulfil their purpose, I have no other resource than to wait for winter to cross with the flotilla. That operation is risky; it would be more so if, pressed by time, political events should oblige me to postpone it to the month of April. Such being the case, I hasten to meet the most pressing danger: I raise my camp here, and by September 23 I shall have in Germany two hundred thousand men, and twenty-five thousand in Naples. I march upon Vienna, and do not lay down my arms until I have Naples and Venice, and have no more to fear from Austria. Austria will certainly thus be quieted during the winter." These words were a prophecy. The same day numerous orders, strictly preparatory as yet, were issued to the troops in Hanover, Holland, and Italy, and other provision made for the contemplated change of purpose. At the same time, still clinging to every hope of arresting Austria, and so being left free for the invasion of England, he sent Duroc to Berlin to offer Hanover to Prussia, upon condition that the latter should move troops toward Bohemia or at least make a clear declaration to Austria.

The issue was already decided. On the 13th of August, after three fruitless attempts, Villeneuve got to sea with his twenty-nine ships-of-the-line. The frigate "Didon" was sent to seek the Rochefort squadron and direct it also upon Brest. Yet the unfortunate admiral was even then hesitating whether he should go there with his vastly greater force, and the orders were likely seriously to endanger the smaller division. As he sailed, he penned these significant words to the Minister of Marine: "The enemy's forces, more concentrated than ever, leave me little other resource than to go to Cadiz."[1]

Shortly after he cleared the harbor the wind shifted to

[1] Chevalier, Marine Française sous l'Empire, p. 180.

north-east, foul for his purpose. The fleet stood to the north-west; but the ships were badly handled and several received damage. On the morning of the 15th they were two hundred and fifty miles west-north-west from Cape Finisterre; the wind blowing a moderate gale, still from the north-east. Three ships of war were in sight, — two British, the third the frigate that had been sent to seek the Rochefort squadron, but which had been captured. A Danish merchantman reported that they were lookouts from a hostile body of twenty-five ships. The story had no foundation, for Cornwallis had not yet divided his fleet; but Villeneuve pictured to himself his inefficient command meeting a force with which it was wholly unable to cope. Losing sight of the great whole of which his own enterprise was but a part, though one of vital importance, his resolution finally broke down. That evening he ordered the fleet to bear up for Cadiz. On the 20th [1] it was sighted from the three ships commanded by Collingwood, who with a small division of varying strength had watched the port since the previous May. With steady judgment, that admiral in retiring kept just out of gun-shot, determined, as he said, not to be driven into the Mediterranean without dragging the enemy too through the Straits. Villeneuve had little heart to pursue. That afternoon he anchored in Cadiz, where were then assembled thirty-five French and Spanish ships-of-the-line. Collingwood at once resumed his station outside. That night one ship-of-the-line joined him, and on the 22d Sir Richard Bickerton arrived with four from the Mediterranean. On the 30th Calder appeared, bringing with him the eighteen detached by Cornwallis. In compliance with his orders he had been before Ferrol, found the port empty, and, learning that Villeneuve had sailed for Cadiz, had hastened to re-enforce the blockade. With twenty-six ships-of-the-line Collingwood held the enemy

---

[1] Collingwood's Correspondence, August 21, 1805.

securely checked, and remained in chief command until the 28th of September, when Nelson arrived from England.

Thus ended, and forever, Napoleon's profoundly conceived and laboriously prepared scheme for the invasion of England. If it be sought to fix a definite moment which marked the final failure of so vast a plan, that one may well be chosen when Villeneuve made signal to bear up for Cadiz. When, precisely, Napoleon learned the truth, does not appear. Decrès, the Minister of Marine, had however prepared him in some measure for Villeneuve's action; and, after a momentary outburst of rage against the unfortunate admiral, he at once issued in rapid succession the directions, by which, to use his own graphic expression, his legions were made to "pirouette," and the march toward the Rhine and Upper Danube was begun. "My decision is taken," he writes to Talleyrand, August 25; "my movement is begun. Three weeks hence I shall be in Germany with two hundred thousand men." During that and the two following days order after order issued from his headquarters; and on the 28th he wrote to Duroc that the army was in full movement. To conceal his change of purpose and to gain all-important time, by lulling the suspicions of Austria, he himself remained at Boulogne, with his eyes seemingly fixed seaward, until the 3d of September, when he went to Paris. On the 24th he left the capital for the army, on the 26th he was at Strasbourg, and on the 7th of October the French army, numbering near two hundred thousand, struck the Danube below Ulm; cutting off some eighty thousand Austrians there assembled under General Mack. On the 20th, the day before Trafalgar, Ulm capitulated; thirty thousand men laying down their arms. Thirty thousand more had been taken in the actions preceding this event.[1] On the 13th of November French troops entered Vienna, and on

[1] Thiers, Cons. et Emp., livre xxii. pp. 125, 128.

the 2d of December the battle of Austerlitz was won over the combined Russians and Austrians. On the 26th the emperor of Germany signed the Peace of Presburg. By it he relinquished Venice with all other possessions in Italy, and ceded the Tyrol to Bavaria, the ally of France.

Austria was thus quieted for three years, but the expedition against Great Britain was never resumed. In the course of the following year difficulties arose between Prussia and France, which led to war and the overthrow of the North German kingdom at Auerstadt and Jena. Yet another campaign was needed to bring Russia to peace in 1807. Meanwhile the Boulogne flotilla was rotting on the beach. In October, 1807, Decrès, by Napoleon's orders, made an inspection of the boats and the four ports. Of the twelve hundred of the former, specially built for the invasion, not over three hundred were fit to put to sea; of the nine hundred transports nearly all were past service. The circular port at Boulogne was covered two feet deep with sand; those of Vimereux and Ambleteuse, three feet. A very few years more would suffice to bury them.[1] In 1814 an English lady, visiting Boulogne after Napoleon's first abdication, noted in her journal that the mud walls of the encampment were still to be seen on the heights behind the town, — the crumbling record of a great failure.

The question will naturally here arise, What at any time were the chances of success? To a purely speculative question, involving so many elements and into which the conditions of sea war then introduced so many varying quantities, it would be folly to reply with a positive assertion. Certain determining factors may, however, be profitably noted. It is, for instance, evident that, if Villeneuve on leaving the West Indies had had with him the Ferrol squadron, and still more if he had been joined by Ganteaume, he could have steered at once for the

[1] Thiers, Cons. et Emp., livre xxviii. p. 233.

Channel; and, by attending to well-known weather conditions, could have entered it with a favoring wind sure to last him to Boulogne. The difficulty of effecting such a combination in the West Indies, which was Napoleon's favorite project, was owing to the presence of British divisions before the hostile ports; and step by step this circumstance drove the emperor back on what he pronounced the worst alternative, — a concentration in front of Brest. As has been noticed, at the critical moment when this final concentration was to be attempted, the British, by a series of movements which resulted naturally from their strategic policy, were before that port in force superior to either of the French detachments seeking there to make their junction. Cornwallis's blunder in dividing that force cannot obscure the military lesson involved.

Nor can Calder's error, in suffering Villeneuve to escape him in July, detract from the equally significant and precisely similar lesson then illustrated. There also the British fleet was on hand to check an important junction — at a point so far from Ferrol as to be out of supporting distance by the division in the port — by virtue of an intelligent use of interior positions and interior lines.

To the strategic advantage conferred by these interior positions, for clinging to which credit is due above all to St. Vincent, is to be added the very superior character of the British personnel, — particularly of the officers; for the immense demand for seamen made it hard to maintain the quality of the crews. Continually cruising, not singly but in squadrons more or less numerous, the ships were ever on the drill ground, — nay, on the battle-field, — experiencing all the varying phases impressed upon it by the changes of the ocean. Thus practised and hardened into perfect machines, though inferior in numbers, they were continually superior in force and in mobility to their opponents.

Possessing, therefore, strategic advantage and superior force, the probabilities favored Great Britain. Nevertheless, there remained to Napoleon enough chances of success to forbid saying that his enterprise was hopeless. A seaman can scarcely deny that, despite the genius of Nelson and the tenacity of the British officers, it was possible that some favorable concurrence of circumstances might have brought forty or more French ships into the Channel, and given Napoleon the mastery of the Straits for the few days he asked. The very removal of the squadrons of observation from before Rochefort and Ferrol, in order to constitute the fleet with which Calder fought Villeneuve, though admirable as a display of generalship, shows that the British navy, so far as numbers were concerned, was not adequate to perfect security, and might, by some conceivable combination of circumstances, have been outwitted and overwhelmed at the decisive point.

The importance attached by the emperor to his project was not exaggerated. He might, or he might not, succeed; but, if he failed against Great Britain, he failed everywhere. This he, with the intuition of genius, felt; and to this the record of his after history now bears witness. To the strife of arms with the great Sea Power succeeded the strife of endurance. Amid all the pomp and circumstance of the war which for ten years to come desolated the Continent, amid all the tramping to and fro over Europe of the French armies and their auxiliary legions, there went on unceasingly that noiseless pressure upon the vitals of France, that compulsion, whose silence, when once noted, becomes to the observer the most striking and awful mark of the working of Sea Power. Under it the resources of the Continent wasted more and more with each succeeding year; and Napoleon, amid all the splendor of his imperial position, was ever needy. To this, and to the immense expenditures required to enforce the Continental System, are to be attributed most of those arbitrary acts which made him the hated of the peoples, for whose enfranchisement he did so much. Lack of revenue and lack of credit, such was the price paid by Napoleon for the Continental System, through which alone, after Trafalgar, he hoped to crush the Power of the Sea. It may be doubted whether, amid all his glory, he ever felt secure after the failure of the invasion of England. To borrow his own vigorous words, in the address to the nation issued before he joined the army, "To live without commerce, without shipping, without colonies, subjected to the unjust will of our enemies, is to live as Frenchmen should not." Yet so had France to live throughout his reign, by the will of the one enemy never conquered.

On the 14th of September, before quitting Paris, Napoleon sent Villeneuve orders to take the first favorable opportunity to leave Cadiz, to enter the Mediterranean, join the ships at Cartagena, and with this combined force move upon southern Italy. There, at any suitable point, he was to land the troops embarked in the fleet to reenforce General St. Cyr, who already had instructions to be ready to attack Naples at a moment's notice.[1] The next day these orders were reiterated to Decrès, enforcing the importance to the general campaign of so powerful a diversion as the presence of this great fleet in the Mediterranean; but, as "Villeneuve's excessive pusillanimity will prevent him from undertaking this, you will send to replace him Admiral Rosily, who will bear letters directing Villeneuve to return to France and give an account of his conduct."[2] The emperor had already formulated his complaints against the admiral under seven distinct heads.[3] On the 15th of September, the same day the orders to relieve Villeneuve were issued, Nelson, having spent at home only twenty-five days, left England for the last time. On the 28th, when he joined the fleet off

---

[1] Napoleon to St. Cyr, Sept. 2, 1805.
[2] Napoleon to Decrès, Sept. 15.   [3] Ibid., Sept. 4.

Cadiz, he found under his command twenty-nine ships-of-the-line, which successive arrivals raised to thirty-three by the day of the battle; but, water running short, it became necessary to send the ships, by divisions of six, to fill up at Gibraltar. To this cause was due that only twenty-seven British vessels were present in the action,—an unfortunate circumstance; for, as Nelson said, what the country wanted was not merely a splendid victory, but annihilation; "numbers only can annihilate."[1] The force under his command was thus disposed: the main body about fifty miles west-south-west of Cadiz, seven lookout frigates close in with the port, and between these extremes, two small detachments of ships-of-the-line,—the one twenty miles from the harbor, the other about thirty-five. "By this chain," he wrote, "I hope to have constant communication with the frigates."

Napoleon's commands to enter the Mediterranean reached Villeneuve on September 27. The following day, when Nelson was joining his fleet, the admiral acknowledged their receipt, and submissively reported his intention to obey as soon as the wind served. Before he could do so, accurate intelligence was received of the strength of Nelson's force, which the emperor had not known. Villeneuve assembled a council of war to consider the situation, and the general opinion was adverse to sailing; but the commander-in-chief, alleging the orders of Napoleon, announced his determination to follow them. To this all submitted. An event, then unforeseen by Villeneuve, precipitated his action.

Admiral Rosily's approach was known in Cadiz some time before he could arrive. It at first made little impression upon Villeneuve, who was not expecting to be superseded. On the 11th of October, however, along with the news that his successor had reached Madrid, there came to him a rumor of the truth. His honor took alarm.

[1] Nels. Disp., vol. vii. p. 80.

If not allowed to remain afloat, how remove the undeserved imputation of cowardice which he knew had by some been attached to his name.   He at once wrote to Décrès that he would have been well content if permitted to continue with the fleet in a subordinate capacity; and closed with the words, "I will sail to-morrow, if circumstances favor."

The wind next day was fair, and the combined fleets began to weigh.   On the 19th eight ships got clear of the harbor, and by ten A. M. Nelson, far at sea, knew by signal that the long-expected movement had begun.   He at once made sail toward the Straits of Gibraltar to bar the entrance of the Mediterranean to the allies.   On the 20th, all the latter, thirty-three ships-of-the-line accompanied by five frigates and two brigs, were at sea, steering with a south-west wind to the northward and westward to gain the offing needed before heading direct for the Straits. That morning Nelson, for whom the wind had been fair, was lying to off Cape Spartel to intercept the enemy; and learning from his frigates that they were north of him, he stood in that direction to meet them.

During the day the wind shifted to west, still fair for the British and allowing the allies, by going about, to head south.   It was still very weak, so that the progress of the fleets was slow.   During the night both manœuvred; the allies to gain, the British to retain, the position they wished.   At daybreak of the 21st they were in presence, the French and Spaniards steering south in five columns; of which the two to windward, containing together twelve ships, constituted a detached squadron of observation under Admiral Gravina.   The remaining twenty-one formed the main body, commanded by Villeneuve.   Cape Trafalgar, from which the battle took its name, was on the south-eastern horizon, ten or twelve miles from the allies; and the British fleet was at the same distance from them to the westward.

Soon after daylight Villeneuve signalled to form line of battle on the starboard tack, on which they were then sailing, heading south. In performing this evolution Gravina with his twelve ships took post in the van of the allied fleet, his own flag-ship heading the column. It is disputed between the French and Spaniards whether this step was taken by Villeneuve's order, or of Gravina's own motion. In either case, these twelve, by abandoning their central and windward position, sacrificed to a great extent their power to re-enforce any threatened part of the order, and also unduly extended a line already too long. In the end, instead of being a reserve well in hand, they became the helpless victims of the British concentration.

At 8 A. M. Villeneuve saw that battle could not be shunned. Wishing to have Cadiz under his lee in case of disaster, he ordered the combined fleet to wear together. The signal was clumsily executed; but by ten all had gone round and were heading north in inverse order, Gravina's squadron in the rear. At eleven Villeneuve directed this squadron to keep well to windward, so as to be in position to succor the centre, upon which the enemy seemed about to make his chief attack; a judicious order, but rendered fruitless by the purpose of the British to concentrate on the rear itself. When this signal was made, Cadiz was twenty miles distant in the north-north-east, and the course of the allies was carrying them toward it.

Owing to the lightness of the wind Nelson would lose no time in manœuvring. He formed his fleet rapidly in two divisions, each in single column, the simplest and most flexible order of attack, and the one whose regularity is most easily preserved. The simple column, however, unflanked, sacrifices during the critical period of closing the support given by the rear ships to the leader, and draws upon the latter the concentrated fire of the enemy's line. Its use by Nelson on this occasion has been much criticised. It is therefore to be remarked that, although his orders, issued several days previous to the battle, are somewhat ambiguous on this point, their natural meaning seems to indicate the intention, if attacking from to windward, to draw up with his fleet in two columns parallel to the enemy and abreast his rear. Then the column nearest the enemy, the lee, keeping away together, would advance in line against the twelve rear ships; while the weather column, moving forward, would hold in check the remainder of the hostile fleet. In either event, whether attacking in column or in line, the essential feature of his plan was to overpower twelve of the enemy by sixteen British, while the remainder of his force covered this operation. The destruction of the rear was entrusted to the second in command; he himself with a smaller body took charge of the more uncertain duties of the containing force. "The second in command," wrote he in his memorable order, "will, after my instructions are made known to him, have the entire direction of his line."

The justification of Nelson's dispositions for battle at Trafalgar rests therefore primarily upon the sluggish breeze, which would so have delayed formations as to risk the loss of the opportunity. It must also be observed that, although a column of ships does not possess the sustained momentum of a column of men, whose depth and mass combine to drive it through the relatively thin resistance of a line, and so cut the latter in twain, the results nevertheless are closely analogous. The leaders in either case are sacrificed,— success is won over their prostrate forms; but the continued impact upon one part of the enemy's order is essentially a concentration, the issue of which, if long enough maintained, cannot be doubtful. Penetration, severance, and the enveloping of one of the parted fragments, must be the result. So, exactly, it was at Trafalgar. It must also be noted that the rear ships of either column, until they reached the hostile line, swept with their broadsides the sea over which enemy's ships from either flank might try to come to the support of the attacked centre. No such attempt was in fact made from either extremity of the combined fleet.

The two British columns were nearly a mile apart and advanced on parallel courses, — heading nearly east, but a little to the northward to allow for the gradual advance in that direction of the hostile fleet. The northern or left-hand column, commonly called the "weather line" because the wind came rather from that side, contained twelve ships, and was led by Nelson himself in the "Victory," a ship of one hundred guns. The "Royal Sovereign," of the same size and carrying Collingwood's flag, headed the right column, of fifteen ships.

To the British advance the allies opposed the traditional order of battle, a long single line, closehauled, — in this case heading north, with the wind from west-north-west. The distance from one flank to the other was nearly five miles. Owing partly to the lightness of the breeze, partly to the great number of ships, and partly to the inefficiency of many of the units of the fleet, the line was very imperfectly formed. Ships were not in their places, intervals were of irregular width, here vessels were not closed up, there two overlapped, one masking the other's fire. The general result was that, instead of a line, the allied order showed a curve of gradual sweep, convex toward the east. To the British approach from the west, therefore, it presented a disposition resembling a re-entrant angle; and Collingwood, noting with observant eye the advantage of this arrangement for a cross-fire, commented favorably upon it in his report of the battle. It was, however, the result of chance, not of intention, — due, not to the talent of the chief, but to the want of skill in his subordinates.

The commander-in-chief of the allies, Villeneuve, was in the "Bucentaure," an eighty-gun ship, the twelfth in order from the van of the line. Immediately ahead of

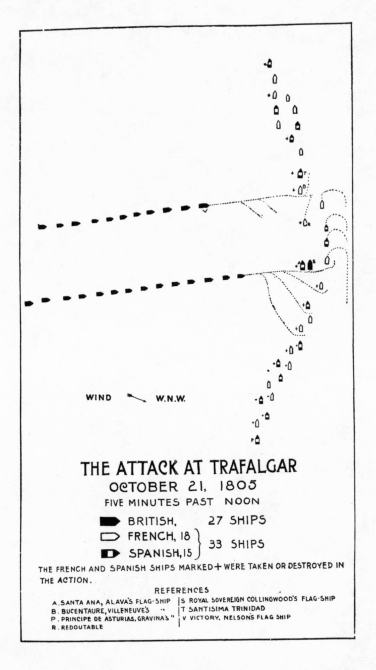

THE ATTACK AT TRAFALGAR

OCTOBER 21, 1805

FIVE MINUTES PAST NOON

WIND W.N.W.

BRITISH, 27 SHIPS

FRENCH, 18 } 33 SHIPS

SPANISH, 15 }

THE FRENCH AND SPANISH SHIPS MARKED + WERE TAKEN OR DESTROYED IN THE ACTION.

REFERENCES

A. SANTA ANA, ALAVA'S FLAG-SHIP | S ROYAL SOVEREIGN COLLINGWOOD'S FLAG-SHIP
B. BUCENTAURE, VILLENEUVE'S " | T SANTISIMA TRINIDAD
P. PRINCIPE DE ASTURIAS, GRAVINA'S " | V VICTORY, NELSON'S FLAG SHIP
R. REDOUTABLE

him was the huge Spanish four-decker, the "Santisima
Trinidad," a Goliath among ships, which had now come
forth to her last battle. Sixth behind the "Bucentaure,"
and therefore eighteenth in the order, came a Spanish three-
decker, the "Santa Ana," flying the flag of Vice-Admiral
Alava. These two admirals marked the right and left of
the allied centre, and upon them, therefore, the British
leaders respectively directed their course, — Nelson upon
the "Bucentaure," Collingwood upon the "Santa Ana."

The "Royal Sovereign" had recently been refitted, and
with clean new copper easily outsailed her more worn
followers. Thus it happened that, as Collingwood came
within range, his ship, outstripping the others by three
quarters of a mile, entered alone, and for twenty minutes
endured, unsupported, the fire of all the hostile ships that
could reach her. A proud deed, surely, but surely also
not a deed to be commended as a pattern. The first shot
of the battle was fired at her by the "Fougueux," the next
astern of the "Santa Ana." This was just at noon, and
with the opening guns the ships of both fleets hoisted their
ensigns; the Spaniards also hanging large wooden crosses
from their spanker booms.

The "Royal Sovereign" advanced in silence until, ten
minutes later, she passed close under the stern of the
"Santa Ana." Then she fired a double-shotted broadside
which struck down four hundred of the enemy's crew,
and, luffing rapidly, took her position close alongside,
the muzzles of the hostile guns nearly touching. Here
the "Royal Sovereign" underwent the fire not only of her
chief antagonist, but of four other ships; three of which
belonged to the division of five that ought closely to have
knit the "Santa Ana" to the "Bucentaure," and so fixed
an impassable barrier to the enemy seeking to pierce the
centre. The fact shows strikingly the looseness of the
allied order, these three being all in rear and to leeward of their proper stations.

For fifteen minutes the "Royal Sovereign" was the only British ship in close action. Then her next astern entered the battle, followed successively by the rest of the column. In rear of the "Santa Ana" were fifteen ships. Among these, Collingwood's vessels penetrated in various directions; chiefly, however, at first near the spot where his flag had led the way, enveloping and destroying in detail the enemy's centre and leading rear ships, and then passing on to subdue the rest. Much doubtless was determined by chance in such confusion and obscurity; but the original tactical plan insured an overwhelming concentration upon a limited portion of the enemy's order. This being subdued with the less loss, because so outnumbered, the intelligence and skill of the various British captains readily compassed the destruction of the dwindling remnant. Of the sixteen ships, including the "Santa Ana," which composed the allied rear, twelve were taken or destroyed.

Not till one o'clock, or nearly half an hour after the vessels next following Collingwood came into action, did the "Victory" reach the "Bucentaure." The latter was raked with the same dire results that befell the "Santa Ana;" but a ship close to leeward blocked the way, and Nelson was not able to grapple with the enemy's commander-in-chief. The "Victory," prevented from going through the line, fell on board the "Redoutable," a French seventy-four, between which and herself a furious action followed, — the two lying in close contact. At half-past one Nelson fell mortally wounded, the battle still raging fiercely.

The ship immediately following Nelson's came also into collision with the "Redoutable," which thus found herself in combat with two antagonists. The next three of the British weather column each in succession raked the "Bucentaure," complying thus with Nelson's order that every effort must be made to capture the enemy's commander-in-chief. Passing on, these three concentrated their efforts, first upon the "Bucentaure," and next upon the

"Santisima Trinidad." Thus it happened that upon the allied commander-in-chief, upon his next ahead, and upon the ship which, though not his natural supporter astern, had sought and filled that honorable post, — upon the key, in short, of the allied order, — were combined under the most advantageous conditions the fires of five hostile vessels, three of them first-rates. Consequently, not only were the three added to the prizes, but also a great breach was made between the van and rear of the combined fleets. This breach became yet wider by the singular conduct of Villeneuve's proper next astern. Soon after the "Victory" came into action, that ship bore up out of the line, wore round, and stood toward the rear, followed by three others. This movement is attributed to a wish to succor the rear. If so, it was at best an indiscreet and ill-timed act, which finds little palliation in the fact that not one of these ships was taken.

Thus, two hours after the battle began, the allied fleet was cut in two, the rear enveloped and in process of being destroyed in detail, the "Bucentaure," "Santisima Trinidad," and "Redoutable" practically reduced, though not yet surrendered. Ahead of the "Santisima Trinidad" were ten ships, which as yet had not been engaged. The inaction of the van, though partly accounted for by the slackness of the wind, has given just cause for censure. To it, at ten minutes before two, Villeneuve made signal to get into action and to wear together. This was accomplished with difficulty, owing to the heavy swell and want of wind. At three, however, all the ships were about, but by an extraordinary fatality they did not keep together. Five with Admiral Dumanoir stood along to windward of the battle, three passed to leeward of it, and two, keeping away, left the field entirely. Of the whole number, three were intercepted, raising the loss of the allies to eighteen ships-of-the-line taken, one of which caught fire and was burned. The approach of Admiral Dumanoir, if made an

hour earlier, might have conduced to save Villeneuve; it
was now too late. Exchanging a few distant broadsides
with enemy's ships, he stood off to the south-west with
four vessels; one of those at first with him having been
cut off.

At quarter before five Admiral Gravina, whose ship
had been the rear of the order during the battle and had
lost heavily, retreated toward Cadiz, making signal to the
vessels which had not struck to form around his flag. Five
other Spanish ships and five French followed him. As he
was withdrawing, the last two to resist of the allied fleet
struck their colors.

During the night of the 21st these eleven ships anchored
at the mouth of Cadiz harbor, which they could not then
enter, on account of a land wind from south-east. At the
same time the British and their prizes were being carried
shoreward by the heavy swell which had prevailed during
the battle; the light air blowing from the sea not enabling
them to haul off. The situation was one of imminent
peril. At midnight the wind freshened much, but fortunately hauled to the southward, whence it blew a gale all
the 22d. The ships got their heads to the westward and
drew off shore, with thirteen of the prizes; the other four
having had to anchor off Cape Trafalgar. That morning
the "Bucentaure," Villeneuve's late flag-ship, was wrecked
on some rocks off the entrance to Cadiz; and toward
evening the "Redoutable," that had so nobly supported her,
was found to be sinking astern of the British ship that had
her in tow. During the night of the 22d she went down,
with a hundred and fifty of her people still on board. On
the 24th the same fate befell the great "Santisima Trinidad," which had been the French admiral's next ahead.
Thus his own ship and his two supports vanished from
the seas.

For several days the wind continued violent from north-
west and south-west. On the 23d five of the ships that had

escaped with Gravina put out, to cut off some of the prizes that were near the coast. They succeeded in taking two; but as these were battered to pieces, while three of the five rescuers were carried on the beach and wrecked with great loss of life, little advantage resulted from this well-meant and gallant sortie. Two other prizes were given up to their own crews by the British prize-masters, because the latter were not able with their scanty force to save them. These got into Cadiz. Of the remaining British prizes, all but four either went ashore or were destroyed by the orders of Collingwood, who despaired of saving them. No British ship was lost.

Of thirty-three combined French and Spanish ships which sailed out of Cadiz on the 20th of October, eleven, five French and six Spanish, mostly now disabled hulks, lay there at anchor on the last day of the month. The four that escaped to sea under Dumanoir fell in with a British squadron of the same size near Cape Ortegal, on the 4th of November, and were all taken. This raised the allied loss to twenty-two,— two more than the twenty for which Nelson, in his dying hour, declared that he had bargained.

No attempt to move from Cadiz was again made by the shattered relics of the fight. On the 25th of October Rosily arrived and took up his now blasted command. Nearly three years later, when the Spanish monarchy, so long the submissive tool of the Directory and of Napoleon, had been overthrown by the latter, and the Spanish people had risen against the usurper, the five French ships were still in the port. Surprised between the British blockade and the now hostile batteries of the coast, Rosily, after an engagement of two days with the latter, surrendered his squadron, with the four thousand seamen then on board. This event occurred on the 14th of June, 1808. It was the last echo of Trafalgar.

Such, in its leading outlines and direct consequences,

was the famous battle of Trafalgar. Its lasting significance and far-reaching results have been well stated by a recent historian, more keenly alive than most of his fellows to the paramount, though silent, influence of Sea Power upon the course of events: "Trafalgar was not only the greatest naval victory, it was the greatest and most momentous victory won either by land or by sea during the whole of the Revolutionary War. No victory, and no series of victories, of Napoleon produced the same effect upon Europe. . . . A generation passed after Trafalgar before France again seriously threatened England at sea. The prospect of crushing the British navy, so long as England had the means to equip a navy, vanished. Napoleon henceforth set his hopes on exhausting England's resources, by compelling every state on the Continent to exclude her commerce. Trafalgar forced him to impose his yoke upon *all* Europe, or to abandon the hope of conquering Great Britain. . . . Nelson's last triumph left England in such a position that no means remained to injure her but those which *must result in the ultimate deliverance of the Continent.*" [1]

These words may be accepted with very slight modification. Napoleon's scheme for the invasion of Great Britain, thwarted once and again by the strategic difficulties attendant upon its execution, was finally frustrated when Villeneuve gave up the attempt to reach Brest and headed for Cadiz. On the part of the allies Trafalgar was, in itself, a useless holocaust, precipitated in the end by the despair of the unfortunate admiral, upon whose irresolution Napoleon not unjustly visited the anger caused by the wreck of his plans. Villeneuve was perfectly clear-sighted and right in his appreciation of the deficiencies of his command, — of the many chances against success. Where he wretchedly failed was in not recognizing the simple duty of obedience, — the obligation to

---

[1] Fyffe's History of Modern Europe, vol. i. p. 281.

persist at all hazards in the part of a great scheme assigned to him, even though it led to the destruction of his whole force. Had he, upon leaving Ferrol, been visited by a little of the desperation which brought him to Trafalgar, the invasion of England might possibly — not probably — have been effected.

An event so striking as the battle of Trafalgar becomes, however, to mankind the symbol of all the circumstances — more important, perhaps, but less obvious — which culminate in it. In this sense it may be said that Trafalgar was the cause — as it certainly marked the period — of Napoleon's resolution to crush Great Britain by excluding her commerce from the Continent. Here, therefore, the story of the influence of Sea Power upon this great conflict, ceases to follow the strictly naval events, and becomes concerned simply with commerce-destroying, ordinarily a secondary operation of maritime war, but exalted in the later years of Napoleon's reign to be the principal, if not the sole, means of action.

To this the two next chapters are devoted. Of these, the first deals with commerce-destroying in the ordinary sense of the words, directed against enemies' property on the high seas; beginning with the outbreak of war in 1793, and narrating the series of measures by which the republic sought to break down British commerce and foreshadowed the policy of Napoleon's Berlin and Milan decrees. The second begins with the Berlin decree, in 1806; and, tracing one by one the steps which carried the emperor from violence to violence, seeks to show how these found their necessary outcome in the Russian expedition and the fall of the Empire. Detached thus, as far as may be, from the maze of contemporary history in which they are commonly lost, these successive acts of the French government are seen to form a logical sequence, connected by one motive and dominated by one necessity. The motive is the destruction of Great

Britain, the necessity that of self-preservation. Each nation, unassailable on its own element, stood like an impregnable fortress that can be brought to surrender only by the exhaustion of its resources. In this struggle of endurance Napoleon fell.

CHAPTER XVII.

THE Warfare against Commerce during the French Revolution, alike under the Republic and under Napoleon, was marked by the same passionate vehemence, the same extreme and far-reaching conceptions, the same obstinate resolve utterly to overthrow and extirpate every opposing force, that characterized the political and military enterprises of the period. In the effort to bring under the yoke of their own policy the commerce of the whole world, the two chief contestants, France and Great Britain, swayed back and forth in deadly grapple over the vast arena, trampling under foot the rights and interests of the weaker parties; who, whether as neutrals, or as subjects of friendly or allied powers, looked helplessly on, and found that in this great struggle for self-preservation, neither outcries, nor threats, nor despairing submission, availed to lessen the pressure that was gradually crushing out both hope and life. The question between Napoleon and the British people became simply one of endurance, as was tersely and powerfully shown by the emperor himself. Both were expending their capital, and drawing freely drafts upon the future, the one in money, the other in men, to sustain their present strength. Like two infuriated dogs, they had locked jaws over Commerce, as the decisive element in the contest. Neither would let go his grip until failing vitality should loose it, or until some bystander should deal one a wound through which the powers of life should

drain away. All now know that in the latter way the
end came. The commercial policy of the great monarch,
who, from the confines of Europe, had watched the tussle
with all the eagerness of self-interest, angered Napoleon.
To enforce his will, he made new and offensive annexa-
tions of territory. The czar replied by a commercial
edict, sharp and decisive, and war was determined. "It
is all a scene in the Opera," wrote Napoleon,[1] "and the
English are the scene shifters." Words failed the men of
that day to represent the grandeur and apparent solidity
of the Empire in 1811, when Napoleon's heir was born.
In December, 1812, it was shattered from turret to foundation stone; wrecked in the attempt "to conquer the sea
by the land." The scene was shifted indeed.

Great Britain remained victorious on the field, but she
had touched the verge of ruin. Confronted with the fixed
resolution of her enemy to break down her commerce by
an absolute exclusion from the continent of Europe, and
as far as possible from the rest of the world, she met the
challenge by a measure equally extreme, forbidding all
neutral vessels to enter ports hostile to her, unless they
had first touched at one of her own. Shut out herself from
the Continent, she announced that while this exclusion
lasted she would shut the Continent off from all external
intercourse. "No trade except *through* England," was the
formula under which her leaders expressed their purpose.
The entrance of Russia into this strife, under the provo-
cations of Napoleon, prevented the problem, which of these
two policies would overthrow the other, from reaching a
natural solution; and the final result of the measures which
it is one object of this and the following chapter to narrate
must remain for ever uncertain. It is, however, evident
that a commercial and manufacturing country like Great
Britain must, in a strife the essence of which was the
restriction of trade, suffer more than one depending, as

[1] To the King of Wurtemburg, April 2, 1811 ; Corr., vol. xxii. p. 19.

France did, mainly npon her internal resources.   The
question, as before stated, was whether she could endure the greater drain by her greater wealth.   Upon the
whole, the indications were, and to the end continued
to be, that she could do so; that Napoleon, in entering
upon this particular struggle, miscalculated his enemy's
strength.

But besides this, here, as in every contest where the
opponents are closely matched, where power and disci-
pline and leadership are nearly equal, there was a further
question: which of the two would make the first and
greatest mistakes, and how ready the other party was to
profit by his errors.   In so even a balance, the wisest
prophet cannot foresee how the scale will turn.   The
result will depend not merely upon the skill of the
swordsman in handling his weapons, but also upon the
wariness of his fence and the quickness of his returns;
much, too, upon his temper.   Here also Napoleon was
worsted.   Scarcely was the battle over commerce joined,
when the uprising of Spain was precipitated by over-
confidence; Great Britain hastened at once to place herself by the side of the insurgents.   Four years later, when
the British people were groaning in a protracted financial
crisis, — when, if ever, there was a hope that the expected
convulsion and ruin were at hand, — Napoleon, instead of
waiting for his already rigorous blockade to finish the
work he attributed to it, strove to draw it yet closer, by
demands which were unnecessary and to which the czar
could not yield.   Again Great Britain seized her opportunity, received her late enemy's fleet, and filled his treasury.   Admit the difficulties of Napoleon; allow as we
may for the intricacy of the problem before him; the fact
remains that he wholly misunderstood the temper of the
Spanish people, the dangers of the Spanish enterprise, the
resolution of Alexander.   On the other hand, looking
upon the principal charge against the policy of the Brit-

ish government, that it alienated the United States, it is
still true that there was no miscalculation as to the long-
suffering of the latter under the guidance of Jefferson,
with his passion for peace.   The submission of the
United States lasted until Napoleon was committed to
his final blunder, thus justifying the risk taken by Great
Britain and awarding to her the strategic triumph.

The Continental System of Napoleon, here briefly
alluded to, and to be described more fully further on, was,
however, only the continuation, in its spirit and aims, of
a policy outlined and initiated by the Republic under the
Directory; which in turn but carried into its efforts
against commerce the savage thoroughness which the
Convention had sought to impress upon the general war.
The principal measures of the emperor found antitypes in
the decrees of the Directory; the only important difference
being, that the execution of the latter reflected the feeble
planning and intermittent energy of the government which
issued them; whereas Napoleon, as always, impressed upon
his system a vigor, and employed for its fulfilment means,
proportioned to the arduousness of the task and the greatness of the expected results.   The one series being therefore but the successor and fulfilment of the other, it has
been thought best to present them in the same close connection in which they stand in the order of events, so as
to show more clearly the unity of design running throughout the whole history, — a unity due to the inexorable logic
of facts, to the existence of an external compulsion, which
could in no other way be removed or resisted.   Both in
common owed their origin to the inability of France
seriously to embarrass, by the ordinary operations of war,
the great commerce of her rival, though she launched her
national cruisers and privateers by dozens on every sea.
The Sea Power of England held its way so steadily, preserved its trade in the main so successfully, and was
withal so evidently the principal enemy, the key of the

hostile effort against France, that it drove not only the weak Directors, but the great soldier and statesman who followed them, into the course which led straight to destruction.

The declarations of war were followed by the customary instructions to commanders of ships-of-war and privateers to seize and bring into port the merchant vessels of the enemy, as well as neutrals found violating the generally acknowledged principles of international law. So far there was nothing in the course of either belligerent that differed from the usual and expected acts of States at war. At once the sea swarmed with hastily equipped cruisers; and, as always happens on an unexpected, or even sudden, outbreak of hostilities, many valuable prizes were made by ships of either nation. The victims were taken un- awares, and the offence on each side was more active and efficient than the defence. This first surprise, however, soon passed, and was succeeded by the more regular course of maritime war. The great British fleets gradu- ally established a distinct preponderance over the masses of the enemy, and the latter was quickly reduced to the ordinary operations of commerce-destroying, in the sense usually given to that word, — a policy, moreover, to which the national tradition and the opinion of many eminent naval officers particularly inclined.

To these raids upon their shipping, by numerous scat- tered cruisers, the British opposed a twofold system. By the one, their merchant vessels bound to different quarters of the globe were gathered in specified ports, and when assembled sailed together under the care of a body of ships of war, charged to conduct them to their voyage's end. This was the convoy system, the essence of which was to concentrate the exposed wealth of the country, under the protection of a force adequate to meet and drive away any probable enemy. Immense numbers of ships thus sailed together; from two to three hundred was not an

unusual gathering; and five hundred, or even a thousand,[1]
were at times seen together in localities like the Chops
of the Channel or the entrance to the Baltic, where the
especial danger necessitated a stronger guard and a more
careful acceptance of protection by the trader,—thus
emphasizing and enlarging the peculiar features of the
practice. It is scarcely necessary to remark that much
time was lost in collecting such huge bodies, and that the
common rate of sailing was far below the powers of many
of their members; while the simultaneous arrival of great
quantities of the same goods tended to lower prices. Consequently, many owners, relying upon the speed of their
vessels and upon good luck, sailed without convoy upon
completing their cargoes,—willing, after the manner of
merchants, to take great risks for the sake of great returns, by being first in the market. To protect these, and
others, which, by misfortune or bad management parted
from their convoy, as well as to maintain their general
command of the sea, the British resorted to another system, which may be called that of patrol. Fast frigates
and sloops-of-war, with a host of smaller vessels, were disseminated over the ocean, upon the tracks which commerce
follows and to which the hostile cruisers were therefore
constrained. To each was assigned his cruising ground,
the distribution being regulated by the comparative dangers, and by the necessary accumulation of merchant shipping in particular localities, as the North Sea, the approach
to the English Channel, and, generally, the centres to
which the routes of commerce converge. The forces thus
especially assigned to patrol duty, the ships " on a cruise,"
to use the technical expression, were casually increased by
the large number of vessels going backward and forward
between England and their respective stations, dispatch-
boats, ships going in for repairs or returning from them,

[1] Life of Sir Wm. Parker, vol. i. p. 39. Ross's Life of Lord de Saumarez,
vol. ii. p. 214. Naval Chronicle, Plymouth Report, Dec. 10, 1800.

so that the seas about Europe were alive with British cruisers; each one of which was wide-awake for prizes. To these again were added the many privateers, whose cruising ground was not indeed assigned by the government, but which were constrained in their choice by the same conditions that dictated at once the course of the trader and the lair of the commerce-destroyer.

Through this cloud of friends and foes the unprotected merchantman had to run the gantlet, trusting to his heels. If he were taken, all indeed was not lost, for there remained the chance of re-capture by a friendly cruiser; but in that case the salvage made a large deduction from the profits of the voyage. The dangers thus run were not, however, solely at the risk of the owner; for, not to speak of the embarrassment caused to others by the failure of one merchant, the crews of the ships, the sailors, constituted a great potential element of the combatant force of the nation. A good seaman, especially in those days of simple weapons, was more than half ready to become at once a fighting man. In this he differed from an untrained landsman, and the customs of war therefore kept him, whenever taken afloat, a prisoner till exchanged. Every merchant ship captured thus diminished the fighting power of Great Britain, and the losses were so numerous that an act, known as the Convoy Act, was passed in 1798, compelling the taking of convoy and the payment of a certain sum for the protection. In the first year of its imposition this tax brought in £1,292,000 to the Treasury, while resulting in a yet greater saving of insurance to owners; and the diminished number of prizes taken by the French was thought to be a serious inconvenience to them, at a time when, by the admission of the Directory, foreign commerce under their own flag was annihilated. This remarkable confession, and the experience which dictated the Convoy Act, may together be taken as an indication that, in the defence and attack of commerce, as in other operations of war, concentration of effort will as a rule be found a sounder policy than dissemination. In 1795 the French formally abandoned the policy of keeping great fleets together, as they had before done in their history, and took to the *guerre de course*. Within three years, ending in December, 1798, "privateers alone put more than twenty thousand individuals in the balance of exchanges favorable to England," and "not a single merchant vessel sailed under the French flag." [1] "The fate of almost all mere cruisers (*bâtimens armés en course*) is to fall, a little sooner or later, into the hands of the enemy," and in consequence, "out of a maritime conscription of eighty thousand seamen, to-day but half remain" with which to man the fleet.   British contemporary authority gives 743 as the number of privateers taken from France alone, between the outbreak of war in 1793 and the 31st of December, 1800, — not to speak of 273 ships of war of the cruiser classes. [2] The absolute loss inflicted by the efforts of these vessels and their more fortunate comrades cannot be given with precision; but as the result of an inquiry, the details of which will be presented further on, the author is convinced that it did not exceed two and a half per cent, and probably fell below two per cent of the total volume of British trade.   This loss may be looked upon as a war tax, onerous indeed, but by no means insupportable; and which it would be folly to think could, by itself alone, exercise any decisive influence upon the policy of a wealthy and resolute nation.   Yet no country is so favorably situated as France then was for operations against British commerce, whether in the home waters or in the West Indies, at that time the source of at least a fourth part of the trade of the Empire.

[1] Message of Directory to Council of Five Hundred, Jan., 1799; Moniteur, An 7, p. 482.

[2] McArthur, Financial and Political Facts of the Eighteenth Century, London, 1801, p. 308.   Norman (Corsairs of France, London, 1887, App.) gives the number of French privateers taken in the same period as 556.

The indecisiveness of the results obtained by the French in their war against British shipping was not due to want of effort on their part. On the contrary, the activity displayed by their corsairs, though somewhat intermittent, was at times phenomenal; and this fact, as well as the extraordinarily favorable position of France, must be kept in view in estimating the probable advantages to be obtained from this mode of warfare. At the period in question London carried on more than half the commerce of Great Britain; in addition to its foreign trade it was the great distributing centre of a domestic traffic, carried on principally by the coasters which clustered by hundreds in the Thames. The annual trade of export and import to the metropolis was over £60,000,000, and the entries and departures of vessels averaged between thirteen and fourteen thousand. Of this great going and coming of ships and wealth, nearly two thirds had to pass through the English Channel, nowhere more than eighty miles wide and narrowing to twenty at the Straits of Dover; while the remaining third, comprising the trade from Holland, Germany, and the Baltic, as well as the coasting trade to North Britain, was easily accessible from the ports of Boulogne, Dunkirk, and Calais, and was still further exposed after the French, in 1794 and 1795, obtained complete control of Belgium and Holland. From St. Malo to the Texel, a distance of over three hundred miles, the whole coast became a nest of privateers of all kinds and sizes, — from row-boats armed only with musketry and manned by a dozen men, or even less, up to vessels carrying from ten to twenty guns and having crews of one hundred and fifty. In the principal Channel ports of France alone, independent of Belgium and Holland, there were at one time in the winter of 1800 eighty-seven privateers, mounting from fourteen to twenty-eight guns, besides numerous row-boats. These were actually employed in commerce-destroying, and the fishing-boats of the coast were capable upon short notice of being fitted for that service, in which they often engaged.

The nearness of the prey, the character of the seas, and the ease of making shelter either on the French or English shore in case of bad weather, modified very greatly the necessity for size and perfect sea-worthiness in the vessels thus used; and also, from the shortness of the run necessary to reach the cruising ground, each one placed on this line of coast was easily equal to ten starting for the same object from a more remote base of operations. Privateers sailing at sundown with a fair wind from St. Malo, or Dieppe, or Dunkirk to cruise in the Channel, would reach their cruising ground before morning of the long winter nights of that latitude. The length of stay would be determined by their good fortune in making prizes, if unmolested by a British cruiser. They ventured over close to the English side; they were seen at times from the shore seizing their prizes.[1] At Dover, in the latter part of 1810, "signals were out almost every day, on account of enemy's privateers appearing in sight."[2] Innocent-looking fishing-boats, showing only their half-dozen men busy at their work, lay at anchor upon, or within, the lines joining headland to headland of the enemy's coast, watching the character and appearance of passing vessels. When night or other favorable opportunity offered, they pulled quickly alongside the unsuspecting merchantman, which, under-manned and unwatchful, from the scarcity of seamen, was often first awakened to the danger by a

[1] Sir J. Barrow, then a Secretary to the Admiralty, mentions in a letter to J. W. Croker, July 18, 1810, that two colliers had been captured in sight of Ramsgate, close under the North Foreland; and on July 27 an ordnance hoy taken close under Galloper Light, in the face of the whole squadron in the Downs not one of which moved. (Croker's Diary, vol. i. p. 33.)

[2] Naval Chronicle, vol. xxiv. p. 327. For further curious particulars concerning French privateering in the narrow seas, see Nav. Chron., vol. xxii p. 279; vol. xxiv. pp. 327, 448, 460–462, 490; vol. xxv. pp. 32–34, 44, 203 293; vol. xxvii. pp. 102, 237.

volley of musketry, followed by the clambering of the enemy to the decks. The crews, few in number, poor in quality, and not paid for fighting, offered usually but slight resistance to the overpowering assault. Boarding was the corsair's game, because he carried many men.

It seems extraordinary that even the comparative impunity enjoyed by the privateers — for that it was only comparative is shown by the fact that an average of fifty were yearly captured — should have been attained in the face of the immense navy of Great Britain, and the large number of cruisers assigned to the protection of the coasts and the Channel. There were, however, many reasons for it. The privateering spirit is essentially that of the gambler and the lottery, and at no time was that spirit more widely diffused in France than in the period before us. The odds are not only great, but they are not easy to calculate. The element of chance enters very unduly, and when, as in the present case, the gain may be very great, while the immediate risk to the owner, who does not accompany his ship, is comparatively small, the disposition to push venture after venture becomes irresistible. The seaman, who risks his liberty, is readily tempted by high wages and the same hope of sudden profits that moves the owner; and this was more especially true at a time when the laying up of the fleets, and the disappearance of the merchant shipping, threw seafaring men wholly upon the coasting trade or privateering. The number of ships and men so engaged is thus accounted for; but among them and among the owners there was a certain proportion who pursued the occupation with a thoughtfulness and method which would distinguish a more regular business, and which, while diminishing the risk of this, very much increased the returns. Vessels were selected, or built, with special reference to speed and handiness; captains were chosen in whom seamanlike qualities were joined to particular knowledge of the British coast and the routes of

British trade; the conditions of wind and weather were studied; the long winter nights were preferred because of the cover they afforded; they knew and reckoned upon the habits of the enemy's ships-of-war; account was kept of the times of sailing and arrival of the large convoys.[1] On the British side, a considerable deduction must be made from the efficiency indicated by the mere number of the coast cruisers. Many of them were poor sailers, quite unable to overtake the better and more dangerous class of privateers. The inducements to exertion were not great; for the privateer meant little money at best, and the abuses that gathered round the proceedings of the Admiralty Courts often swallowed up that little in costs. The command of the small vessels thus employed fell largely into the hands of men who had dropped hopelessly out of the race of life, while their more fortunate competitors were scattered on distant seas, and in better ships. To such, the slight chance of a bootless prize was but a poor inducement to exposure and activity, on the blustering nights and in the dangerous spots where the nimble privateer, looking for rich plunder, was wont to be found. It was worth more money to recapture a British merchantman than to take a French cruiser.

Privateering from the Atlantic, or Biscay, coast of France was necessarily carried on in vessels of a very different class from those which frequented the Channel. There was no inducement for the merchant ships of Great Britain to pass within the line from Ushant to Cape Finisterre; while, on the other hand, her ships-of-war abounded there, for the double purpose of watching the French fleets in the ports, and intercepting both the enemy's cruisers and their prizes, as they attempted to enter. For these reasons, privateers leaving Bordeaux, Bayonne, or Nantes, needed to be large and seaworthy,

[1] See, for example, the account of the privateer captain, Jean Blackeman Nav. Chron., vol. xii. p. 454.

provisioned and equipped for distant voyages and for a long stay at sea.   Their greatest danger was met near their home ports, either going or returning; and their hopes were set, not upon the small and often unprofitable coaster, but upon the richly laden trader from the East or West Indies or the Mediterranean.   Out, therefore, beyond the line of the enemy's blockade, upon the deep sea and on one of the great commercial highways converging toward the Channel, was their post; there to remain as long as possible, and not lightly to encounter again the perils of the Bay of Biscay.   Moreover, being larger and more valuable, the owner had to think upon their defence; they could not, like the cheap Channel gropers, be thrown away in case of any hostile meeting.   While they could not cope with the big frigates of the enemy, there were still his smaller cruisers, and the hosts of his privateers, that might be met; and many a stout battle was fought by those French corsairs.   One of these, the "Bordelais," taken in 1799, was said then to be the largest of her kind sailing out of France.   She had the keel of a 38-gun frigate, carried twenty-four 12-pounder guns, and a crew of two hundred and twenty men.   In four years this ship had captured one hundred and sixty prizes, and was said to have cleared to her owners in Bordeaux a million sterling.[1]

A third most important and lucrative field for the enterprise of French privateers was found in the West Indies. The islands of Guadaloupe and Martinique served as excellent bases of operations.   The latter indeed was for many years in British possession, but the former remained, practically without interruption, in the hands of France until its capture in 1810.   During the many years of close alliance, from 1796 to 1808, between France and Spain, the West Indian ports of the latter served not only to maintain her own privateers, but to give a wide exten-

[1] Naval Chronicle, vol. ii. p. 535; vol. iii. p. 151.

sion to the efforts of her more active partner.   The geographical and climatic conditions of this region tended also
to modify the character both of the cruisers and of their
methods.   Along with a very large European trade, carried on by ships of an average burden of two hundred and
fifty tons, there was also a considerable traffic from island
to island by much smaller vessels.   This local trade was
not only between the possessions of the same nation or of
friendly States, but existed also, by means of neutrals or
contraband, between those of powers at war; and through
these and her system of free ports, together with liberal
modifications of her commercial code wherever an advantage could thereby be gained, Great Britain succeeded
in drawing into her own currents, in war as well as
in peace, the course of much of the export and import of
the whole Caribbean Sea and Spanish Main.   From these
two kinds of trade — combined with the general good
weather prevailing, with the contiguity of the islands to
each other, and with the numerous ports and inlets scattered throughout their extent — there arose two kinds of
privateering enterprise.   The one, carried on mainly by
large and fast-sailing schooners or brigs, was found generally suitable for undertakings directed against ships
bound to or from Europe; while for the other the various
islands abounded with small row-boats or other petty craft,
each with its group of plunderers, which lay in wait and
usually in profound concealment to issue out upon the
passing trader.[1]   The uncertain character of the wind in
some parts of the day particularly favored an attack, by
two or three heavily manned rowing boats, upon a vessel
large enough to take them all on board bodily, but fettered
by calm and with a small crew.   On one occasion a United
States sloop-of-war, lying thus motionless with her ports

[1] In 1806, on the Jamaica station alone, were captured by the British
forty-eight public or private armed vessels, two of which were frigates, the
rest small.   (Nav. Chron., vol. xvii. pp. 255, 337.)

closed, was taken for a merchantman and assailed by several of these marauders, who then paid dearly for the mistake into which they had been led by her seemingly unarmed and helpless condition.

The remoteness of this region from Europe covered very great irregularities, both by the privateers and in the courts. This evil became greater in the French and Spanish islands, when, by the progress of the war, the Sea Power of Great Britain more and more broke off correspondence between them and the mother countries; and when Napoleon's aggression drove the Spaniards into revolution and anarchy, the control of Spain, always inert, became merely nominal. These circumstances, coinciding with the presence of a very large neutral shipping, mainly belonging to the United States, whose geographical nearness made her one of the chief sources of supplies to these colonies, caused the privateering of the Latin and mixed races to degenerate rapidly into piracy, towards which that mode of warfare naturally tends. As early as 1805, an American insurance company complained to the Secretary of State that "property plundered by real or pretended French privateers was uniformly taken into the ports of Cuba, and there, with the connivance of the Spanish government, was sold and distributed, *without any form of trial,* or pretence for legal condemnation." [1] And the United States consul at Santiago de Cuba reported officially that more than a thousand American seamen had been landed in that port, most of them without clothes or any means of support; and that "the scene of robbery, destruction, evasion, perjury, cruelty, and insult, to which the Americans captured by French pirates, and brought into this and adjacent ports, have been subjected, has perhaps not been equalled in a century past." [1] This lawlessness ended, as is generally known, in an actual prevalence of piracy on an extensive scale, about the

[1] American State Papers, vol. ii. pp. 670, 771.

south side of Cuba and other unfrequented parts of the archipelago, for some years after the war. From the character of the ground and the slow communications of the day, these desperadoes were finally put down only by the systematic and long continued efforts of the various governments concerned.

The Eastern trade of Great Britain was in the hands of the East India Company; and its ships, which carried on the intercourse between India and Europe, were of a size altogether exceptional in those days. At a time when a small ship-of-the-line measured from fourteen to sixteen hundred tons, and the traders between America and Europe averaged under three hundred, a large proportion of the East Indiamen were of twelve hundred tons burden, exceeding considerably the dimensions of a first-class frigate.[1] Being pierced for numerous guns and carrying many men, both crew and passengers, among whom often figured considerable detachments of troops, they presented a very formidable appearance, and were more than once mistaken for ships of war by French cruisers; so much so that in the year 1804 a body of them in the China seas, by their firm bearing and compact order, imposed upon a hostile squadron of respectable size, commanded by an admiral of cautious temper though of proved courage, making him for a brief period the laughing stock of both hemispheres, and bringing down on his head a scathing letter from the emperor. Their armament, however, was actually feeble, especially in the earlier part of the French Revolution. About the year 1801, it was determined to increase it so that the larger ships should carry thirty-eight 18-pounders;[2] but the change seems to have been but imperfectly effected, and

---

[1] James (Naval Hist., ed. 1878, vol. iii. p. 249) says that though denominated 1,200-ton ships, the registered tonnage of most exceeds 1,300, and in some cases amounts to 1,500 tons.

[2] Nav. Chronicle, vol. vi. p. 251.

upon the occasion in question the ships which thus "bluffed" Admiral Linois were none of them a match for a medium frigate. It is, indeed, manifestly impossible to combine within the same space the stowage of a rich and bulky cargo and the fighting efficiency of a ship of war of the same tonnage. Still, the batteries, though proportionately weak, were too powerful for ordinary privateers to encounter, unless by a fortunate surprise; and, as the French entertained great, if not exaggerated, ideas of the dependence of Great Britain upon her Indian possessions, considerable efforts were made to carry on commerce-destroying in the Eastern seas by squadrons of heavy frigates, re-enforced occasionally by ships-of-the-line. These were the backbone of the *guerre de course*, but their efforts were supplemented by those of numerous privateers of less size, that preyed upon the coasting trade and the smaller ships, which, from China to the Red Sea, and throughout the Indian Ocean, whether under British or neutral flags, were carrying goods of British origin.

At the outbreak of the war Great Britain was taken unawares in India, as everywhere; and, as the operations in Europe and in the West Indies called for the first care of the government, the Indian seas were practically abandoned to the enemy for over a year. After the fall of Pondicherry, in September, 1793, Admiral Cornwallis returned to Europe with all his small squadron, leaving but a single sloop-of-war to protect the vast expanse of ocean covered by the commerce of the East India Company.[1] Not till the month of October, 1794, did his successor reach the station. Under these circumstances the losses were inevitably severe, and would have been yet more heavy had not the company itself fitted out several

[1] Brenton's Naval Hist. (first ed.) vol. i. p. 346. Low's Indian Navy vol. i. 204.

ships to cruise for the protection of trade.[1] An animated warfare, directed solely toward the destruction and protection of commerce, now ensued for several years, and was marked by some exceedingly desperate and well-contested frigate actions; as well as by many brilliant exploits of French privateersmen, among whom the name of Robert Surcouf has attained a lasting celebrity. Depending at first upon the islands of France and Bourbon as their base of operations, the distance of these from the peninsula of Hindoostan, combined with the size of the East India ships, compelled the employment of relatively large vessels, able to keep the sea for long periods and to carry crews which would admit of many detachments to man prizes without unduly weakening the fighting capacity. When, in 1795, the conquest of Holland and flight of the Orange government turned the Dutch from enemies into allies of France, their colonies and ports became accessories of great importance to the cruisers, owing to their nearness to the scene of action and especially to the great trade route between China and Europe. On the other hand the British, long debarred from rewards for their efforts, other than recaptures of their own merchant ships, now found the whole of the Dutch trade thrown open to them, and the returns bear witness both to its numbers and to their activity.

Notwithstanding, however, the unprotected state of British commerce in the early years of the war, and the distinguished activity of the French cruisers, the insurance premiums at no time rose to the sums demanded in 1782, when a concentrated effort to control the sea by a fleet, under Admiral Suffren, was made by France.[2] At

---

[1] Low's Indian Navy, vol. i. 205. Milburn's Oriental Commerce, vol. i. 405.

[2] The premium of insurance, which had in 1782 been fifteen guineas per cent on ships engaged in the trade with China and India, did not exceed half that rate at any period between the spring of 1793 and the end of the struggle. (Lindsay's Merchant Shipping, vol. ii. 265. See also Chalmer's Historical View, pp. 308–310.)

that time the premiums were fifteen per cent; between 1798 and 1805 they fluctuated between eight and twelve per cent. ˉ In 1805 the chief command in the Indian seas was given to Rear-Admiral Sir Edward Pellew, afterwards Lord Exmouth, and by his skilful arrangements such security was afforded to the trade from Bombay to China, one of the most exposed parts of the Eastern commercial routes, that the premium fell to eight per cent, with a return of three per cent, if sailing with convoy. Under this systematic care the losses by capture amounted to but one per cent on the property insured, being less than those by the dangers of the sea.[1] But during the very period that these happy results were obtained by wisely applying the principle of concentration of effort to the protection of commerce, disaster was overtaking the trade of Calcutta; which lost nineteen vessels in two months through the neglect of its merchants to accept the convoys of the admiral.[2] In fact, as the small proportionate loss inflicted by scattered cruisers appears to indicate the inconclusiveness of that mode of warfare, so the result of the convoy system, in this and other instances, warrants the inference that, when properly systematized and applied, it will have more success as a defensive measure than hunting for individual marauders, — a process which, even when most thoroughly planned, still resembles looking for a needle in a haystack.

Soon after this time the British government reverted most properly to the policy of Pitt, by directing expeditions against the enemies' colonies, the foreign bases of their Sea Power, and, in the absence of great fleets, the only possible support upon which commerce-destroying can depend; with whose fall it must also fall. The

---

[1] Letter of Bombay merchants to Sir Edward Pellew; Nav. Chron., vol. xxiii. 107.

[2] Robert Surcouf, by J. K. Laughton; Colburn's United Service Magazine, 1883, part i. pp. 331, 332.

islands of Bourbon and of France capitulated in 1810, the
same year that saw the surrender of Guadaloupe, the last
survivor of the French West India Islands. This was
followed in 1811 by the reduction of the Dutch colony of
Java. Thus "an end was put to the predatory warfare
which had been successfully carried on against the British
trade in India for a number of years." [1]

While the scattered cruisers of France were thus worry-
ing, by a petty and inconclusive warfare, the commerce of
Great Britain and its neutral carriers, the great British
fleets, being left in quiet possession of the seas by the
avowed purpose of the Directory to limit its efforts to the
guerre de course, swept from the ocean every merchant
ship wearing a hostile flag, and imposed upon the neutral
trade with France the extreme limitations of maritime
international law, as held by the British courts. Toward
the end of the war, indeed, those principles were given an
extension, which the government itself admitted was beyond
anything before claimed as reconcilable with recognized
law. The precise amount of the injury done, the exact
number of the vessels detained, sent in, and finally condemned, in all parts of the world will perhaps never be
known; it is certainly not within the power of the present
writer to determine them. The frequent, though not complete, returns of British admirals give some idea of the
prevailing activity, which will also appear from the occasional details that must be cited in the latter part of this
chapter. Into the single port of Plymouth, in the eight
years and a half ending September 29, 1801, there were
sent 948 vessels of all nations; [2] of which 447 were
enemy's property, 156 recaptured British, and the remainder neutrals, belonging mostly to America, Denmark, and
Sweden, the three chief neutral maritime states. From
Jamaica, the British commander-in-chief reports that,

---

[1] Milburn's Oriental Commerce, vol. i. p. xci.
[2] Naval Chronicle, vol. vii. 276.

between March 1 and August 3, 1800,— that is, in five
months,— 203 vessels have been captured, detained, or
destroyed.[1] This was in but one part of the West Indian
Seas. The admiral at the Leeward Islands reports that
in two months of the same year 62 vessels had been sent
in.[1] In five months, ending September 3, 1800, Lord
Keith reports from the Mediterranean 180 captures.[1]
How far these instances may be accepted as a fair example
of the usual results of British cruising, it is impossible to
say; but it may be remarked that they all occur at a
period when the war had been raging for seven years,
and that captures are more numerous at the beginning
than at the latter end of long hostilities. In war, as in
all states of life, people learn to accommodate themselves
to their conditions, to minimize risks; and even prize lists
become subject to the uniformity of results observed in
other statistics.

Whatever the particulars of French losses, however,
they are all summed up in the unprecedented admission
of the Directory, in 1799, that "not a single merchant
ship is on the sea carrying the French flag." This was
by no means a figure of speech, to express forcibly an
extreme depression. It was the statement of a literal
fact. "The former sources of our prosperity," wrote M.
Arnould, Chef du Bureau du Commerce, as early as 1797,
"are either lost or dried up. Our agricultural, manufacturing, and industrial power is almost extinct." And
again he says, "The total number of registers issued to
French ships from September, 1793, to September, 1796,
amounts only to 6028." Of these, 3351 were undecked
and of less than thirty tons burden. "The maritime war
paralyzes our distant navigation and even diminishes
considerably that on our coasts; so that a great number
of French ships remain inactive, and perhaps decaying, in
our ports. This remark applies principally to ships of

[1] Naval Chronicle, vol. iv. pp. 150, 151, 326.

over two hundred tons, the number of which, according
to the subjoined table,[1] amounts only to 248.   Before the
revolution the navigation of the seas of Europe and to the
French colonies employed more than 2,000 ships."

In the year ending September 20, 1800, according to a
report submitted to the consuls,[2] France received directly
from Asia, Africa, and America, all together, less than
$300,000 worth of goods; while her exports to those three
quarters of the world amounted to only $56,000.   Whether
these small amounts were carried in French or neutral
bottoms is immaterial; the annihilation of French shipping is proved by them.   The same report shows that the
average size of the vessels, which, by hugging closely the
coast, avoided British cruisers and maintained the water
traffic between France and her neighbors, Holland, Spain,
and Italy, was but thirty-six tons.   Intercourse by water
is always easier and, for a great bulk, quicker than by
land; but in those days of wagon carriage and often poor
roads it was especially so.   In certain districts of France
great distress for food was frequently felt in those wars,
although grain abounded in other parts; because the surplus could not be distributed rapidly by land, nor freely
by water.   For the latter conveyance it was necessary to
depend upon very small vessels, unfit for distant voyages,
but which could take refuge from pursuers in the smallest
port, or be readily beached; and which, if captured, would
not singly be a serious loss.

[1] Registration of vessels made in all ports of France (except the newly
acquired departments) from September 1793, to September 1796 : —

Under 30 tons	3,351 (undecked)
Between 30 and 100 tons	1,897
" 100 and 200 tons	532
" 200 and 400 tons	193
Above 400 tons	55
	6,028

It should be explained that as all ships, old as well as new, had to register,
this gives the total of French shipping without deduction for losses.

[2] Moniteur, 26 Floréal, An 9 (May 16, 1801).

Towards the end of 1795, a contemporary British authority states that over three thousand British ships had been captured, and about eight hundred French.[1] This was, however, confessedly only an estimate, and probably, so far as concerns the British losses, a large exaggeration. Ten years later a member of the House of Commons, speaking with a view rather to disparage the earlier administration, gave the British losses for the same years as 1,395.[2] Lloyd's lists give the whole number of British captured, for the years 1793–1800, both inclusive, as 4,344, of which 705 were recaptured; leaving a total loss of 3,639.[3] Assuming, what is only for this purpose admissible, that the average loss each year was nearly the same, these figures would give for the three years, 1793–1795, 1,365 as the number of captures made by hostile cruisers. In the tables appended to Norman's " Corsairs of France" the losses for the same period are given as 1,636.[4]

Finally, the number of prizes brought into French ports up to September 16, 1798, was stated by M. Arnould, in the Conseil des Anciens, as being 2,658. The table from which his figures were taken he called " an authentic list, just printed, drawn up in the office of the French Ministry of Marine, of all prizes made since the outbreak of the war."[5] It included vessels of all nationalities, during a period when France had not only been at war with several states, but had made large seizures of neutral vessels upon various pretexts. Of the entire number M. Arnould

---

[1] Macpherson's Annals of Commerce, vol. iv. 359.

[2] Cobbett's Parl. Debates, March 15, 1804, p. 921.

[3] Naval Chronicle, vol. xvii. p. 369.

[4] Norman gives the total number of captures, 1793–1800, as 5,158 against Lloyd's 3,639. Through the kindness of Captain H. M. Hozier, Secretary of Lloyd's, the author has received a list of British ships taken, annually, 1793–1814. This list makes the numbers considerably less than the earlier one used in the text. By it, between 1793 and 1800, both inclusive, only 3,466 British ships were captured.

[5] Moniteur, 16 Pluviôse, An 7 (Feb. 5, 1799), pp. 582, 583.

considered that not more than 2,000 were British. If we accept his estimate, only 900 British ships would have been taken in three years. It is to be observed, however, as tending to reconcile the discrepancy between this and the English accounts, that the tables used by him probably did not give, or at most gave very imperfectly, the French captures made in the East and West Indies; and, furthermore, the aggregate British losses, as given by Lloyd's lists, and by Norman's tables, include captures made by the Dutch and Spaniards as well as by the French.[1]

The British reports of their own losses are thus seen largely to exceed those made by the French. According equal confidence to the statements of Sir William Curtis, of Norman, and of Lloyd's list, we should reach an annual loss by capture of 488 British ships; which would give a total, in the twenty-one years of war, from 1793–1814,[2] of 10,248. Norman's grand total of 10,871 considerably exceeds this amount; but it will be safer, in considering a subject of so great importance as the absolute injury done, and effect produced, by war upon commerce, to accept the larger figure, or to say, in round numbers, that eleven

---

[1] Guérin gives the total number of captures by France from Great Britain, from 1793 to the Peace of Amiens, March 25, 1802, including both ships of war and merchant vessels, as 2,172; while the French lost in all, from ships-of-the-line to fishing-boats, between 1,520 and 1,550. Of this total, 27 were ships-of-the-line and 70 frigates, — a number considerably below that given by James, the painstaking English naval historian. Allowing 150 as the number of smaller naval vessels taken, there would remain, by Guérin's estimate, about 1,300 French trading vessels which fell into British hands. Of these a large proportion must have been the chasse-marées that carried on the coasting trade (as their expressive name implies); attacks on which formed so frequent and lucrative a diversion from the monotony of blockade service. (Hist. Mar de la France, vol. iii. p. 674.)

Guérin claims great carefulness, but the author owns to much distrust of his accuracy It is evident, however, from all the quotations, that Fox's statement, May 24, 1795, that in the second year of the war France had taken 860 ships, was much exaggerated. (Speeches, vol. v. p. 419. Longman's, 1815.)

[2] In this period of twenty-two years there were eighteen months of maritime peace.

thousand British vessels were captured by the enemy during the protracted and desperate wars caused by the French Revolution. It is the great and conspicuous instance of commerce-destroying, carried on over a long series of years, with a vigor and thoroughness never surpassed, and supported, moreover, by an unparalleled closure of the continental markets of Great Britain. The Directory first, and Napoleon afterwards, abandoned all attempts to contest the control of the sea, and threw themselves, as Louis XIV. had done before them, wholly upon a cruising war against commerce. It will be well in this day, when the same tendency so extensively prevails, to examine somewhat carefully what this accepted loss really meant, how it was felt by the British people at the time, and what expectation can reasonably be deduced from it that, by abandoning military control of the sea, and depending exclusively upon scattered cruisers, a country dependent as Great Britain is upon external commerce can be brought to terms.

Evidently, a mere statement of numbers, such as the above, without any particulars as to size, or the value of cargoes, affords but a poor indication of the absolute or relative loss sustained by British commerce. It may, however, be used as a basis, both for comparison with the actual number of vessels entering and clearing annually from British ports, and also for an estimate as to the probable tonnage captured. The annual average of capture, deduced from 11,000 ships in twenty-one years is 524. In the three years 1793–1795, the average annual number of British vessels entering and clearing from ports of Great Britain was 21,560.[1] Dividing by 524, it is found that one fortieth, or two and a half per cent of British shipping, reckoning by numbers, was taken by the enemy. In the three years 1798–1800, 1801 being the year of broken hostilities, the average annual entries and depart-

[1] Macpherson's Annals of Commerce, vol. iv.

ures were 21,369,[1] which again gives two and a half as
the percentage of the captures.   It must be noted, also,
that only the commerce of England and Scotland with
foreign countries, with the colonies, with Ireland and the
Channel Islands, and with British India enters into these
lists of arrivals and departures.   The returns of that day
did not take account of British coasters, nor of the local
trade of the colonies, nor again of the direct intercourse
between Ireland and ports other than those of Great
Britain.   Yet all these contributed victims to swell the
list of prizes,[1] and so to increase very materially the
apparent proportion of the latter to a commerce of which
the returns cited present only a fraction.   Unfortunately,
the amount of the coasting trade cannot now be ascertained,[2] and the consequent deduction from the calculated two and a half per cent of loss can only be
conjectured.

To obtain the tonnage loss there appears to the writer
no fairer means than to determine the average tonnage of
the vessels entering and departing as above, at different
periods of the war.   In the three years 1793–1795, the
average size of each ship entering or sailing from the
ports of Great Britain, including the Irish trade, was 121
tons.   In the year 1800 the average is 126 tons.   In 1809
it has fallen again to 121, and in 1812 to 115 tons.   We
cannot then go far wrong in allowing 125 tons as the
average size of British vessels employed in carrying on
the foreign and the coasting trade of Great Britain itself

[1] Thus it is told of one of the most active of French privateersmen, sailing out of Dunkirk, that "the trade from London to Berwick, in the smacks,
was his favorite object; not only from the value of the cargoes, but because
they required few hands to man them, and from their good sailing were
almost sure to escape British cruisers and get safely into ports of France or
Holland."   Between 1793 and 1801 this one man had taken thirty-four prizes.
(Nav. Chron., vol. xii. p. 454.)

[2] Returns of the coasting trade were not made until 1824.   Porter's
Progress of the Nation, section iii. p. 77.

during the war.[1] On this allowance the aggregate tonnage lost in the 11,000 British prizes, would be 1,375,000 in twenty-one years. In these years the aggregate British tonnage entering and leaving the ports of Great Britain, exclusive of the great neutral tonnage employed in carrying for the same trade, amounted to over 55,000,000;[2] so that the loss is again somewhat less than one fortieth, or $2\frac{1}{2}$ per cent.

Another slight indication of the amount of loss, curious from its coincidence with the above deductions, is derived from the report of prize goods received into France in the year ending September, 1800, which amounted to 29,201,676 francs. At the then current value of the franc this was equivalent to £1,216,000. The real value of British exports for 1800 was £56,000,000, the prize goods again being rather less than one fortieth of the amount. The imports, however, being also nearly £56,000,000, the loss

---

[1] The merchant vessels of that day were generally small. From Macpherson's tables it appears that those trading between Great Britain and the United States, between 1792 and 1800, averaged from 200 to 230 tons; those to the West Indies and the Baltic about 250; to Germany, to Italy, and the Western Mediterranean, 150; to the Levant, 250 to 300, with some of 500 tons. The East India Company's ships, as has been said, were larger, averaging nearly 800 tons. The general average is reduced to that above given (125) by the large number of vessels in the Irish trade. In 1796 there were 13,558 entries and clearances from English and Scotch ports for Ireland, being more than half the entire number (not tonnage) of British ships employed in so-called foreign trade. The average size of these was only 80 tons. (Macpherson.) In 1806 there were 13,939 for Ireland to 5,211 for all other parts of the world, the average tonnage again being 80. (Porter's Progress of the Nation, part ii. pp. 85, 174.)

Sir William Parker, an active frigate captain, who commanded the same ship from 1801 to 1811, was in that period interested in 52 prizes. The average tonnage of these, excluding a ship-of-the-line and a frigate, was 126 tons. (Life, vol. i. p. 412.)

In 1798, 6,844 coasters entered or left London, their average size being 73 tons. The colliers were larger. Of the latter 3,289 entered or sailed, having a mean tonnage of 228. (Colquhoun's Commerce of the Thames, p. 13.)

[2] The returns for 1813 were destroyed by fire, and so an exact aggregate cannot be given. Two million tons are allowed for that year, which is probably too little.

on the entire amount falls to one eightieth. It is true that many of these prize goods were probably taken in neutrals, but on the other hand the report does not take into account French capture in the colonies and East Indies; nor those made by Holland and Spain, the allies of France.

If the total number of vessels *belonging* to Great Britain and all her dependencies be taken, as the standard by which to judge her loss by captures, it will be found that in 1795 they amounted to 16,728; [1] in 1800, 17,885; [1] in 1805, 22,051; [2] in 1810, 23,703. [2] Using again 524 as the annual number of captures, the annual proportion of loss is seen gradually to fall from a very little over 3 per cent, in the first year, to somewhat less than $2\frac{1}{2}$ per cent, in the last.

Finally, it may be added that the Lloyd's list before quoted gives the total number of losses by sea risks, 1793–1800, as 2,967; which, being contrasted with the losses by capture, 3,639, shows that the danger from enemy's cruisers very little exceeded those of the ocean. To offset, though only partially, her own losses, Great Britain received prize goods, during the same years, to the amount of over £5,000,000. [3] There were also engaged in carrying on her commerce, in 1801, under the British flag, 2,779 vessels, measuring 369,563 tons, that had been brought into her ports as prizes; which numbers had increased in 1811 to 4,023 ships and 536,240 tons. [4]

Taking everything together, it seems reasonable to conclude that the direct loss to the nation, by the operation of hostile cruisers, did not exceed $2\frac{1}{2}$ per cent of the commerce of the Empire; and that this loss was partially made good by the prize ships and merchandise taken by

---

[1] Macpherson's Annals of Commerce, vol. iv. 368, 535.

[2] Porter's Progress of the Nation, part ii. p. 171.

[3] Chalmer's Historical View, p. 307.

[4] Porter, part ii. p. 173. The Naval Chronicle, vol. xxix. p. 453, gives an official tabular statement of prize-vessels admitted to registry between 1793 and 1812. In 1792 there were but 609, total tonnage 93,994.

its own naval vessels and privateers. A partial, if not a complete, compensation for her remaining loss is also to be found in the great expansion of her mercantile operations carried on under neutral flags; for, although this too was undoubtedly harassed by the enemy, yet to it almost entirely was due the increasing volume of trade, that poured through Great Britain to and from the continent of Europe, every ton of which left a part of its value to swell the bulk of British wealth. The writings of the period show that the injuries due to captured shipping passed unremarked amid the common incidents and misfortunes of life; neither their size nor their effects were great enough to attract public' notice, amid the steady increase of national wealth and the activities concerned in amassing it. "During all the operations of war and finance," says one writer, "the gains of our enterprising people were beyond all calculation, however the unproductive classes may have suffered from the depreciation of money and the inequalities of taxation. Our commerce has become more than double its greatest extent during the happiest years of peace."[1] There were, indeed, darker shades to the picture, for war means suffering as well as effort; but with regard to the subject-matter of this chapter, Commerce, and its fate in this war, there was for many years but one voice, for but one was possible. The minister, essentially a master of trade and finance, delighted year by year to enlarge upon the swelling volume of business and the growing returns of the revenue. Not only did the new taxes bring in liberally, but the older ones were increasingly productive. These signs of prosperity were not seen all at once. The first plunge into the war was followed, as it always is, by a shrinking of the system and a contraction of the muscles; but as the enemy more and more surrendered the control of the sea, as the naval victories of the years 1797 and 1798 empha-

[1] Chalmer's Historical View, p. 351.

sized more and more the absolute dominion of Great Britain over it, and as the new channels of enterprise became familiar, the energies of the people expanded to meet the new opportunities.

The share borne by neutral shipping in the extension and maintenance of this extraordinary fabric of prosperity, thus existing in the midst of all the sorrow, suffering, and waste of war, must next be considered; for it was the cause of the remarkable measures taken by both belligerents against neutral trade, which imparted so singular and desolating a character to the closing years of the struggle and affected deeply the commerce of the whole world. At the very beginning of the war Great Britain proceeded to avail herself of the services of neutrals, by a remission of that part of the Navigation Act which required three fourths of the crews of British merchantmen to be British subjects. On the 30th of April, 1793, this was so modified as to permit three fourths to be foreigners, to replace the large body taken for the fleets. This was followed, from time to time, as the number of enemies multiplied through the extending conquests and alliances of France, by a series of orders and proclamations, infringing more and more upon the spirit of the Act, with the direct and obvious purpose of employing neutral vessels to carry on operations hitherto limited to the British flag. The demands of the navy for seamen, the risks of capture, the delays of convoy, entirely arrested, and even slightly set back, the development of the British carrying trade; while at the same time the important position of Great Britain as the great manufacturing nation, coinciding with a diminution in the productions of the Continent, consequent upon the war, and a steadily growing demand for manufactured goods on the part of the United States, called imperiously for more carriers. The material of British traffic was increasing with quickened steps, at the very time that her own shipping was becoming less able to bear it. Thus in 1797, when the British navy was forced to leave the Mediterranean, all the Levant trade, previously confined to British ships, was thrown open to every neutral. In 1798, being then at war with Spain, the great raw material, Spanish wool, essential to the cloth manufactures, was allowed to enter in vessels of any neutral country. The produce even of hostile colonies could be imported by British subjects in neutral bottoms, though not for consumption in England, but for re-exportation; a process by which it paid a toll to Great Britain, without directly affecting the reserved market of the British colonist. The effect of these various conditions and measures can best be shown by a few figures, which indicate at once the expansion of British commerce, the arrest of British carrying trade, and the consequent growth of the neutral shipping. In 1792, the last year of peace, the total British exports and imports amounted to £44,565,000; in 1796 to £53,706,000; in 1800, the last unbroken year of war, to £73,723,000.[1] For the same years the carrying of this trade was done, in 1792, by 3,151,389 tons of British, and 479,630 tons of foreign shipping; in 1796, by 2,629,575 British, and 998,427 foreign; in 1800, by 2,825,078 British and 1,448,287 foreign. Thus, while there was so great an increase in the commerce of the kingdom, and it employed nearly 650,000 more tons of shipping in 1800 than in 1792, the amount carried in British ships had fallen off; and the proportion of neutral bottoms had risen from thirteen to nearly thirty-four per cent.

[1] The amounts given are those known as the "official values," assigned arbitrarily to the specific articles a century before. The advantage attaching to this system is, that, no fluctuation of price entering as a factor, the values continue to represent from year to year the proportion of trade done. Official values are used throughout this chapter when not otherwise stated. The "real values," deduced from current prices, were generally much greater than the official. Thus, in 1800, the whole volume of trade, by official value £73,723,000, was by real value £111,231,000. The figures are taken from Macpherson's Annals of Commerce.

The significance of these facts could not escape the French government, nor yet the jealousies of certain classes connected with the carrying trade in Great Britain herself; but in the first war the latter were not joined by the other powerful and suffering interests, which gradually impelled the ministry into a series of acts deeply injurious to all neutrals, but chiefly to the United States. In France, the early effusiveness of the revolutionists toward England, based upon the hope that she too would be swept into the torrent of their movement, had been quickly chilled and turned to bitterness, greater even than that which had so long divided the two nations. Victorious everywhere upon the Continent, the government saw before it only one unconquerable enemy, the Power of the Sea; it knew that she, by her subsidies and her exhortations, maintained the continental states in their recurring hostilities, and it saw her alone, amid the general confusion and impoverishment, preserve quiet and increase a wealth which was not only brilliant, but solid. The Directory therefore reached the conclusion, which Napoleon made the basis of his policy and which he never wearied of proclaiming, that Great Britain maintained the war and promoted the discord of nations for the simple purpose of founding her own prosperity upon the ruin of all other commerce, her power upon the ruin of all other navies.[1] At the same time the French government held tenaciously to that profound delusion, the bequest to it from past generations of naval officers and statesmen, that a war directed against the commerce of Great Britain was a sure means of destroying her. It knew that hosts of privateers were employed, and that very many British

[1] The French will not suffer a Power which seeks to found its prosperity upon the misfortunes of other states, to raise its commerce upon the ruin of that of other states, and which, aspiring to the dominion of the seas, wishes to introduce everywhere the articles of its own manufacture and to receive nothing from foreign industry, any longer to enjoy the fruit of its guilty speculations. — *Message of Directory to the Council of Five Hundred*, Jan. 4, 1798.

prizes were brought in; yet, withal, the great Sea Power moved steadily on, evidently greater and stronger as the years went by. It knew also that her manufactures were increasing, that their products filled the Continent; that the produce of the East and of the West, of the Baltic and of the Mediterranean, centred in Great Britain; and that through her, not the Continent only, but France herself, drew most of her tropical articles of consumption. There was but one solution for this persistent escape from apparently sure destruction; and that was to be found in the support of the neutral carrier and the pockets of the neutral consumer. From this premise the fatal logic of the French Revolution was irresistibly drawn to the conclusion that, as every neutral ship engaged in the British carrying trade was a help to England, it was consequently an enemy to France and liable to capture.[1] Napoleon but amplified this precedent when he declared that there were no more neutrals, and placed before Sweden, longing only for quiet, the option "war with France or cannon-balls for English vessels approaching your ports."

The exceptionally intense spirit which animated the parties to this war trenched with unusual severity upon the interests of neutral powers, always more or less in conflict with the aims of belligerents. These questions also received new importance, because now appeared for the first time a neutral maritime state, of great extent and rapidly growing, whose interests and ambitions at that time pointed to shipping and carrying trade as forms of enterprise for which it had received from nature peculiar facilities. In all previous wars the Americans had acted as the colonists of Great Britain, either loyal or in revolt. In 1793 they had for four years been a nation in the real sense of the word, and Washington's first term closed. In the very first Congress measures were taken for developing American shipping, by differential duties upon native and

[1] **Message** of Directory to Council of Five Hundred, Jan. 4, 1798.

foreign ships.[1] From the impulse thus given, combined
with the opening offered by the increase of British trade
and the diminished employment of British shipping, the
ship-builders and merchants extended their operations
rapidly.   By the report of a committee of the House,
January 10, 1803, it appears that the merchant tonnage of
the United States was then inferior to that of no other
country, except Great Britain.[2] In 1790 there had entered her ports from abroad 355,000 tons of her own
shipping and 251,000 foreign, of which 217,000 were
British.[3] In the year 1801 there entered 799,304 tons of
native shipping,[4] and of foreign but 138,000.[5] The amount
of British among the latter is not stated; but in the year
1800 there cleared from Great Britain under her own flag,
for the United States, but 14,381 tons.[6] Figures like these
give but a comparative and partial view of the activity of
American shipping, leaving out of account all the carrying
done by it outside the ken of the home authorities; but it is
safe to say that the United States contributed annually at
least six hundred thousand tons to maintain the traffic of
the world, which, during those eventful years, centred in
Great Britain and ministered to her power.   Among the
forms of gain thus opened to American traders there was
one to which allusion only will here be made, because at
a later period it became the source of very great trouble,
leading step by step to the war of 1812.   This was the
carriage of the productions of French and other colonies,
enemies of Great Britain, to the United States, and thence
re-exporting them to Europe.

[1] The act imposing these duties went into effect Aug. 15, 1789. Vessels
built in the United States, and owned by her citizens, paid an entrance duty
of six cents per ton; all other vessels fifty cents. A discount of ten per
cent on the established duties was also allowed upon articles imported in
vessels built and owned in the country. (Annals of Congress. First Congress, pp. 2131, 2132.)

[2] Am. State Papers, vol. x. 502.   [3] Ibid., p. 389.
[4] Ibid., p. 528.   [5] Ibid., p. 584.
[6] Macpherson's Annals of Commerce, vol. iv. 535.

Besides the new state in the Western Hemisphere, there were three others whose isolated position had hitherto given them the character of neutrals in the maritime wars of the eighteenth century. These were the Baltic countries, Russia, Denmark, and Sweden, which had combined in 1780 to defend their neutral rights, if need were, by force of arms. The power of this confederacy to assume the same attitude in 1793 was broken by the policy of Russia. By whatever motives swayed, the Empress Catharine took decided ground against the French Revolution. On the 25th of March, 1793, a convention between her and the British government was signed, by which both parties agreed, not only to close their own ports against France and not to permit the exportation of food to that country, but also "to unite all their efforts *to prevent other powers*, not implicated in the war, from giving, on this occasion of common concern to every civilized state, any protection whatever, directly or indirectly in consequence of their neutrality, to the commerce or property of the French on the sea."[1] How the empress understood this engagement was shown by her notification, during the same summer, to the courts of Sweden and Denmark, that she would station a fleet in the North Sea to prevent neutrals bound to France from proceeding.[2] Great Britain had already — June 8, 1793 — directed the commanders of cruisers to detain all vessels loaded with flour or grain, bound to French ports, and to send them to England, where the cargo would be purchased and freight paid by the British government.[3] These instructions were duly communicated to the government of the neutral states, which protested with more or less vigor and tenacity, but found themselves helpless to resist force with force. Sin-

---

[1] Am. State Papers, vol. i. 243.

[2] Annual Register, 1793, p. 346 *.

[3] Am. State Papers, i. 240. A complete series of the orders injuriously affecting United States commerce, issued by Great Britain and France, from 1791 to 1808, can be found in the Am. State Papers, vol. iii. p. 262.

gularly enough, the French government had preceded the
British on this occasion, having issued orders to the same
effect on the 9th of the previous May; but the fact appears
to have escaped the ministry, for, in justifying their action
to the United States, they do not allude to it. Their
course is defended on the broad ground that, from the
character of the war and the situation of France, there
was a fair prospect of starving her into submission,[1] and
that under such circumstances provisions, always a questionable article, became contraband of war. The answer
was not satisfactory to the neutral, deprived of part of his
expected gains, but the argument was one of those that
admit of no appeal except to arms. A further justification of the order was found by the British ministry in the
undoubted fact that "the French government itself was the
sole legal importer of grain in France" at that time; and
therefore "the trade was no longer to be regarded as a
mercantile speculation of individuals, but as an immediate
operation of the very persons who have declared war, and
are now carrying it on, against Great Britain." The
American minister to France, Monroe, confirms this, in
his letter of October 16, 1794: "The whole commerce of
France, to the absolute exclusion of individuals, is
carried on by the government itself." [2]

Soon after, on the 6th of November, 1793, another order
was issued by the British ministry, directing the seizure
of "all ships laden with goods the produce of any colony
belonging to France, or carrying provisions or other supplies for the use of any such colony." This order was
based upon the Rule of 1756, so called from the war in
which it first came conspicuously into notice, and the principle of which, as stated by British authorities, was that

---

[1] Am. State Papers, i. 240, 241. How probable this result was may be
seen from the letters of Gouverneur Morris, Oct. 19, 1793, and March 6,
1794. State Papers, vol. i. pp. 375, 404.

[2] Am. State Papers, vol. i. p. 679.

a trade forbidden to neutrals by the laws of a country, during peace, could not be lawfully carried on by them in
time of war, for the convenience of the belligerent; because, by such employment, their ships " were in effect
incorporated in the 'enemy's navigation, having adopted
his commerce and character and identified themselves with
his interests and purposes." [1] At that time the colonial
trade was generally reserved to the mother country; and
against it particularly, together with the coasting trade,
similarly restricted, was this ruling of the British courts
and government directed. Neutrals replied, " Because the
parent country monopolizes in peace the whole commerce
of its colonies, does it follow that in war it should have no
right to regulate it at all ?" [2] " We deny that municipal
regulations, established in peace, can in any wise limit
the public rights of neutrals in time of war." [3] It is evident that these two lines of argument do not fairly meet
each other; they resemble rather opposite and equal weights
in a balance, which will quickly be overturned when passion or interest, combined with power, is thrown in upon
either side. Starting from such fundamentally different
premises, interested parties might argue on indefinitely
in parallel lines, without ever approaching a point of
contact.

The chief present interest in this question, referring as
it does to an obsolete colonial policy, is as illustrative of
one of those dead-locks, which, occurring at a critical
moment, when passion or interest is aroused, offer no
solution but by war. It was useless to point out that
Great Britain relaxed in every direction her own peace
regulations, for the advantage of British commerce in the

[1] Wheaton's International Law, p. 753.

[2] Monroe to the British Minister of Foreign Affairs. Am. State Papers
vol. ii. p. 735.

[3] Reply to " War in Disguise, or Frauds of the Neutral Flag," by Gouverneur Morris, New York, 1806, p. 22.

present contest. The reply was perfectly apt, that she did not dispute the right of her enemy to avail himself of any help the neutral could give; she only asserted the determination not to permit the neutral to extend it with impunity. There was no doubt, in the mind of any considerable body of Englishmen, as to the perfect soundness of the English doctrine. Lord Howick, who, as Mr. Grey, had embarrassed his party in 1792 by the exuberance of his liberalism,[1] as foreign minister in 1807 wrote: "Neutrality, properly considered, does not consist in taking advantage of every situation between belligerent states by which emolument may accrue to the neutral, whatever may be the consequences to either belligerent party; but in observing a strict and honest impartiality, so as not to afford advantage in the war to either; and, particularly, in so far restraining its trade to the accustomed course which it held in time of peace, as not to render assistance to one belligerent in escaping the effects of the other's hostilities."[2] An agreement among any number of the subjects of the interested nation proves nothing as to the right of the question, but the irreconcilable divergence of views at this time shows most clearly the necessity, under which every country lies, to be ready to support its own sense of its rights and honor by force, if necessary.

Under the order of November 6, some hundreds of American ships were seized and brought into West Indian ports by British cruisers.[3] The application of the order to them was, however, liable to two serious objections, even admitting the principle. In the first place, it was made without warning, under a rule that was at least not

[1] Russell's Life of Fox, vol. ii. p. 281.

[2] Letter to Danish Minister, March 17, 1807. Cobbett's Parl. Debates, vol. x. p. 406.

[3] A letter from an American consul in the West Indies, dated March 7, 1794, gives 220 as the number. This was, however, only a partial account, the orders having been recently received. (Am. State Papers, i. p. 429.)

generally accepted; and in the second place, the trade between the French West India Islands and the United States had been permitted, before the war, in vessels of sixty tons and upwards.[1] In the year ending September 30, 1790, fifty-seven thousand tons of American shipping entered home ports from the French colonies. The trade, therefore, was one that existed prior to the war, and so did not come under the rule of 1756.[2] The order of November 6 was not made public until nearly the end of the year; the United States minister in London not receiving a copy until Christmas Day. He hastened at once to protest, but before he could obtain an audience a second was issued, January 8, 1794, revoking the former and limiting the operations of the rule to vessels bound from the colonies direct to Europe. Although the principle was maintained by the new order, and not admitted by the United States, still, as their own trade was excepted, much dissatisfaction was removed.

The serious nature of the difficulties that had already arisen determined the government to send an extraordinary envoy to England. John Jay was nominated to this office, and reached London in June, 1794. The British government, having already receded from its first position, as well as revoked the order of June 8, 1793, for the seizure of provisions, found no difficulty in assuming a conciliatory attitude. The result of Jay's mission was a treaty of Commerce and Navigation, concluded November 19, 1794, the first contracted between the two countries since the separation. The injuries done to American commerce, under the orders of November 6, were to be submitted to

---

[1] By the ordinance of Aug. 30, 1784. See Annals of Congress, Jan. 13, 1794, p. 192.

[2] The National Convention, immediately after the outbreak of war, on the 17th of February, 1793, gave a great extension to the existing permission of trade between the United States and the French colonies; but this could not affect the essential fact that the trade, under some conditions, had been allowed in peace.

a joint commission. The report of the latter was not made until 1804, but by it compensation was made for most of the seizures; and it was claimed in the following year by Mr. Monroe, then envoy in London, that the decision of the commission definitely disposed of the principle of the Rule of 1756. It does not appear, however, that its power extended further than the settlement of the cases. There, its decision was to be final; but it had no power to commit either government to any general principle of international law not otherwise established.[1] The Rule of 1756 was not mentioned in the treaty, and the failure to do so may be construed as a tacit acquiescence, or at least submission, on the part of the United States.[2] On the other hand, considerable commercial advantages were obtained. Great Britain conceded to American ships the privilege of direct trade between their own country and the British East and West Indies, but they were precluded from carrying the produce of those colonies to other foreign ports. Indeed, so great was the anxiety of the British ministers to prevent coffee and sugar from being taken to Europe, indirectly, by neutral ships, that they insisted upon, and Jay admitted, a stipulation that while the trade with the British West Indies was permitted, the United States would not allow the carrying of any molasses, sugar, coffee, cocoa, or cotton in American vessels to any other part of the world than to the United States. This would have stopped a profitable

[1] In fact Monroe, in another part of the same letter, avows: " The doctrine of Great Britain in every decision is the same. . . . Every departure from it is claimed as a relaxation of the principle, gratuitously conceded by Great Britain."

[2] Mr. Jay seems to have been under some misapprehension in this matter, for upon his return he wrote to the Secretary of State: " The treaty does prohibit re-exportation from the United States of West India commodities in neutral vessels; . . . but we may carry them direct from French and other West India islands to Europe." (Am. State Papers, i. 520.) This the treaty certainly did not admit.

trade already open to American merchants, who first imported, and then re-exported to France, the produce of the French islands; the broken voyage being considered to purge the origin of the commodities. This article (the twelfth) was accordingly rejected by the Senate, and only as thus modified was the treaty ratified by both powers.

The French government had viewed with distrust the negotiation between Great Britain and the United States. Although assured by Mr. Jay, through the American minister at Paris, that the treaty contained an express stipulation guarding the existing conventions between France and his own country, the Directory had the insolence to demand a copy of the instrument, to which it considered itself entitled, although it had not yet been communicated to the United States government. When the terms finally became known, its indignation passed bounds. The principal points to which it took exception were two, wherein the United States admitted conditions favoring the interests of belligerents relatively to neutrals, and against which the chief efforts of the weaker maritime states had been addressed. The first of these was the well-settled principle that a neutral ship did not protect property belonging to an enemy, laden on board it. The United States had always admitted this as valid, while trying to introduce, as an innovation, the contrary rule. In the treaty of 1778 with France, the two countries had stipulated that in any future war in which one of them should be engaged the belligerent should respect his enemy's property, if under the flag of the other party to the compact; but the United States did not think that this agreement between two nations overturned for all others a settled usage. The interests of Great Britain indisposed her to accept the proposed change, and the old principle was explicitly accepted in the seventeenth article of Jay's treaty. The other point objected to by France referred to the definitions of contraband of war. This has

always been, and still is, one of the most difficult problems of international law; for an article may be of the
first importance in the wars of one age or one country,
and of slight consequence in another century or a different
scene. By Jay's treaty the United States allowed that
naval stores were, and under some circumstances provisions might be, contraband of war, and therefore liable
to seizure. A free trade in these articles was of great
importance to the Americans; but they were weak then, as
in a military sense they, with far less excuse, are now;
and then, as now, they must submit in questions of doubtful right. The material interests of United States citizens, as distinguished from the national self-respect, were
in part saved by Great Britain undertaking to pay for provisions when seized as contraband. All these conditions
bore against the wishes of the French, who regarded the
Americans as owing an undischarged debt of gratitude to
them for the scanty, though certainly most important, aid
extended in the Revolutionary struggle by the monarch
whom his people had since beheaded; and from this time
the arrogance with which the French government had
treated that of the United States became tinged with
acrimony. It refused to see the difficulties and weakness
of the new and still scarcely cemented body of states; or
that, indirectly, the bargain struck by the latter was upon
the whole as advantageous to France herself as could be
expected, when Great Britain had an absolute control
over the sea and all that floated upon it. To imperious
rebukes and reproaches succeeded a series of measures,
outraging neutral and treaty rights, which finally led to
hostilities between the two countries.

From the time of Jay's treaty to the peace of Amiens,
and until the year 1804 in the following war, the relations
between Great Britain and the United States remained
on a fairly settled basis. Innumerable vexations, indeed,
attended neutral commerce at the hands of cruisers who

were willing on slight grounds to seize a prize, taking the chance of the courts deciding in their favor, and the delays of prize courts added greatly to the annoyance; but upon the whole American trade throve greatly. In June, 1797, the Secretary of State reported, in reply to a resolution of the House, that "captures and losses by British cruisers, it is presumed, have not been numerous; for the citizens of the United States having, these three years past, been accustomed to look to the government for aid in prosecuting these claims, it is not to be doubted that, generally, these cases have been reported to the Department." In 1801 there was an outbreak of lawless seizure in the West Indies.[1] The American vessels engaged in that trade were small, and, as legal expenses were the same for a large as for a small prize, the cost of a contest amounted to a sum very disproportionate to the value of the ship; so the captors hoped, by the well-known delays of procedure, to extort a compromise. An abuse of this kind, however outrageous, is different in principle from the direct action of a government; nor are such cases the only ones in which men have been willing to take dishonest advantage of the imperfections, ambiguities, or delays of the law.[2] The Secretary of State, in transmitting a report on the subject to the House of Representatives, said, "Neither the communications from our minister at London, nor my conversations with the Chargé d'Affaires of his Britannic Majesty in the United States, would lead to an opinion that any additional orders have lately been given by the British government, authorizing the system of depredation alluded to."[3]

In fact, at this time Pitt's government seems to have considered all trade, which did not go direct to hostile

[1] See letter of Thos. Fitzsimmons, Am. State Papers, vol. ii. 347.

[2] The pretexts for these seizures seem usually to have been the alleged contraband character of the cargoes.

[3] Am. State Papers, vol. ii. 345.

countries, an advantage to Great Britain, and especially if it could be drawn to pass through her own ports. Accordingly, in January, 1798, a further relaxation of the Rule of 1756 was promulgated, extending to European neutrals the concession made in 1794 to the United States. British cruisers were now directed not to capture neutral ships, bound from the hostile colonies to Europe and laden with colonial produce, provided the latter had become neutral property and its destination was to their own country, or to a port of Great Britain. The final clause foreshadowed the policy of the Orders in Council of ten years later, towards which Great Britain, under the stress of war, was steadily gravitating. The law of self-preservation, divined by the instinct of the state, demanded that the United Kingdom should become, for that war, the storehouse of the world's commerce. The more thriving that commerce, the better for her, if it could be concentrated in her own borders. Thus France and the whole world should become tributary to a wealth and to a power by which, not Great Britain only, but the world should be saved. It was a great conception, of slow growth and gradual realization; it was disfigured in its progress by imperfections, blunders, and crimes; but it was radically sound and in the end victorious, for upon Great Britain and upon commerce hung the destinies of the world.

The action of France towards neutral, and especially towards American, vessels reflected the instability and excitement of the successive French governments, the violent passions of the time, and the uncertainty necessarily attendant upon the course of a nation which, having cut adrift from fixed principles and precedents, is guided only by changing impressions of right and wrong. The decree of the 9th of May, 1793, arresting vessels laden with provisions or carrying enemy's goods, was revoked as regards the United States on the 23d of the same month, because

contrary to the treaty of 1778.   On the 28th, five days
later, the revocation was revoked, and the original order
established.[1]   On the first of July the decision was
again reversed and the treaty ordered to be observed; notwithstanding which the United States minister found it
impossible to obtain the release of vessels seized contrary
to its terms, and on the 27th of the month the last decision was again repealed.[2]   On the 22d of September the
American minister writes: "I understand it is still in
contemplation to repeal the decree I complained of, and
that in the mean time it has not been transmitted to the
tribunals.   In effect, it can do very little harm; because
the fleets of this country are confined by the enemy, and
the privateers by a decree of the Convention."[3]   Here
matters rested during the Reign of Terror and until
November 15, 1794, after the fall of Robespierre, when
the Directory issued its first edict on the subject; reiter-
ating that enemy's goods under the neutral flag would be
considered liable to seizure, until the powers, enemies of
France, should declare French property free on board neutral ships.   This made the treatment of cargoes on American vessels depend, not upon the formal engagements of
France with the United States, but upon the conduct of
Great Britain; and it was succeeded, on the 3d of January, 1795, by a decree of revocation.   Enemy's goods
under neutral flags now remained exempt from capture
until the 2d of July, 1796; when proclamation was issued,
notifying neutral powers that the ships of the French Republic would be used against their merchant vessels, were it
for the purpose of confiscation, search or detention, in the
same manner that they suffered the English to act in regard

---

[1] It will be remembered that the closing days of May witnessed the culmination of the death struggle between the Jacobins and Girondists, and that
the latter finally fell on the second of June.

[2] Am. State Papers, vol. i. pp. 284, 286, 748.

[3] Ibid., p. 372.

to them.   Great Britain was thus made supreme arbiter
of the conduct of France towards neutrals.

This last step of the French government was directly
traceable to its dissatisfaction with Jay's treaty, the ratifications of which had been exchanged at London on the
28th of October, 1795.   On the 16th of February, 1796,
the Minister of Foreign Affairs told Mr. Monroe, the
American minister, that his government considered the
alliance between the two countries, formed by the treaty
of 1778, to be terminated, *ipso facto*, by Jay's treaty; and
on the 7th of October he was further informed that the
minister to the United States had been recalled and would
not be replaced.   Meanwhile President Washington, being
dissatisfied with Monroe's conduct, had summoned him
home and sent out Mr. Pinckney as his relief; but the
Directory, on the 11th of December, refused to receive
any minister plenipotentiary from the United States until
the grievances it had alleged were redressed,[1] and on the
25th of January, 1797, Pinckney was ordered to leave the
country as an unauthorized foreigner.

France was now fully embarked on a course of violence
toward the United States, which arose, not from any
reasonable cause of discontent given, but from the disposition, identical with that shown toward the weaker
European nations, to compel all countries to follow the
dictates of the French policy.   The utterly loose terms of
the decree of July 2, 1796, authorized the seizure of any
neutral vessel by a French captain, if, in his judgment, the
conduct of Great Britain toward the neutral justified it;
and left the ultimate fate of the prize to a tribunal governed only by its own opinion upon the same subject.
"You are mistaken," said a French deputy, "if you think

---

[1] One of these complaints was that the United States now prohibited the
sale, in her ports, of prizes taken from the British by French cruisers.   This
practice, not accorded by the treaty with France, and which had made an unfriendly distinction against Great Britain, was forbidden by Jay's treaty.

that a privateer sails furnished with instructions from the
Minister of Marine, who ought to direct their action. The
instructions are drawn up by his owners; they indicate to
the captain what he may seize and what release. They com-
pile for him his duties under all the rules, under all the
laws, contradictory or otherwise, from the year 1400 up to
the law of Nivôse 29, An 6" (Jan. 18, 1798).[1]

In the West Indies the French agents, practically removed from all control of the home government by the
British command of the sea, issued on the 27th of November, 1796, a decree for the capture of Americans bound to,
or coming from, British ports. They had already, on the
first of August, directed that all vessels having contraband
goods on board should be seized and condemned, whatever their destination, and although the accepted law condemned only the contraband articles themselves, not the
ship nor the rest of the cargo. On the first of the following February the same commissioners ordered the capture
of all neutrals sailing for the French islands which had
surrendered to the enemy, and declared them good prize.
That these acts fairly represented the purpose of the
Directory may be inferred from the capture of American
ships in European waters under the decree of July 2, and
from the fact that the French consuls at Malaga and Cadiz
interpreted the decree to authorize seizure and condemnation for the single circumstance of being destined for a
British port.[2] Over three hundred American vessels were
thus seized, and most of them condemned. Envoys sent
from the United States to treat concerning these matters
said, in October, 1797, that France had violently taken
from America over fifteen million dollars.[3] "At no
period of the war," wrote they again, February 7, 1798,
"has Britain undertaken to exercise such a power. At

---

[1] Speech of M. Dentzel in the Conseil des Anciens. Moniteur, An 7,
p. 555.

[2] Am. State Papers, vol. ii. p. 28.   [3] Ibid., vol. ii. p. 163.

no period has she asserted such a right."[1] "Was there ever anything," said the deputy before quoted, "like the injustice of the condemnations in the Antilles ? "

These irregular and arbitrary proceedings are chiefly significant as showing the lack of any fixed principles of action on the part of the French government and its agents; and they were closely connected with similar courses towards neutral vessels in French ports. At the outbreak of hostilities in 1793, one hundred and three American ships were embargoed at Bordeaux and detained more than a year, without any reason given; nor had the owners been indemnified in 1796.[2] Cargoes were forcibly taken from vessels and payment either refused or offered in kind, and so delayed that in the West Indies alone the American losses were calculated at two million dollars. Besides these acts, which had the character of spoliations, the contracts and other financial obligations of the French government and its agents with citizens of the United States remained undischarged. The irritation between the two governments, and on the part of American merchants, continued to increase rapidly. The decree of July 2, the essence of which was the formal repudiation of a clause of the treaty of 1778, at the time when alone it became applicable, remained in force; and was rendered more obnoxious by a further order, of March 2, 1797, making more stringent the proofs of neutrality to be adduced before French tribunals and requiring papers which had long been disused.

At this time the astonishing successes of Bonaparte's Italian campaigns were approaching their triumphant conclusion. The battle of Rivoli had been fought on the 14th of January, 1797,[3] Mantua capitulated on the 2d of

---

[1] Letter to Talleyrand, Am. State Papers, vol. ii. p. 178.

[2] Ibid., vol. i. pp. 740, 748.

[3] The day after the news of Rivoli was received, Mr. Pinckney, who had remained in Paris, though unrecognized, was curtly directed to leave France.

February, and the Pope had been compelled to sue for peace. To Austria there remained only the hope of contesting the approach to her German dominions. The confidence of the Directors knew no bounds, and they now began to formulate the policy toward British commerce which Napoleon inherited from them. The design was formed of forcing the United States to recede from the obnoxious conventions of Jay's treaty; and the government of Holland, then entirely dependent upon that of France, was pressed to demand that Dutch property on board American vessels should be protected against British seizure, and to suggest the concurrence of the three republics against Great Britain.[1] The Dutch accordingly represented "that, when circumstances oblige our commerce to confide its interests to the neutral flag of American vessels, it has a just right to insist that that flag be protected with energy;"[2] in other words, that, when the British control of the sea forced the Dutch ships from it, Dutch trade should be carried on under the American flag, and that the United States should fight to prevent the seizure of the Dutch property, although it admitted that the traditional law of nations would not justify it in so doing. On the 6th of May, 1797, Spain also, doubtless under the dictation of France, made the same demand.[2] Similar representations were made to the other neutral country, Denmark. Here is seen the fore-runner of Napoleon's contention that, as against Great Britain's control of the sea, no state had a right to be neutral. Soon afterward the idea was carried farther. Denmark was requested to close the mouth of the Elbe to British commerce. "The French," wrote our minister to London on the 12th of March, 1797, "assign our treaty with England as the cause of their maritime conduct toward us, but they have recently demanded of Hamburg and Bremen to suspend all commerce with England. These have not

[1] Am. State Papers, vol. ii. p. 13.   [2] Ibid., p. 14.

complied, and the French minister has been recalled from Hamburg. The same demand has been made at Copenhagen, and the refusal has produced a sharp diplomatic controversy. These powers have made no late treaty with England."[1]

Hostilities with Austria had ceased by the preliminaries of Leoben, April 18, followed, after long negotiations, by the treaty of Campo Formio, October 17, 1797. Of the coalition against France, Great Britain alone remained upright and defiant. She had in 1797, after Austria had yielded, offered to negotiate; but the terms demanded were such that she refused to accept them, and her envoy was ordered out of France as peremptorily as Mr. Pinckney had been a few months before. The Directory thought that the time was now come when she could be brought to unconditional surrender, and the weapon by which her commerce should be annihilated was already forged to its hand. On the 31st of October, 1796 (Brumaire 10, An 5),[2] a law had been passed by the Legislature forbidding entirely the admission of any British manufactured goods, directing that all persons who already had such in possession should declare them within three days, and that they should be at once packed and stored for re-exportation. In order to insure the execution of the statute, domiciliary visits were authorized everywhere within three leagues of the frontiers or sea-board, and throughout France the dwellings of all tradesmen were also open to search. Laws of similar purpose had been passed early in the war;[3] but they either had been found insufficient or were no longer applicable to the changed conditions of affairs. "Now that," to use the words of a deputy, "the flags of the Republic or those of its allies float over the sea from Embden to Trieste, and almost all the ports of the Euro-

---

[1] American State Papers, vol. ii. p. 14.
[2] Moniteur, An v. pp. 164, 167.
[3] March 1, and October 8, 1793. Ibid.

pean seas are closed to England, we must stop the voluntary subsidies which are paid her by the consumers of English merchandise."[1] With Belgium annexed, with Spain and Holland vassals rather than allies, with the greater part of Italy in military occupation, it seemed possible to repel the entrance points of British goods to the Continent far from the French frontier, and by strict watchfulness to close the latter against such as worked their way to it.

The expectation, however, was deceived; the superior quality and abundance of British manufactures created a demand which evaded all watchfulness and enlisted all classes against the officials. The Directory therefore determined, toward the end· of 1797, to put the law into force with all severity and to introduce another and final rigor into its maritime prize code. On the 4th of January, 1798, a message was sent to the council of Five Hundred, announcing that "on that very day the municipal administrators, the justices of the peace, the commissaries of the Directory, and the superintendents of customs, are proceeding in all the chief places of the departments, in all the ports, and in all the principal communes, to seize all English merchandise now in France in contravention of the law of Brumaire 10, An 5. Such is the *first act* by which, now that peace is given to the Continent, the war declared long since against England is about to assume the real character that belongs to it." But more was needed. Neutral vessels were in the habit of entering British ports, shipping British goods, and carrying on British trade; they were even known, when opportunity offered, to introduce articles of British manufacture, directly or indirectly, into France. By so doing they aided Great Britain and actually took part in the war. "The Directory, therefore, thinks it urgent and necessary to pass a law declaring that the character of vessels, rela-

[1] Speech of Lecouteulx; Moniteur, An v. p. 176.

tive to their quality of neutral or enemy, shall be determined by their cargo; . . . in consequence, that every
vessel found at sea, having on board English merchandise
as her cargo, in whole or in part, shall be declared lawful
prize, whosoever shall be the proprietor of this merchandise, *which shall be reputed contraband for this cause alone*,
that it comes from England or her possessions." This
decree was adopted without discussion, in the very terms of
the Directory's message, on the 18th of January, 1798.
From that time forward, to use the expression of a French
deputy, speaking a year later on the proposed, repeal of
the law, "if a handkerchief of English origin is found on
board a neutral ship, both the rest of the cargo and the
ship itself are subject to condemnation." It is, perhaps,
well to point out that this differed from the Rule of 1756,
by forbidding a trade which at all times had been open to
neutrals, in peace as in war. It differed from the old rule
condemning enemy's property found in neutral bottoms,
by condemning also neutral property of hostile origin,
.together with the whole cargo and the ship, as contami-
nated by the presence of any British goods.

Nevertheless, British commerce continued to thrive,
and was rather benefited than injured by the new law.
What the indomitable purpose, unlimited power, and
extraordinary mental and physical activity of Napoleon
could only partially accomplish, proved to be wholly
beyond the weak arm of the Directory. When war first,
shut the ports of France to Great Britain, her trade
thither passed through the Netherlands and Holland.
When the Netherlands were overrun, Amsterdam monopolized the traffic. With the fall of Holland, it passed
away to Bremen and Hamburg. The latter port, being
farther east and more remote from the French armies,
naturally drew the greater part and became the real heir
of Amsterdam.[1] It was the emporium of Northern Ger-

[1] Macpherson's Annals of Commerce, vol. iv. 463.

many, through which poured the colonial produce of the world and the manufactures of the British Islands, and from which they were distributed over the Continent. The enormous subsidies paid by the United Kingdom to Germany found their way back, in part at least, by the increased purchasing power of the belligerent countries,[1] which consumed the manufactures of Great Britain and the coffee and sugar which had passed through her ports and paid toll to her revenues.[2] The shipping clearing for Hamburg from British ports, which was naught in 1793, rose to fifty-three thousand tons in 1795; and in 1798, the year during which the new French law operated, increased to seventy-four thousand. But, while Hamburg was the great centre, all the northern German ports shared the same prosperity. After Prussia retired from the war against France, in April, 1795, a neutral North German territory was established, behind a line agreed upon between the two countries. The total tonnage entering the ports of this region increased from one hundred and twenty thousand in 1792 to two hundred and six thousand in 1795; and in 1798 reached three hundred and three thousand. The value of merchandise imported rose from £2,200,000 in 1792, to £8,300,000 in 1795, £11,000,000 in 1798, and £13,500,000 in 1800.[3]

A similar elasticity was shown by British trade throughout the world. Only in the Mediterranean was there a marked decrease both of exports and imports, — a loss partly filled by the enterprise of American merchants;[4] but only partly, for the Barbary pirates seconded the sweeping French decrees in excluding neutrals from that sea. But it was in the West Indies, together with the

[1] Macpherson's Annals of Commerce, vol. iv. 413, note.

[2] Of the imports into Germany, three fifths were foreign merchandise re-exported from Great Britain.

[3] These figures are all taken from Macpherson's Annals of Commerce, vol. iv.

[4] See Am. State Papers, vol. x. p. 487.

German ports, that the commercial activity of Great Britain found its greatest resources; and in the steady support contributed by that region to her financial stability is to be found the justification of the much derided policy of Pitt in capturing sugar islands. Alike as valuable pieces of property, as possessions to be exchanged when framing a treaty, and as bases for cruisers, which not merely seized upon British shipping but disturbed the commercial development of the whole region, each hostile island should at once have been seized by Great Britain. In a contest between equal navies for the control of the sea, to waste military effort upon the capture of small islands, as the French did in 1778, is a preposterous misdirection of effort; but when one navy is overwhelmingly preponderant, as the British was after 1794, when the enemy confines himself to commerce-destroying by crowds of small privateers, then the true military policy is to stamp out the nests where they swarm. If, by so doing, control is also gained of a rich commercial region, as the Caribbean Sea then was, the action is doubly justified. The produce of the West Indies, as of the East, figured doubly in the returns of British commerce, — as imports, and as re-exported to the Continent.[1] Each captured

[1] The importance of the West India region to the commercial system of Great Britain in the last decade of the 18th century will be seen from the following table, showing the distribution per cent of British trade in 1792 and 1800 : —

	Imports from,		Exports to,	
	1792.	1800.	1792.	1800.
British West Indies	20	28	11	10
United States	5	7	17	15
Russia	9	8	3	2
Germany and Prussia	5	12	9	31
France, Belgium, and Holland . .	8	4	15	12
Mediterranean	7	2	6	2
Spain and Portugal	9	5	6	3
Ireland	13	7	9	9
Asia (not Levant)	14	16	10	7
Miscellaneous	10	11	14	9
	100	100	100	100

The significance of these figures lies not only in the amounts set down directly to the West Indies, but also in the great increase of exports to Ger-

island contributed to swell the revenues by which the war was maintained.[1] The disappearance of the merchant fleets of France, Spain, and Holland, the ruin of San Domingo, and the general disorganization of such French islands as were not taken, threw the greater part of the production of tropical articles into British hands; and the practice of the day, which confined its transport to British ships, helped to support the shipping interest also in the strain brought upon it by the war. The Americans alone could compete in the continental market as carriers of such produce. Debarred from going with it direct to Europe by the Rule of 1756, the rise in price, due to the diminished production and decrease of transport just mentioned, allowed them to take the sugar and coffee of the colonies at war with England to American ports, reship it to the Continent, and yet make a good profit on the transaction. As the British colonists were in full possession of the home market, and their produce commanded high prices, the outcry which caused so much trouble ten years later was not now raised. On the contrary, their prosperous condition facilitated the British orders of January, 1798, exempting from capture Danes, Swedes, and other neutral ships, when carrying coffee and sugar of hostile origin to their own country, or to England.

It was against this great system of trade that the law of Nivôse 29 was launched. British manufactured goods, rather than British gold and silver, bought and paid for the produce of the East and West Indies, for that of the United States and of the Levant. The Continent consumed the manufactures of Great Britain, the sugar and coffee of her colonies, and obtained through British merchants the spices and wares of the East; for all which it for the most

many, and the high rate maintained to France, Belgium, and Holland, with which war existed. Of these exports 25 per cent in 1792, and 43 per cent in 1800, were foreign merchandise, chiefly West Indian — *re-exported.*

[1] In 1800 the captured islands sent 9 per cent of the British imports.

part paid back specie. The United States took specie from France herself for the colonial produce carried there in its vessels, and with it paid Great Britain for her manufactures. France herself received British goods through continental channels, and paid hard cash for them. The money thus coming to London had flowed back as subsidies to the armies of the coalitions. Now, thanks to Bonaparte, Great Britain stood alone. The French navy was powerless to contend with her fleets; but, by actual possession or by treaty, the Directory had excluded her ships from a great part of the Continent. Nevertheless, British goods abounded in all parts through the complicity of neutral carriers. If these could be stopped, the market for British manufactures would be closed; therefore against them were launched the cruisers of France, with the authority of the decree to capture any one of them found with a bale or box of British origin on board. The result was curious.

After the lapse of a year, on the 13th of January, 1799, the Directory addressed a message to the lower house of the Legislature [1] on the subject of maritime prizes, in which occurred the celebrated avowal, already quoted, that not a single merchant ship under French colors sailed the deep seas. But this was not all. The irregularities and outrages of privateers had so terrified neutrals that there had been an immense diminution in the entries of neutral tonnage, although Great Britain had rather relaxed than increased the severe rules she had adopted early in the war. In consequence of the smaller importations from abroad, there were necessarily smaller sales of French goods, and the decrease of neutral carriers impeded the export of agricultural produce and manufactures, as well as the importation of raw materials essential to the latter. The Directory attributed the evil to an existing ordinance, which left the final determination of prize cases in the

[1] *Moniteur, An vii.* pp. 478, 482.

hands of the courts, instead of attributing it to the executive. It argued that if there were a right of final appeal
to the latter, it could check the arbitrary proceedings of
the cruisers and the erroneous decisions of the judges.
If, as was represented by the American consulate at
Paris, the courts of first instance were chiefly composed
of merchants in the sea-ports, most of whom were,
directly or indirectly, interested in fitting out privateers,[1]
there was certainly need of some change in the existing
legislation. In the Conseil des Anciens, however, a
different view prevailed. On the 17th of January, 1799,
a debate began in that body, on a resolution fixing the
date when the law of January 18, 1798, became operative.[2]
The consequent discussion took a wide range over the
policy and results of the enactment, as shown by the year
it had been in force. The disastrous commercial condition
of France was freely admitted on all sides; but in several
powerful speeches it was attributed directly and convinc-
ingly to the working of the law itself. "Neutrals repelled from our ports; our agricultural products without
any outlet abroad; our industry and commerce annihilated;
our colonies helpless; our shipping ways deserted; a balance of twenty thousand sailors in English prisons; our
ships of war without seamen, — such are the political effects
of the law which is ruining, crushing us."[3]

In less impassioned words, other deputies showed the
unfairness of the law. If, on the land frontier, a wagon
was stopped carrying a bale of British goods, the bale was
confiscated, but the rest of the load escaped. If in a
ship a like bale was found, not only it, but all the rest
of the cargo and the ship itself were condemned. Even
in the fiercest heat of the Revolution and the utmost danger to the country, it had never been attempted, as now,

[1] Am. State Papers, vol. ii. p. 8.
[2] Moniteur, An vii. p. 502.
[3] Ibid., p. 716; Couzard's speech.

to forbid neutrals carrying British goods to their own country.[1] The step could not be justified under the plea of reprisals; for "if the English have seized French goods on these same neutrals, they have not confiscated the rest of the cargo. These are, therefore, not reprisals, but new proceedings on our part, which neutrals could neither expect nor guard against."[2] A neutral ship came within reach of the French coast only at her extreme peril. A small package of British goods would justify her capture by a French privateer, whatever her destination; nay, even if she were bringing to France articles urgently needed, and intended to take away French produce in exchange for them. Neutrals, allies, even French vessels themselves, carrying on the little trade with neighboring states, were preyed on by French corsairs. This condition reacted on the enterprise of the cruisers themselves. It was much safer, and quite as profitable, to keep close to the home coast and board passing vessels. The merest trifle, smuggled on board by one of the crew, or shipped unknown to the master and owner, made them good prize. Owing to this caution, the captures brought into French home ports had dropped, from six hundred and sixty-two in the previous year, to four hundred and fifty-two, notwithstanding the vast extension of the field for seizures.[3]

The loss of prizes, however, was far from being the worst effect of the law. Neutrals being repelled, friendly and French shipping scared away, commerce had been seriously crippled for want of carriage. In the year

[1] Moniteur, An vii. p. 555; Dentzel's speech.

[2] Ibid.; Lenglet's speech.

[3] Ibid., pp. 582, 583. The figures are chiefly taken from the speech of M. Arnould. A person of the same name, who was Chef du Bureau du Commerce, published in 1797 a book called "Système Maritime et Politique des Européens," containing much detailed information about French maritime affairs, and displaying bitter hatred of England. If the deputy himself was not the author, he doubtless had access to the best official intelligence.

before the enactment the coasting trade employed 895,000 tons; of which 120,000 were neutrals, by whom goods were transported from one sea frontier of France to another, as from the Bay of Biscay to the French Mediterranean coast. In the year following, the total fell to 746,000; but the neutrals dropped to 38,000. In the foreign trade 860,000 tons were employed in the year before the law, of which 623,000 were neutral. In the year following, the total fell to 688,000, of which 468,000 were neutrals. There thus resulted a total loss of 322,000 tons in a commerce of only 1,750,000. To this the speaker added a striking comparison: "In the same year in which we lost 322,000 tons by the operation of the law, we took four hundred and fifty-two prizes. Assuming — what is not the case — that these were all English, and that they averaged two hundred tons burden — an excessive allowance — we have taken from our enemy 90,400 tons against 322,000 we have lost." "All the sufferings of ourselves and allies might be borne, if good resulted to ourselves or harm to England; but it has not." "English ships are insured at a premium of five per cent, while neutrals bound to France have to pay twenty to thirty per cent. Neutrals themselves seek English convoy.[1] French merchants would gladly charter neutral ships to carry to San Domingo the produce that is overflowing our storehouses, and to bring back the coffee and sugar for which we are paying such extravagant rates; but they will not come near us. So, instead of paying a moderate price with French goods, we are paying exorbitant rates in specie, which goes straight to England, our most cruel foe."[2] The policy of the law was condemned by the results. In support of its justice, it was alleged that there were at

---

[1] In consequence of the law of Jan. 18, 1798, the British government appointed a ship-of-the-line and two frigates to convoy a fleet of American vessels to their own coast. — *Macpherson's Annals of Commerce,* vol. iv. p. 440.

[2] Moniteur, An vii. p. 564; Cornet's speech.

sea only French and British ships, whence it followed that all which were not French could be seized, — a contention which derives its sole present interest from being the same as that put forth by Napoleon ten years later. It shows again — what can scarcely be too often asserted in the interests of truth — that the emperor was but the full and perfect incarnation of the spirit that animated the Convention and the Directory.

The Government of the United States had not yet, in 1798, passed into the hands of men with an undue "passion for peace." Upon the unceremonious dismissal of Mr. Pinckney, not for personal objections but as rejecting any minister from America, the President had called a special meeting of Congress in May, 1797, and recommended an increase of the naval establishment. When the news of the law of January 18, 1798, reached the United States, Congress was in session. On the 28th of May an act was approved, authorizing the capture of any French armed vessel which shall, upon the coast of the United States, have committed any depredation upon her commerce.[1] On the 7th of July another act abrogated all existing treaties between the two countries;[2] and on the 9th was decreed the seizure of French armed vessels anywhere on the high seas, not only by public armed ships, but by privateers, which the President was authorized to commission.[3] Thereupon followed a period of maritime hostilities, though without a formal declaration of war, which lasted three years; the first prize being taken from the French in June, 1798, and peace being restored by a treaty, signed in Paris September 30, 1800, and ratified the following February. The small force of the United States was principally occupied in the West Indies, protecting their trade, — both by the patrol system directed against the enemy's cruisers, and by convoying bodies of

[1] Annals of Congress, 1798, p. 3733.
[2] Ibid., p. 3754.   [3] Ibid.

merchantmen to and from the islands. As the condition of the French navy did not allow keeping large fleets afloat, the ships of the United States, though generally small, were able to hold their ground, capture many of the enemy, and preserve their own commerce from molestation. The mercantile shipping of France, however, had already been so entirely destroyed by Great Britain, that she suffered far more from the cessation of the carrying trade, which Americans had maintained for her, than from the attacks of the American navy.

The year 1798, which opened with the unlucky law of January 18, was in all respects unfortunate for France. In May Bonaparte sailed for Egypt, the country thus parting with its ablest general, with thirty-two thousand of its best troops, and its only available fleet, of thirteen sail-of-the-line, which the government with the utmost difficulty had been able to equip. On the first of August Nelson destroyed the fleet in the Báttle of the Nile; and the British navy, forced to leave the Mediterranean in 1796, again asserted its preponderance throughout the whole of that sea, opposing an effectual barrier to the return of the army in Egypt. The entire face of affairs changed, not only in the East but in Europe. The Porte, at first hesitating, declared openly against France. A second coalition was formed between Great Britain, Austria, and Russia, to which Naples acceded; and the armies of the latter entered upon their campaign in November. They were, indeed, quickly overthrown; but the very march of the French troops against them left the armies in northern Italy hopelessly inferior to their opponents. The year 1799 was full of reverses. In Germany and in Italy the French were steadily driven back; in Switzerland only did they, under Masséna, hold their ground. The British indeed were repelled in their attack upon Holland, but they carried away with them the Dutch navy. A Russo-Turkish fleet, entering the Mediterranean, retook the Ionian Islands from the French; and Admiral Bruix escaped from Brest only to find it impossible to achieve any substantial results in the face of the British superiority on the sea. In the midst of this confusion and disaster, and amid the commercial and internal distress caused by the maritime legislation, Bonaparte returned. Landing on the 9th of October, he on the 9th of November overthrew the Directory. Preparations for war were at once begun, and the successes of the first consul in Italy and of Moreau in Germany, in 1800, combined with the defection of the czar from the coalition, restored peace to the Continent and internal quiet to France.

Upon this followed the renewal of the Armed Neutrality of the Baltic powers. Great Britain found herself again without an ally, face to face with France, now supported by the naval combination of the northern states. Still she stood resolute, abating not a jot of her asserted maritime rights. As before, the allies demanded that the neutral flag should cover the enemy's property that floated under it, and that the term "contraband of war" should apply only to articles strictly and solely applicable to warlike purposes, which, they claimed, naval stores and provisions were not. They proposed also to deprive Great Britain of the belligerent right of search, by sending ships of war with the merchant ships, and requiring that the assertion of the naval captain should be received as establishing the lawful character of the two or three hundred cargoes under his convoy. "The question," said Pitt, "is whether we are to permit the navy of our enemy to be recruited and supplied, — whether we are to suffer blockaded ports to be furnished with warlike stores and provisions, — whether we are to suffer neutral nations, by hoisting a flag upon a sloop or a fishing boat, to convey the treasures of South America to the harbors of Spain, or the naval stores of the Baltic to Brest and Toulon. I would ask, too, has there ever been a period, since we have been a naval country, in which we have acted upon this principle?"[1] and he alleged not only the unbroken practice of Great Britain, but her old treaties with the allied states, and especially the convention with Russia in 1793. So far as precedent and tradition went, England's case was unimpeachable. She was called upon to surrender, not a new pretension, but an old right important to her military position. "I have no hesitation," said Fox, Pitt's great opponent, "in saying that, as a general proposition, 'free bottoms do not make free goods;' and that, as an axiom, it is supported neither by the law of nations nor by common-sense."[2]

At this time the British navy was superior to the combined forces of all Europe. A fleet, of which Nelson was the animating spirit though not the nominal head, entered the Baltic. Denmark was struck down on the 2d of April, 1801; and this blow, coinciding with the murder of the Czar Paul, dissolved a coalition more menacing in appearance than in reality. The young man who succeeded to the Russian throne met with dignity the imposing attitude of Nelson, now left in chief command; but he had not inherited his father's fantastic ambitions, and the material interests of Russia in that day pointed to peace with Great Britain. The treaty, signed June 5, 1801,[3] permitted the neutral to trade from port to port on the coast of a nation at war; but renounced, on the part of Russia, the claim that the neutral flag covered the enemy's goods. On the other hand Great Britain admitted that property of a belligerent, sold *bonâ fide* to a neutral, became neutral in character and as such not liable to seizure; but from the operation of this admission obtained the special exception of produce from the hostile colonies.[4] This, Russia conceded, could not be carried directly from the colony to the mother country, even though it had become

---

[1] Speech of February 2, 1801.   [2] Speech of March 25, 1801.
[3] Annual Register, 1801; State Papers, p. 212.   [4] Ibid., p. 217.

neutral property by a real sale; and similarly the direct trade from the mother country to the colony was renounced.   Great Britain thus obtained an explicit acknowledgment of the Rule of 1756 from the most formidable of the maritime powers, and strengthened her hands for the approaching dispute with the United States. In return, she abandoned the claim, far more injurious to Russia, to seize naval stores as contraband of war.   Four months later, hostilities between Great Britain and France also ceased.

The maritime commercial interests, both of belligerents and neutrals, received convincing and conspicuous illustration from this, the first of the two sea wars growing out of the French Revolution.   It was the interest of the neutrals to step in and take up the trade necessarily abandoned, to a greater or less degree, by the belligerents; and it was also useful to both parties to the war that they should do so.   But it was very much less to the advantage of the more purely maritime state than it was to its antagonist; for not only did she need help less, but such temporary changes in the course of trade tend to become permanent.   The immediate gain may become a final and irretrievable loss.   Hence Great Britain is seen to yield readily the restrictions of the Navigation Act, wherever it is clearly advisable to avail herself of neutral seamen or neutral carriers; but the concession goes no further than immediately necessary, and is always expressly guarded as temporary.   The relaxation is a purely warlike measure, and she is perfectly consistent in refusing to allow it to her enemies.   Every slackening of the Navigation Act was a violation in principle of the Rule of 1756,[1] which she was quite content to have her enemy imitate; as the big boy at school offers the small one the opportunity of

---

[1] The *principle* of the Rule of 1756, it will be remembered, was that the neutral had no right to carry on, for a belligerent, a trade from which the latter excluded him in peace.

returning an injury in kind. France might employ
neutrals contrary to what Great Britain claimed as the
law of nations, as the latter herself did; but there was the
difference that Great Britain could put a stop to the
operations favorable to her opponent, while France could
only partially impede those that advantaged hers. It was,
therefore, clearly the policy of the British to yield nothing
to neutrals except when they could not avoid it, and then
explicitly to assert the principle, while conceding a relaxation; they thus kept control over the neutral trade,
and impeded operations that both helped their enemy
and might also supplant their own commerce. In the
latter part of the war, as the purpose of France to cripple
their trade took shape, and the exclusion of British goods
from the Continent became an evident and avowed intention, the ministry strengthened itself with the reflection
that the measure was impracticable so long as neutral
'bottoms abounded; but a few months later the denial of
intercourse between hostile nations and their colonies by
neutral intermediaries was inserted in the Russian treaty.
The intention to use neutrals to the utmost extent desirable for British interests thus coincided with the determination to stop a traffic esteemed contrary to them.
The permission to neutrals, by the orders of January,
1798, to carry the produce of French and Dutch colonies
to Great Britain, when they were threatened with seizure
if they sailed with the same for France or Holland, illustrates both motives of action; while it betrays the gradual
shaping of the policy — which grew up over against
Bonaparte's Continental System — of forcing neutrals
to make England the storehouse and toll-gate of the
world's commerce. Superficially, Great Britain seems
rather to relax toward neutrals between 1793 and 1801;
but the appearance is only superficial. The tendencies
that issued in the ever famous Orders in Council of 1807
were alive and working in 1798.

The question for British statesmen to determine, therefore, was how far to acquiesce in the expansion of
neutral trade, and where to draw their line,— always a
difficult task, dependent upon many considerations and
liable to result in inconsistencies, real or apparent. For
France the problem was less intricate. Her commerce
even before the war was chiefly in foreign hands;[1] she
had therefore little cause to fear ultimate injury by concessions. Immediate loss by neutral competition was
impossible, for the British navy left her no ships to lose.
Hence it was her interest to avail herself of neutral carriers to the fullest extent, to recognize that the freer their
operations the better for her, and that, even could restrictions upon their carrying for her enemy be enforced, the
result would be to compel the British people to develop
further their own merchant shipping. Every blow at a
neutral was really, even though not seemingly, a blow for
Great Britain. In a general way this was seen clearly
enough, and a policy favoring neutrals was traditional in
France, but the blind passions of the Revolution overthrew
it. To use the vigorous words of a deputy: "The French
people is the victim of an ill-devised scheme, of a too
blind trust in commerce-destroying, *an auxiliary measure,*
which, to be really useful, should strike only the enemy,
and not reach the navigation of neutrals and allies, and
still less paralyze the circulation and export of our
agriculture and of the national industries."[2] Such were
the results of the direct action of successive French governments, and of the indirect embarrassment caused by
the delays and inconsistencies of the executive and the
tribunals. It was thought that neutrals could be coerced
by French severities into resisting British restrictions,

[1] By a report submitted to the National Convention, July 3, 1793, it appears that in the years 1787–1789 two tenths only of French commerce was
done in French bottoms. In 1792, the last of maritime peace, three tenths
was carried by French ships. (Moniteur, 1793, p. 804.)

[2] Moniteur, An vii. p. 582 ; Arnould's speech.

whether countenanced or not by international law. But Great Britain, though a hard taskmaster, did not so lay her burdens as to lose services which were essential to her, nor compel a resistance that under the military conditions was hopeless; and the series of wild measures, which culminated in the law of January 18, 1798, only frightened neutrals from French coasts, while leaving Great Britain in full control of the sea. The year 1797 saw the lowest depression of British trade; coincidently with the law of January 18 began a development, which, at first gradual, soon became rapid, and in which the neutrals driven from France bore an increasing proportion.

The short peace of Amiens lasted long enough to indicate how thoroughly Great Britain, while using neutrals, had preserved her own maritime advantages intact. The preliminaries were signed October 1, 1801, and war was again declared May 16, 1803; but, notwithstanding the delays in paying off the ships of war, and the maintenance of an unusually large number of seamen in the peace establishment, the neutral shipping employed fell from twenty-eight per cent, in 1801, to eighteen and a half per cent in 1802.

On the outbreak of the second war Napoleon reverted at once to the commercial policy of the Convention and the Directory. On the 20th of June, 1803, a decree was issued by him directing the confiscation of any produce of the British colonies, and of any manufactures of Great Britain, introduced into France. Neutral vessels arriving were required to present a certificate from the French consul at the port of embarkation, certifying that the cargo was in no part of British origin. The same measure was forcibly carried out in Holland, though nominally an independent state;[1] and the occupation of Hanover, while dictated also by the general principle of injuring Great

[1] Annual Register, 1804. State Papers, p. 286.

Britain as much as possible, had mainly in view the closure of the Elbe and the Weser to British commerce. Beyond this, however, Bonaparte being then engrossed with the purpose of a direct attack by armed force upon the British islands, the indirect hostilities upon their commercial prosperity were, for the moment, neglected.

At the same period Great Britain began to feel that neutral rivalry was being carried too far for her own welfare, and determined to tighten the reins previously slackened. She obtained from Sweden in July, 1803, a special concession, allowing her to arrest Swedish vessels laden with naval stores for France, and to purchase the cargoes at a fair price, — a stipulation identical with that about provisions in Jay's treaty; and when the French occupation of Hanover excluded her ships from the Elbe and Weser, she by a blockade of the rivers shut out neutrals also. But it was in the West Indies, so long a fruitful source of wealth, that the pressure of neutral competition was most heavily felt. The utter ruin of San Domingo, and the embarrassments of the other islands hostile to Great Britain, had in the former war combined with the dangers of the seas to raise the price of colonial produce on the Continent,[1] and, consequently, to give a great development to the British growth of sugar and coffee, the transport of which was confined by law to British vessels. The planters, the shipping business, and the British merchants dealing with the West Indies, together with the various commercial interests and industries connected with them, all participated in the benefits of this traffic, which supplied over one fourth of the imports of the kingdom, and took off besides a large amount

---

[1] The exports of the French West India islands in 1788 amounted to $52,000,000, of which $40,000,000 were from San Domingo alone. (Traité. d'Économie Politique et de Commerce des Colonies, par P. F. Page. Paris, An 9 (1800) p. 15.) This being for the time almost wholly lost, the effect upon prices can be imagined.

of manufactures. As production increased, however, and prices lowered, the West India business began to feel keenly the competition by the produce of the hostile islands, exported by American merchants.

Of the extent of this commerce, and of its dependence upon the interruption, by Great Britain, of the ordinary channels for French and Dutch trade, a few figures will give an idea. In 1792, before the war, the United States exported to Europe 1,122,000 pounds of sugar, and 2,136,742 of coffee; in 1796, 35,000,000 of sugar and 62,000,000 of coffee; in 1800, 82,000,000 of sugar and 47,000,000 coffee. In 1803, during the short peace, the exports fell to 20,000,000 of sugar and 10,000,000 coffee; in 1804, a year of war, they again rose to 74,000,000 sugar, and 48,000,000 coffee. The precise destination cannot be given; but the trade between France and her West India Islands, carried on by American ships, amounted in 1805 to over $20,000,000, of which only $6,000,000 were United States produce. In like manner the trade with Holland was over $17,000,000, of which $2,000,000 were of American origin.

Upon the return of Mr. Pitt to power, in 1804, the attempt was made to strengthen the fabric of British commercial prosperity in the Caribbean, by an extension of the system of free ports in the different colonies; by means of which, and of their large merchant shipping, the British collected in their own hands, by both authorized and contraband traffic, so much of the carrying trade of this region, extending their operations to the mainland as well as throughout the islands. More, however, was needed to restrain the operations of the Americans, who, by reducing the price of coffee on the Continent, diminished the re-exportation from Great Britain, thus affecting the revenue of the kingdom and the profits of the planters; and who also, by acting as carriers, interfered with the accumulations at the free ports and the consequent employment of British ships. All the classes interested joined in urging the government to find some relief; and the clamor was increased by a sense of indignation at the tricks by which belligerent rights were believed to be evaded by the Americans. The Rule of 1756 did not allow the latter to carry their cargoes direct to Europe; but, as the trade winds compelled vessels to run to the northward until they reached the westerly winds prevailing in the higher latitudes, no great delay was involved in making an American port, or even in trans-shipping the cargo to a vessel bound for Europe.[1] Great Britain admitted that articles of hostile origin, but become neutral property, could be carried freely to the neutral country; and, when so imported, became part of the neutral stock and could then be freely re-exported to a hostile state.

The question of a *bonâ fide* importation, like all others involving a question of intention, could be determined only by the character of the transactions attending it; but it was held generally that actual landing and storage, with payment of the duties, was sufficient proof, unless rebutted by other circumstances. Early in the war following the peace of Amiens, the British courts awoke to the fact that the duties paid on goods so imported were simply secured by a bond, and that on re-exportation a drawback was given, so that a very small percentage of the nominal duties was actually paid.[2] Upon this ground a ship was condemned in May, 1805, and great numbers

---

[1] An American vessel arrived in Marblehead May 29, landed her cargo on the 30th and 31st, reloaded, and cleared June 3. (Robinson's Admiralty Reports, vol. v. p. 396.)

[2] In the case of the brig "Aurora," Mr. Madison, the Secretary of State, wrote: "The duties were paid or secured, according to law, in like manner as they are required to be secured on a like cargo meant for home consumption; when reshipped, the duties were drawn back with a deduction of three and a half per cent (on them), as is permitted to imported articles in all cases." (Am. State Papers, vol. ii. p. 732.)

In the case of the American ship "William," captured and sent in, on duties to the amount of $1,239 the drawback was $1,211. (Robinson's Ad-of American vessels carrying colonial produce to Europe were seized and brought into port, as well as others proceeding from the United States to the West Indies, with cargoes originating in the mother countries; and when, in the opinion of the court, the duties had been only nominally paid, they were condemned. It is hard to see the soundness of an objection to these decisions, based on the validity of the payments; but the action of the British government is open to severe censure in that no warning was given of its purpose no longer to accept, as proof of importation, the payment of duties by bond, on which drawback was given. Whether it had known the law of the United States or not, that law had been open to it, and ignorance of its provisions was due not to any want of publicity, but to the carelessness of British authorities. Under the circumstances, the first seizures were little short of robbery.

The reclamations of the United States met with little attention during Pitt's brief second administration; but after his death, in January, 1806, and the accession to office of Grenville and Fox, a more conciliatory attitude was shown,— especially by the latter, who became Minister of Foreign Affairs. Favorably inclined to the Americans since his opposition to the policy of the Revolutionary War, he seemed desirous of conceding their wishes; but the pressure from without, joined to opposition within the ministry, prevented a frank reversal of the course pursued. Instead of the Rule of 1756, Fox obtained an Order in Council, dated May 16, 1806, placing the coast of the Continent, from Brest to the Elbe, in a state of blockade. The blockade, however, was only to be enforced strictly between the mouth of the Seine and Ostend. Into ports between those two points no neutral would be admitted

miralty Reports, vol. v. p. 396.) In the celebrated case of the " Essex," with which began the seizures in 1804, on duties amounting to $5,278, the drawback was $5,080. (Ibid., 405)

on any pretext, and, if attempting to enter, would be condemned; but on either side, neutral ships could go in and out freely, provided they "had not been laden at any port belonging to his Majesty's enemies, or, if departing, were not destined to any port belonging to his Majesty's enemies." The wording of the order was evidently framed to avoid all question as to the origin of cargoes, upon which the Rule of 1756 hinged. Not the origin of the cargo, but the port of lading, determined the admission of the neutral ship to the harbors partially blockaded; and if to them, then, *a fortiori*, to all open ports of the enemy. On the other hand, the strict blockade already established of the Elbe and Weser was by this order partially relieved, in the expectation that neutrals would carry British manufactures to those northern markets. In short, the Order was a compromise, granting something both to the mercantile interest and to the Americans, though not conceding the full demands of either. It is at best doubtful whether the British were able to establish an effective blockade over the extent of coast from Brest to the Elbe, but the United States and Napoleon had no doubts whatever about it; and it thus fell, by a singular irony of fate, to the most liberal of the British statesmen, the friend of the Americans and of Napoleon, as almost the last act of his life, to fire the train which led to the Berlin and Milan decrees, to the Orders in Council of 1807, and to the war with the United States six years later.

Fox died on the 13th of September, 1806, and was succeeded as Minister of Foreign Affairs by Lord Howick. On the 25th of the same month the partial restrictions still imposed on the Elbe and the Weser were removed; so that neutral ships, even though from the ports of an enemy of Great Britain, were able to enter. In the mean time, war had broken out between France and Prussia; the battle of Jena was fought October 14, and on the 26th Napoleon entered Berlin. The battle of Trafalgar, a twelvemonth before, had shattered all his confidence in the French navy and destroyed his hopes of directly invading Great Britain. On the other hand the short campaign of 1805 had overthrown the Austrian power, and that of 1806 had just laid Prussia at his feet. The dream of reducing Great Britain by the destruction of her commercial prosperity, long floating in his mind, now became tangible, and was formulated into the phrase that he "would conquer the sea by the land." Two of the great military monarchies were already prostrate. Spain, Holland, Italy, and the smaller German states were vassals, more or less unwilling, but completely under his control; there seemed no reason to doubt that he could impose his will on the Continent and force it to close every port to British trade. On the 21st of November, 1806, the emperor issued the famous Berlin Decree; and then, having taken the first in the series of fated steps which led to his ruin, he turned to the eastward and plunged with his army into the rigors of a Polish winter to fulfil his destiny.

CHAPTER XVIII.

THE WARFARE AGAINST COMMERCE, 1806–1812.

THE BERLIN AND MILAN DECREES OF NAPOLEON, 1806 AND 1807. — THE BRITISH ORDERS IN COUNCIL, 1807–1809. — ANALYSIS OF THE POLICY OF THESE MEASURES OF THE TWO BELLIGERENTS. — OUTLINE OF CONTEMPORARY LEADING EVENTS.

NAPOLEON'S Berlin decree alleged many reasons and contained many provisions; but the essential underlying idea was to crush the commerce of Great Britain by closing the Continent to her products of every kind.[1] The pretext was found in the Order in Council of May 16, 1806, issued by the ministry of Grenville and Fox, putting the coast of the Continent from Brest to the Elbe under blockade. Napoleon asserted that the right to blockade applied only to fortified, not to commercial, ports, which was not true; and further, that the united forces of Great Britain were unable to maintain so extensive an operation, which, if not certainly true, was at least plausible. Retaliating an abuse, if it were one, with a yet greater excess, the Berlin decree began by declaring the British islands blockaded, at a time when the emperor could not keep a ship at sea, except as a fugitive from the omnipresent fleets of his enemy. From this condition of phantom blockade it resulted that all commerce with the British Islands was forbidden; and consequently all merchandise exported from them, having been unlawfully carried, became good prize. Vessels from Great Britain could not be admitted into French ports. Further, as the

---

[1] The text of the Berlin decree can be found among the series beginning in American State Papers, vol. iii. p. 262.

British refused to surrender the old rule, by which the goods of individual enemies at sea were liable to capture, Napoleon decreed that not only the property of individual Englishmen on the Continent was to be seized, but also that of individual neutrals, if of British origin. The preamble ended with a clause defining the duration of the edict, by which the emperor burned his ships, laying down conditions which Great Britain would never accept until at her last gasp. "The present decree shall be considered as a fundamental principle of the Empire, until England has acknowledged that the law of war is one and the same on the land as on the sea; that it cannot be extended to private property of whatever kind, nor to the person of individuals not in the profession of arms, and that the right of blockade must be restricted to fortified places, actually invested by sufficient forces."

Having launched his missile, Napoleon became at once engaged in the campaign against Russia. The bloody and doubtful battle of Eylau was fought on the 8th of February, 1807, and for the next few months the emperor was too busily engaged, holding on by his teeth on the banks of the Vistula, to superintend the working of his decree.[1] Immediately upon its promulgation in Paris, the American minister demanded an explanation on several points from the Minister of Marine, who replied that he did not understand it to make any alterations in the laws respecting maritime captures, and that an American vessel could not be taken at sea merely on the ground that she was bound to, or coming from, a British port; this he inferred from the fact that such vessels were, by the seventh article, denied admission to French ports.[2]

---

[1] A curious indication of the dependence of the Continent upon British manufactures is afforded by the fact that the French army, during this awful winter, was clad and shod with British goods, imported by the French minister at Hamburg, in face of the Berlin decree. (Bourrienne's Memoirs, vol. vii. p. 292.)

[2] Am. State Papers, vol. ii. p. 805.

The inference, natural though it was, only showed how
elastic and slippery the terms of Napoleon's orders could
be. The whole edict, in fact, remained a dead letter
until the struggle with Russia was decided. At first,
British merchants desisted from sending to the Continent;
but, as advices showed that the decree was inoperative,
shipments by neutral vessels became as brisk as at any
time before, and so continued until August or September,
1807.[1] The battle of Friedland, resulting in the total
defeat of the Russian army, was fought on the 14th of
June; on the 22d an armistice was signed; and on
the 25th Alexander and Napoleon had their first interview upon the raft in the Niemen. On the 8th of July
was concluded the remarkable and, to Europe, threatening
Treaty of Tilsit. The czar recognized all the new states
created by the emperor, and ceded to him the maritime
positions of the Ionian Islands, and the mouths of the
Cattaro in the Adriatic; in return for which Napoleon
acquiesced in Russia's taking Finland from Sweden, and
also, under certain conditions, the European provinces of
the Turkish Empire as far as the Balkans. A further
clause, buried in the most profound secrecy, bound Russia
and France to make common cause in all circumstances;
to unite their forces by land and sea in any war they
should have to maintain; to take arms against Great
Britain, if she would not subscribe to this treaty; and to
summon, jointly, Sweden, Denmark, Portugal, and Austria
to concur in the projects of Russia and France, — that is
to say, to shut their ports to England and to declare war
against her.[2]

At the time the Berlin decree was issued, negotiations
were proceeding in London, between the United States
envoys and the British ministry, concerning the several
matters in dispute between the two countries; and on the

---

[1] Cobbett's Parl. Debates, vol. xiii. Appendix, pp. xxxiv–xlv.
[2] Thiers, Consulat et Empire, vol. vii. pp. 666–669.

31st of December, 1806, a commercial treaty was signed by the respective commissioners. The vexed question of the trade between the hostile countries and their colonies was arranged, by a stipulation that goods imported from the colonies to the United States might be re-exported, provided, after deducting the drawback, they had paid full two per cent duties, *ad valorem*, to the Treasury; and that articles coming from the mother countries might likewise be re-shipped to the colonies, provided they remained subject to one per cent duty, after recovering the drawback. These, as well as other features of the treaty, were not acceptable to the United States, and it was not ratified by that government.

Meantime the British ministry had been considering the terms of the Berlin decree, and, instead of waiting to see how far it would become operative, determined to retort by a measure of retaliation. On the 7th of January, 1807, an Order in Council was issued by the Whig ministers, which often returned to plague them in the succeeding years, when they, in opposition, were severely criticising the better known measures of the following November. The January Order, after quoting Napoleon's decree, avowed his Majesty's unwillingness to carry to extremes his undoubted right of retaliation; and therefore, for the present, went no further than to forbid all trade by neutral vessels "from one port to another, both of which ports shall belong to, or be in possession of, France or her allies, or shall be so far under their control as that British vessels may not freely trade thereat." [1] The direct object of this step was to stop the coastwise trade in Europe; its principle was the right of retaliation; in its effect, it was an extension of the prohibition laid by the Rule of 1756. The latter forbade the direct trade between hostile colonies and the mother countries;

[1] Letter of Lord Howick to Mr. Monroe, Jan. 10, 1807; Am. State Papers, vol. iii. p. 5.

the order of January, 1807, extended the restriction to trade between any two hostile ports. It bore particularly hard upon American ships, which were in the habit of going from place to place in Europe, either seeking the best markets or gathering a cargo. Under it, "American trade in the Mediterranean was swept away by seizures and condemnations, and that in other seas threatened with the same fate." [1]

Matters were in this state when Napoleon returned to Paris at the end of July, full of his projects against Great Britain, and against neutrals as the abettors of her prosperity. His aims were not limited to crushing her by commercial oppression; in the not distant future he intended to seize the navies of Europe and combine them in a direct assault upon her maritime power. On the 19th of July, while he was still at Dresden, Portugal was notified that she must choose between war with France or with Great Britain; and on the 31st, from Paris, a similar intimation was given to Denmark. [2] To constrain the latter, a corps under Bernadotte was collecting on her frontiers; while another, under Junot, was assembling in the south of France to invade Portugal. But in both countries Napoleon was anticipated by Great Britain. The ministry had received certain information [3] of the secret articles agreed to at Tilsit, and foresaw the danger of allowing the two navies of Denmark and Portugal to fall into the hands of the emperor. Early in August twenty-five sail-of-the-line entered the Baltic, convoying transports with twenty-seven thousand troops; the island on which Copenhagen stands was invested by the ships, and the town itself by the army. The Danish government

[1] President's Message to Congress, Oct. 27, 1807 ; Am. State Papers, vol. iii. p. 5.

[2] Correspondance de Napoléon.

[3] British Declaration of September 25, 1807, — a paper which ably and completely vindicates the action of Great Britain ; Annual Register, 1807, p. 735.

was then summoned to surrender its fleet into the safe keeping of Great Britain, a pledge being offered that it, and all other maritime equipment delivered, should be held only as a deposit and restored at a general peace. The offer being refused, the city was bombarded from the 2d to the 5th of September, at the expiration of which time the terms demanded were yielded, the British took possession of eighteen sail-of-the-line besides a number of frigates, stripped the dock-yards of their stores, and returned to England. The transaction has been visited with the most severe, yet uncalled-for, condemnation. The British ministry knew the intention of Napoleon to invade Denmark, to force her into war, and that the fleet would soon pass into his hands, if not snatched away. They avoided the mistake made by Pitt, in seizing the Spanish frigates in 1804; for the force sent to Copenhagen was sufficient to make opposition hopeless and to justify submission. To have receded before the obstinacy of the Danish government would have been utter weakness.

In Portugal Great Britain had to deal with a friendly nation, instead of the hostile prepossessions of Denmark. The French corps of invasion, under Junot, entered Spain on its way to Portugal on the 17th of October. Under the urgent and unsparing orders of Napoleon it made a march of extreme suffering with great rapidity, losing most of its numbers by the way from privation, exposure, or straggling; but when the handful that kept together entered Lisbon on the 30th of November, it found the Portuguese fleet gone, and that the court and its treasure had departed with it. The British government had for some time past expected such an attempt by Napoleon, and at the critical moment a squadron on the spot determined the vacillating regent to withdraw to Brazil.

Though foiled in his endeavors to seize the fleets, Napoleon had succeeded in formally closing the ports of the two countries to the introduction of British goods; while the bombardment at Copenhagen had served as a colorable pretext for the declaration of hostility against Great Britain made by Russia on the 20th of October. The mediation proposed by the czar had already been refused by the British ministry, unless the articles of the Treaty of Tilsit were first communicated to it;[1] but those articles were not of a character to bear such an exposure. Prussia, under the compulsion of the two empires, closed her ports against Great Britain by a proclamation dated September 2d; no navigation nor trade with England or her colonies was to be permitted, either in British or in neutral vessels.[2] Austria also acceded to the Continental System, and excluded British goods from her borders.[3] In Italy, the new kingdom of Etruria showed little zeal in enforcing Napoleon's commands to co-operate in his measures; the British carried on commerce at Leghorn, as freely as at any port in their own country. By the emperor's orders the viceroy of Italy therefore took possession of the city; and at the same time French detachments entered also the Papal States, occupied their coasts, and drove the British from them. Joseph Bonaparte being already king of Naples, the control of Napoleon and the exclusion of his enemies were thus extended over both coasts of Italy. Turkey being at this time involved in hostilities with Great Britain, the emperor was able to assert that " England sees her merchandise repelled by all Europe; and her ships, loaded with useless wealth, seek in vain, from the Sound to the Hellespont, a port open to receive them."[4] Decrees applying extreme rigor to the examination of vessels entering the Elbe and the Weser were issued on the 6th of August and 13th of November.[5]

---

[1] Annual Register, 1807. State Papers, p. 771.
[2] Ibid., p. 739.
[3] Lanfrey's Napoleon (French ed.), vol. iv. p. 153.
[4] Corr. de Nap., vol. xv. p. 659.
[5] Annual Register, 1807, p. 777.

Napoleon had a special grudge against the two Hanseatic cities, Bremen and Hamburg, which had long mocked his efforts to prevent the introduction of British merchandise to the Continent; for which the commercial aptitudes of their merchants, their extensive intelligence abroad, and their noble rivers, afforded peculiar facilities. Despite all these efforts and the external appearances of universal submission, there still occurred wide-spread evasions of the emperor's orders, to which allusion must be made later. It is necessary, before doing so, to give the contemporary measures of other nations, in order that the whole situation, at once of public regulation and private disobedience, together with the final results, may come distinctly before the reader.

Great as was the power of Napoleon, it ceased, like that of certain wizards, when it reached the water. Enemies and neutrals alike bowed to his invincible armies and his superb genius when he could reach them by land; but beyond the water there was one enemy, Great Britain, and one neutral, America, whom he could not directly touch. The spirit of his course toward England and his initiatory steps have been given; it remained now to define his action toward the United States. Weak as the latter was, feeble to humiliation as had been the course of its government hitherto, and although the prepossessions of the party in power were undoubtedly strongly against Great Britain, the question was one of immense importance; but the emperor, who respected nothing but force, failed so to realize it. He stood just where the Directory stood at the end of 1797, every enemy but Great Britain overthrown, but seeing her defiant still and prosperous. Napoleon, however, had, what the Directory had not, experimental evidence of the results of such restrictions upon neutrals as were imposed by the law of January 18, 1798. It was possible to ascribe the disastrous effects to France of that measure, and its total failure to achieve the object

intended, to one of two totally distinct causes. Either the
law had been inadequately enforced, owing to the feeble
executive efforts of the Directors and the comparatively
limited extent of their influence, or else it was in its
nature and essence so contrary to the true interest and
policy of France that the very limitations imposed by
defective power had saved her, and the ability to carry it
further would have ended in utter ruin. Pursued some
what further, the question became: Will it be possible,
not for France only but for all Europe, — for the concurrence of all Europe is necessary to the effectual working
of the scheme, — to ˙ dispense with the neutral carrier
(whom it is the tendency of the Berlin decree to repel)
for a length of time sufficient to ruin Great Britain ? Can
Europe forego external commerce for a longer time than
Great Britain can spare the European market ? Can the
intercourse between the continental nations be so facilitated, the accustomed routes of import and export so
modified, such changes introduced into the habits of
manufacture and consumption, as will render bearable the
demands made upon the patience of nations ? If, as the
Order in Council of January seems to indicate, Great
Britain resent the attempt to keep neutrals from her ports,
by retaliatory measures impeding their traffic with the
Continent, upon whom will these combined French and
English restrictions fall most heavily ? — upon the state
having a large body of merchant ships, to which neutrals
are the natural rivals; or upon the nations whose shipping is small, and to whom therefore neutrals are useful,
if not necessary, auxiliaries ?

In a commercial war, as in any other, the question must
be faced whether with ten thousand it is possible to meet
him who is coming with twenty thousand. As a matter of
fact, while Napoleon was contemplating a measure which
would most injuriously affect neutrals, already largely
employed in transporting British goods, the jealousy of

British merchants and statesmen was keenly excited by the growth of this neutral carrying trade,[1] and they were casting about for a pretext and a means to cripple it. The Berlin decree revived the clamor of these men, who, being then in opposition, had condemned the Order of January, 1807, for not carrying retaliation far enough, and for directing it upon the coasting trade, which could only partially be reached, instead of upon the neutral carriage of colonial goods, which lay open everywhere to the British navy. A change of ministry in the latter part of March, 1807, brought this party again into power, after an absence from it of fourteen months since the death of Pitt. In the mean time, however, the decree had remained inoperative, through the absence of Napoleon in Poland, the decisions of the Minister of Marine as to its scope, and the connivance of the local authorities everywhere in its neglect. No further steps therefore had been taken by the new British ministry up to the time of the emperor's return to Paris. The latter at first only issued some additional regulations of a municipal character, to ensure a stricter observance, but he was soon called upon to give a momentous decision. The opinion of the Minister of Marine, as to the meaning of certain clauses of the decree,[2] was submitted to him by the Minister of Justice; and he stated that the true original intention was that French armed vessels should seize and bring into port neutrals having on board any goods of British origin, even though at the time neutral property. As to whether they should also arrest neutrals for the simple reason that they were going to, or coming from, the British Islands, his Majesty reserved his decision. This dictum of the emperor, which threw to the winds the ruling of the Min-

---

[1] See, for example, Cobbett's Parl. Debates, vol. viii. pp. 636 and 641–644; vol. ix. p. 87, petition of West India planters; p. 100, speech of Mr. Hibbert, and p. 684, speech of Mr. George Rose.

[2] See *ante*, p. 273.

ister of Marine, was given to the prize courts on the 18th
of September, 1807, and shortly afterward the latter
acted upon it in the case of an American ship wrecked
upon the French coast; that part of her cargo which was
of British origin was ordered to be sold for the benefit of
the state.[1] The effect of Napoleon's pronouncements was
at once seen in Great Britain. The insurance of neutral
ships bound to continental ports, especially to those of
Holland and Hamburg, rose from four guineas in August
to eight and twelve in October, and some insurers refused
to take risks even at twenty-five and thirty. In the two
months of September and October sixty-five permits were
issued by the Custom House to re-land and store cargoes
that had actually been shipped for the Continent.[2] The Tory
ministry now had the pretext it wanted for a far-reaching
and exhaustive measure of retaliation.

Napoleon's decisions of September 18 were communicated to the Congress of the United States on December
18 by the President; who at the same time transmitted a
proclamation from the king of Great Britain, dated October 16, directing the impressment of British seamen found
serving on board any foreign merchant ship.[3] In view of
the dangers to which American vessels were exposed by
the action of the two belligerents, an embargo was recommended, to insure their safety by keeping them in their
own ports; the real purpose, however, being to retaliate
upon Great Britain, in pursuance of the policy of a Non-
Importation Act directed against that country, which had
gone into effect the previous July. An Act of Embargo
was accordingly at once passed, and was approved on the
22d of December.[4] All registered vessels belonging to
the United States were forbidden to depart from the ports

[1] Am. State Papers, vol. iii. pp. 245–247.
[2] Cobbett's Parl. Debates, vol. xiii. Appendix. pp. xxxiv–xlv.
[3] Am. State Papers, vol. iii. pp. 23, 24.
[4] Annals of Congress, 1807, p. 2814.

in which they were then lying, except upon giving bond that their cargoes would be landed in another port of the country. This continued in force throughout the year 1808 and until March 1, 1809, when it was repealed; and for it was substituted a Non-Intercourse Act,[1] which allowed the merchant ships of the United States to go abroad in search of employment and to traffic between their own and other countries, except Great Britain and France and the colonies occupied by them, which were wholly forbidden to American vessels. They not only could not clear from home for those countries, but they were required to give bond that they would not, during the voyage, enter any of their ports, nor be directly or indirectly engaged in any trade with them. French or British ships entering a port of the United States were to be seized and condemned. This act was to continue in force until the end of the next session of Congress; and it accordingly remained the law governing the intercourse of the United States with Great Britain and France until May, 1810.

On the 11th of November, 1807, were published the great retaliatory measures of Great Britain, which for the moment filled the cup of neutrals. Setting forth the Berlin Decree as the justifying ground for their action, the Orders in Council of that date[2] proclaimed a paper blockade, of the barest form and most extensive scope, of all enemies' ports. "All ports and places of France and her allies, or of any other country at war with his Majesty, and all other ports or places in Europe from which, although not at war with his Majesty, the British flag is

[1] Annals of Congress, 1808–1809, p. 1824.

[2] There were three Orders in Council published on the 11th of November, all relating to the same general subject. They were followed by three others, issued November 25, further explaining or modifying the former three. The author, in his analysis, has omitted reference to particular ones; and has tried to present simply the essential features of the whole, suppressing details.

excluded, and all ports in the colonies of his Majesty's enemies, *shall from henceforth be subject to the same restrictions*, in point of trade and navigation, *as if the same were actually blockaded in the most strict and rigorous manner.*" All trade in hostile colonial produce was likewise declared unlawful for neutrals.

An actual blockade, such as is here mentioned, requires the presence off the blockaded port of a force sufficient to make entrance or departure manifestly dangerous; in which case a vessel attempting to pass in either direction is, by that common consent of nations called International Law, justly liable to capture. To place such a force before each of the many and widely scattered harbors embraced by these Orders, was evidently beyond the power of even the vast numbers of the British navy. The object which could not be attained by the use of means acknowledged to be lawful, the British ministry determined to compass by sheer force, by that maritime supremacy which they unquestionably wielded, and which they could make effectual to the ends they had in view, namely: to maintain the commerce and shipping of Great Britain, upon which her naval strength depended, to force the enemy's trade to pass through her ports, and thus to raise her revenues to the point necessary to her salvation in the life and death struggle in which she was embarked.[1]

The entire suppression of trade with the restricted coasts, whether by neutral carriers or in the articles of import or export the world needed, was in no sense whatever the object of the British ministers. To retaliate on

[1] The attention paid to sustaining the commerce of Great Britain was shown most clearly in the second Order of November 11, which overrode the Navigation Act by permitting *any* friendly vessel to import articles the produce of hostile countries; a permission extended later (by Act of Parliament, April 14, 1808) to *any* ship, "belonging to *any* country, *whether in amity with his Majesty or not.*" Enemy's merchant ships were thus accepted as carriers for British trade with restricted ports. See Am. State Papers, vol iii. pp. 270, 282.

their enemy was the first aim, to make him suffer as he had meant to make them; but, withal, to turn his own measures against him, so that while he was straitened, Great Britain should reap some amelioration for her own troubles. Throughout this stormy and woeful period, the instinct of the British nation recognized that the hearts of the continental peoples were with them rather than with Napoleon,— and for much the same reason that the United States, contrary alike to the general interests of mankind and to her own, sided upon the whole, though by no means unanimously, against Great Britain. In either case the immediate oppressor was the object of hatred. Throughout the five years or more that the Continental blockade was in force, the Continental nations saw the British trying everywhere, with more or less success, to come to their relief,— to break through the iron barrier which Napoleon had established. During great part of that time a considerable intercourse did prevail; and the mutual intelligence thus maintained made clear to all parties the community of interests that bound them together, notwithstanding the political hostilities. Nothing appears more clearly, between the lines of the British diplomatic correspondence, than the conviction that the people were ready to further their efforts to circumvent the measures of Napoleon.

Keeping in view the purpose of making the United Kingdom the centre and warehouse of the world's commerce, it was evident that, provided this end — the chief object of the Orders in Council — were attained, the greater the commerce of the outside world was, the greater would be the advantage, or toll, resulting to Great Britain. The Orders therefore contained, besides the general principle of blockade, certain exceptions, narrow in wording but wide in application. By the first, neutrals were permitted to trade directly between their own country and the hostile colonies. They were also

allowed to trade direct between the latter and the free
ports of the British colonies, which were thus enabled,
in their degree, to become the centres of local commerce,
as Britain herself was to be the entrepôt of European and
general commerce.

The second exception, which was particularly odious to
neutrals, permitted the latter to go direct from a port of
the United Kingdom to a restricted hostile port, although
they might not start from their own country for the same,
nor for any other place in Europe from which the British
flag was excluded.   Conversely, neutrals were at liberty
to sail from any port of his Majesty's enemies forbidden
to them by the Orders, provided they went direct to some
port in Europe belonging to Great Britain;[1] but they
might not return to their own land without first stopping
at a British port.

Such, stripped of their verbiage, appears to be the gist
of the Orders in Council of November 11, 1807.   Neutrals
might not trade directly with any ports in Europe not open
to British ships; but they might trade with them by going
first to a British port, there landing their cargo, reship-
ping it subject to certain duties,[2] and thence proceeding
to a hostile port.   The same process was to be observed
on the return voyage; it might not be direct home, but
must first be to Great Britain.   The commerce of the Continent thus paid toll, going and coming; or, to repeat the
words of the ministry, there was for the enemy "no trade
except through Great Britain."   British cruisers were

---

[1] Gibraltar and Malta are especially named, they being natural depots
for the Mediterranean, whence a large contraband trade was busied in
evading Napoleon's measures. The governors of those places were authorized to license even enemy's vessels, if unarmed and not over one hundred
tons burthen, to carry on British trade, contrary to the emperor's decrees.

[2] On March 28, 1808, an Act of Parliament was passed, fixing the duties
on exportations from Great Britain in furtherance of the provisions of the
Orders. This Act contained a clause excepting American ships, ordered
into British ports, from the tonnage duties laid on those which entered
voluntarily.

"instructed to warn any vessel which shall have com-
menced her voyage prior to any notice of this Order, to
discontinue it; and to proceed instead to some port in
this kingdom, or to Gibraltar or Malta; and any vessel
which, after being so warned, shall be found in the prosecution of a forbidden voyage, shall be captured." Vessels
which in obedience to the warning came into a British
port were to be permitted, after landing their cargo, to
"re-port it for exportation, and allowed to proceed to their
original port of destination, or to any other port at amity
with his Majesty, upon receiving a certificate from the
collector of the port" setting forth these facts; but from
this general permission to "re-port," were specially excepted "sugar, coffee, wine, brandy, snuff, and tobacco,"
which could be exported to a restricted port only "under
such conditions as his Majesty, by any license to be
granted for that purpose, may direct." Licenses were
generally necessary for export of any foreign produce or
manufacture; while goods of British origin could be
taken to a hostile country without such license. In the
end, the export of cotton to the Continent was wholly forbidden, the object being to cripple the foreign manufactures. Upon the license requirements was soon built up
the extraordinary licensed traffic, which played so important a subordinate part in the workings both of the Orders
and of the Continental System.

Anything more humiliating and vexatious to neutrals than these Orders can scarcely be conceived.
They trampled upon all previously received law, upon
men's inbred ideas of their rights; and that by sheer
uncontrolled force, the law of the strongest. There
was also not only denial of right, but positive injury
and loss, direct and indirect. Yet it must not be for-
gotten that they were a very real and severe measure
of retaliation upon Napoleon's government; of which
a contemporary German writer had truly said it was

already wound up so tight the springs could almost
be heard to crack. It must be remembered, too, that
Great Britain was fighting for her life. The additional
expense entailed upon every cargo which reached the
Continent after passing through her ports, the expenses
of delay, of unloading and reloading, wharfage, licenses,
maintenance, fell chiefly upon the continental consumer;
upon the subjects of Napoleon, or upon those whom he
was holding in military bondage. Nor was this all. Although Great Britain was not able to blockade all the individual French or continental ports,— an inability due
more to the dangers of the sea than to the number of the
harbors,— she was able to make the approach to the French
coast exceedingly dangerous, so much so that it was more
to the interest of the ordinary trader to submit to the Orders
than to attempt to evade them; especially as, upon arriving
at a port under Napoleon's control, he found the emperor
possessed with every disposition to confiscate his cargo, if
a plausible pretext could be made. In the English Channel Great Britain controlled the approaches from the Atlantic to all the northern continental ports; and at Gibraltar
those to the Mediterranean. The Orders were therefore
by no means an empty threat. They could not but exercise a very serious influence upon the imports to the Continent, and especially upon those exotic objects of
consumption, sugar, coffee, and other tropical growths,
which had become so essential to the comfort of people;
and upon certain raw materials, such as cotton, dye-woods
and indigo. Naval stores from the Baltic for England
passed so near the French coast that they might be slipped
in by a lucky chance; but the neutral from the Atlantic,
who was found near the coast of France or Spain, had to
account for the appearances which were against him.
These obstacles to direct import tended therefore to increase prices by diminishing supplies, and combined with
the duties laid by Great Britain, upon the cargoes forced

into her ports, to raise the cost of living throughout the Continent. The embarrassments of its unfortunate inhabitants were further augmented by the difficulty of exporting their own products; and nowhere was this more keenly felt than in Russia, where the revenues of the nobility depended largely on the British demand for naval stores, and where the French alliance and the Continental System were proportionately detested.

The object of the Orders in Council was therefore twofold: to embarrass France and Napoleon by the prohibition of direct import and export trade, of all external commerce, which for them could only be carried on by neutrals; and at the same time to force into the Continent all the British products or manufactures that it could take. A preference was secured for the latter over foreign products by the license practice, which left the course of traffic to the constant manipulation of the Board of Trade. The whole system was then, and has since been, roundly abused as being in no sense a military measure, but merely a gigantic exhibition of commercial greed; but this simply begs the question. To win her fight Great Britain was obliged not only to weaken Napoleon, but to increase her own strength. The battle between the sea and the land was to be fought out on Commerce. England had no army wherewith to meet Napoleon; Napoleon had no navy to cope with that of his enemy. As in the case of an impregnable fortress, the only alternative for either of these contestants was to reduce the other by starvation. On the common frontier, the coast line, they met in a deadly strife in which no weapon was drawn. The imperial soldiers were turned into coast-guards-men to shut out Great Britain from her markets; the British ships became revenue cutters to prohibit the trade of France. The neutral carrier, pocketing his pride, offered his service to either for pay, and the other then regarded him as taking part in hostilities. The ministry, in the exi-

gencies of debate, betrayed some lack of definite conviction as to their precise aim. Sometimes the Orders were
justified as a military measure of retaliation; sometimes
the need of supporting British commerce as essential to
her life and to her naval strength was alleged; and their
opponents in either case taunted them with inconsistency.[1]
Napoleon, with despotic simplicity, announced clearly his
purpose of ruining England through her trade, and the
ministry really needed no other arguments than his
avowals. *Salus civitatis suprema lex.* To call the measures of either not military, is as inaccurate as it would be
to call the ancient practice of circumvallation unmilitary,
because the only weapon used for it was the spade.

Napoleon was not the man to accept silently the Orders
in Council. On the 27th of October he had signed the
treaty of Fontainebleau with Spain, arranging the parti-
tion of Portugal and taking thus the first step in the
invasion of the Peninsula. On November 16 he left Fontainebleau to visit his kingdom of Italy. From the
capital, Milan, he issued the decree which bears its name,
on the 17th of December, 1807. Alleging the Orders as
its motive, the Milan Decree declared that any ship which

---

[1] In a debate on the Orders, March 3, 1812, the words of Spencer Perceval,
one among the ministers chiefly responsible for them, are thus reported :
" With respect to the principle upon which the Orders in Council were
founded, he begged to state that he had always considered them as *strictly
retaliatory ;* and as far as he could understand the matter they were most
completely justified upon the principle of retaliation. . . . *The object of the
government was to protect and force the trade of this country,* which had been
assailed in such an unprecedented manner by the French decrees. If the
Orders in Council had not been issued, France would have had free colonial
trade by means of neutrals, and we should have been shut out from the Continent. . . . *The object of the Orders in Council was, not to destroy the trade of
the Continent, but to force the Continent to trade with us.*" (Cobbett's Parl.
Debates, vol. xxi. p. 1152.)

As regards the retaliatory effect upon France, Perceval stated that the
revenue from customs in France fell from sixty million francs, in 1807, to
eighteen and a half million in 1808, and eleven and a half in 1809. (Ibid.
p. 1157.)

submitted to search by a British cruiser was thereby "denationalized;" a word for which, at sea, "outlaw" is the only equivalent. It lost the character of its own country, so far as French cruisers were concerned, and was liable to arrest as a vagrant. The decree further declared that all vessels going to, or sailing from, Great Britain, were for that fact alone good prize,— a point which, under the Berlin decree, had as yet been left open. French privateers were still sufficiently numerous to make these regulations a great additional danger to ships at sea; and the decree went on to say that, when coming under the previous provisions, they should be seized whenever they entered a French port.

The two belligerents had now laid down the general lines of policy on which they intended to act. The Orders in Council received various modifications, due largely to the importance to Great Britain of the American market, which absorbed a great part of her manufactures; but these modifications, though sensibly lightening the burden upon neutrals and introducing some changes of form, in no sense departed from the spirit of the originals. The entire series was finally withdrawn in June, 1812, but too late to avert the war with the United States, which was declared in the same month. Napoleon never revoked his Berlin and Milan decrees, although by a trick he induced an over-eager President of the United States to believe that he had done so.

In the year 1808 the emperor's purpose to overthrow the Spanish monarchy, and place one of his own family upon the throne, finally matured. He left Paris on the 2d of April, and, after a long delay at Bordeaux, on the 14th reached Bayonne. There took place his meetings with the king and infante of Spain which resulted in the former resigning his crown, to be disposed of as to Napoleon might seem best. While at Bayonne, on April 17, the emperor issued an order, directing the sequestration

of all American ships which should enter the ports of
France, Italy, Holland, and the Hanse towns, as being
under suspicion of having come from Great Britain. The
justification for this step was found in the Embargo Act
of December, 1807, in consequence of which, Napoleon
argued, as such ships could not lawfully have left their
own country, they came really from England, and their
papers were fabricated.[1] Under this ruling sequestrations
continued to be made until March 23, 1810; when the Decree
of Rambouillet confiscated finally the vessels and cargoes
thus seized.[2] After May, 1810, the Non-Intercourse Act,
which had replaced the Embargo, was temporarily suspended as regarded both Great Britain and France, and
never renewed as to the latter; so the plea upon which
these confiscations had proceeded was no longer valid.

Meanwhile the emperor's plans for the Peninsula met
with unexpected reverses. An insurrection on the 2d of
May in Madrid was followed by spontaneous popular risings in all parts of the country. On the 21st of July an
army corps under General Dupont was cut off by the insurgents in Andalusia and surrendered, to the number of
eighteen thousand, at Baylen; and on the 29th the new
king of Spain, Joseph Bonaparte, fled from Madrid, which
he had only entered on the 20th. On the 1st of August a
British fleet appeared off the coast of Portugal, bearing
the first division of troops destined to•act in the Peninsula,
under the command of Sir Arthur Wellesley. On the 21st
the battle of Vimiero was fought, resulting in the defeat
of Junot; who, by the Convention of Cintra, signed on the
30th, was permitted to evacuate Portugal and was conveyed

---

[1] Correspondance de Napoléon, vol. xvii. p. 19.

[2] Mr. Henry Adams (History of the United States, 1801–1817) gives
134 as the number of American ships seized between April, 1809, and April,
1810, and estimates the value of the vessels and cargoes at $10,000,000
(Vol. v. p. 242.) The author takes this opportunity of acknowledging his
great indebtedness to Mr. Adams's able and exhaustive work, in threading the
diplomatic intricacies of this time.

to France with his army in British transports. At the same time a division of the Russian fleet which had taken refuge in Lisbon, on its return from the Mediterranean, was, by a separate convention, left in the hands of Great Britain until the conclusion of the war. The admiral had steadily refused to co-operate with Junot; in which course he probably reflected the strong feeling of the Russian upper classes against the French alliance. In consequence of these successive disasters Portugal was wholly lost, and the French army in Spain fell back to the line of the Ebro.

Napoleon realized the necessity of vigorous measures to suppress the general uprising, before it had attained organization and consistency, and determined to take the field in person; but, before removing to this distant scene of action, he thought advisable to confirm and establish his understanding with the czar, upon whose support depended so much of his position in Central Europe. The two sovereigns met for the second time, September 27, 1808, at Erfurt. The alliance formed at Tilsit was renewed; France undertook not to consent to peace until Russia obtained Finland from Sweden, Moldavia and Wallachia from Turkey; Russia guaranteed the crown of Spain to Joseph; and it was agreed that a formal proposition for peace should at once be made to England, as publicly and conspicuously as possible. The czar had already in the preceding February begun hostilities against Sweden, giving as a pretext her leaning toward Great Britain and her refusal to join with Russia and Denmark in shutting the Baltic to British fleets. Denmark also had declared war against Sweden, for carrying on which the possession of Norway then gave her facilities which she no longer has; and Prussia, on the 6th of March, had closed her ports against Swedish commerce "at the solicitation of the imperial courts of Paris and St. Petersburgh."

The vital importance of the Baltic to Great Britain,

both as the source whence her naval stores were drawn
and as a channel whereby her commerce might find a
way into the Continent remote from the active vigilance of
Napoleon, imposed upon her the necessity of strenuously
supporting Sweden. A fleet of sixty-two sail, of which
sixteen were of the line, was acordingly sent through the
Sound in April, under Sir James Saumarez, one of the
most distinguished of British admirals; who, to an unusually brilliant reputation for seamanship, activity, and
hard fighting, joined a calm and well-balanced temper,
peculiarly fitted to deal with the delicate political situation that obtained in the North during the four years of
his Baltic command. The fleet was shortly followed by
a body of ten thousand troops under the celebrated Sir
John Moore; but the rapid progress of the Russian arms
rendered this assistance abortive, and Moore was soon
transported to that scene of action in the Peninsula in
connection with which his name has been immortalized.

A joint letter, addressed to the king of Great Britain by
the allied emperors, was forwarded through the usual
channels by the foreign ministers of both powers on the
12th of October. The British reply, dated October 28,
expressed a willingness to enter into the proposed negotiations, provided the king of Sweden and the government
acting in the name of the king of Spain, then a prisoner
in the hands of Napoleon, were understood to be parties
to any negotiation in which Great Britain was engaged.
"To Spain," said the British note, "his Majesty is not
bound by any formal instrument; but his Majesty has, in
the face of the world, contracted with that nation engagements not less sacred, and not less binding upon his Majesty's mind, than the most solemn treaties." This reply
was, in one point at least, open to severe criticism for
uncalled-for insolence. To that part of the letter of the
two sovereigns which attributed the sufferings of the Continent to the cessation of maritime commerce, it was re-

torted: " His Majesty cannot be expected to hear with
unqualified regret that the system devised for the destruction of the commerce of his subjects has recoiled upon
its authors, or its instruments." Nevertheless, it is impossible to withhold admiration for the undaunted attitude of the solitary Power that ruled the sea, in the face
of the two mighty sovereigns who between them controlled
the forces of the Continent, or to refuse recognition of the
fidelity with which, against overwhelming odds, she now,
as always in the time of Pitt, refused to separate her cause
from that of her allies. The decision of the British court
was made known to Europe by a public declaration, dated
December 15, which, while expressing the same firm resolve, allowed to appear plainly the sense entertained by
the ministry of the restiveness of the Continent under the
yoke it was bearing.

The proposal to include the Spanish people in the
negotiations was rejected by both France and Russia.
Napoleon, having in the mean time returned to Paris, left
there on the 29th of October to take command of the
armies, which, to the number of over three hundred thousand men of all arms, had either entered Spain or were
rapidly converging upon it. On the 8th of November he
crossed the frontier, and on the 4th of December Madrid
surrendered. Northern Spain being overrun and subdued,
the capital having fallen without any real resistance, and
the political prestige of the insurrection being thus seriously, if not hopelessly, injured, the emperor now proposed to divide the mass of soldiers that had so far acted
under his own supreme direction. In the disorganized
and helpless condition of the Spanish people, with the
proved weakness and imbecility of the provisional governments, a dispersion that might otherwise be unwise became admissible. Army corps under his marshals were to
overrun the southern provinces of the Peninsula, while an
overwhelming force under his personal leadership was to

cross the frontier, and carry the eagles to Lisbon, in accordance with his boast made before leaving Paris. From
this determination he was turned aside by the sudden intelligence that the small body of British troops, commanded by Sir John Moore, which he supposed to be
retreating toward Lisbon, and which he expected to drive
on board the ships there, had cut loose from their connection with it, and, by a daring move to the north, were
threatening his own lines of communication with France.
Upon the receipt of this news, on the 21st of December, he
at once postponed his previous purposes to the necessity of
dislodging and driving out of Spain the little force, of
less than twenty-five thousand men, that had dared thus
to traverse his plans. Thus was Napoleon headed from
his course by an imperious military necessity, and Spain
saved at a most critical moment, by the petty army which
had come from the sea, and which had only dared to make
this move — well nigh desperate at the best — because it
knew that, in the inevitable retreat, it would find in the
sea no impassable barrier, but a hospitable host, — in truth,
its own country. The Peninsula gained the time to breathe,
which, unless under stern compulsion, Napoleon never
granted to an enemy; and the opportunity thus lost to
him never again returned.

Thus opened the year 1809. Napoleon at the head of
eighty thousand men was driving before him, through the
snows of northwestern Spain, some twenty thousand British troops, with the relentless energy that distinguished
all his movements of pursuit. In the north, Russia, having completed the conquest of Finland, was now preparing
to invade Sweden on the west of the Baltic, the king of
that country was on the point of being dethroned on account of insanity, and the policy of the nation was tending to a peace with its gigantic enemy; which the latter
refused to grant except upon the condition of joining the
alliance against Great Britain. To this Sweden was most

unwilling to accede. Her people depended wholly upon their produce of naval stores and grain and upon maritime commerce. Hence, to lose the freedom of their trade was almost tantamount to destruction, and the British ministry from the first saw that, whatever steps Sweden might be forced to take, its real wishes must be to keep open intercourse with Great Britain. From the anxious and delicate position of this small country, between these opposing claims, arose the necessity of great prudence and caution on the part of the British government, of its diplomatic representative, and of the admiral commanding the fleet. The task ultimately devolved upon the latter, when Sweden was at last forced into formal war; and to his sound judgment and self-restraint was largely due that no actual collision took place, and that, in the decisive moments of 1812, she, despite her serious causes of complaint against the czar, sided with Russia, instead of against her.

In Central Europe, Austria, since the peace of Presburg,[1] three years before, had been quietly engaged in restoring her military strength. The various changes which had taken place in Germany during that time, the establishment and growth of the Confederation of the Rhine, the destruction of the power of Prussia, the foundation of the Duchy of Warsaw, combined with the great losses of territory which she had herself undergone, had left Austria in a position that she could not possibly accept as final; while the alliance between Russia and France placed her in a state of isolation, which Napoleon had been careful to emphasize during the meeting at Erfurt. The renewal of the war between herself and France was therefore in the nature of things. The only question to be decided was when to declare it;[2] but this was a matter which Napoleon, who fully understood the political situation, was not

[1] December 26, 1805.
[2] Metternich's Memoirs, vol. i. p. 82.

in the habit of allowing an enemy to determine. He undertook his Spanish enterprise with the full knowledge that his absence; and that of his Grand Army, in the Peninsula must be short; he understood that a prolonged stay there, caused by lack of immediate and decisive success, would give Austria the opportunity she needed; but he had reasonable expectation of accomplishing his task, and returning with his army to his eastern frontiers, within a safe period of time. This hope was frustrated by the action of Sir John Moore. The year 1809 therefore opened with the prospect of war impending over the two empires. "From the frontiers of Austria to the centre of Paris," wrote Metternich, "I have found but one opinion accepted by the public,— that is, that in the spring at latest, Austria will take the field against France. This conclusion is drawn from the relative position of the two powers."[1]

Underlying the other contentions, affecting them all with the unheeded, quiet, but persistent action which ordinarily characterizes the exertions of sea power, fermenting continually in the hearts of the people, was the commercial warfare, the absence of that maritime peace for which the nations sighed. The Berlin and Milan decrees on the one side, the Orders in Council on the other, were still, at the opening of 1809, in full force. France, which especially needed the concurrence of neutral carriers, had taken away even the slight chances of reaching her ports which British cruisers might leave, by pronouncing confiscation on any ship which had submitted to a search, though it was powerless to resist. Great Britain, on the other hand, having shut out all competition with her own trade to the Continent by the blockade, which forbade direct access to neutral ships, was prepared to avail herself of every chance to force upon Europe, at any point, and by any means, neutral or other, any and all

[1] Metternich to Stadion, Jan. 11, 1809; Memoirs, vol. ii. p. 312.

merchandise, manufactured or colonial, which came from her own warehouses. For this the license system offered a means of which neutrals were only too ready to avail themselves. A British license could admit them to any port from which a British blockade excluded them; and, as it was only to be obtained legitimately in a British port, the neutral carriers, when there, naturally filled up with the most paying cargo, whatever its origin.

In the years from 1806 to 1810, as at earlier periods of the revolutionary wars, Holland and the Hanse towns competed for the profits of this indirect and often contraband trade. In June, 1806, Napoleon, in pursuance of his policy of placing members of his own family upon the thrones of the Continent, had obtained the conversion of Holland from a republic to a monarchy and bestowed its crown upon his brother Louis. The latter sought from the first to identify himself with his new subjects, and constantly withstood the commands of Napoleon in favor of their interests. Foremost among these was maritime commerce, for which geographical position and generations of habit especially fitted the Dutch. With such dispositions on the part of the king, notwithstanding the jealous watchfulness and sharp remonstrances of the emperor, evasions were frequent, and the decrees even openly disregarded on different pretences. The whole community naturally engaged in undertakings at once so consonant to its habits and so remunerative when successful. From the time the Berlin decree was issued until after the war with Austria in 1809, Napoleon's attention, though often angrily attracted by Holland and the neglect of his orders, was still too much diverted to admit of the decisive measures needed to enforce them. First, the Russian war in 1807, then the affairs of the Peninsula extending through 1808, finally the Austrian war in 1809 with his hazardous position between the battles of Essling and Wagram, accompanied as the whole period was with financial difficulties and expedients due to the straits of the empire under the cessation of maritime commerce, occupied his mind almost wholly, and allowed but partial attention to the Continental System.

Neutral ships therefore continued to be openly admitted into Holland, and the emperor's demands for their confiscation to be eluded; and there was besides much smuggling, for which the character of the coast and its nearness to England offered ample facilities. From Holland the goods usually found their way without great difficulty into France, though on two occasions Napoleon, to punish Holland for her waywardness, closed the frontier against her. "Your Majesty," wrote he to Louis, "took advantage of the moment in which I had embarrassments upon the Continent, to allow the relations between Holland and England to be resumed; to violate the laws of the blockade, the only measure by which that power can be seriously injured. I showed my dissatisfaction by forbidding France to you, and made you feel that, without having recourse to my armies, I could, by closing the Rhine, the Weser, the Scheldt, and the Meuse to Holland, place her in a position more critical than by declaring war against her. I was so isolating her as to annihilate her. The blow resounded in Holland. Your Majesty appealed to my generosity. . . . I removed the line of custom-houses; but your Majesty returned to your former system. It is true I was then at Vienna, and had a grievous war upon my hands. All the American ships which entered the ports of Holland, while they were repelled from those of France, your Majesty received. I have been obliged a second time to close my custom-houses to Dutch commerce. . . . I will not conceal my intention to re-unite Holland to France, to round off her territory, as the most disastrous blow I can deal to England." He consented, however, to suspend his action, upon condition that the existing stores of colonial merchandise were confiscated, as well as the cargoes of the American ships.[1]

The important part played in the former war by Hamburg and Bremen, as commercial centres and warehouses for continental trade, has already been mentioned. To a certain extent they still fulfilled the same function, but under greatly altered conditions. The political changes following the war of 1806 and 1807, and the presence of French troops in Prussian fortresses and throughout Northern Germany, combined to make them subservient, as Prussia was, to the emperor's wishes. In point of form the continental blockade extended throughout all this region, as in Holland; everywhere vessels and merchandise coming from Great Britain were proscribed and should be confiscated, whenever found.[2] All the shores of the North Sea, those of Denmark, and, by the co-operation of the czar, the coasts of the Baltic, shared the general prohibition. The minister of France at Hamburg found his chief occupations in either demanding subsidies — contributions in money or kind — for the French troops, or in insisting, much against his will, upon increased severity against the introduction of British goods. The distress occasioned by these stringent requirements was very great, even while Napoleon's other preoccupations lasted; but the general consent of all the people in passive resistance, the activity of smugglers, and the corruption that ever hangs about custom-houses and increases with the duties, conspired to mitigate the privations. The coasts of the

[1] Letter of Napoleon to Louis, dated Trianon, Dec. 20, 1808; Mémoires de Bourrienne, vol. viii. p. 134. Garnier's Louis Bonaparte, p. 351. The date should be 1809. On Dec. 20, 1808, Napoleon was at Madrid, in 1809 at Trianon; not to speak of the allusion to the Austrian war of 1809.

[2] Napoleon issued orders to this effect in August, 1807. Cargoes of goods such as England might furnish were sequestrated; those that could not possibly be of British origin, as naval stores and French wines, were admitted. All vessels were to be prevented from leaving the Weser. No notification of this action was given to foreign agents. See Cobbett's Political Register, 1807, pp. 857–859.

North Sea, between the mouths of the Ems, the Weser, and the Elbe, and those of Danish Holstein, low, of difficult approach for large vessels, and hence favorable to the multiplication of small boats and the operations of those having local knowledge, fostered smuggling; to which also conduced the numbers of fishermen, and the fringe of offlying islands, out of the reach of the ordinary custom-house officer.

To support this contraband trade, the British, on the 5th of September, 1807, seized Heligoland and converted it into a depot for goods waiting to be introduced into Germany or Holstein. "A garrison of six hundred men defended the island, and ships of war cruised continually in its neighborhood. From there contraband traders obtained merchandise, with which they supplied the Continent. Farmers along the coast received these smuggled goods, which were taken from them during the night and spread far and wide. The populations of the various countries aided the smugglers, joined them in opposing the revenue officers and in seducing the latter from their duty." [1] Between Holstein and Hamburg was drawn up a close line of custom-house officials; but the forbidden goods leaked through all barriers. "More than six thousand persons of the lower and middle classes passed their day in going more than twenty times from Altona, in Holstein, to Hamburg. Punishments and confiscations fell upon the guilty; but this did not put an end to the incessant strife, sometimes by cunning, sometimes by force, against this fiscal tyranny." [2] Between five and six hundred women were employed by the merchants of Hamburg daily to convey into the city, each of them, fourteen pounds of coffee and other produce, concealed beneath their garments. [3]

[1] Thiers, Consulate and Empire (Forbes's translation), vol. xii. p. 21.

[2] Mémoires de Bourrienne, French Minister at Hamburg, vol. viii. pp 193–198.

[3] Annual Register, 1809; State Papers, 747.

In the Baltic conditions were somewhat different. Much there depended upon the heartiness of the czar in the cause; upon whether he would content himself with a bare perfunctory compliance with the letter of his engagements at Tilsit and Erfurt, or would decisively enforce an entire cessation of traffic with Great Britain. The latter course, however, was impossible to Alexander. Impulsive and ambitious, he yet lacked the hardness of character needed to disregard the cold disapproval of the nobles and the distress of his subjects. Under the influence of Napoleon's presence, of his fascination and his promises, it had seemed possible to do that which in the isolation of his court, and deprived of sympathy, became drearily monotonous; nor did Napoleon, by fidelity to his word, make the task easier. Decrees of great severity were issued,[1] and the British flag was honestly excluded; but the quick mercantile intelligence soon detected that no ill-timed curiosity as to ships' papers would be exercised,[2] nor vexatious impediments thrown in the way of exporting the national products, which, if essential to Great Britain's naval supremacy, were no less the source of Russia's wealth. In truth, British consumption of naval stores, and British capital invested in Russia, had been leading elements in the prosperity of the country; and it had been no light sacrifice to concede such advantages as the czar had already yielded.

Such was the working condition of the Continental System between 1806 and 1810. Despite the general disquietude in Great Britain and the undoubted impediments raised to that free export upon which her prosperity was

---

[1] April 1, 1808 ; Naval Chronicle, vol. xxi. p. 48. May 7, 1809 ; Annual Register, 1809, p. 698.

[2] Napoleon saw, in 1809, that his work at Tilsit was all to be done over, since the only war Russia could make against the English was by commerce, which was protected nearly as before. There was sold in Mayence sugar and coffee which came from Riga. — *Mémoires de Savary, duc de Rovigo* (Imperial Chief of Police), vol. iii. p. 135.

based, the general confidence was unabated.[1] Much was
hoped from the resistance of the continental peoples, more
from their steadfast evasion of the edicts. In 1806, just
before the Berlin decree was issued, but when the system
was already in force, a commercial magazine wrote: "The
regulations adopted only show the ignorance of the French
government of commercial principles. When the blockade of the Elbe was removed, instead of finding markets
exhausted and prices enhanced, they were found over-
stocked."[2] "In spite of every prohibition British goods
continue (Dec. 1, 1806) to find their way in vast quantities into France. They are exported hence on French
orders. It is easy to insure them for the whole transit to
the town in France where they are to be delivered to the
purchaser. They are introduced at almost all parts of the
land confines of the French Empire. No sooner are they
received into the French merchant's warehouse, than evidence is procured that they are of French manufacture;
the proper marks are stamped, and the goods are in a
state to be exhibited, in proof that the manufactures of
France quite outrival those of England. The writer had
this information from gentlemen who have a concern in
the trade to which it relates."[3] "Though the port of
Venice is now totally shut against British commerce, as
also the peninsula of Istria from whence Italian silk has
always been obtained, yet through neutral vessels we now
obtain Piedmont silk, which is the best and finest, direct
from Leghorn, Lucca, and Genoa."[4] "From Malta a brisk

[1] D'Ivernois, Effects of the Continental blockade, London, Jan., 1810.
Lord Grenville, one of the leaders of the Opposition, expressed a similar confidence when speaking in the House of Lords, Feb. 8, 1810. (Cobbett's Parl.
Debates, vol. xv. p. 347.) So also the King's speech at the opening of Parliament, Jan. 19, 1809: "The public revenues, notwithstanding we are shut
out from almost all the continent of Europe and entirely from the United
States, has increased to a degree never expected, even by those persons who
were most sanguine." (Naval Chronicle, vol. xxi. p. 48.)

[2] Monthly Magazine, vol. xxi. p. 195.   [3] Ibid., vol. xxii. p. 514.
[4] Ibid., vol. xxi. p. 539.

trade, yielding quick returns, is kept up with the ports of Italy. Malta is the emporium, the storehouse. From Malta we supply Leghorn and other places in the power of France. But the British goods are sold, even before they are landed, for ready money; and scarcely a pound's worth of British property is at any moment hazarded where the French might seize it." [1]

Indications of embarrassment now begin to accumulate, but still, in January, 1808, we read: "Several ships from Holland have lately entered our harbors, and brought over large quantities of goods usually imported from Hamburg. This is a proof of the futility of Bonaparte's commercial speculations." [2] Russia had by this declared against Great Britain, causing a rise in all Russian produce; and the Embargo Act of the United States had just gone into operation. There is a vast falling off in the Baltic and American trade. In 1805 over eleven thousand ships had passed through the Sound, going and coming; in 1807 barely six thousand, and British ships are excluded from all but Swedish harbors. In August, 1808, the ports of Holland are opened for the export of Dutch butter, and two hundred bales of silk are allowed to be smuggled out, for which a bribe of six thousand guineas was extorted by some person in authority. [3] In 1809 a notice again occurs of the ports of Holland being opened by the king; and concurrently, West India produce, which has been for some months dull, is found more in demand and commanding good prices. [4] Malta is doing a famous business at the same time, and has become one of the greatest depots in the Mediterranean. [5]

The year 1809 was marked by a great, though temporary, revival of trade, due to several causes. Napoleon himself was detained during great part of the year in the

---

[1] Monthly Magazine, vol. xxii. p. 618.
[2] Ibid., vol. xxiv. p. 611.
[3] Ibid., vol. xxvi. p. 11.
[4] Ibid., vol. xxvii. pp. 417, 641.
[5] Ibid., p. 135.

heart of Austria, absorbed in one of his most doubtful contests with the empire; and in his absence trade with the North Sea ports went on almost as in time of peace. In the United States an eager British minister, of politics opposed to the party in power, had committed himself without due authority to an official statement to the government that the Orders in Council would be rescinded by June 10. The President, without waiting to hear further, removed the restrictions of the Non-Intercourse Act on that date; and accordingly, for some months there was free traffic and a very great interchange of goods between the United States and Great Britain. In South America, the withdrawal of the Portuguese court to Brazil and the uprising of Spain against Napoleon had resulted in throwing open the colonial ports to Great Britain; and an immense wave of speculative shipments, heavily employing the manufactories, was setting in that direction. In the Baltic, the czar was wearying of his engagements with France, and of the emperor's tergiversations; wearying too, of the opposition of his court and subjects. He adhered faithfully, indeed, to the letter of his bargain and refused admission to British ships; but he would not open his eyes to the fact that British commerce was being carried on in his ports by neutrals with British licenses. He had never promised to exclude neutrals, or forbid all export and import; and it was none of his business to pry behind the papers that covered transactions essential to his people. The imports to Great Britain of naval stores, mainly from the Baltic, more than doubled from 1808 to 1809, and were even greater the following year.[1] Wool from Spain and silk from Italy experienced a similar rise. Even West India produce, so vigorously excluded from the Continent, shared the general advance; and there was a great, though feverish and unsound, hope of returning prosperity. It was evident that Napoleon's measures were meeting

[1] Tooke's History of Prices, vol. i. pp. 300, 301.

only partial success, and men were willing to believe that
their failure lay in the nature of things,— in the impossibility of his attempt. They had yet to learn that per-
secution fails only when it is not, or cannot be, thorough
and unrelenting.

Among the multiplied impediments to intercourse between nations, due first of all to the narrow ideas of commercial policy prevalent at that epoch, increased by the
state of open maritime war or hostile exclusion existing
between Great Britain and most of the continental countries, and further complicated by the continental blockade
of Napoleon and the retaliatory orders of the British government, there arose an obscure but extensive usage of
"licenses;" which served, though but partially, and in a
wholly arbitrary manner, to remove some of the difficulties
that prevented the exchange of commodities. A license,
from its name, implies a prohibition which is intended to
be removed in the particular case; and the license practice of the Napoleonic wars was for the most part not so
much a system, as an aggregation of individual permis-
sions to carry on a traffic forbidden by the existing laws
of the authority granting them. The licenses were issued
both by the British government and by Napoleon; and
they were addressed, according to the character of the
sway borne by one party or the other, either to the police
of the seas, the armed cruisers, or to the customs authorities of the continental ports. It was generally admitted
in Great Britain that the Board of Trade was actuated
only by upright motives in its action, though the practice
was vigorously attacked on many grounds,— chiefly in
order to impugn the Orders in Council to which alone
their origin was attributed; but in France the taint of
court corruption, or favoritism, in the issue of licenses
was clearly asserted.[1]

---

[1] Salgues, Mémoires pour servir à l'histoire de la France, vol. viii. pp.
350–355. Mémoires de Marmont, duc de Raguse, vol. iii. p. 365. Mémoires
de Savary, duc de Rovigo, vol. v. p. 115.

The "License System," in the peculiar and extensive form to which the phrase was commonly applied, was adopted by the British government in 1808,[1] immediately after the Orders in Council and the alliance of Russia with Napoleon. Licenses did not then first begin to be issued, nor were they then for the first time necessary;[2] but then began the development which carried their numbers from two thousand six hundred and six in 1807, to over fifteen thousand in 1809 and over eighteen thousand in 1810. After the last year there was a rapid falling off, due, not to a change of system, but to the bitter experience that the license, which protected against a British cruiser, did not save the ship and cargo upon arrival in a port under Napoleon's control, when he had at last devoted his indomitable energy to the thorough enforcement of his decrees. During the years in which the practice flourished, it was principally to the Baltic ports that the licensed vessels went, though they also made their way to those of Holland, France, Spain, and other countries on the Continent. The trade to the British East and West Indies was confined to British vessels, as in time of profound peace.

The true origin of the later license trade is to be found in that supremacy and omnipresence of the British navy, which made it impossible for vessels under an enemy's flag to keep the sea. In order to employ their vessels, hostile owners transferred them to a neutral ownership, ordinarily by a fraudulent process which received the name of "neutralization." A neutralized ship remained

---

[1] Quarterly Review, May, 1811, p. 465.

[2] For instance, a license was necessary for a British subject to ship any articles to an enemy's port, though in a neutral vessel. In principle, licenses are essential to trade with an enemy. In 1805 and 1807 Orders in Council dispensed with the necessity of a license in particular instances; but even then merchants preferred to take out a license, because it cut short any questions raised by British cruisers, and especially by privateers. See Cobbett's Parl. Debates, vol. x. p. 924.

the property of the hostile merchant; but, for a stipulated price, a neutral firm, who made this their regular business, gave their name as the owners and obtained from the authorities of the neutral country all the requisite papers and attestations by which the British cruisers, on search-ing, might be deceived. As a regular systematic business, fraudulent from beginning to end, the practice first arose during the war of the American Revolution, in 1780, when Holland became a party to the war, having a large mer-cantile tonnage with very inadequate means of protecting it. At that time a firm established itself in Embden, on the Prussian side of the Ems, which divides Prussia from Holland, and within the two years that remained of the war "neutralized," under Prussian flags, a hundred thou-sand tons of foreign shipping, besides cargoes to an im-mense value for those days. In the wars of Napoleon it was the fate of Holland to be again dragged in the wake of France, and the same practice of neutralization, sup-ported by false oaths and false papers, again sprang up and flourished extensively in the Prussian province of East Friesland, — Prussia carefully maintaining her neutrality from 1795 to the unfortunate Jena campaign of 1806.

In the year 1806 it was asserted that there were up-wards of three thousand sail belonging to merchants of Holland, France, and Spain navigating under the Prussian flag; and the practice doubtless was not confined to Prussia. "It is notorious," wrote Lord Howick, the British foreign minister, "that the coasting trade of the enemy is carried on not only by neutral ships but by the shameful miscon-duct of neutral merchants, who lend their names for a small percentage, not only to cover the goods, but in num-berless instances to mask the ships of the enemy." [1] The fact becoming known, British cruisers, when meeting a valuable ship with Prussian papers, were apt to take the

[1] Cobbett's Parl. Debates, vol. x. p. 406.

chance of her being condemned and send her in; but
even in British ports and admiralty courts the neutralizing agent was prepared to cover his transaction.
The captain ,and crew of the detained vessel were all
carefully instructed and prepared to swear to the false-
hoods, which were attested by equally false papers
sworn to before Prussian judges. To this trade, it
was alleged, France owed the power to obtain naval
stores despite the British blockade of her arsenals. The
frauds recoiled in a curious way on the head of Prussia;
for, in the later stage of the Jena campaign, the neutralized ships supplied French magazines in the Baltic
ports, the French hospitals at Lubeck, and the army
that besieged Dantzic. The capture of vessels, the character of whose papers was suspected, served to swell
the cry against Great Britain for violating neutral rights,
induced greater severity in the British naval measures,
and so directly contributed to the Berlin Decree and the
Orders in Council.[1]

Thus had stood the neutralizing trade toward the end of
1805. After Napoleon had finally abandoned all thought of
invading England, the victorious campaign of Austerlitz and
the peace of Presburg, extending by conquest the boundaries
of the empire, extended also the sweep of those municipal
regulations, already in force, which excluded British goods
from French territory. Early in 1806, beguiling Prussia
into hostilities with Great Britain through the occupation
of Hanover, the emperor compassed also the closure of the
great German rivers. Peace was indeed soon restored;
but the Jena campaign, quickly following, delivered Prussia, bound hand and foot, to Napoleon's dictates. In the
summer of 1807 the Peace of Tilsit united the empires of

---

[1] For an interesting account of the neutralizing trade, see Naval Chronicle,
vol. xxxi. pp. 288–295, and vol. xxxii. p. 119. On the License System, the
Parliamentary Debates (table of contents), and the Quarterly Review of May,
1811, may be consulted.

the East and West in a common exclusion of British
trade, to which Prussia could not but accede. Great
Britain thus found herself face to face with no mere
municipal regulations of one or two countries, but with a
great political combination aiming at her destruction
through the commerce which was her life. Nor was this
combination merely one of those unfriendly acts which
seeks its end by peaceful means, like the Non-Intercourse
Acts of America. The British cabinet was perfectly informed that the minor states were to be coerced, by direct
military force, into concurrence with the commercial
policy of France and Russia,— a concurrence essential
to its success.

It was necessary for Great Britain to meet this threatening conjunction, with such measures as should reduce the
proposed injury to an amount possible for her to bear, until
the inevitable revulsion came. She found ready to her
hand the immense unprincipled system of neutralized vessels, and by means of them and of veritable neutrals she
proposed to maintain her trade with the Continent. To do
so, without reversing the general lines of her policy, as laid
down in the Orders in Council, it was necessary to supply
each neutral employed with a clear and unmistakable
paper, which would insure beyond peradventure the respect of British cruisers for a class of vessels they had
been accustomed to regard with suspicion. It would not
do that a ship engaged in maintaining a British trade that
was in great danger of extinction should be stopped by
their own cruisers. The wording of the licenses was
therefore emphatically sweeping and forcible. They protected against detention the vessel carrying one, whatever
the flag she flew (the French flag alone being excepted),
and directed that "the vessel shall be allowed to proceed,
notwithstanding all the documents which accompany the
ship and cargo may represent the same to be destined to
any neutral or hostile port, or to whomsoever such prop-

erty may belong." [1] These broad provisions were necessary, for the flags flown, except that of the United States, were those of nations which had, willingly or under duress, entered the Continental System; and the papers, having to undergo the scrutiny of hostile agents at the ports of arrival, had to be falsified, or, as it was euphoniously called, "simulated," to deceive the customs officer, if zealous, or to give him, if lukewarm, fair ground for admitting the goods. The license protected against the British cruiser, which otherwise would have detained the vessel on the ground of her papers, intended to deceive the port officers. "The system of licenses," said an adverse petition, "renders it necessary for the ships employed to be provided with sets of forged, or, as they are termed, simulated papers." [2] Of these, two sets were commonly carried, the paper, the wax for the seals, and other accompaniments being carefully imitated, and signatures of foreign rulers, as of Napoleon and of the President and Secretary of State of the United States, skilfully forged. [3] The firms conducting this business made themselves known to the mercantile community by circular letters. [4]

In this way large fleets of licensed vessels under the flags of Prussia, Denmark, Mecklenburg, Oldenburg, Kniphausen, and other almost unknown German principalities, as well as many American merchant ships, went yearly to the Baltic laden with British and colonial produce, and returned with the timber, hemp, tallow, and grain of the North. They entered St. Petersburg and every port in the Baltic, discharged, loaded with the return cargo, and then repaired to a common rendezvous; whence, when col-

---

[1] Quarterly Review, May, 1811, p. 461. Lindsay's History of Merchant Shipping, vol. ii. p. 316.

[2] Petition of Hull merchants, 1812; Cobbett's Parl. Debates, vol. xxi. p. 979.

[3] Am. State Papers, vol. iii. p. 341.

[4] Cobbett's Parliamentary Debates, vol. xxi. p. 1113.

lected to the number of about five hundred, they sailed for
Great Britain under convoy of ships of war, to protect them
against the privateers that swarmed in the Sound and North
Sea.[1] Crushed between England and France, the Danish
seamen, who would not come into the licensed service of
the former, had lost their livelihood and had turned in a
body to privateering, in the practice of which they fell
little short of piracy;[2] and French privateers also found
the ground profitable for cruising.

It was to this disposition of the north countries, as well
as to conciliate the United States, that was probably due
the Order in Council of April 26, 1809; which, while
preserving the spirit, and probably securing the advantages of those of November, 1807, nevertheless formally
and in terms revoked the latter, except so far as expressly
stated in the new edict. The constructive, or paper,
blockade, which under the former orders extended to
every port whence the British flag was excluded, was
now narrowed down to the coasts of Holland, France, and
so much of Italy as was under Napoleon's immediate
dominion. The reasons assigned for this new measure
were "the divers events which had taken place since
the date of the former orders, affecting the relations
between Great Britain and the territories of other powers." The Spanish peninsula, being now in open and
general revolt against Napoleon, was of course exempted;
and southern Italy, by its nearness to Malta and Sicily,
one a possession and the other an ally of England, might
more readily be supplied from them than by neutrals
coming from a greater distance. The maintenance of the
blockade of Holland was particularly favorable to British
trade. By that means the great articles of continental

---

[1] Ross's Life of Admiral Saumarez, vol. ii. pp. 196, 241.

[2] In the years 1809 and 1810 one hundred and sixty American vessels
alone were seized by Danish privateers. Only a part, however, vere condemned. (Am. State Papers, vol. iii. p. 521.)

consumption could reach Holland and France, direct, only by British license, which meant that they came from England; while, if carried from a neutral country to the German rivers, to the Hanse towns, or to the Baltic, as the new Order allowed them to be, they had to be brought thence to the regions more immediately under Napoleon's government by land carriage, which would so raise their price as not to conflict with the British licensed trade. Thus the condition of the suffering neutral populations was relieved, without loosening the pressure upon France; and some of the offence given to the neutral carriers was removed. Another advantage accrued to Great Britain from thus throwing open the trade to the Baltic to all neutrals; for the great demand and high prices of naval equipment would induce them to bring these to the British market and arsenals, in preference to other countries.

This Order was issued at the moment when the British minister at Washington was assuring the American government that the Orders in Council would be wholly withdrawn on the 10th of June following.[1] At the same time the French and Austrians were drawing near to each other on the fields of Germany. On the 6th of April the Archduke Charles issued his address to the Austrian army, and on the 10th crossed the Inn, moving toward Bavaria. On the 12th Napoleon quitted Paris to place himself at the head of his troops, which had already preceded him, but were then scattered in different positions, in sore need of his directing hand. On the 17th he was in their midst. On the same day the first collision occurred with Davout's corps under the walls of Ratisbon. Five days of active manœuvring and hard fighting succeeded, ending with the battle of Eckmuhl; after which the Archduke, outgeneralled and defeated, fell back into Bohemia. On the 12th of May

---

[1] Erskine's note to that effect was dated April 19, 1809.

Vienna surrendered, and on the 13th Napoleon entered the Austrian capital for the second time in his career.

In the same eventful week, and on the very day of the battle of Eckmuhl, Sir Arthur Wellesley again landed at Lisbon to begin his memorable four years of command in the Peninsula. Napoleon had relinquished to Soult the pursuit of Sir John Moore, while still in mid-career; and after the embarkation of the British army from Coruña and the surrender of that city, January 16-26, 1809, the marshal was ordered to invade Portugal. After a difficult series of operations, Oporto was reached and stormed on the 29th of March; but Soult lacked the means to push further south. Wellesley, on his arrival, at once decided to march against him, in preference to attacking the French forces in Spain on the line of the Tagus. On the 12th of May, the same day that Vienna surrendered, the British troops crossed the Douro, Soult was forced to evacuate Oporto in haste, retreated to the northward, and re-entered Spain. The British general then returned with his army to the Tagus, and on the 27th of June advanced along that line into Spain. On the 28th of July he fought the battle of Talavera; but, though victorious, the failure of the Spanish troops to support him, their unreliable character as soldiers, and the want of provisions, compelled him to return at the end of August into Portugal, where he took up a position close to the frontier.

The French movements in Spain were rendered indecisive by lack of unity in the direction of the armies, due to the military incapacity of the king and the jealousies of the different marshals. The same early summer months were passed by Napoleon in a desperate struggle on the banks of the Danube, below Vienna. Though the capital had fallen, the Austrian army still remained, chastened but not subdued, and now confronted him on the north side of the stream under a general of a high order of merit, if inferior to the great emperor. To cross from the south to the north bank of the broad river, in the face of such a foe, was no light undertaking even for Napoleon. The first attempt began on the 20th of May; and during the two succeeding days the French army passed slowly across the insufficient bridges which alone could be thrown, for lack of proper material. During the 21st and 22d continued the strife, known in history as the battle of Essling; and on the latter day some sixty thousand French troops were in action with the Austrians, when the great bridge, joining the south shore to the island of Lobau in mid-stream, gave way before a freshet, which had already raised the waters of the Danube by fourteen feet. The supply of ammunition to the engaged troops ceased, and it therefore became impossible to retain the positions already gained. During the night of the 22d the corps on the north side were withdrawn into the island; and for the next six weeks Napoleon was untiringly occupied in providing materials for bridges which would be sure not to fail him. At last, when all was prepared, the army again crossed, and on the 6th of July was fought the memorable battle of Wagram. Terminating in the defeat of the Austrians, it was followed on the 12th by an armistice; and a definitive treaty of peace was ratified at Vienna on the 15th of October. Austria surrendered all her remaining seaboard on the Adriatic, besides portions of her interior territory, and again acceded to the prohibition of British goods of all kinds within her dominions.

A month before, September 17, 1809, peace had been concluded between Russia and Sweden; the latter ceding Finland and engaging to close her ports to all British ships, "with the exception of the importation of salt and colonial productions, which habit had rendered necessary to the people of Sweden." [1] On the 6th of January Napoleon, less merciful than the czar, exacted a convention which allowed only the entry of salt, excluding explicitly

[1] Annual Register, 1809, p. 726.

the colonial produce permitted by the Russian treaty; in return for which he restored Pomerania to Sweden.[1] Thus were formally closed to Great Britain all the northern ports through which, by the license trade, she had continued to pour her merchandise into the Continent, though in much diminished volume.

It now became Napoleon's great object to enforce the restrictions, which had thus been wrested from vanquished opponents in support of his continental policy, by increased personal vigilance and by urgently reiterated demands, for which he had an undeniable ground in the express terms of his treaties with the sea-board powers. Upon the Continent, except in the Spanish peninsula, the treaty of Vienna was followed by a peace of exhaustion, which lasted nearly three years. The emperor returned to Fontainebleau on the 26th of October, and at once began the dispositions from which he hoped the reduction of Great Britain, but which irresistibly led, step by step, to his own final overthrow. The French army was withdrawn from southern Germany, but gradually; remaining long enough in the various conquered or allied countries to ease the imperial treasury from the expense of their support, according to Napoleon's invariable policy. The evacuation was not completed until the first of June, 1810. A hundred thousand men, chiefly new levies, were directed on Spain, together with the Imperial Guard, the supposed precursor of the emperor himself; but the best of the troops, the hardened corps of Davout and Masséna, were reserved for northern Germany and the Dutch frontiers, to enforce the submission of the people to the continental blockade. Napoleon himself did not go to Spain, and that tedious war dragged wearily on, with greater or less vigor here or there, according to the qualities of the different leaders; but lacking the unity of aim, the concert of action, which nothing but the presence

[1] *Moniteur,* Feb. 24, 1810.

of a master spirit could insure among so many generals of
equal rank, imbued with mutual jealousy, and each taxed
with a burden that demanded his utmost strength. Around
Lisbon, Wellington was preparing the lines of Torres
Vedras, and thus striking deep into the soil of the Peninsula a grip from which all the armies of France could not
shake him, so long as the navy of Great Britain stood at
his back, securing his communications and his line of
retreat; but of this Napoleon knew nothing.

It was above all things necessary to bring the Spanish
war to an end, and the emperor was heartily weary of it;
but still the Continental System constrained him. "Duroc
assured me," writes Bourrienne,[1] "that the emperor had
more than once shown regret at being engaged in the Spanish war; but since he had the English to fight there, no
consideration could have induced him to abandon it, the
more so as all that he was then doing was to defend the
honor of the Continental System. . . . He said to Duroc
one day, 'I no longer hold to Joseph being king of Spain,
and he himself cares little about it. I would place there
the first comer, if he could close his ports to the English.'"
The military situation in Spain imperatively demanded his
own presence; without it the war was interminable. The
Spanish ulcer, as he himself aptly termed it, was drain-
ing away both men and money; and the seat of the trouble
was at Lisbon, where the British sea power had at last
found the place to set its fangs in his side and gnaw unceasingly. But Napoleon could not resolve either to withdraw from the contest or to superintend it in person. The
Spaniards and Portuguese, in the prevailing anarchy,
could contribute little, as consumers, to British commerce;
whereas the north of Europe, from Holland to St. Petersburg, while yielding a nominal acquiescence, everywhere
evaded the blockades with the connivance of their governments. Here, then, in his opinion, was the quarter to strike

[1] *Mémoires*, vol. ix. pp. 21–24.

Great Britain; the Peninsula was to her but a drain of men and money, which the custom of northern and central Europe alone enabled her to endure. The emperor therefore decided to sustain both efforts, the peninsular war and the northern continental blockade; to divide his strength between the two, instead of combining it upon either; and to give his immediate attention to the North. Thus it was that the Sea Power of Great Britain, defying his efforts otherwise, forced him into the field of its own choosing, lured him, the great exemplar of concentrated effort, to scatter his forces, and led him along a path which at last gave no choice except retreat in discomfiture or advance to certain ruin.

Napoleon advanced. Since the Jena campaign he had occupied with French and Polish troops the fortresses of Glogau, Custrin, Stettin, and Dantzic. By these he controlled the Oder and the Vistula, and kept a constant rein upon Prussia, so as to exact the war indemnities she still owed, to check any movement upon her part, and to enforce the demands of his policy. Davout, the most severe and thorough of the French marshals, took command of these fortresses, as also of Hanover and of the Hanse towns, on which likewise imperial troops were quartered. At the mouth of the Ems his corps was in touch with that of Marshal Oudinot, which stretched thence along the frontiers of Holland to Belgium and Boulogne. Thus the whole sea-board from Boulogne to the Baltic was gripped by French divisions, which in any dispute or doubt powerfully supported the emperor's arguments and sustained the Continental System, both by actual interference and by the constant threat contained in their presence. These measures "were necessary," says M. Thiers,[1] "in order to compel the Hanse towns to renounce commercial intercourse with Great Britain, and to coerce Holland, which paid no more attention to the commercial blockade than

[1] Cons. et Empire (Forbes's Trans.), xii. 15.

if it had been governed by an English or a German prince. Even when the governments attempted to keep good faith the communities were little affected, and pursued a contraband trade which the most vigorous measures failed to prevent. Napoleon determined to conduct in person this kind of warfare."

Holland was the first victim. As has before been said, Louis Bonaparte strove continually to thwart the operation of the system. Napoleon now demanded a strict execution of the blockade, and for that purpose that the guard of the Dutch coasts and of the mouths of the rivers should be entrusted to French custom-house officers.[1] He also required that the American vessels which had entered Dutch ports under the king's permission should be confiscated. Louis, though willing to concede the former conditions and to exclude Americans and other neutrals thenceforward, could not bring himself to give up those that had entered under his own authority; but, having been induced to visit his brother in Paris in November, 1809, he was by threats and persuasion brought to yield every point demanded. It was during these interviews that Napoleon, giving way to one of those transports of passion which increased with him as years went by, again betrayed the fatal compulsion under which England held him, and the purposes already forming in his mind. "It is the English," he cried, "who have forced me to aggrandize myself unceasingly.[2] But for them I would not have united Naples, Spain, Portugal to my empire. I have willed to struggle and to extend my coasts, in order to increase my resources. If they keep on, they will oblige me to join Holland to my shore lines, then the Hanse towns, finally Pomerania, and perhaps even Dantzic." Then he suggested that Louis should, by indirect means, convey to the British cabinet the impending dan-

---

[1] Corr. de Nap., vol. xx. p. 235.

[2] Compare Metternich's Memoirs, vol. ii. p. 188.

ger of Napoleon's proceeding to these extremities, in the hopes that apprehension might induce it to offer terms of peace, in order to avert the union of Holland to the empire.

A Dutch banker, M. Labouchère, who had extensive relations with prominent houses, was accordingly dispatched, though without formal credentials, and opened the matter to the ministers; but the latter showed little interest. Whatever the nominal state of Holland, they said, it is really only a French dependency; and as for the extension of the Continental System, they expected no less than an increase of tyranny with the increase of the emperor's sway. Louis was then sent back to Holland, having further agreed to cede to France all his provinces west of the Rhine, and to line the coasts of the remainder with an army partly Dutch, partly French, but commanded by a French general. Overwhelmed with mortification, he cherished at times impotent thoughts of resistance, which issued only in insults to the French Chargé and in impediments thrown in the way of the French army of occupation and the customs officers. Finally, in June, 1810, a body of French troops having presented themselves before Harlem were denied entrance; and at about the same time a servant of the French embassy was mobbed at the Hague. Napoleon at once ordered Oudinot to enter, not only Harlem, but Amsterdam, with drums beating and colors flying, while the French corps to the north and south of Holland crossed the frontiers to support the army of occupation. On the first of July Louis signed his abdication, which was published on the 3d; by which time he had secretly left the kingdom for an unknown destination. On the 9th Holland was united to the empire by an imperial decree. The coveted American ships with their cargoes were sequestrated, and the large accumulations of colonial produce formed under Louis's lax blockade were made to contribute to the imperial treasury, by being admitted into France upon payment of a duty of fifty per cent. But, for this immediate benefit, the thrifty Hollanders were to pay by an unrelenting exclusion of trade, by the quartering of foreign troops, and by the conscription, both land and naval.

The empire now extended to the Ems; but still, with persevering cunning, smugglers and neutrals contrived to introduce tropical produce and British manufactures to some extent. Owing to the restrictions, indeed, the goods rose from fifty to a hundred per cent over the London prices, but still they came; and, in consequence at once of the British blockade of the French coast and of the emperor's jealous support of that blockade by his own decrees, the people of France had to pay far dearer than the other continental nations.[1] Thus were Napoleon's objects doubly thwarted; for, while he aimed at breaking down Great Britain by exclusion from the rest of Europe, he also meant to make France, as the corner stone of his power, the most prosperous nation, and to secure for her the continental market which her rival was to lose.[2] All foreign articles decreased in price in proportion as the distance from Paris increased. Before the union, coffee and sugar cost in his capital three and four times what they did in Holland. He now became unremitting and threatening in his representations to the Northern states. Exacting the last farthing of Prussia at one breath, with the next he offered to deduct from the debt the value of all licensed cargoes seized by her. He menaced Sweden with the reoccupation of Pomerania, if the great fleets under British license were admitted to Stralsund. It was indeed to the Northern and Baltic ports that four fifths of the licensed vessels went; only a small proportion sailed to the blockaded ports of France and Holland.[3] By dint of urgent

---

[1] Thiers, Cons. et Emp., Book xxxviii. p. 182.

[2] Corr. de Nap., vol. xxi. p. 70: "Mon principe est, La France avant tout." (Letter to viceroy of Italy.)

[3] Parl. Debates, vol. xxi. p. 1050; xxiii. p. 540.

representations and the presence of the French troops, he contrived to have seized the greater part of a convoy of six hundred sail, which entered the Baltic in the summer of 1810; but which, being delayed by head winds, had not reached their ports in time to escape the movements of his troops. The Northern trade had taken on immense dimensions in 1809, when Napoleon was battling about Vienna and the governments were not under his eye; but this year he could make himself felt, and some forty million dollars' worth of British property was seized in the northern ports.[1] The blow seriously affected the already overstrained commercial system of Great Britain, and its results were shown by the fall in the number of licenses issued, from eighteen thousand in 1810 to seventy-five hundred in 1811.

The emperor went further. Deciding, after long consideration, that fifty per cent on the London prices represented the profits of smugglers of colonial goods, he determined to allow the introduction of the latter upon payment of duty to that extent. Characteristically unwilling to appear to take a step backward, he extended this permission only to produce not coming from British colonies; but it was understood, and officially intimated to the customs authorities, that the inquiry should not be rigorous. In this subterfuge, says M. Thiers, consisted the whole combination.[2] Having thus constituted a lawful variety of colonial products in the empire and in the subject countries, the emperor felt at liberty to execute one of those vast confiscations, which contributed so

[1] Cobbett's Parl. Debates, vol. xxi. pp. 1056, 1117.

[2] The decree was also shrouded in secrecy, and its existence denied in the Moniteur (Cobbett's Pol. Register, xviii. p. 701). Napoleon wrote to the viceroy of Italy, Aug. 6, 1810: "You will receive a decree which I have just issued to regulate duties on colonial produce. . . . It is to be executed in Italy; it is secret and to be kept in your hands. You will therefore give orders in pursuance of this decree only by ministerial letters." (Corr., vol. xxi. p. 28.)

materially to his military chest. All collections of these
goods existing within his reach were to be seized at the
same time, and, if they had not been declared, should be
condemned; if they had, should pay half their value, in
money or in kind. "Thus it was hoped to seize everywhere at the same time, and to take for the treasury of
Napoleon, or for that of his allies, the half in case of
declaration, the whole in case of dissimulation. It can
be conceived what terror would be caused to the numerous
accomplices of British commerce."[1] This measure was
established by a decree of August 5, 1810, and accepted
by all the continental states, except Russia. The latter
refused to go beyond her obligations by the treaty of
Tilsit, and took the occasion to express her uneasiness
at seeing the French troops gradually extending along the
northern seas, and even as close to her own borders as
Dantzic. The impossibility of cordial co-operation in the
immense sacrifices demanded by the Continental System
was clearly shown by this refusal; but by no less vigorous means could Great Britain be reached, and Napoleon
could not recede. The decree was extended outside the
boundaries of the empire, to any depot of colonial goods
within four days' march of the frontiers, in Switzerland,
in Germany, in Prussia, in the Hanse towns. Large
sums of money were realized, and the government became
a dealer in groceries when the payments were made in
kind. The pressure of the French troops extended everywhere, and French flotillas cruised along the coasts of the
North Sea, whether within the limits of the empire or not,
in the mouths and along the course of the great rivers,
to seal them more completely.

The decree of August 5 was carried out by the armed
hand. "*Wherever my troops are,*" wrote Napoleon to
Prussia, "I suffer no English smuggling." On this
ground French authorities executed the mandate in the

[1] Thiers, Cons. et Empire, Book xxxviii. pp. 181–189.

Prussian port of Stettin, which was in the military occupation only of his troops. "All the ports of this once potent kingdom," says a contemporary magazine, "are filled with French soldiers, who seize and burn every article which can possibly have passed through British hands. Prussia is described as in a deplorable state, almost disorganized and no employment for industry."[1] Similar action was taken in the Hanse towns with no other justification. The king of Westphalia was ordered to withdraw his army from the northern part of the kingdom, that French soldiers might enter for the same purpose. In Switzerland the native authorities were permitted to act, but a French customs officer supervised. On the 18th of August the emperor directed the military occupation of the territory of Lubeck, Lauenburg, Hamburg, and all the west bank of the Elbe, for a length of fifty miles from its mouth; thence the line extended, at about the same distance from the sea, to Bremen, and thence to the frontiers of Holland, taking in the little states of Arenberg and Oldenburg. This military occupation was but the precursor of the annexation of these countries a few months later, which led to the first overt act of displeasure on the part of the czar. In justification of the step, one of a series which alienated Alexander and led up to the Russian war, was alleged the purpose of sustaining the continental blockade as the only means of destroying Great Britain. "General Morand," so read the orders, "is charged to take all necessary measures for the prevention of smuggling. For this purpose he will 'establish a first line of troops from Holstein to East-Frisia, and a second line in rear of the first."[2]

On the 6th of October the viceroy of Italy was directed to occupy with Italian troops all the Italian cantons of Switzerland, and to sequestrate at once all colonial or

[1] Monthly Magazine, Feb. 1811, vol. xxxi. p. 67.
[2] Corr. de Nap., vol. xxi. p. 58.

other contraband merchandise. The order was accompanied with Napoleon's usual formula: "This ought to bring in several millions." Eugene was to explain that this was only a step similar to the occupation of northern Germany, that it did not invade the neutrality of Switzerland; and he was to be particularly careful that the emperor's hand did not appear. "That there should be a quarrel between *you* and Switzerland will do no harm."[1] On the 19th of October Prussia was notified that, if she did not efficiently preclude the passage of British and colonial merchandise through her states, the French army would enter them; and the French minister was directed to leave Berlin if satisfaction was not given.[2]

Coincidently with these principal measures, the correspondence of Napoleon teems with orders, complaints, remonstrances, reprimands, queries, all showing how bent his mind was on the one purpose. Having turned over the command of the army in Portugal, directed against the British, to his ablest marshal, Masséna, he was concentrating his own energies on the blockade. At the same time, he occupied himself with stringent measures for protecting the industries of France in the European market. No man ever held more thoroughly than the emperor that element of the theory of protection, that the government can manage the business of the people better than themselves. His kingdom of Italy should not use Swiss nor German cottons; such goods must come only from France.[3] Italian raw silks shall go nowhere but to France,[4] and then only to Lyon. The whole export trade is in his hands by a system of licenses,[5] apparently borrowed from Great Britain, and which at this time he greatly extended. On the 25th of July an order was given that no ship could clear from a port of the empire for abroad without a license, signed by the emperor him-

---

[1] Corr. de Nap., vol. xxi. p. 224.
[2] Ibid., p. 268.
[3] Ibid., p. 77.
[4] Ibid., pp. 70, 71.
[5] Ibid., pp. 61, 62.

self. On September 15 another decree was issued,[1] allowing licensed vessels to sail from Hamburg, Bremen, and
Lubeck for French ports. The license was to cost twelve
dollars per ton, and was good only for the return voyage;
but the vessel upon arriving in France was exempt from
all question as to search by British cruisers, and might
even land all her cargo in a British port, — in other words,
she was excepted from the Berlin and Milan decrees. She
could not, however, enter France with any British goods.
Returning, she was to load with wines or other French
produce, except grain or flour. Under the rival license
systems new and curious methods of evasion grew up.
Compelled to take French articles which were not wanted
in Great Britain, as well as those that were, the former
were put on board of so inferior a quality that they could
be thrown into the sea without loss. At either end smuggling boats met the licensed vessel before entering port,
and took from her forbidden articles. Ships of either
nation, with foreign flag, and simulated papers, were to
be seen in each other's ports.[2] The British, as a commercial people, were naturally willing to give a larger extension to this evasive trade; but the emperor would not
grant anything that he thought could help his enemy,
even though it benefited his own people. He believed, and
rightly, that Great Britain was receiving more harm than
France; he did not realize that, from her immense wealth
and commercial aptitudes, she could endure the process
longer.

The decree of August 5 admitted colonial goods, but
excluded British manufactures. On the 19th of October
was issued another edict, directing that all such manufactured goods, wherever found in the emperor's dominions,

---

[1] Cobbett's Pol. Register, vol. xviii. pp. 704, 722.

[2] At Bordeaux licensed vessels were known to take on board wines and
brandies for the British army in Portugal. (Mémoires du duc de Rovigo,
vol. v. p. 60.)

or even in countries in the mere military occupation of his troops, should be publicly burned. This was remorselessly done. "Persons who at this epoch were living in the interior of France can form no idea of the desolation which so savage a measure spread through countries accustomed to live by commerce. What a spectacle offered to peoples impoverished and lacking everything, to see the burning of articles the distribution of which would have been an alleviation to their sufferings! . . . What a means of attaching conquered peoples, to irritate their privations by the destruction of a number of articles of the first necessity!"[1] "The tampering with the mails," says Savary, the Minister of Police, "caused me to make some very sad reflections, and forced me to admit that we were not advancing toward tranquillity; and that, if the party against us were not yet formed, at least all sentiments were agreed, and that a single reverse would be enough to ruin us. . . . The more we disturbed the relations of Europe with England, the more, on all sides, men sought to draw together; and we remained with the odious epithets given to us by all those whom our measures thwarted."[2] "There was already an understanding from one end of Europe to the other; every cabinet earnestly wished the overthrow of Napoleon, as the people also wished, with at least equal ardor, a state of things less stifling for their industry and trade. Despite the terror inspired by Napoleon's name, there was, side by side with that terror, that damnable Continental System which settled the question; it was necessary either to fight or to succumb. The people of the North were under an imperious necessity to break that yoke of lead, which made the custom house the prime agent of the governments of Europe."[3]

[1] Bourrienne, Mémoires, vol viii. p. 261.
[2] Mémoires du duc de Rovigo, vol. v. p. 66.
[3] Mémoires de Bourrienne, vol. ix. p. 60.

Russia had refused to accede to any steps beyond her engagements of Tilsit; but nowhere was discontent more profound, nowhere opposition more to be dreaded. While Napoleon was indisputably leading Great Britain into greater and greater embarrassment, by the depreciation of her manufactures and by the accumulations of unsalable sugars and coffees in her warehouses, he was also ruining the agriculture of Russia and the revenues of her nobles. Despite the relief afforded by the great licensed fleets, the Tilsit agreements so embarrassed trade, that hemp, which in 1802 was worth £32 the ton in London, had reached, in 1809, £118;[1] and other products of the North rose in the same proportion. At the same time sixty thousand tons of coffee lay in the London warehouses, unsalable at sixpence the pound, while the price on the Continent was from four to five shillings, and in places even seven shillings.[2] No better proof of the efficacious co-working of Napoleon's system and of the British Orders can be offered; but the question was one of endurance. Which could stand such a strain longer? In Russia matters were fast approaching a climax. The czar felt the ground trembling under his feet;[3] and, while he renewed his protestations of fidelity to Tilsit and Erfurt, he had to see Napoleon, by his licenses, evading the restrictions which he at the same time was pressing his ally to enforce more rigorously. In vain was the explanation offered that these licenses were but in furtherance of the restrictive system; that France was unloading her surplus products upon England, while refusing to receive aught but specie in return; and that in consequence the exchange was going more and more against Great Britain. The czar knew better; and the repeated and urgent letters of the emperor,

---

[1] Porter's Progress of the Nation, sect. iii. p. 205. In 1815, after Napoleon's overthrow, the price fell to £34.

[2] Tooke's Hist. of Prices, vol. i. p. 354.

[3] Souvenirs du duc de Vicence, vol. i. p. 88.

becoming, as was the wont of Napoleon's requests, rather peremptory than entreating, to seize and confiscate all neutral ships entering Russian ports, fell on deaf ears. Alexander feared war; but he remembered his father's fate, and feared assassination more.

On the 10th of December, 1810, the emperor sent a message to the Senate announcing that he had annexed to the empire the Hanse towns, together with the region on the North Sea intervening between them and Holland, which had been as yet only in military occupation. In the same paper he expressed his intention of making a canal from the Elbe to Lubeck, by which the empire should be brought into direct water communication with the Baltic. This assurance was not calculated to ease the anxiety of the czar as to the eastward progress of France; but the measure was accompanied by a circumstance of personal affront, peculiarly dangerous to an alliance which depended chiefly upon the personal relations of two absolute sovereigns. The Grand Duke of Oldenburg, one of the countries thus unceremoniously annexed, was uncle to the czar; and though Napoleon proposed to indemnify him for the material loss, by territory taken in the interior of Germany, Alexander would not accept such satisfaction nor name any compensation that he would think adequate. He did not threaten war, but he refused to surrender his grievance, and reserved his right to retaliate an injury.

Meantime very serious results were developing, both in Great Britain and France, from the strained and abnormal conditions of commerce and the shocks caused by Napoleon's sudden and tremendous blows at credit, by his wide-spread confiscations, and by the Baltic seizures. The triple array of French troops that lined the shores of the Continent, re-enforced by the belt of British cruisers girding the coasts from the Ems to Bayonne, and from the Pyrenees to Orbitello, created a barrier which neither mercantile ingenuity nor popular want could longer evade to a degree that afforded any real measure of relief. The stolid, though as yet peaceable, measures of resistance taken by the United States had added seriously to the embarrassments of Great Britain, while rather furthering the policy of Napoleon, however contrary this was to the interests of France. During the years 1808 and 1809, the continuance of the embargo and of the non-intercourse acts, closing the North American market, coincided with the opening of the South American; and a great rush was made by the British mercantile community for the latter, although it was not, by the number of the inhabitants, nor by their wealth, nor by their habits of life, at all able to take the place of the consumers lost in Europe and North America. The goods sent out in great quantities were injudiciously chosen, as well as far in excess of the possible requirements; so they remained unsold, and for the most part uncared for and unhoused, on the beach in South American ports. The judgment of men seemed to become unhinged amid the gloom and perplexity of the time, and the frantic desire of each to save himself increased the confusion. Mere movement, however aimless or dangerous, is less intolerable than passive waiting.

The years 1809 and 1810 were consequently marked by an extensive movement in trade, which carried with it an appearance of prosperity in great part delusive. Immense imports were made from the Baltic, and from Italy, at the moment that Napoleon's coils were tightening around them; large shipments also to the North, to South America, and to the West Indies. In the United States only was there a transient period of solid transactions; for in May, 1810, the Non-Intercourse Act expired by its own limitations. A proviso, however, was immediately enacted that if, before the 3d of March, 1811, either Great Britain or France should recall their decrees so far as they affected the United States, the Act should, within three months of the revocation, revive against the power that maintained its edicts.   Napoleon contrived to satisfy President Madison that his Berlin and Milan decrees were so recalled on the first of November; but Great Britain refused to consider the terms of the withdrawal satisfactory, as in truth they were not.   The Order in Council of April 26, 1809, remained in force; and non-intercourse between the United States and Great Britain again obtained in February, 1811, and continued to the outbreak of the war in 1812.

Toward the end of 1810 the results of the various causes of trouble began to be heavily felt.   Very scant returns coming from South America, the shippers were unable to discharge their debts to the manufacturers; and the embarrassments of the latter were felt by their workmen.   From the West Indies the returns came in tropical produce, which could be realized only on the Continent, long since partly and now effectually closed.   A succession of bad seasons had necessitated the importation of large quantities of grain from Holland and France, especially in 1809, when an abundant harvest there, coinciding with a very bad crop in England, induced Napoleon to enter upon his license system, and to authorize an export which in three years drained £10,000,000 in specie from the enemy.   The freights to the licensed carriers, mostly neutrals' or hostile, at least in name, were also paid in specie, which was thus taken out of the country; and there was a further drain of gold for the maintenance of the fleets in distant parts of the world and for the war in Spain, which now took the place of the former subsidies to allies as a consumer of British treasure.   Thus arose a scarcity of specie.   In November, 1810, the bankruptcies were two hundred and seventy-three, against one hundred and thirty of the same month a year before.   Stoppages and compositions equalled in number half the traders of the kingdom.   " The general failures have wonderfully affected manufactures, and want of confidence prevails between manufacturer and merchant." A month later "bankruptcies continue to increase, and confidence is nearly at an end. Neither gold nor silver is often to be seen. The trade of the manufacturing towns is at stand; and houses fail, not every day, but every hour. In the great seaports, the king's stores are full of all kinds of colonial produce which find no sale. Despondency is increased by the accounts from the Continent, which represent all the seaports and internal depots of trade to be full of French soldiers, who seize and burn every article which can possibly have passed through British hands." As the shadows darkened, murmurs grew louder and louder against the once popular [1] Orders in Council, to which all the evil was now attributed. The press changed its tone upon them, and a gradual agitation for their repeal grew up around the Opposition leaders; who, from the moment they lost power, had never ceased' to inveigh against the retaliatory system framed by the ministry.

But while disaster was thus thickening about Great Britain, the case of France was worse. It was quite true, as the emperor said, that the people could live without sugar and coffee, and that necessity would in time find ways to produce many articles the import of which was denied her; but such warped applications of her industry and ingenuity, even when finally realized, could neither replace the loss of her natural channels of effort nor for any length of time cope with a nation, which, however momentarily shaken by unprecedented conditions, yet kept power continually to renew her strength by contact, through the sea, with new sources. That Great Britain would do this, her traditions and the habits of her people were the pledge; and the credit of the government bore witness to it through all. In the early part of 1811 a

---

[1] Both Monroe and Pinkney, while ministers in London, informed the United States government that the extreme measures taken were popular. (Am. State Papers, vol. iii. pp. 188, 206.)

serious commercial crisis occurred in France, causing great anxiety to Napoleon. It was his particular wish to keep this corner-stone of the empire prosperous and contented under the immense demands made upon it for men, and the bitter sufferings entailed by the conscription. But prosperity was hard to secure with all the sea outlets of her manufactures and agriculture closed, with only a continental market, and that impoverished by the universal cessation of trade and further enfeebled by the exhausting demands made upon the peoples to support the armies quartered upon them. The British blockade of the French, Dutch, and Italian coasts forbade absolutely, except to the limited license trade, the water carriage of raw materials essential to manufactures, and prevented the export of French luxuries. "The state of France as it fell under my observation in 1807," wrote an American traveller, "exhibited a very different perspective" from that of Great Britain. "The effects of the loss of external trade were everywhere visible,— in the commercial cities half-deserted, and reduced to a state of inaction and gloom truly deplorable; in the inland towns, in which the populace is eminently wretched, and where I saw not one indication of improvement, but on the contrary numbers of edifices falling to ruin; on the high roads, where the infrequency of vehicles and travellers denoted but too strongly the decrease of internal consumption, and the languor of internal trade; and among the inhabitants of the country, particularly of the South, whose misery is extreme, in consequence of the exorbitant taxes, and of the want of outlet for their surplus produce. In 1807 the number of mendicants in the inland towns was almost incredible. . . . The fields were principally cultivated by women." [1]

---

[1] Letter on the Genius and Disposition of the French Government; oy an American lately returned from Europe, pp. 189–192. Baltimore, 1810. See also Metternich's Memoirs, vol. ii. p. 476, for the unhappiness of France.

All the genius of Napoleon could not create demands when there was not means to gratify them, and the exquisite products of French taste and skill labored under the same disadvantage as coffee and sugar, than which they were even less necessary; men could dispense with them. Production, stimulated by an exaggerated protection, became for a time excessive and then ceased; even the exclusion of British manufactures and the frequent burnings could not secure the continental market to articles, the raw materials for which were made so dear by the sea blockade, or by the long land carriage. Levant cotton made its weary way on horse and mule back, from Turkey, through Illyria, to Trieste, and thence was duly forwarded to France;[1] but even so, when made into stuffs, found itself in competition with British cottons which were landed in Salonica, conveyed on horses and mules through Servia and Hungary into Vienna, and thence distributed over Germany.[2] In the same manner was British colonial produce introduced. Despite all Napoleon's efforts, smuggling continued to compete with and undersell the fair trader, and his own licenses were used to evade his own decrees.[3] Many firms in Holland went out of business altogether, the factories of Lyon closed their doors, and several Paris houses were in distress; although, like the British warehouses, their stores were crowded with goods for which they could find no purchasers. Banks could not recover their advances, internal commerce fell into confusion, and general disaster followed.

At the same time there was in France, as in Great Britain, much suffering from bad harvests, and this was aggravated for the former by the interruption of the coast-

---

[1] Mémoires du duc de Raguse, vol. iii. p. 423. Marmont adds: "This was a powerful help to French industry *during that time of suffering and misery.*"

[2] Tooke's History of Prices, vol. i. p. 311.

[3] In like manner, vessels with British licenses frequently slipped into French ports, especially with naval stores from the Baltic.

ing trade by the British cruisers, and by the indifferent character of the inland roads, which, except when they served the military plans of the emperor, were neglected from the straitened state of the finances. The government came to the rescue with various measures of relief, necessarily partial and arbitrary; designed rather to stave off immediate trouble than to afford a radical cure for existing difficulties. Yet serious remedies were needed; for the growing distress of the Continent must continue to react upon France, which found therein its only customers. In Holland almost all the former sources of wealth had one by one been cut off; and even money-lending, which survived the others, became a losing business from the wide-spread ruin in Europe.[1] In Russia the ruble had fallen to one third of the value it had before the institution of the Continental System; although the czar had refused to impose upon his people and their commerce the decrees of August 5 and October 19, which Napoleon had forced upon other states. With growing poverty in Europe, the empire must grow poorer, and in proportion to its loss of wealth must be the diminution of the revenue. Yet already the revenue was insufficient to the wants of the state, despite all the extraordinary resources which had been called up during the past year, and which could not again be expected. It was not to be hoped that many American ships would again place themselves within reach of the emperor's confiscations. The enormous seizures of colonial produce, made by surprise in the previous August, could not, to any similar extent, be repeated. The duty of fifty per cent, levied throughout the states occupied by his troops, on the coffee and sugar which was declared by the owners, had fallen upon accumulations made during the years of lax blockade and had brought in large sums; but it now served only as an inducement to smuggling.

---

1 "There was not a Dutchman," says M. Thiers, "who had not lost fifty per cent by foreign loans." (Cons. et Empire (Forbes's trans.), xii. 47.)

Great ingenuity had been shown in devising extraordinary means for extracting money from the subject peoples, but every year saw these supplies diminishing. Like slavery, like bad farming, Napoleon's administration, and especially his army, required continually new soil[1] and did little to renew or develop the powers which it taxed; beneficent plans were formed, multitudinous orders issued, but they received rare fulfilment except when they conduced to the military efficiency of the state.

There remained two resources. One was economy; and the correspondence of Napoleon at this period teems with exhortations to his lieutenants, with denials of money, and with precepts to get all they can out of the annexed territories, and ask as little as possible from him.[2] The emperor held in reserve, subject only to his own orders, a great military treasure which had begun with war contributions, and into which poured the results of the extraordinary transactions just mentioned. Five wars had brought into this chest 805,000,000 francs; but in 1810 there remained but 354,000,000, and he was unwilling to trench further upon it, unless some grave emergency arose. He hoped to spare, if not to add to it, by the confiscation of the property of Spanish nobles who had resisted his change of dynasty, as well as by the seizure of "false neutrals." Evidently, however, such resources are precarious, and cannot be compared to those

---

[1] "The emperor does desire war, because he needs more or less virgin soil to explore, because he has need to occupy his armies and to entertain them at the expense of others. . . . M. Romanzow has repeated to me a long conversation he had had with the emperor. 'He wants money,' said he, — 'he does not hide it; he wishes war against Austria to procure it.'" (Metternich to Stadion, Feb. 17, 1809 ; Memoirs, ii. 329.) The Austrian war of 1809 brought $34,000,000 into Napoleon's military chest. (Thiers, Cons. et Emp., Book xxxviii. p. 34.)

[2] Thus to Davout, commanding the Army of Germany : "I shall need much money, which should make you feel the importance of obtaining for me as much as you can, and asking of me as little as possible." (Corr., March 24, 1811.)

of a commercial state. Contrasted with Great Britain, the financial expedients of Napoleon resembled those of a mediæval prince or an Oriental potentate; and in a strain of endurance, in a question of time, the very artificial, not to say unnatural, framework of power which he had built could not hope to outlast the highly organized, essentially modern, and above all consistently developed society which confronted him. A state of long standing and fixed traditions may endure the evils of a bad system, disadvantaged by it, but not ruined; but when the system is new and rests upon a single man, it asks in vain for the confidence inspired by a closely knit, yet wide-spreading, body politic whose established character guarantees the future.

This was clearly shown in the ability of either government to use the other resource — borrowing — as a means to supplement its deficient income. Napoleon steadfastly refused to resort to this, alleging that it was an unjustifiable draft upon the future, and could have but one result — bankruptcy. He proved easily that Great Britain could not go on borrowing indefinitely at her present rate. A better reason for his own abstinence was to be found in the condition of his credit. The public debt of France under his rule was small, and, as he did not add to it, it stood at a good figure in the market.[1] His military genius, the wide flight of his arms, the war contributions, the iniquitous plan by which he quartered his troops on foreign countries, not merely in war but in peace, and made them responsible for their maintenance, — measures such as these, facilitated by frequently recurrent wars and combined with exactions like those narrated in this chapter, enabled him to meet his expenditures, accumulate the large reserve fund mentioned, and at the same time

[1] This condition of the debt was partly factitious, Napoleon maintaining the public funds at eighty, by the secret intervention of the military chest. (Thiers, Cons. et Emp., Book xli. p. 18.)

distribute in France an amount of coin which greatly aided the circulation. But his success imposed upon no one. Everybody understood that such expedients were essentially transient, that to renew them meant renewed wars, invasions growing ever wider and wider, and results dependent always upon military prestige, which a single lost battle might overthrow. Compared with insecurity such as this, the fast growing debt of Great Britain possessed a relative solidity; which even exceeded the absolute confidence felt that the interest would be regularly paid. Behind her stood the history and the prestige of a Sea Power which men knew had met many a heavy reverse, yet had never failed; and which stood before Napoleon more mighty than ever. Far and wide, through many a sea and in many a land, stretched the roots of her strength; never more glorious, because never more sorely tried than by the great emperor. She had credit, he had none.

Savary, one of the most devoted of Napoleon's followers, quotes with conviction the following words to him of a Parisian banker, in the early part of 1811: "A humiliating fact, and one which gives the key to many others, is the state of credit in France and in England. The English debt amounts to about $3,500,000,000, ours only to $250,000,000; and yet the English could borrow at need sums much more considerable than we ourselves could, and above all at an infinitely more favorable rate. Why this difference? Why is the credit of the State, in France, lower than the credit of the leading merchants and bankers; while the reverse is the permanent condition in England? A word suffices to explain it: To restore one's credit in England, you have only to work with the government; while to lose one's credit in France it is only necessary *not* to keep out of government transactions. All England is, so to say, a single commercial house, of which ministers are the directors, the laws the contract, which power itself cannot infringe. Here the Council of State usurps the powers of the tribunals, and I could almost say that nothing useful is done, because *nothing is really guaranteed.*" [1] A competent American witness, before quoted, who had spent two years in France, wrote, in 1809: "The French rulers, whatever may be their power, are unable to obtain supplies at home except by *sacrifices equivalent to the risk which is incurred by contracting with them.* Their credit abroad may be estimated by the fact, which is so well known to us all, that no intelligent merchant in this country can be induced, by any consideration, to make advances in their favor, or to accept a bill on their treasury, from their highest accredited agent." [2]

While the public credit, that touchstone of prosperity, stood thus in the two states, the same eye-witness thus describes the relative condition of the two peoples: "In France the extinction of all public spirit and of the influence of public opinion, the depopulation and decay of the great towns, the stern dominion of a military police, incessantly checked the exultation, natural to the mind, on viewing the profusion of the bounties bestowed by nature. The pressure of the taxes was aggravated by the most oppressive rigor in the collection. The condition of the peasantry as to their food, clothing, and habitations bore no comparison with the state of the same class in England. . . . In England, whatever may be the representations of those who, with little knowledge of the facts, affect to deplore her condition, it is nevertheless true that there does not exist, and never has existed elsewhere, so beautiful and perfect a model of public and private prosperity. . . . I pay this just tribute of admiration with the more pleasure, as it is to me in the light of an atonement for the errors and prejudices under which

[1] Mémoires du duc de Rovigo, vol. v. p. 116.
[2] Genius and Disposition of French Govt. p. 166. Baltimore, 1810.

I labored on this subject, before I enjoyed the advantage of a personal experience. A residence of nearly two years in that country — during which period I visited and studied nearly every part of it, with no other view or purpose than that of obtaining correct information, and I may add, with previous studies well fitted to promote my object — convinced me I had been egregiously deceived." [1]

The writer saw England before her sorest trial came. Since 1807, and especially after 1809, the condition of both nations had grown sensibly worse. The commercial embarrassments of Great Britain under the dislocation of her trade and the loss of her markets, occasioned partly by the Continental System and partly by the American Non-Intercourse Act, and aggravated by the wild speculations that followed the year 1808, resulted in 1811 in wide-spread disaster, — merchants' failing, manufactories closing, workmen out of employment and starving. In France the commercial crisis of the same year, extending over the Continent, soon became a chaos of firms crashing one upon the other and dragging down, each the other, in its fall. [2] Soon great numbers of workmen in all the provinces found themselves, like their English brethren, deprived of occupation. Council upon council was held by the emperor to ascertain how, by government interference, to remedy the ills for which governmental interference was immediately responsible. But, underneath the apparently similar conditions of distress in the two countries, lay the real difference between a nation shut in, and thrown back upon itself, and one that kept open its communications with the world at large. In 1811 Great Britain had already begun to react through her natural channels; the energies of her people under the load upon them had been like a strong spring, whose tension remains,

---

[1] Genius and Disposition of French Govt., pp. 181–192.
[2] Thiers, Cons. et Emp., Book xli. p. 22.

though compressed. The South American trade revived; the Spanish Main took off the accumulations in the West India Islands, and the latter in turn began to call for supplies from home; Russia was visibly relenting; in the Peninsula, Masséna, whose progress had been stopped at the lines of Torres Vedras, was forced to retreat into Spain in the month of March, and through a liberated Portugal were found new openings for British commerce. For France there could be no return of prosperity until the sea was again free to her, either through her own or through neutral ships; but the latter could not safely repair to her ports until her rival revoked the still existing Order in Council, blockading the whole French and Dutch coast, and this she would not do before the emperor recalled the decrees upon which rested his Continental System. And while Great Britain was making appalling drafts upon the future in her ever-mounting debt, France was exhausting a capital which no forcing power could replace, by her anticipated conscriptions, which led to a revolt far more menacing than the riots of English workmen. Sixty thousand "refractory" conscripts were scattered through the departments, and among the forests of western, central, and southern France, refusing to join their regiments and defying the authorities. They were pursued by flying columns of old soldiers; who, often long strangers to their own countrymen, took with their property the same liberties they had practised in foreign parts. In January, 1811, the whole conscription for the year was called out, and in midsummer that for 1812; but no legal measures could make men of the boys sent to die before the virile age,[1] more often of exposure than by the hands of the enemy, in the gloomy mountains and parched plains of Spain.

The great struggle of endurance, " of the highest individual genius against the resources and institutions of

[1] Thiers, Cons. et Emp., Book xli. p. 11.

a great nation "[1] who stayed its power on the sea, was now drawing near its close; the battle between the sea and the land was about to terminate in one of the most impressive and gigantic military catastrophes recorded by history. But the inevitable end was already clearly indicated before Napoleon started for Russia, although the dim vision of weary eyes in England, strained by long watching, saw not that which the apprehensions of Frenchmen, troubled with the anguish of France, tremblingly felt. The credit of France was gone; nor could her people bear any added burdens, until the sea, over which Great Britain still moved unresisted, was open to them. The people of the Continent had become bitterly hostile through the sufferings caused by the blockade, and the imperial power could only be maintained by an army which was itself filled by borrowing upon the future; its capital, its reserve, was fast being exhausted.[2] The question of physical endurance was settled; the only point really left in doubt was that of moral endurance. Would Great Britain and the British government have the nerve to hold out till the emperor was exhausted ? "[3] Already the agitation for the repeal of the Orders in Council, with which the existing ministry was identified, was becoming ominous. The leaders of the Opposition were opposed to the Peninsular war; and Napier has vividly shown the doubts and hesitations of the ministry as to sustaining that great enterprise which compelled Napoleon to such waste of life, to such a fatal division of his force. Time was not allowed to test to the utmost British

[1] Arnold's History of Rome, opening of chap. xliii.

[2] It is interesting to observe in Metternich's letters, while ambassador at Paris, how he counts upon this exhausting of the capital of French soldiers as the ultimate solution of the subjection of Austria. "For some time Napoleon has lived on anticipations. The reserves are destroyed." (April 11, 1809.) Compare also his exclamation to the emperor in 1813 : "Is not your present army anticipated by a generation ? I have seen your soldiers; they are mere children." (Memoirs, vol. i. p. 189).

[3] See Metternich's Memoirs, vol. ii. p. 477.

tenacity; the darkest hour was fast passing away, the clouds began to break and the day to dawn.

Three weeks after Napoleon's annexation of the Hanse towns and of the Duchy of Oldenburg, on the last day of the year 1810, Alexander put forth a commercial ukase which under all the circumstances had the appearance of retaliatory action; and at the least drew a sharp line between his commercial policy and the Continental System as inculcated by Napoleon. The decree expressly permitted the entrance of colonial produce under neutral flags; and many articles of French manufacture were virtually denied admission, by not being included in a list of goods which could be introduced on payment of duty. In vain did the czar assert that his object was to develop, by protection, Russian manufactures of the excluded articles. Napoleon rejected the explanation. "The last ukase," he wrote in a personal letter to Alexander, "is at bottom, but yet more in form, specially directed against France."[1] But while the exclusion of French products was the most open, the admission of neutral ships with colonial produce was the most significant, feature of the edict. This was the point upon which the emperor had been most importunate; here was the leak which, in his judgment, was sinking the ship. "Six hundred English merchant ships," he had written in a previous letter, October 23, 1810,[2] "wandering in the Baltic, have been refused admission to Prussian ports and those of Mecklenburg, and have steered for your Majesty's states. If you admit them the war still lasts. . . . Your Majesty knows that if you confiscate them we shall have peace. Whatever their papers, under whatever names they are masked, French, German, Spanish, Danish, Russian, your Majesty may be sure they are English."

Later, on the 4th of November,[3] Napoleon wrote through

[1] Corr. de Nap., vol. xxi. p. 497 (Feb. 28, 1811).   [2] Ibid., p. 275.
[3] Ibid., p. 296.

the ordinary ministerial channels: "There are no neutrals.
Whatever the papers produced, they are false. Not a
single ship enters Russia with so-called American papers
but comes really from England.[1] Peace or war is in the
hands of Russia. Let her confiscate all ships brought in
by the English, and join France in demanding of Sweden
the seizure of the immense quantity of merchandise the
English have landed at Gottenburg under various flags.
If Russia wishes peace with England, she has here the
means. But Russia has followed opposite principles, and
of this but one proof need be given: that is, that the
colonial merchandise which appeared at the last Leipzig
fair was brought there by seven hundred wagons coming
from Russia; that to-day all the traffic in that merchandise is done through Russia; finally, that the twelve hundred ships which the English have convoyed by twenty
ships of war, disguised under Swedish, Portuguese,
Spanish, American flags, have in part landed their cargoes in Russia." To these complaints Alexander had
replied that he had adhered, and would adhere, to his engagements and exclude British ships; but that he would
not, and could not, go beyond them and forbid neutrals.
The ukase of December 31 took the matter out of diplomatic discussion, and, coming so immediately upon the
annexation of Oldenburg, had the appearance of defiance.
As such Napoleon accepted it. "This seems," he wrote

---

[1] These contentions of Napoleon were for the most part perfectly correct.
Some interesting facts, bearing upon the true character of the so-called
neutral trade in the Baltic, may be gathered from Ross's Life of Saumarez,
vol. ii. chaps. ix.–xiii. See also representations made by a number of American ship-captains, Am. State Papers, vol. iii. pp. 329–333. On the other hand,
the scrupulously upright John Quincy Adams, U. S. minister to Russia,
affirmed that he positively knew some of the American ships to be direct
from the United States. The facts, however, only show the dependence of
the world at that time upon the Sea Power of Great Britain, which made
Napoleon's Continental System impossible; yet, on the other hand, it was his
only means of reaching his enemy. If he advanced, he was ruined; if he
receded, he failed.

in the personal letter of February 28 above quoted, "a change of system. All Europe so regards it; and already our alliance no longer exists, in the opinion of England and of Europe. . . . If your Majesty abandons the alliance and burns the conventions of Tilsit, it would be evident that war would follow a few months sooner or later. The result must be, on either side, to strain the resources of our empires in preparations. . . . If your Majesty has not the purpose of reconciliation with England, you will see the necessity, for yourself and for me, of dissipating all these clouds." From that time both sovereigns prepared for war.

The turn of affairs in the North at this time, and during the succeeding critical twelvemonth, was powerfully influenced by the presence of a great British fleet in the Baltic and by the extreme discretion of its admiral. Napoleon had compelled Sweden to follow up her exclusion of British ships by a formal declaration of war, which was issued November 17, 1810. The British minister had to leave Stockholm; and, after his departure, the political as well as military direction of affairs on the spot was under the conduct of Sir James Saumarez. That most distinguished and admirable officer had thoroughly appreciated, during his three summers in the Baltic, the feelings of the Swedish rulers and people; and it was chiefly owing to his representations to his own government, and to his steadily conciliatory action, that the formal war never became actual. He resisted with dignity and firmness every attempt on the part of the Swedish authorities to carry out Napoleon's orders to confiscate; but he did not allow himself to be moved, by such occasional yielding on their part, to any act of retaliation. Good feeling between the two nations centred around his attractive personality, and facilitated the essential, but difficult, conciliation between Sweden and Russia. The entire license trade was under the protection of his fleet, which had charge also of the suppression of privateering, of the police of the hostile coasts, and of the interruption of communications between Denmark and Norway.[1] Its presence virtually insured the independence of Sweden against France and Russia, except during the winter months, when compelled to leave the Baltic; and its numbers and character gave the Swedish government a sufficient excuse for not proceeding to the extremities demanded by Napoleon. During the summer of 1811 the flag-ship was the centre of the secret consultations which went on between the two states, to which Russia also, having finally rejected Napoleon's terms, soon became a party; and towards the end of the season the negotiation, practically completed by the admiral, was formally concluded with a British plenipotentiary. It was determined to keep up the appearance of war, but with the understanding that Sweden would 'join the alliance of Great Britain and Russia. The czar had then no cause to fear that, in the approaching contest with the great conqueror, he should find a hostile Sweden on his flank and rear.[2]

The preparations of Napoleon for the great Russian campaign occupied the year 1811. It was his intention to carry on a vigorous warfare in the Spanish peninsula, while collecting the immense forces of every kind needed in the north of Germany. But the unsatisfactory character of many of the soldiers gathering on the Elbe, among them being tens of thousands of refractory conscripts and foreign nationalities, compelled him to withdraw from

[1] During one year, 1809, this fleet captured 430 vessels, averaging sixty tons each, of which 340 were Danes. Among these were between thirty and forty armed cutters and schooners, of which Denmark had to employ a great many to supply Norway with grain. The remaining ninety vessels were Russian. (Naval Chronicle, vol. xxii. p. 517.)

[2] "Once more I must tell you," wrote a Swedish statesman to Saumarez, "that you were the first cause that Russia dared to make war against France. Had you fired one shot when we declared war against England, all had been ended and Europe would have been enslaved." (Ross's Saumarez, vol. ii p. 294.)

Spain in the latter part of 1811 some forty thousand veterans, whose place was to be filled by levies of an inferior character, which, moreover, did not at once appear. The fortune of war in the Peninsula during the year had varied in different quarters. On the east coast General Suchet had brought Tortosa to capitulate on the 1st of January. Thence advancing to the south he reduced Tarragona by siege and assault on the 28th of June,— an exploit which obtained for him his grade of Marshal of France. Still moving forward, according to Napoleon's general plan and instructions to him, the end of the year found him before the city of Valencia, which surrendered on the 9th of January, 1812. But to obtain these later successes, at the time that so many hardened warriors were removed from the Peninsula, it had been necessary to support Suchet with divisions taken from the centre and west, to abandon the hope entertained of combining another great attempt against Lisbon, and also to withdraw Marmont's corps from the valley of the Tagus to a more northern position, around Salamanca and Valladolid. At this time Wellington occupied a line on the frontiers of Portugal, north of the Tagus, resting on the city of Almeida and facing Ciudad Rodrigo. The latter, with Badajoz, on the Guadiana, constituted the two supports to the strong barrier by which the emperor proposed to check any offensive movements of the enemy upon Spain.

The year had been passed by the British general in patient contention with the innumerable difficulties, political and military, of his situation. Masséna had indeed been forced to withdraw from Portugal in April, but since that time Wellington had been balked, in every attempt, by superior numbers and by the strength of the positions opposed to him. His reward was now near at hand. On the 8th of January, 1812, he suddenly appeared before Ciudad Rodrigo, favored in his movements

by the pre-occupation of Marmont, who was engaged in
the reorganization and arrangements necessitated by the
withdrawal of so many troops for the Russian war, and
also deceived by the apparent inactivity in the British
lines. The siege was pushed with a vigor that disregarded the ordinary rules of war, and the place was successfully stormed on the 19th of January. As rapidly as
the nature of the country, the season, and other difficulties
would permit, Wellington moved to the south, intending
to attack Badajoz. On the 16th of March the place was
invested, and though most ably defended by a governor of
unusual ability, it was snatched out of the hands of Marshal Soult by the same audacity and disregard of ordinary
methods that had bereft Marmont of the sister fortress.
Badajoz was stormed on the night of the 6th of April;
and the Spanish frontier then lay open to the British, to
be crossed as soon as their numbers, or the mistakes of
the enemy, should justify the attempt.

Thus opened the fatal year 1812. The clouds breaking
away, though scarce yet perceptibly, for Great Britain,
were gathering in threatening masses on the horizon of
Napoleon. A painful picture is drawn by his eulogist,
M. Thiers, of the internal state of the empire at this time.
An excessively dry season had caused very short crops
throughout Europe, and want had produced bread riots in
England, as well as in France and elsewhere. But such
demonstrations of popular fury were far more dangerous
and significant, in a country where all expression of
opinion had been so rigorously controlled as in the empire, and in a capital which concentrates and leads, as
only Paris does, the feelings of a nation. The discontent
was heightened and deepened by the miseries of the conscription, which ate ever deeper and deeper, wringing the
heart of every family, and becoming more and more extreme as each succeeding enterprise became vaster than
those before it, and as the excessive demands, by reduc-

ing the quality of the individual victims, required ever
growing numbers. Six hundred thousand men had been
poured into Spain, three hundred thousand of whom had
died there.[1] Besides the immense masses carried forward
to the confines of Poland, and those destined for the Peninsula, there was to be a powerful reserve between the Elbe
and the Rhine, another behind the Rhine in France itself,
and to these Napoleon now proposed to add yet a third, of
one hundred and twenty thousand so-called national
guards, taken from the conscription of the four last years
and legally not liable to the call. Throughout the great
cities there was growing irritation, rising frequently to
mutiny, with loud popular outcries, and again the number
of refractory conscripts, of whom forty thousand had been
arrested the year before, rose to fifty thousand; again
flying columns pursued them through all the departments.
Caught, shut up in the islands off the coasts, whence they
could not escape, and, when drilled, marched under strong
guard to the ends of Europe, they none the less contrived
often to desert; and everywhere the people, hating the
emperor, received them with open arms and passed them
back, from hand to hand, to their homes. Thus amid
starvation, misery, weeping, and violence, the time drew
near for Napoleon to complete his great military undertaking of conquering the sea by the land.

In the North the situation had finally developed
according to the wishes of Great Britain. The secret
understanding of 1811 had resulted in January, 1812, in
another commercial ukase, allowing many British manufactures to be introduced into Russia. On the 5th of April
a secret treaty was concluded with Sweden, ceding Finland to Russia, but assuring to the former power Norway,
of which Denmark was to be deprived. Relieved now on
her northern flank, Russia soon after made peace with
Turkey under the mediation of Great Britain. Thus with
both hands freed she awaited the oncoming of Napoleon.

[1] Thiers, Cons. et Emp., Book xlii. p. 383.

On the 9th of May, 1812, the emperor left Paris to take
command of his forces in Poland; and on the 24th of June
the imperial army, to the number of four hundred thousand men, crossed the Niemen and entered Russia. Two
hundred thousand more followed close behind. The preceding day, June 23, the British Orders in Council of
1807 and 1809 were revoked, as to the United States of
America. It was too late. War had been declared by
Congress, and the declaration approved by the President,
five days before, on the 18th of June, 1812.

In narrating the extraordinary, and indeed unparalleled, series of events which reach their climax in the
Berlin and Milan Decrees and the Orders in Council, the
aim has been to compress the story within the closest limits
consistent with clearness, and at the same time to indicate the mutual connection of the links in the chain; how
one step led to another; and how throughout the whole,
amid apparent inconsistencies, there is an identity of
characteristics, not impossible to trace, from the outbreak
of the Revolution to the downfall of Napoleon. To do this
it has been thought expedient to suppress a mass of details,
much of a very interesting character, bearing upon the
working of the two opposing systems. The influence of
the military element of Sea Power, the function of the
British navy, after Trafalgar, has also been passed over in
silence. When that great disaster wrecked Napoleon's
naval hopes, and convinced him that not for many years
could he possibly gather the ships and train the seamen
necessary to meet his enemy in battle upon the ocean, he
seized with his usual sagacity the one only remaining
means of ruining her, and upon that concentrated his
great energies. The history of Europe and of the civilized
world, after 1805, turned upon this determination to destroy Great Britain through her commerce; and the decision was forced upon the mighty emperor by the power

of the British navy, and the wise resolve of the government
not to expose her land forces to his blows, until peculiarly
favorable circumstances should justify so doing.   The opportunity came with the Spanish uprising; and, by one of
those coincidences not uncommon in history, with the
hour came the man.   The situation was indeed of the most
favorable for Great Britain.   The theatre of war, sur-
rounded on three sides by water, was for the French a
salient thrust far out into the enemy's domain on the sea,
while its interior features and the political character of
the people, incapable of cohesion and organized effort,
made the struggle one eminently alien to the emperor's
genius; for it gave no opportunity for those brilliant combinations and lightning-like blows in which he delighted.
To the British the Peninsula offered the advantage that
the whole coast line was a base of operations; while every
friendly port was a bridge-head by which to penetrate, or
upon which, in case of reverse, to retire, with a sure retreat in the sea beyond.

The course pursued by each of the two governments, in
this great enterprise of commerce-destroying, may be
looked at from the two points of view, of policy and of
rightfulness.

In the matter of policy, both Napoleon's decrees and the
Orders in Council have been fiercely assailed and extensively argued.   In so broad and complicated a subject, a
probable conclusion can only be reached by disregarding
the mass of details, of statistics, with which the disputants have rather obscured than elucidated the subject,
and by seeking the underlying principle which guided, or
should have guided, either government.   It is possible to
form a very strong argument, for or against either, by
fastening upon the inevitable inconveniences entailed
upon each nation by the measures of its adversary and by
its own course.   It is by impressions received from these
incidents — or accidents — the accompaniments rather

than the essentials of the two systems, that the debates of Parliament and the conclusions of historians have been colored.

As the combined tendency of the two policies, fully carried out, was to destroy neutral trade in Europe, the preponderance of injury must fall upon the nation which most needed the concurrence of the neutral carrier. That nation unquestionably was France.[1] Even in peace, as before stated, much more than half her trade was done in neutral bottoms; the war left her wholly dependent upon them. Alike to export and to import she must have free admission of neutral ships to her ports. Prior to the Berlin decree the British made no pretence to stop this; but they did, by reviving in 1804 the Rule of 1756, and by Fox's decree of May, 1806, blockading the coast from Brest to the Elbe, betray an apprehension of the result to themselves of the neutral trade with France. This should have put the emperor upon his guard. The very anxieties shown by a people of such mercantile aptitudes should have been most seriously regarded, as betraying where their immediate danger lay. The American market was a most important benefit to them, but American merchant ships threatened to be a yet more important injury. These having, under the circumstances of the war, a practical monopoly of carrying West India produce which exceeded in quality and quantity that of the British Islands, were underselling the latter on the Continent. The ill effect of this was partially obviated by the Rule of 1756; but there remained the fear that they would absorb, and be absorbed by, the commerce of the Continent; that to it, and to it alone, they would carry both articles of consumption and raw materials for manufacture; and that from it, and from it alone, they would take away manufactured articles with which Great Britain up to the present time

---

[1] Compare Metternich's argument with the French Minister of Foreign Affairs, October 1807. (Memoirs, vol. ii. p. 161.)

had supplied them,—and, through them, large tracts of Spanish America.

Up to 1804 the course of trade had' been for American ships to. load for continental ports, receive there the greater part of the payment for their cargoes in bills of exchange on the Continent, and with these to go to British ports and pay for British manufactures, with which they completed their lading.   If, on the other hand, they went from home direct to Great Britain, the cargoes they carried were in excess of British consumption, and so far were profitable to Great Britain chiefly as to a middleman, who re-exported them to the Continent.   But, when Pitt returned to power, this course of trade was being sensibly modified.   American ships were going more and more direct to the Continent, there completing their cargoes and sailing direct for home. ·Continental manufactures were supplanting British, though not in all kinds, because the American carrier found it more profitable to take them as his return freight; just as the produce of continental colonies was, through the same medium, cutting under British coffees, sugars, and other tropical products. British merchants were alarmed because, not only their merchant shipping, but the trade it carried was being taken away; and British statesmen saw, in the decay of their commerce, the fall of the British navy which depended upon it.

It was plainly the policy of Napoleon to further a change which of itself was naturally growing, and which yet depended wholly upon the neutral carrier.   The latter was the key of the position; he was, while war lasted, essentially the enemy of Great Britain, who needed him little, and the friend of France, who needed him much.   Truth would have justified England in saying, as she felt, that every neutral was more or less serving France.   But in so doing the neutral was protected by the conventions of international law and precedent, which the British mind instinctively reveres, and for violating which it must have an excuse. This the emperor, whose genius inclined essentially to aggressive and violent action, promptly afforded. Overlooking the evident tendency of events, unmindful of the experience of 1798, he chose to regard the order of blockade of May, 1806, as a challenge, and issued the Berlin decree, which he was powerless to carry out unless the neutral ship came into a port under his control. He thus drove the latter away, lost its services, and gave Great Britain the excuse she was seeking for still further limiting its sphere of action, under the plea of retaliation upon France and her associates. And a most real retaliation it was. Opposition orators might harp on the definition of the word, and carp at the method as striking neutrals and not the enemy. Like Napoleon, they blinked at the fundamental fact that, while Great Britain ruled the sea, the neutral was the ally of her enemy.

The same simple principle vindicates the policy of the British ministry. Folios of argument and oratory have been produced to show the harm suffered by Great Britain in this battle over Commerce. Undoubtedly she suffered, — perhaps it would not be an exaggeration to say she nearly died; but when two combatants enter the lists, not for a chivalric parade but for life and death, it is not the incidental injuries, but the preponderance of harm done and the relative endurance, which determine the issue. To the same test of principle must be referred the mistakes in details charged against British ministries. Military writers say that, when the right strategic line of effort is chosen, mistakes of detail are comparatively harmless, and even a lost battle is not fatal. When France decided, practically, to suppress the concurrence of the neutral carrier, she made a strategic blunder; and when Great Britain took advantage of the mistake, she achieved a strategic success, which became a triumph.

As regards the rightfulness of the action of the two parties, viewed separately from their policy, opinions will probably always differ, according to the authority attributed by individuals to the *dicta* of International Law. It may be admitted at once that neither Napoleon's decrees nor the British orders can be justified at that bar, except by the simple plea of self-preservation,— the first law of states even more than of men; for no government is empowered to assent to that last sacrifice, which the individual may make for the noblest motives. The beneficent influence of the mass of conventions known as International Law is indisputable, nor should its authority be lightly undermined; but it cannot prevent the interests of belligerents and neutrals from clashing, nor speak with perfect clearness in all cases where they do. Of this the Rule of 1756 offered, in its day, a conspicuous instance. The belligerent claimed that the neutral, by covering with his flag a trade previously the monopoly of the enemy, not only inflicted a grave injury by snatching from him a lawful prey, but was guilty likewise of a breach of neutrality; the neutral contended that the enemy had a right to change his commercial regulations, in war as well as in peace. To the author, though an American, the belligerent argument seems the stronger; nor was the laudable desire of the neutral for gain a nobler motive than the solicitude, about their national resources, of men who rightly believed themselves engaged in a struggle for national existence. The measure meted to Austria and Prussia was an ominous indication of the fate Great Britain might expect, if her strength failed her. But, whatever the decision of our older and milder civilization on the merits of the particular question, there can be no doubt of the passionate earnestness of the two disputants in their day, nor of the conviction of right held by either. In such a dilemma, the last answer of International Law has to be that every state is the final judge as to whether it should or should not make war; to its own self alone is it responsible for the rightfulness of this action. If, however, the condition of injury entailed by the neutral's course is such as to justify war, it justifies all lesser means of control. The question of the rightfulness of these disappears, and that of policy alone remains.

It is the business of the neutral, by his prepared condition, to make impolitic that which he claims is also wrong. The neutral which fails to do so, which leaves its ports defenceless and its navy stunted until the emergency comes, will then find, as the United States found in the early years of this century, an admirable opportunity to write State Papers.

CHAPTER XIX.

SUMMARY. — THE FUNCTION OF SEA POWER AND THE POLICY OF GREAT BRITAIN IN THE REVOLUTIONARY AND NAPOLEONIC WARS.

THE outbreak of the French Revolutionary War found Great Britain unprepared. For nearly ten years her course had been directed by the second Pitt, who, though inheriting the lofty spirit and indomitable constancy of his father, yet loved peace rather than war, and sought the greatness and prosperity of his country through the development of her commerce and manufactures and the skilful management of her finances. He strove also consistently for the reduction of expenditure, including that for the military, and even for the naval establishment. As late as February 17, 1792, when the Revolution had already been nearly three years in progress and France was on the eve of declaring war against Prussia and Austria, he avowed his expectation of many years of peace for the British empire; and the estimates provided for only sixteen thousand seamen and marines. "Unquestionably," said he, "there never was a time in the history of this country, when, from the situation of Europe, we might more reasonably expect fifteen years of peace than at the present moment." When the war with Germany began, Great Britain proclaimed and steadily maintained an attitude of neutrality; and the Minister asserted over and over again; to France and to her enemies, the intention not to interfere with the internal affairs of that country. This purpose continued unshaken through the tremendous events of the succeeding summer and autumn;

through the assaults on the Tuileries on June 20 and
August 10, through the suspension of the king which
immediately followed the latter date, through the revolt-
ing massacres of September, finally through the deposi-
tion of the King and the proclamation of the Republic.
Doubtless these events gave a series of shocks to public
opinion in Great Britain, alienating the friends and em-
bittering the enemies of the Revolution; doubtless whatever sympathy with the French advance towards freedom
the ministers felt was chilled and repelled by the excesses
and anarchy which marked its. steps; but, whatever their
personal feelings, no indication appears, either in their
public actions or in their private correspondence as since
revealed, of any intention to depart from a strict, even
though cold, neutrality, until near the end of the year
1792.

The leaders of the party in France, which at this time
was exerting the greatest influence upon the course of
the Revolution, had long favored war with foreign
nations, as the surest means to destroy the monarchy and
unite public feeling in favor of the Republic and of the
Revolution. The course of events had justified their
forecast. Prussia and Austria had given provocation;
and, although the latter at least would not have proceeded to extremes, war had been proclaimed and the
fall of the monarchy had followed. There was, however,
one nation with which the revolutionists imagined themselves to be in sympathy, and which they thought also as
a whole sympathized with them. That nation was the
English; between England and France there was to be
friendship, and concurrence of effort to a common end.
Herein the French leaders fatally misconceived the character of English freedom, and the nature of its successive
advances to the conditions in which it then stood, and
through which Englishmen hoped for yet further enlargement. Reverence for the past, and, in the main, for the

existing order of things; profound regard for law and for an orderly method of making needful changes; a constant reference to the old rights and customs of the English people; respect for vested rights, for agreements, for treaties,— such were the checks which had modified and controlled the actions of the English, even when most profoundly moved. The spirit which dominated the French Revolution was that of destruction. The standard, by which all things human were to be tried, was a declaration of human rights put forth by its leaders, which contained indeed many noble, true, and most essential principles; but, if aught existing did not at once square with those principles, the forces of the Revolution were to advance against it and sweep it from the face of the earth. No respect for the past, no existent prescriptive rights, no treaties that seemed contrary to natural rights, were to control the actions of the revolutionists. They were to destroy, and to rebuild from the foundation, according to their own interpretation of what justice demanded.

The courses and aims, therefore, of the two nations were wholly divergent, and, as these were but the expression in either case of the national temper, the hope of sympathy and concurrence was delusive; but it was a natural delusion, fostered in the hearts of the sanguine Frenchmen by the utterances of many warm-hearted friends of freedom in the rival nation, and by the more violent words of a limited number of revolutionary societies. The former of these were, however, quickly alienated by the atrocities which began to stain the progress of the Revolution; while the latter, being supposed by the French leaders to represent the feeling of the British nation, as distinguished from its Government, contributed to draw them further in that path of reckless enmity to existing institutions which led to the war with Great Britain.

Still, so long as the exponents of French public feeling confined themselves to violent and irregular action within their own borders, and to declamations, which did not go beyond words, against the governments and institutions of other nations, the British ministry remained quiet, though watchful. There are extant private letters, written in the early part of November, 1792, by the Prime Minister, and by his relative, Lord Grenville, the Minister of Foreign Affairs, which indicate that they rejoiced in having maintained the neutrality of Great Britain, and that they looked forward to its continuance, though with anxiety. But on the 19th of that month the National Convention, which then comprised within itself both the executive and legislative functions of the French Government, adopted a declaration that it would grant fraternity and succor to *all* people who should wish to recover their liberty;[1] and it charged administrative officers to give republican generals the necessary orders to carry help to those people and to defend their citizens who had been molested, or who might be subject to molestation, on account of their devotion to the cause of liberty. As if further to emphasize the scope of this decree, for such in effect it was, it was ordered to be translated and printed in all languages.

By this official action the French Government had taken a great and important step, radically modifying its relations to all other states. The decree did not mention the governments with which France was then at war, limiting to their people the application of its terms. On the contrary, when a member of the Convention, a month later, proposed to insert words which should restrict its operation to those peoples "against whose tyrants France was, or should hereafter be, at war," and gave, as his reason, to remove the uneasiness of Great Britain, the motion found no support. The previous question was

---

[1] Annual Register, 1792; State Papers, p. 355.

moved, and the Convention passed on to other business.[1]

The men who then wielded the power of France had
thus gone beyond a simple inveighing against other governments, and the mere use of words calculated to excite
discontent among the people of other states, and had
announced an intention to interfere forcibly in their internal affairs whenever called upon to do so by citizens
who, in the opinion of the French Government, were deprived of their just liberty or molested in their efforts to
recover it. The anarchist of our own day, who contents
himself with verbally attacking existing laws and institutions, however vehemently, may remain untouched so long
as he confines himself to the expression and advocacy of his
opinions; but when he incites others to action in order to
carry out his ideas, he is held responsible for the effect of
his words; and when he takes measures leading to violence, he is open to arrest and punishment. Such as this,
among governments, was the step taken by France in
November, 1792. She not only incited the citizens of
other states to rebellion, but announced her intention of
supporting them, and gave to her generals the necessary
orders for carrying that purpose into effect.

Meanwhile the Austrian Netherlands was rapidly overrun and annexed to the French Republic, which thus
abandoned the lofty posture of disinterestedness, and the
disclaimers of all desire for conquest which the leaders of
the Revolution had made from the tribune of the Convention. Soon after followed a decree declaring the navigation of the Scheldt, the great artery of Belgium, open to
the sea. This set aside, without negotiation, the compacts of the previous owners of the Netherlands, by which
the navigation of the river from the sea was reserved to
Holland, within whose territory the mouth lay, — an
agreement consecrated by renewed treaties, and which,

[1] Moniteur, Dec. 25, 1792; Proposition of M. Barailon.

by long standing, had become part of the public law of
Europe. The act strikingly showed the determination of
the French leaders to disregard treaties which conflicted
with their construction of the natural rights of man; for
they were at peace with Holland, yet made no attempt to
obtain their end by negotiation.

The interests and the peace of Great Britain were now
seriously threatened. For over a century her statesmen
had held, and held rightly, that the possession of Belgium
by France was incompatible with her security. They had
supported the legal, though iniquitous, claim of the
Dutch to the exclusive navigation of the Scheldt; and,
above all, the country was bound by a treaty of alliance
to defend Holland, whose rights as defined by treaty had
been rudely set aside by France. Moreover, on the 28th
of November deputations from the British revolutionary
societies were received at the bar of the Convention, and
the President of the latter, in reply to their address,
made a speech strongly hostile to the British Government,
affecting to distinguish between it and the people over
whom it ruled; a pretence which was equally maintained
in the United States of America, where the French minister the following year dared to appeal openly to the
people against the policy of their government.

On the 1st of December the British Government issued
a proclamation, calling out the militia on account of
seditions and insurrectionary movements dangerous to
the state, and at the same time, as required by law, summoned Parliament to meet on the 15th. The hopes
and the patience of Pitt were alike exhausted; and
although he still continued to listen to any overtures
that contained a promise of peace, he had determined to
exact guarantees, amounting to more than words, which
should assure the safety of Great Britain and her ally,
Holland. Meantime the British forces should be organized and got ready to act. The French Government had

proclaimed its intention of interfering in the affairs and overthrowing the institutions of all states, when, in its judgment, their citizens were molested in their efforts for freedom. To await supinely the moment when it should please France to act would be the decision of folly; nor was it possible, for one imbued with English traditions, to view without distrust a government which appeared to look for justice by disregarding law, and avowedly disowned existing compacts and treaties in favor of a speculative somewhat called the Rights of Man, concerning which, its own passions being the judge, revelations as numerous might be expected as were vouchsafed to Mahomet.

There are some who can only account for the different lines of action followed by Pitt, before and after 1792, in both cases with the indomitable tenacity of his race and lineage, by conceiving two entirely different personalities in the same man,— a sudden and portentous change, unprecedented save by miracle as in the case of St. Paul. More truly may be seen in him the same man acting under circumstances wholly different, and in the later instance unforeseen. It was not given to Pitt to read the future of the French Revolution with the prophetic eye of Burke. He had the genius, not of the seer, but of the man of affairs; but that he had the latter in an eminent degree is evident from the very rapidity of the change, when he was at last forced to the conviction that external conditions were wholly changed. He was at heart the minister of peace, the financier, the promoter of commerce and of gradual and healthy reforms; but in a great speech, delivered before he had begun to fear that peace would end in his time, he impressed upon his hearers his own profound conviction that all the blessings which England then enjoyed rested upon the union of liberty with law. Having enumerated the material circumstances to which the existing prosperity of the nation was to be ascribed, he continued : —

" But these are connected with others more important. They are obviously and necessarily connected with the duration of peace, the continuance of which, on a secure and durable footing, must ever be the first object of the foreign policy of this country. They are connected *still more* with its internal tranquillity, and with the natural effects of a free but well-regulated government. . . . This is the great and governing cause, the operation of which has given scope to all the other circumstances which I have enumerated. It is the union of liberty with law, which, by raising a barrier equally firm against the encroachments of power and the violence of popular commotion, affords to property its just security, produces the exertion of genius and labor, the extent and solidity of credit, the circulation and increase of capital ; which forms and upholds the national character and sets in motion all the springs which actuate the great mass of the community through all its various descriptions. . . . On this point, therefore, let us principally fix our attention ; let us preserve this first and most essential object, and every other is in our power." [1]

It was perfectly consistent with this position that, when Pitt saw a neighboring state in convulsions from the struggle of a turbulent minority for liberty without law ; when that state had not only proclaimed its purpose, but taken steps to promote a similar condition in other nations ; when societies representing a small, but active and radical, minority in England were openly fraternizing with France ; when the great leader of the English Opposition had, from his seat in Parliament, praised the French soldiery for joining the mobs, — it was perfectly consistent with his past that Pitt should oppose with all his powers a course of action which not only endangered the internal peace upon which the prosperity

[1] Pitt's Speeches, vol. ii. pp. 46, 47.

of England rested, but also carried into the realm of international relations the same disorganizing principles, the same disregard for law, covenant, and vested right that had reduced France to her then pitiful condition. Not only Great Britain, but the European world was threatened with subversion. That Pitt did not bewail aloud the wreck of his hopes, the frustration of his career, the diversion of his energies from the path that was dearest to him, shows the strength, not the instability, of the man. That he laid aside the reforms he had projected, and discouraged all movements towards internal change, which, by dividing the wills of the people, might weaken their power for external action, proves but that concentration of purpose which, sacrificing present gratification to future good, achieves great ends. Never does the trained seaman appear greater, has well said the naval novelist Cooper, than when, confronted with unexpected peril, he turns all his energies from the path in which they were before directed, to meet the new danger. "Never," writes Lanfrey of the critical period between Essling and Wagram, "had the maxim of sacrificing the accessory to the principal, of which Napoleon's military conceptions afford so many admirable examples, *and which is true in every art*, been applied with more activity and fitness. . . . The complications which he most feared were to him, for the moment, as though they did not exist. No secondary event had power to draw him off from the great task he had primarily assigned to himself." [1] All instinctively recognize the courage as well as the wisdom of this conduct in the dangers which the seaman and the soldier are called to meet; why deny its application to the no less urgent, and at times more momentous, issues presented to the statesman? If, as may fairly be claimed, it is to the maritime power of Great Britain that Europe owes the arrest of a subversive

[1] Lanfrey's Napoleon, vol. iv. p. 112 (Eng. trans., ed. 1886).

revolution, if to that 'maritime power is due that a great, irresistible, and beneficent movement toward the liberty and welfare of the masses survived a convulsion that threatened its destruction, then to Pitt, as the master spirit who directed the movements of the British nation, the gratitude of Europe is also due.

When Parliament met on the 15th of December, the king's speech mentioned the disturbances that had taken place in the country and the threatening state of affairs in Europe, and recommended an increase in the land and sea forces of the kingdom. This measure was alleged, among other grievances by France, as indicating an unfriendly feeling toward her on the part of the British Government; but it has been reasonably urged that she had already manned a fleet superior to that which Great Britain had in commission, besides keeping ready for instant service a large number of other ships, which could have no possible enemy except the British navy. Viewed simply as measures of precaution, of the necessity for which every state is its own judge, it is difficult to criticise severely either government; but the fact remains that France had been the first to arm her fleet, and that Great Britain did not do the same until substantial grounds of offence had been given.

By a singular coincidence, on the same day that Parliament met, the National Convention issued a second celebrated decree, yet more decisive in its character than that of November 19, which it was evidently meant to emphasize and supplement. The generals of the Republic were now directed "in every country which the armies of the French Republic shall occupy, to announce the abolition of all existing authorities, of nobility, of serfage, of every feudal right and every monopoly; to proclaim the sovereignty of the people and convoke the inhabitants in assemblies to form a provisional government, to which no officer of a former government, no noble, nor any member

of the former privileged corporations, shall be eligible."
To this was added the singular and most significant declaration that "the French nation will treat as enemies
any people which, refusing liberty and equality, desires
to preserve its prince and privileged castes, or to make
any accommodation with them." It was impossible to
announce more clearly that this was no mere war of
opinions, but, on the contrary, one of principles and
methods fraught with serious and practical consequences;
nor could any despot have worded a more contemptuous
denial of the rights of a people concerning their form of
government. The revolutionary spirit, which underlay
the frequent changes of men in the French Government,
showed how fixed was its purpose to alter forcibly the
institutions of other states, regardless of the habits and
affections of their citizens, by the systems imposed upon
the smaller neighboring nations, hammered all upon the
anvil of French centralization, in defiance of the wishes
and the struggles of the people concerned. Europe thus
found itself face to face with a movement as enthusiastic
in its temper and as radical in its demands as the
invasions of the Mahometans.

To this fanatical, yet lofty, and in the masses of the
French people generous and devoted spirit, continental Europe had no equal force to oppose. It is a common remark
that the eighteenth century saw the appearance of several
ruling princes who were possessed with the liberal views of
the rising school of philosophers, and who sincerely desired to effect the improvement and elevation of their
people, — to remove grievances, to lighten burdens, to
advance the general welfare. The wisdom or strength
of these men had not been equal to the task they had
assumed. There still remained unjustifiable inequalities
of conditions, grievous abuses; a depression of the lower
orders, and a stagnation among the upper, which seemed
to place insurmountable obstacles in the way of advance,

and made it impossible for the masses to feel a living, national interest in governments which contributed so little to their happiness. This good-will among the sovereigns of the day was indeed a most encouraging symptom. It made it possible to effect the needed changes and to advance without a violent break with the past, — to have reform and progress without revolution; but to achieve these ends was beyond the power of the ruler alone: there was needed the voice and co-operation of all classes in the state. This Louis XVI. had sought to obtain; but unfortunately, not only for France but for Europe, the most numerous and important of the orders of the States-General had met the difficulties of the situation, the outcome of centuries, not with firmness, but with impatience. From the beginning was shown the determination to break with the past, — to proceed at a bound to the desired goal. No regard was had to the fitness of the people for such sudden change, to the immense conservative force of established custom, nor to the value of continuity in the life of a nation. Nor was this all. Law, as well as custom, was lightly set at nought. The first Assembly threw off the fetters imposed by its instructions, and assumed powers which had not been confided to it. By means of these usurped faculties the Constituent Assembly radically changed the constitution of France.

The instantaneous effect upon the French people and upon the internal condition of the state is well known. As the far-reaching character of the movement, and its lack of efficient elements for self-control, became evident, the anxieties of conservative men in other nations, however desirous of steady progress in human liberty, could not fail to be aroused. It was notorious, long before 1792, that ill-balanced as was the new constitutional frame of government in France, and radical as was the temper of the leading members of the Legislative Assembly, the deliberations of the latter were overawed by the clubs and the populace of Paris, and that government had practically passed into the hands of the mob which was worked by the clubs and the radical municipality of the city. The grotesque yet terrible scenes of June 20 and August 10, the hideous massacres of September, not merely showed the frantic excesses of which a French mob is capable, but also and more solemnly evinced how completely governmental control was swallowed up in anarchy. Still, all these things were internal to France, and it might be hoped would so remain until the French people had worked their own solution of their troubles. The decrees of November 19 and December 15 blasted this hope, and formally announced that French beliefs and methods were to be forcibly spread throughout Europe. How was the assault to be met?

Few statesmen of that day expected that this mighty and furious spirit of misrule would so soon bend its neck to an uncontrolled and energetic despotism. The coming of the one man, Napoleon, was dimly seen in the distance by the thoughtful, who knew that anarchy clears the way for absolute power; but the speedy appearance and tyrannous efficiency of the Committee of Public Safety, with its handmaid the Revolutionary Tribunal, were not foreseen. The statesmen of 1793 saw the strength, but were more impressed by the superficial exhibition of disorder in the popular outburst. They expected to repress it, to drive it back within the limits of France, and impose the guarantees necessary for the security of Europe, by meeting it with numerous, well-organized armies of veteran troops, and by a solid, orderly financial system, wielding plentiful resources. In short, they thought to cope with a mighty spirit by means of elaborate and powerful machinery. The means were insufficient. The living spirit developed the rude but efficient organism which was needed to direct its energies and which was in sympathy with its aims; the elaborate machinery of armies and finances failed, because not quickened by the life of the nations by whose rulers it was wielded.

Fortunately for Europe and for freedom, another spirit, less demonstrative but equally powerful, was already living and animating another great nation, peculiarly fitted by position and by the character of its power to grapple with and exhaust that which was vicious and destructive in the temper of the French Revolution. As already said, the great feature of English freedom was its respect for law, for established authority, for existing rights; its conservative while progressive character, in which it was directly opposed to the subversive principles of the French. But the English temper, when once aroused, was marked also by a tenacity of purpose, a constancy of endurance, which strongly supported the conservative tendencies of the race and were equally foreign to the French character. Once embarked in the strife, and definitely committed for the time to the preservation, rather than to the progress, of society, under leaders who strongly embodied the national traits, hatred of the enemy's principles became more conspicuous, superficially, than the love of freedom, which yet retained its hold deep in the hearts of both rulers and people. War does not live on the benevolent emotions, though it may be excited by them. The position and the maritime power of England were great factors, great determining factors in the final issue of the French Revolutionary wars; but these were but the machinery of the British power. The great gain to the cause of stability in human history was made when the spirit of order and law, embodied in the great nation which it had created, rose against the spirit of lawlessness and anarchy, which had now possessed a people who for long years and by nature had been submissively subject to external authority. Two living forces had met in a desperate struggle, which was not indeed for life and death, for both would survive; but from which should result the predominance of the one that was compatible with reasonable freedom, and the subjection of the other, which knew no mean between anarchy and servile submission. Less ebullient, but more steadfast and deeply rooted, the former wore out the latter; it forced it back through the stage of prostration under absolute power until it had returned to the point whence it started, there to renew its journey under conditions that made it no longer a danger to the whole world.

Such being the profound nature of the strife, its course may be regarded under two aspects, not necessarily opposed, but rather complementary. First, and obviously, there is the policy of the leaders on either side, the objects which they proposed to themselves, the steps by which they sought to compass those objects, and the results of their various movements. Secondly, there is the more obscure and wider question as to the relative influence of the great elements of power which entered as unconscious factors in the strife,— mighty forces, wielded or directed by statesmen, and yet after all their masters. Of these factors Sea Power was one, and among the most important.

The circumstances of the times had placed this force wholly in the hands of Great Britain. She wielded it as absolute mistress. Its action, like that of all the other forces in the strife, depended in part upon the direction given it by the British leaders for the purposes of war. From this point of view, its structure appears to be simple and rudimentary; the related movements of a few principal parts are open to inspection and susceptible of criticism. But from another point of view, in its course and influence, this wonderful and mysterious Power is seen to be a complex organism, endued with a life of its own, receiving and imparting countless impulses, moving in a thousand currents which twine in and around one another in infinite flexibility, not quite defying the investigation which they provoke, but rendering it exceedingly laborious. This Power feels and is moved by many interests; it has a great history in the past, it is making a great and yet more wonderful history in the present. Grown to the size of a colossus, which overshadows the earth without a second, — unless it be the new rival rising in the Western hemisphere, — it is now assailed with a fury and virulence never before displayed. Attacked in every quarter and by every means, sought to be cut off alike from the sources and from the issues of its enterprise, it adapts itself with the readiness of instinct to every change. It yields here, it pushes there; it gives ground in one quarter, it advances in another; it bears heavy burdens, it receives heavy blows; but throughout all it lives and it grows. It does not grow because of the war, but it does grow in spite of the war. The war impedes and checks, but does not stop, its progress. Drained of its seamen for the war-fleets, it modifies the restrictions of generations, throws open its ports to neutral ships, its decks to neutral seamen, and by means of those allies maintains its fair proportions, until the enemy proclaims that the neutral who carries but a bale of British goods, even to his own country, ceases thereby to be a neutral and becomes the enemy of France; a proclamation which but precipitated the ruin of French commerce, without markedly injuring that of its rival.

The maritime power and commercial prosperity of Great Britain sprang essentially from the genius and aptitudes of her people, and were exceptionally favored and developed by the peculiar situation of the British Islands. To these natural advantages the policy of the government added somewhat, as at times it also ignorantly imposed obstacles; but the actions of statesmen only modified, for good or ill, they did not create the impulses which originated and maintained the maritime activity of the British people. The most celebrated measure designed to foster that activity, Cromwell's Navigation Act, had now been in operation for a century and a quarter; but, while its superficial effects had secured the adherence of the British people and the envy of foreign states, shrewder economists, even a century ago, had come to regard it as an injury to the commercial prosperity of the country. They justified it only as a means of forcing the development of the merchant marine, the nursery of the naval force upon which the safety of Great Britain must depend. Whatever the fluctations of its fortunes or the mistakes of governments in the past, the sea power of Great Britain had at the opening of the French Revolution attained proportions, and shown a tenacity of life, which carried the promise of the vast expansion of our own day. Painfully harassed during the American Revolution, and suffering from the combined attacks of France, Spain, and Holland, seeing then large portions of its carrying trade pass into the hands of neutrals, and bereft by the event of the war of its most powerful colonies, it had not only survived these strains, but by the immediate and sustained reaction of the peace had, in 1793, more than regained its pre-eminence. Once more it stood ready, not only to protect its own country, but to sustain, with its well-proved vitality, the demands of the continental war; where the armies of her allies, long untouched by the fires which breathed in France and England, were but a part of the machinery through which the maritime power of the latter energized.

How far the ministers of the day understood, and how wisely they used, the sea power of Great Britain, is a question that will demand a separate consideration. That is the question of military policy,— of the strategy of the war. We have first to consider the influence of the maritime power in itself, and the functions discharged by Great Britain simply in consequence of possessing this great and unique resource. The existence, powers, and unconscious working of a faculty obviously offer a subject for consideration distinct from the intelligent use of the faculty; though a correct appreciation of the former conduces to an accurate criticism of the latter.

Because of the decay of the French navy during the early years of the war, the Republic, after 1795, virtually abandoned all attempt to contest control of the sea. A necessary consequence was the disappearance of its merchant shipping, a result accelerated by the capture of most of its colonies, and the ruin of its colonial system by the outbreaks of the blacks. So great was this loss, due rather to the natural operation of Great Britain's naval supremacy than to any particular direction by the ministry, that the Executive Directory, in a message to the Council of Five Hundred, January 13, 1799, could use the expression, scarcely exaggerated, "It is unhappily too true that there is not a single merchant vessel sailing under the French flag." Two years later the Minister of the Interior reported to the Consular Government that the commerce with Asia, Africa, and America was almost naught, the importations direct from all those quarters of the globe amounting to only 1,500,000 francs, while the exports to them were but 300,000 francs. As the advancing tide of French conquest extended the territory and alliances of the Republic, the commerce of its new friends was involved in the same disaster that had befallen its own. The shipping of Spain and Holland thus also disappeared from the sea, and a large part of their colonies likewise passed into the hands of Great Britain, to swell the commerce and to employ the shipping of the latter. The navy of neither of these Powers exerted any effect upon the control of the sea, except so far as they occupied the attention of detachments of the British navy, so marked had the numerical and moral superiority of the latter become.

The disappearance of so large a body of merchant shipping as that of France, Holland, and Spain, could not, of course, imply the total loss to commerce and to the world of the traffic previously done by it. Much less could these three countries wholly dispense with the supplies for which, during peace, they had chiefly depended upon the sea. On the contrary, the necessity for importing many articles by sea was increased by the general continental war, which not only created a long hostile frontier, prohibitory of intercourse on the land side, but also, by drawing great numbers of workers from their ordinary occupations to the armies of all parties, caused a material diminution in the products of Europe at large. In France, shut in both by land and sea, with a million of men under arms, and confronted with the stern determination of England to reduce her by starvation, the danger and the suffering were particularly great; and had there not been a singularly abundant and early harvest in 1794, the aim of her enemy might then have been in great measure reached.

Such a condition of things offered of course a great opening to neutral maritime states. They hastened to embrace it, — among others the United States, whose carrying trade grew very rapidly at this time; but the naval power of Great Britain during this period was so overwhelming, and her purpose so strong, that she succeeded in imposing severe restraints upon neutrals as well as enemies, in matters which she considered of prime importance. Sweden and Denmark strenuously resisted her claim to prevent the importation into France of provisions and naval stores; but failing, through the hostile attitude of the Czarina towards France, to receive the powerful support of Russia, as in 1780 they had done, they were forced to succumb to the Power of the Sea. The United States likewise were constrained by their impotence to yield, under protest, before the same overwhelming Power. While reserving the principle, they in practice conceded naval stores to be contraband, and on the subject of provisions accepted a compromise which protected their own citizens without materially injuring France. No serious attempt was made to change the existing rule of international law, by which enemies' property on board neutral ships was good prize. As seizure involved sending the ship into a port of the captor, and a possible detention there during the adjudication of suspected goods, the inconvenience of the process was a powerful deterrent. The English courts also held that the produce of hostile colonies was lawful prize if found in neutral bottoms; because, the trade of those colonies being by the mother countries interdicted to foreigners in peace, the concession of it in war was merely a ruse to defraud the other belligerent of his just rights of capture, — a plea uselessly contested by American writers. All these causes operated to the injury of both hostile and neutral commerce, and to the same extent, in appearance at least, to the benefit of the British; and they are cited simply as illustrative of the natural working of so great a force as the Sea Power of Great Britain then was. The results were due, not to the skill with which the force was used or distributed, but to sheer preponderance of existing brute strength.

By the destruction of the enemies' own shipping and by denying neutrals the right to carry to them many articles of the first importance, Great Britain placed the hostile countries in a state of comparative isolation, and created within their borders a demand for the prohibited merchandise which raised its price and made the supplying of it extremely profitable. When commercial intercourse is thus refused its usual direct roads, it seeks a new path, by the nearest circuitous course, with all the persistency of a natural force. The supply will work its way to the demand, though in diminished volume, through all the obstacles interposed by man. Even the contracted lines about a beleaguered city will thus be pierced by the ingenuity of the trader seeking gain; but when the blockade is extended over a long frontier, total exclusion becomes hopeless. In such cases the tendency of commerce is to seek a centre near the line which it intends to cross, and there to accumulate the goods which are to pass the hostile frontier and reach the belligerent. That centre will usually be in a neutral seaport, to which trade is free, and a clearance for which will afford no pretext for seizure or detention by the opposite belligerent. Thus, in the American Revolution, the neutral Dutch island of St. Eustatius became the rendezvous and depot of traders who purposed to introduce their goods, even contraband of war, into the West India islands of either party to that contest; and it was asserted that upon its capture by the British, in 1781, when war began with Holland, large amounts of property belonging to English merchants, but intended for French customers, were found there. So, in the American Civil War, from 1861 to 1865, the town of Nassau in the British Bahamas became a centre at which were accumulated stores of all kinds intended to break through the blockade of the Southern coast.

So again, in the wars of the French Revolution, as long as Holland remained in alliance with Great Britain, that country was the centre from which foreign goods poured into France and the continent of Europe; but when the United Provinces had been overrun by French troops, and a revolution in their government had attached them to the French policy, commerce, driven from their now blockaded coast, sought another depot farther to the eastward, and found it in Bremen, Hamburg, and some other German ports, — of which, however, Hamburg was by far the most

favored and prosperous. Through Hamburg the coffee
and sugar of the West Indies, the manufactured goods of
Great Britain, the food products of America, the luxuries
of the East, poured into Germany; and also into France,
despite the prohibitive measures of French governments.
An indication of this change in the course of commerce is
found in the fact that the imports from Great Britain
alone into Germany, which amounted to £2,000,000 in
1792, had in 1796, the year after Holland became allied
to France, increased to £8,000,000, although the purchasing power of Germany had meanwhile diminished. In
the same time the tonnage annually clearing from Great
Britain to Germany increased from 120,000 to 266,000.
Similar results, on a much smaller scale, were seen at
Gibraltar when Spain attempted to prevent British goods
entering her own ports; and again at Malta, when the
possession of that island offered British commerce a foothold far advanced in the Central Mediterranean. Somewhat similar, likewise, were the advantages of the islands
of Ceylon and Trinidad with reference to the mainlands
of India and South America, which gave to them a particular commercial as well as strategic value, and led
England to accept them as her compensations at the
Peace of Amiens.

In such cases the temporary commercial centre not only
reaps the profits of the broker, but all classes of its community benefit by the increase of employments, of floating
capital, and of floating population. Precisely analogous
to these was the office which her geographical position
and unrivalled control of the sea enabled Great Britain
to discharge toward the European world during the
French Revolution. Her maritime power and commercial spirit, the gradual though rapid growth of past generations, enabled her at once to become the warehouse where
accumulated the products of all nations and of all seas
then open to commerce, and whence they were trans-

shipped to the tempest-tossed and war-torn Continent
So also her watery bulwarks, traversed in every direction
by her powerful navy, secured her peaceful working as the
great manufactory of Europe, and thus fostered an immense
development of her industries, which had become more
than ever necessary to the welfare of the world, since those
of Holland and France were either crippled for want of
raw material or isolated by their impotence at sea. Great
Britain impeded the direct admission of tropical products
to the Continent; but their re-exportation from her own
ports and the export of British manufactures became the
two chief sources of her singular prosperity. The favorable reaction produced by this concentration within her
borders of so much of the commercial machinery of the
civilized world, is evident. Activities of every kind
sprang up on all sides, increasing the employment of
labor and the circulation of capital; and, while it is vain
to contend that war increases the prosperity of nations, it
must be conceded that such a state of things as we have
depicted affords much compensation to the nation concerned, and may even increase its proportionate prosperity,
when compared with that of its less fortunate enemies.
To quote the words of Lanfrey: "The English nation had
never at any time shown more reliance upon its own resources than when Pitt, in 1801, retired after eight years
of war. The people bore without difficulty the heavy taxes
which the war imposed upon them, and what was more
astonishing still, Pitt had found no opposition in Parliament to his last Budget. The immense increase in the
industrial prosperity of England triumphantly refuted the
predictions of her enemies, as well as the complaints of
alarmists. As the effect of every fresh declaration of
war upon the Continent had been to diminish competition
in the great market of the world and to throw into her
hands the navies and colonies of her adversaries, the English had begun to look upon the loan of millions and the

subsidies as so much premium paid for the development of their own resources. " [1]

It is not, therefore, merely as a weapon of war in the hands of the ministry that the sea power of Great Britain is to be regarded; nor yet only as the fruitful mother of subsidies, upon whose bountiful breasts hung the impoverished and struggling nations of the Continent. Great as were its value and importance in these respects, it had yet a nobler and more vital function. Upon it depended the vigorous life of the great nation which supplied the only power of motive capable of coping with the demoniac energy that then possessed the spirit of the French. Great Britain, though herself unconscious of the future, was in the case of a man called upon to undergo a prolonged period of trial, exposure, and anxiety, severely testing all his powers, physical and mental. However sound the constitution, it is essential that, when thus assailed by adverse external influences, all its vital processes should be protected, nourished, and even stimulated, or else the bodily energies will flag, fail, and collapse. This protection, this nourishment, the maritime power ministered to the body politic of the state. Despite the undeniable sufferings of large classes among the people, the ministry could boast from year to year the general prosperity of the realm, the flourishing condition of commerce, the progressive preponderance and control of the sea exerted by the navy, and a series of naval victories of unprecedented brilliancy, which stimulated to the highest degree the enthusiasm of the nation. Such a combination of encouraging circumstances maintained in full tension the springs of self-confidence and moral energy, in the absence of which no merely material powers or resources are capable of effective action. | \

By the natural and almost unaided working of its intrinsic faculties, the sea power of Great Britain sus-

---

[1] Lanfrey's *Napoleon*, vol. ii. chap. iii. p. 122 (Eng. trans., 2d ed.).

tained the material forces of the state and the spirit of
the people. From these we turn to the consideration of
the more striking, though not more profound, effects produced by the use made of this maritime power by the
British ministry — to the policy and naval strategy of the
war — in curtailing the resources and sapping the strength
of the enemy, and in compelling him to efforts at once
inevitable, exhausting, and fruitless. In undertaking
this examination, it will be first necessary to ascertain
what were the objects the ministers proposed to achieve
by the struggle in which they had embarked the nation.
If these are found to agree, in the main, with the aim
they should have kept before them, through realizing the
character of the general contest, and Great Britain's proper
part in it, the policy of the war will be justified. It will
then only remain to consider how well the general direction given to the naval and military operations furthered
the objects proposed, — whether the strategy of the war
was well adapted to bring its policy to a successful
issue.

The sudden revulsion of feeling in the British ministry,
consequent upon the decrees of November 19 and December
15, has been mentioned. It was then realized that not
only the internal quiet of Great Britain was endangered,
but that the political stability of Europe was threatened
by a Power whose volcanic energy could not be ignored.
There was not merely the fear that extreme democratic
principles would be transmitted from the masses of one
country to those of another still unprepared to receive
them. To say that the British Government went to war
merely to divert the interest of the lower orders from internal to foreign relations is not a fair statement of the
case. The danger that threatened England and Europe
was the violent intervention of the French in the internal
affairs of every country to which their armies could penetrate. This purpose was avowed by the Convention, and

how sincerely was proved by the history of many ·an adjoining state within the next few years. Although the
worst excesses of the Revolution had not yet occurred,
enough had been done to indicate its tendencies, and ·to
show that, where it prevailed, security of life, property,
and social order disappeared.

Security, therefore, was from the first alleged as the
great object of the war by the Prime Minister, who undoubtedly was the exponent of the government, as truly
as he was the foremost man then in England. In his
speech of February 12, 1793, upon the French declaration
of war, he returns again and again to this word, as the
key-note to the British policy.

"Not only had his Majesty entered into no treaty, but no
step even had been taken, and no engagement formed on the
part of our Government, to interfere in the internal affairs of
France, or attempt to dictate to them any form of constitution. I declare that the whole of the interference of Great
Britain has been with the general view of seeing if it was
possible, either by our own exertions or in concert with any
other Power, to *repress this French system of aggrandizement
and aggression*, with the view of seeing whether we could not
re-establish the blessings of peace; whether we could not,
either separately or jointly with other Powers, provide for
the *security* of our own country and *the general security of
Europe*."

It is only fair to Pitt to compare the thought underlying this speech of February 12, 1793, with that of February 17, 1792, already quoted, in order that there may be
realized the identity of principle and conviction which
moved him under circumstances so diverse. This position he continually maintained from year to year; nor
did he, when taunted by the leader of the Opposition with
lack of definiteness in the objects of the war, suffer himself to be goaded into any other statement of policy. It
was in vain that the repeated jeer was uttered, that the

ministry did not know what they were driving at; and
when the constant recurrence of allied disasters and
French successes on the Continent, preceding as they did
the most brilliant successes of the British navy, made yet
more poignant the exultation of the Opposition, Pitt still
refused, with all his father's proud tenacity, to give any
other account of his course than that he sought security —
peace, yes, but only a secure peace. To define precisely
what success on the part of Great Britain, or what reverses suffered by France, would constitute the required
security, was to prophesy the uncertain fortunes of war,
and the endurance of that strange madness which was
impelling the French nation. When a man finds his interests or his life threatened by the persistent malice of
a powerful enemy, he can make no reply to the question,
how long or how far he will carry his resistance, except
this: that when the enemy's power of injury is effectually
curtailed, or when his own power of resistance ends,
then, and then only, will he cease to fight. It fell to
Pitt's lot, at one period of the war, to be brought face to
face with the latter alternative; but the course of the
French Government — of the Directory as well as of
Napoleon — justified fully the presentiment of the British
Government in 1793, that not until the aggressive power
of France was brought within bounds, could Europe know
lasting peace. Peace could not be hoped from the temper of the French rulers.

Whatever shape, therefore, the military operations
might assume, the object of the war in the apprehension
of the British minister was strictly defensive; just as the
French invasion of the Austrian Netherlands, though an
offensive military operation, was, in its inception, part of
a strictly defensive war. To the larger and more general
motive of her own security and that of Europe, there was
also added, for Great Britain, the special treaty obligation to assist Holland in a defensive struggle, — an obliga-

tion which was brought into play by the French declaration
of war against the United Provinces. It is necessary to
note the two causes of war, because the relation of Great
Britain to the wider conflict was different from that which
she bore to the defence of Holland, and entailed a different line of action. The treaty called upon her to contribute a certain quota of land forces, and the character of her
particular interest, in both the Netherlands and Holland,
made it expedient and proper that British troops should
enter the field for their protection; but after the disastrous campaign of 1794 had subdued Holland to France,
and a revolution in its government had changed its relations to Great Britain, the troops were withdrawn, and
did not again appear on the Continent until 1799, when
favorable circumstances induced a second, but futile attempt to rescue the Provinces from French domination.

The part borne by the troops of England in the earlier
continental campaigns was therefore but an episode, depending upon her special relations to Holland, and terminated by the subjection of that country to France. What
was the relation of Great Britain to the wider struggle,
in which, at the beginning, almost all the nations of the
Continent were engaged? What functions could she discharge towards curtailing the power of France, and so
restoring to Europe that security without which peace is
but a vain word? Upon the answers to these questions
should depend the criticism of the use made by the British ministry of the nation's power. To condemn details
without having first considered what should be the leading
outlines of a great design, is as unsafe as it is unfair; for
steps indefensible in themselves may be justified by the
exigencies of the general policy. It is not to be expected
that, in a war of such vast proportions and involving such
unprecedented conditions, serious mistakes of detail should
not be made; but, if the great measures adopted bear a
due proportion both to the powers possessed and to the

end aimed at, then the government will have fulfilled all that can be demanded of it. The sea power which constituted the chief strength of Great Britain furnished her with two principal weapons: naval superiority, which the course of the war soon developed into supremacy, and money. The traditional policy of a strong party in the state, largely represented in the governing classes, was bitterly adverse to a standing army; and the force actually maintained was to a great extent neutralized by the character of the empire, which, involving possessions scattered over all quarters of the globe, necessitated dispersion instead of concentrated action. The embarrassment thus caused was increased by the dangerously discontented condition of Ireland, involving the maintenance of a considerable permanent force there, with the possibility of having to augment it. Furthermore, the thriving condition of the manufactures and commerce of England, protected from the storm of war ravaging the Continent and of such vital importance to the general welfare of Europe, made it inexpedient to withdraw her people from the ranks of labor, at a time when the working classes of other nations were being drained for the armies.

For these reasons great operations on land, or a conspicuous share in the continental campaigns became, if not absolutely impossible to Great Britain, at least clearly unadvisable. It was economically wiser, for the purposes of the coalitions, that she should be controlling the sea, supporting the commerce of the world, making money and managing the finances, while other states, whose industries were exposed to the blast of war and who had not the same commercial aptitudes, did the fighting on land. This defines substantially the course followed by the ministry of the day, for which the younger Pitt has been most severely criticised. It is perhaps impossible to find any historian of repute who will defend the general military conduct of the Cabinet at whose head he stood; while the brilliant successes of the Seven Years' War have offered a ready text for disparagers, from his contemporary, Fox, to those of our own day, to draw a mortifying contrast between his father and himself. Yet what were the military enterprises and achievements of the justly famed Seven Years' War? They were enterprises of exactly the same character as those undertaken in the French Revolutionary War, and as those which, it may be added, are so constant a feature of English history, whether during times of European peace or of European war, that it may reasonably be suspected there is, in the conditions of the British empire, some constant cause for their recurrence. Like the petty wars which occur every few years in our generation, they were mixed military and naval expeditions, based upon the fleet and upon the control of the sea, scattered in all quarters of the world, employing bodies of troops small when compared to the size of continental armies, and therefore for the most part bearing, individually, the character of secondary operations, however much they may have conduced to a great common end.

It is an ungracious task to institute comparisons; but, if just conclusions are to be reached, the real facts of a case must be set forth. The elder Pitt had not to contend with such a navy as confronted his son at the outbreak of the French Revolution. The French navy, as is avowed by its historians, had received great and judicious care throughout the reign of Louis XVI.; it had a large and splendid body of ships in 1793; it enjoyed the proud confidence of the nation, consequent upon its actions in the war of 1778; and, although its efficiency was fatally affected by the legislation of the National Assembly and by the emigrations, it was still an imposing force. Not until years of neglect had passed over it, and the fatal Battle of the Nile had been fought, did its character and

weight sink to the same relative insignificance that the
elder Pitt encountered in the Seven Years' War. The
elder, like the younger, shaped his system of war upon the
control of the sea, upon the acquisition of colonies, upon
subsidizing allies upon the Continent, and, as main outlines of policy, these were undoubtedly correct; but the
former had in his favor heavy odds in the weak condition
of the French navy, and in having on his side the great
military genius of the age. On the side of the elder Pitt
fought Frederick the Great, against a coalition, numerically overwhelming indeed, but half-hearted, ill-knit,
and led by generals far inferior to their great opponent,
often mere creatures of the most corrupt Court favor.
Against the younger Pitt arose a greater than Frederick,
at the very moment of triumph, when the combined effects
of the sea power of England, of the armies of Austria, and
of the incompetency of the Directory had brought the
Revolution "to bay,"—to use the words of a distinguished French naval officer and student.[1] In 1796 and
in 1799 Bonaparte, and Bonaparte alone, rescued from
impending destruction—not France, for France was not
the object of Pitt's efforts—but that "system of aggrandizement and aggression" to which France was then
committed.

The elder Pitt saw his work completed, though by
weaker hands; the younger struggled on through disappointment after disappointment, and died under the
shadow of Austerlitz, worn out in heart and mind by the
dangers of his country. Contemporaries and men of later
generations, British and foreigners, have agreed in attributing to him the leading part in the coalitions against
Revolutionary France; but they have failed to admit the
specific difficulties under which he labored, and how
nearly he achieved success. It is easy to indulge in
criticism of details, and to set one undertaking against

[1] Jurien de la Gravière, Vie de l'Amiral Baudin, p. 9.

another; to show the failures of expeditions landed on
the French coast in the Seven Years' War; to point out
that Wolfe's conquest of Canada in 1759, by freeing the
American colonies from their fear of France, promoted
their revolt against Great Britain, while Nelson in 1798,
and Abercromby in 1801, saved Egypt, and probably India
also, to England; to say that the elder Pitt did not regain
Minorca by arms, while the younger secured both it and
Malta. Martinique fell to the arms of both; the Cape of
Good Hope, Ceylon, Trinidad, prizes of the later war,
may fairly be set against Havana and Manila of the
earlier. In India, Clive, the first and greatest of British
Indian heroes, served the elder Pitt; yet before the arms
of the younger fell Mysore, the realm of Hyder Ali and
Tippoo Saib, the most formidable enemies that Britain
had yet met in the Peninsula. Such comparisons and
arguments are endless; partly because there is much to
be said on both sides, but chiefly because they concern
details only, and do not touch the root of the matter.

The objects of the two Pitts were different, for the circumstances of their generations were essentially diverse.
The task of the one was to extend and establish the great
colonial system, whose foundations had been laid by
previous generations, and to sustain in Europe the
balance of power between rival, but orderly, governments; that of the other was to steady the social order
and political framework of Great Britain herself, and of
Europe, against a hurricane which threatened to tear up
both by the roots. Each in his day, to strengthen his
country and to weaken the enemy, pursued the same great
line of policy, which in the one age and in the other fitted
the situation of Great Britain. To extend and consolidate
her sea power; to lay the world under contribution to her
commerce; to control the sea by an all-powerful navy; to
extend her colonial empire by conquest, thereby increasing her resources, multiplying her naval bases, and depriv-

ing her enemy alike of revenues and of points whence he could trouble English shipping; to embarrass the great enemy, France, by subsidizing continental allies,— such was the policy of both the Pitts; such, alike in the Revolution and in the Seven Years' War, was the policy imposed by a due recognition, not only of the special strength of Great Britain, but of her position in relation to the general struggle. Frederick in the one case, Austria in the other, needed the money, which only the sustained commercial prosperity of England could supply. The difference in the actual careers run by the two statesmen is that the son had to meet far greater obstacles than the father, and that, so far as the part of Great Britain herself was concerned, he achieved equal, if not greater, successes. The father had to contend, not against the mighty fury of the French Revolution, but against the courtier generals and the merely professional soldiery of Louis XV. and his mistresses; he had an allied America; he met no mutiny of the British fleet; he was threatened by no coalition of the Baltic Powers; he encountered no Bonaparte. It was the boast of British merchants that under his rule "Commerce was united to and made to grow by war;" but British commerce increased during the French Revolution even more than it did in the earlier war, and the growth of the British navy, in material strength and in military glory, under the son, exceeded that under the father.

In history the personality of the elder statesman is far more imposing than that of the younger. The salient characteristic of the one was an imperious and fiery impetuosity; that of the other, reserve. The one succeeded in power a minister inefficient as an administrator, weak in nerve, and grotesque in personal appearance; the striking contrast presented by the first William Pitt to the Duke of Newcastle, his aggressive temper, the firm self-reliance of his character, his dazzling personality, around which a dramatic halo clung even in the hour of his death, made a vivid impression upon the imagination of contemporaries, and have descended as a tradition to our own days. Save to a few intimate friends, the second Pitt was known to his fellow-countrymen only on the benches of the House of Commons. A temper as indomitable as his father's bore in silence the vastly greater and more prolonged strain of a most chequered struggle; only a few knew that the strain was endured with a cheerfulness, a calmness, and a presence of mind, which of themselves betoken a born leader of men. In the darkest hour, when the last ally, Austria, had forsaken England and consented to treat with France, when the seamen of the fleet had mutinied, and British ships of war, taken violently from their officers, were blockading the approaches to London, Pitt was awakened during the night by a member of the Cabinet with some disastrous news. He listened quietly, gave his directions calmly and clearly, and dismissed the messenger. The latter, after leaving the house, thought it necessary to return for some further instruction, and found the minister again sleeping quietly. The incident is a drama in itself.

In considering the use made of Great Britain's powers for war by the administration of the second Pitt, the broad outlines should be regarded, not as a simply military question, — such as the combinations of a general officer in a campaign, — but as efforts of statesmanship, directing arms in an attempt to compass by force the requirements considered to be most decisive in a political situation. The office of the statesman is to determine, and to indicate to the military authorities, the national interests most vital to be defended, as well as the objects of conquest or destruction most injurious to the enemy, in view of the political exigencies which the military power only subserves. The methods by which the military force will proceed to the ends thus indicated to it — the numbers, character, equipment of the forces to be employed, and their management in campaign —·are technical matters, to be referred to the military or naval expert by the statesman. If the latter undertakes to dictate in these, he goes beyond his last and commonly incurs misfortune.

It is not likely that such a division of labor, between the statesman, the soldier, and the seaman, is ever formally made. It is enough if it be practically recognized by the due influence of the military element in deciding details, and by its cheerful obedience in carrying out the views of the government whose servant it is. In criticising results it is fair to assume, where not otherwise proved, that for the general direction of the war the government is responsible, and that in the particular management of military movements the advice of professional men has had just weight. A somewhat striking illustration of this is to be found in the change of naval strategy, within the limits of the Channel fleet, when, without any change in the government, the positive convictions and stringent methods of Lord St. Vincent set aside, in 1800, the traditions of Lord Howe and Lord Bridport.

What then was the general direction imparted to military movements by a government which had announced its object in the war to be the attainment of security, by "repressing the French system of aggrandizement and aggression"?

Owing to the distracted condition of France, many confusing cross-lights were at first cast upon that central theatre of European disturbance, by movements whose force it was impossible rightly to estimate. Such were the risings in La Vendée and Brittany, the revolt at Lyon, the delivery of Toulon to the allied fleets. Experience justifies the opinion that such insurgent movements, involving but a part of a nation, are best left to themselves, supported only by money and supplies. If, thus aided, they have not the vitality to make good their

cause, the presence of foreign troops, viewed ever with
jealousy by the natives, will not insure success. It is,
however, the French Revolution itself that furnishes the
surest illustrations of this truth, shedding upon it a light
which Pitt did not have to guide him. Such embarrassments of the French Government were naturally thought
to give opportunity for powerful diversions; the more so
as the amount of disaffection was much exaggerated, and
the practice of partial descents upon the French coasts
had come down unquestioned from previous wars.

To this mistake, as natural as any ever made in war,
and to the treaty obligation to support Holland, is to be
attributed much of the misdirection given to the British
army in the first two years of the war. When the illusion was over, and Holland conquered, the military effort
of Great Britain was at once concentrated on its proper
objects of ruling the sea and securing positions that contributed to naval control and commercial development.
Even in 1793 a respectable force had been sent to the
West Indies, which in 1794 reduced all the Windward
Islands. Stretching its efforts too far, reverses followed;
but in 1795 a powerful fleet was sent with sixteen thousand troops commanded by Sir Ralph Abercromby, the
best general officer revealed by the early part of the war.
From the first, Pitt had seen the necessity of controlling
the West Indies. That necessity was twofold: first, by
far the greatest fraction of British trade, over one fourth
of the whole, depended upon them; and, second, the
enemy's islands were not only valuable as producing,
they were above all the homes of cruisers that endangered
all commerce, neutral as well as British. To control the
whole Caribbean region was, among those objects that lay
within the scope of the British Government, the one most
essential to the success of the general war. To sneer at
the attempt as showing merely a wish for sugar islands is
to ignore the importance of the West Indies to the finan-

cial stability of Great Britain; upon whose solvency depended, not only the maritime war, but the coalitions whose aid was needed to repress "the system of French aggression."

Abercromby restored England's control over the lesser Antilles, except Guadaloupe, and added to her possessions Trinidad and the Dutch colonies on the mainland. Although unable to retain Haïti, whose ports were for some time occupied, the British navy ensured its loss to France and the final success of the negro revolt; and commercial relations were established with the new government. During the same period the Cape of Good Hope, Ceylon, and other Dutch and French possessions in India were reduced by similar expeditions. These not only extended the sphere of British commerce; they contributed yet more to its enlargement by the security resulting from the conversion of hostile to friendly ports, and the consequent diminution of enemy's cruisers.

It is a singular fact that neither the extraordinary commercial prosperity secured by these successes, nor the immense development of the navy during Pitt's administration, is mentioned in the celebrated denunciation of his "drivelling" war policy by Macaulay. Of naval administration the latter speaks, in order to assign the credit to another; on commercial and naval expansion he is silent. Yet no factors in the war were so important. The one sustained Great Britain, on whose shoulders was upborne the whole resistance of Europe; the other crushed France by a process of constriction which, but for Bonaparte, would have reduced her at an early period, and to free her from which Napoleon himself was driven to measures that ruined him. These important results were obtained by lengthening the cords and strengthening the stakes of British commerce, by colonial expansion and safe-guarding the seas, and by the growth of the navy,— none of which objects could have been accomplished without the hearty support of the Prime Minister. From the co-operation of these causes, and the restrictions placed on neutral trade, the commerce of Great Britain increased by 65 [1] per cent between 1792 and 1800, while the loss by capture was less than 2½ per cent on the annual volume of trade.

The directly offensive use of Great Britain's maritime power made by the ministry, in order to repress the French system of aggression, consisted in throwing back France upon herself, while at the same time cutting off her resources. The continental armies which begirt her on the land side were supported by subsidies; and also when practicable, as in the Mediterranean, by the co-operation of the British fleets, to whose influence upon his Italian campaign in 1796 Bonaparte continually alludes. To seaward the colonial system of France was ruined, raw material cut off from her manufactures, her merchant shipping swept from the sea. In 1797 the chief of the Bureau of Commerce in France wrote: "The former sources of our prosperity are either lost or dried up. Our agricultural, manufacturing, and industrial power is almost extinct." [2] At the same time, while not denying the right of neutrals to trade with ports not blockaded, every restriction that could be placed upon such trade by stringent, and even forced, interpretations of international law was rigorously imposed by a navy whose power was irresistible. Even provisions (and it will be well for Great Britain of the present day to recall the fact) were claimed to be contraband of war, on the ground that, in the then condition of France, when there was a reasonable hope of starving her into peace, to supply them contributed to prolong hostilities.

[1] That is, about 8 per cent annually. The increase during the four years of the elder Pitt in the Seven Years' War, 1757–1761, was 29 per cent, about 7 per cent annually.

[2] Système Maritime et Politique des Européens dans le 18ᵐᵉ siècle, par Arnould. Paris, 1797.

So severe was the suffering and poverty caused by this isolation, that in the moment of his greatest triumph, immediately after signing the peace of Campo Formio, which left Great Britain without an ally, in October, 1797, Bonaparte wrote: "Either our government must destroy the English monarchy, or must expect to be itself destroyed by the corruption and intrigue of those active islanders. Let us concentrate all our activity upon the navy and destroy England." The Directory, conscious that its navy was paralyzed and that its *guerre de course*, pursued since 1795 against British commerce, had not seriously affected the latter, although 1797 was the year of its lowest depression, could see no further means of injuring England except by attacking the neutral carriers of her wares. Affecting to regard them as accomplices in Great Britain's crimes against humanity, it procured from the Convention, in January, 1798, a decree that "every vessel found at sea, having on board English merchandise as her cargo, in whole or in part, shall be declared lawful prize, whosoever shall be the proprietor of the merchandise, which shall be reputed contraband for this cause alone, that it comes from England or her possessions." At the same time orders were issued to confiscate property of British origin wherever found on shore, and domiciliary visits were authorized to insure its discovery. Napoleon was therefore perfectly justified in declaring in later years that the Directory outlined the policy of his Continental System, embodied in his Berlin and Milan decrees of 1806 and 1807.

To the Directory the attempt thus to destroy British prosperity worked disaster. To Napoleon it brought ruin, owing to the greater vigor, wider scope, and longer duration which he was able to impart to the process. The aim of his Berlin and Milan decrees, like that of the Directory, was to undermine British trade by depriving it of the necessary concurrence of neutral carriers. As this alone would not be enough, he determined to support the decrees by excluding Great Britain from her principal market, to close the entire Continent to all goods coming from her or her colonies, or even passing through her ports. For this purpose — to carry out this gigantic project — edict after edict was issued to France and her allied countries; for this purpose annexation after annexation to the empire was made; for this purpose a double cordon of French troops lined the shores of the Continent from France to the Baltic; for this purpose British goods were not only seized but publicly burned throughout his dominions; for this purpose demands were made upon all neutral states to exclude British manufactures and colonial produce; for this purpose the calamitous Spanish war was incurred;[1] and finally, for this purpose reiterated and imperious complaints were addressed to the czar on his failure to enforce the exclusion, and, upon his persistence, the fatal invasion of Russia followed.

The justice or wisdom of this course is not here in question. It is enough to say that it nearly ruined Great Britain, but entirely ruined Napoleon. The noticeable point, bearing upon the wisdom of Pitt's military policy, is that Napoleon was forced into it by that policy, because England was destroying him, and he had no other means of injuring her. Great Britain's success not only followed, but was consequent upon steady adherence to the main features of Pitt's policy. Military writers say that success on a battlefield is of slight avail if the strategic line of operations is ill-chosen, and that even a great defeat may be redeemed if the position has been taken in accordance with the strategic conditions of the campaign. This amounts to saying, in non-military language, that hard blows are useless if not struck on the right spot.

[1] For Napoleon's own assertion of this fact, see " Note pour le Ministre des Relations Extérieures," Corr. de Nap., Oct. 7, 1810. See also *ante.* p. 320.

Numerous reverses attended the coalitions against France, although few fell upon Great Britain herself; but none was fatal because the general policy, begun by Pitt and continued by his successors, was strategically sound with reference to the object in view,— namely, "the repression of that system of aggression" which was the very spirit of the French Revolution, formulated by the Convention, adopted by the Directory, inherited and given its full logical development by Napoleon.

It is the fashion with the political heirs of Fox, Pitt's greatest opponent, to draw a marked contrast between the war which preceded and that which followed the Peace of Amiens. In the former it is Great Britain which, in a frenzy of hatred or panic fear toward the French Revolution, becomes the wanton aggressor, and turns a movement that, despite some excesses, was on the whole beneficent, into the stormy torrent of blood that poured over Europe. In the second war, Napoleon is the great culprit, the incarnate spirit of aggression, violence, faithlessness, and insolence; with whom peace was impossible. It is, however, notorious, and conceded by French writers, that the French leaders in 1791 and 1792 wanted war on the Continent;[1] the impartial conduct of the British Cabinet was admitted by the French Government when acknowledging the recall of the British ambassador six months before war broke out;[2] the decrees of November 19 and December 15 are before the reader, as is the refusal of the Convention to give the former a construction conciliatory to Great Britain; the treaty rights of Holland had been set aside by the high hand without an attempt at negotiation, and there can be little doubt that the purpose was already formed to invade her territory shortly. Despite all this,

---

[1] Martin, Hist. de France depuis 1789, vol. i. p. 396.

[2] Annual Register, 1793, p. 163. For the correspondence on that occasion see A. R. 1792; State Papers, pp. 326, 327. See also letter of Le Brun, French Minister of Foreign Affairs, in the Moniteur of Aug. 26, 1792.

not Great Britain, but the Republic, declared war. The treatment, by the Convention and the Directory, of the lesser states that fell under their power,[1] their dealings with Great Britain, their aggressiveness, insolence, and bad faith were identical in spirit with the worst that can be said of Napoleon; the sole difference being that for a weak, incompetent, and many-headed government was substituted the iron rule of a single man of incomparable genius. Scruples were known to neither. The Berlin and Milan decrees, in which was embodied the Continental System that led Napoleon to his ruin, were, as he himself said, but the logical development of the Directory's decree of January, 1798,[2] against which even the long-suffering United States of America rebelled. Both measures struck at Great Britain through the hearts of allies and of neutrals, for whose rights and welfare, when conflicting with the course France wished to take, they showed equal disregard; both were framed in the very spirit of the first National (Constituent) Assembly, which set aside institutions and conventions that did not square with its own ideas of right; which sought justice, as it saw it, by overleaping law.

It is, however, far more important to note, and clearly

[1] The Directory tended to impose upon the smaller states, neighboring to or allies of France, republican constitutions, "unitaires" (centralized) in form, analogous to our own, as Bonaparte had done for the Cisalpine Republic and for Genoa. It had just done so in Holland, where it had raised against the government of the United Provinces a kind of 18th of Fructidor (coup d'état). It now (1798) aimed at revolutionizing Switzerland. Bonaparte urged it on. He had already provoked a revolution in a republic near to and allied with the Swiss, that of the Grisons. — MARTIN: *Hist. de France depuis* 1789, vol. iii. p. 7.

[2] Napoleon's remark referred to the edicts of the Directory, confiscating British goods wherever found on land; but it applies equally to the decree of January, 1798, which extended the edict to the sea: "Le Directoire ébaucha le système du blocus continental; il ordonna la saisie de toutes les marchandises Anglaises qui pouvaient se trouver à Mayence et dans les autres pays cédés à la France." (Commentaires de Napoléon I., Paris, 1867, vol. iii. p. 413.)

to apprehend, that both measures were forced upon the rulers of France by the strategic lines of policy laid down by the ministry of Pitt. The decree of January, 1798, followed close upon the rupture of the peace conferences of Lille, initiated by Pitt in 1797; a rupture brought on by a display of arrogance and insolence on the part of the Directory, similar to that shown by it towards the United States at the same period, that can only be realized by reading the correspondence,[1] and which is now known to have been due, in part at least, to the hope of a bribe from the British ministry.[2] The Berlin decree, which formally began the Continental System, was issued in November, 1806, when Pitt had not been a year in his grave. Both were forced upon the French leaders by the evident hopelessness of reaching Great Britain in any other way, and because her policy of war was hurting France terribly, while sustaining her own strength. In other words, Great Britain, by the strategic direction she gave to her efforts in this war, forced the French spirit of aggression into a line of action which could not but result fatally.[3] But for Bonaparte, the result, nearly attained in 1795 and again in 1799, would have followed then; not even his genius could avert it finally.

It is related that a leader of antiquity once cried to his opponent, "If you are the great general you claim to be, why do you not come down and fight me?" and received the pertinent reply, "If you are the great general you say, why do you not *make* me come down and fight you?" This was precisely what Great Britain effected. By the mastery of the sea, by the destruction of the French colonial system and commerce, by her persistent enmity to

---

[1] This correspondence, so far as published, is to be found in the Annual Register for 1797; State Papers, pp. 181–223.

[2] See Stanhope's Life of Pitt, vol. ii. p. 224 (ed. 1879).

[3] For a graphic description of the effects of the Berlin decree on the Continent, see Fyffe's History of Modern Europe, vol. i. p. 328.

the spirit of aggression which was incarnate in the French Revolution and personified in Napoleon, by her own sustained and unshaken strength, she drove the enemy into the battle-field of the Continental System, where his final ruin was certain. Under the feeble rule of the Directory that ruin came on apace; within a year it was evident that the only gainer by the system was the foe whom it sought to overthrow, that France herself and her allies, as well as neutral Powers, were but being broken down to the profit of Great Britain. Despite the first failure, there was a plausible attraction about the measure which led Napoleon, confident in his strength and genius, to apply it again with the relentless thoroughness characteristic of his reign. For a time it succeeded, owing not only to the vigor with which it was used, but also to Great Britain being exasperated into retaliatory steps which, by forbidding the trade of neutrals to and between all the ports thus closed to British commerce, stopped at its source the contraband trade, which eluded Napoleon's blockade and kept open the way for British exports to the Continent.

The strain, however, was too great to be endured by the great composite political system which the emperor had founded, and through which he hoped to exclude his enemy from every continental market. The privations of all classes, the sufferings of the poorer, turned men's hearts from the foreign ruler, who, in the pursuit of aims which they neither sympathized with nor understood, was causing them daily ills which they understood but too well. All were ready to fall away and rise in rebellion when once the colossus was shaken. The people of Spain, at one extremity of Europe, revolted in 1808; the Czar of Russia, at the other, threw down the gauntlet in 1810, by a proclamation which opened his harbors to all neutral ships bringing colonial produce, the object of Napoleon's bitterest reclamations. In the one case the people refused the ruler put over them to insure a more vigorous enforcement of the continental blockade; in the other the absolute monarch declined longer to burden his subjects with exactions which were ruining them for the same object. The Spanish outbreak gave England a foothold upon the Continent at a point most favorable for support by her maritime strength and most injurious to the emperor, not only from the character of the country and the people, but also because it compelled him to divide his forces between his most remote frontiers. The defection of the czar made a fatal breach in the line of the continental blockade, opening a certain though circuitous access for British goods to all parts of Europe. Incapable of anticipating defeat and of receding from a purpose once formed, Napoleon determined upon war with Russia. He, the great teacher of concentration, proceeded to divide his forces between the two extremes of Europe. The results are well known to all.

It was not by attempting great military operations on land, but by controlling the sea, and through the sea the world outside Europe, that both the first and the second Pitt ensured the triumph of their country in the two contests where either stood as the representative of the nation. Mistakes were made by both; it was the elder who offered to Spain to give Gibraltar for Minorca, which the younger recovered by force of arms. Mistakes many may be charged against the conduct of the war under the younger; but, with one possible exception, they are mistakes of detail in purely military direction, which cannot invalidate the fact that the general line of action chosen and followed was correct. To recur to the simile already borrowed from military art, the mistakes were tactical, not strategic; nor, it may be added, to any great degree administrative.

The possible exception occurred at the beginning of the war, in the spring and summer of 1793. It may be, as has been claimed by many, that a march direct upon

Paris at that time by the forces of the Coalition would have crushed all opposition, and, by reducing the mob of the capital, have insured the submission of the country. It may be so; but in criticising the action of the British ministers, so far as it was theirs, it must be remembered that not only did men of the highest military reputation in Europe advise against the movement, but that the Duke of Brunswick, then second to none in distinction as a soldier, had tried it and failed a few months before. For unprofessional men to insist, against the best professional opinions at their command, is a course whose propriety or prudence can only be shown by the event,— a test to which the advance upon Paris, now so freely prescribed by the wisdom of after-sight, was not brought. One consideration, generally overlooked, may here be presented. To attempt so momentous and hazardous an enterprise, when the leaders to whom its conduct must be intrusted regard it as unwise, is to incur a great probability of disaster. Even Bonaparte would not force his plans upon Moreau, when the latter, in 1800, persisted in preferring his own. Yet this must statesmen have done, had they in 1793 ordered their generals to advance on Paris.

Once lost, the opportunity, if such it were, did not recur. It depended purely upon destroying the resistance of France before it had time to organize. Thenceforward there remained to encounter, not the policy of a court, playing its game upon the chess-board of war, with knights and pawns, castles and armies, but a nation in arms, breathing a fury and inspired by passions which only physical exhaustion could repress. Towards that exhaustion Great Britain could on the land side contribute effectually only by means of allies, and this she did. On the side of the sea, her own sphere of action, there were two things she needed to do. The first was to sustain her own strength, by fostering, widening, and guarding the workings of her commercial system; the second was to cut France off from the same sources of strength and life. Both were most effectually accomplished, — not, as Macaulay asserts, by the able administration of Earl Spencer (whose merit is not disputed), but by the general policy of the ministry in the extension of the colonial sytem, in the wise attention paid to the support of British commerce in all its details, and in the extraordinary augmentation of the navy. Between 1754 and 1760, the period embracing the most brilliant triumphs of the elder Pitt, the British navy increased by 33 per cent. Between 1792 and 1800, under his son, the increase was 82 per cent. How entirely the military management and direction of this mighty force depended upon the sea-officers, and not upon the statesman, when a civilian was at the head of the Admiralty, will be evident to any one studying closely the slackness of the Channel fleet immediately under the eye of Earl Spencer, or the paltry dispositions made in particular emergencies like the Irish invasion of 1796, and contrasting these with the vigor manifested at that very moment under Jervis in the Mediterranean, or later, in the admirable operations of the same officer in command of the Channel fleet.

Few indeed are the statesmen who are not thus dependent upon professional subordinates. Pitt was no exception. He was not a general or an admiral, nor does he appear so to have considered himself; but he realized perfectly where Great Britain's strength lay, and where the sphere of her efforts. By that understanding he guided her movements; and in the final triumph wrought by the spirit of the British nation over the spirit of the French Revolution, the greatest share cannot justly be denied to the chief who, in the long struggle against wind and tide, forced often to swerve from the direct course he would have followed by unforeseen dangers that rose around the ship in her passage through unknown seas, never forgot the goal "Security," upon which from the first his will was set. Fit indeed it was that he should drop at his post just when Trafalgar had been won and Austerlitz lost. That striking contrast of substantial and, in fact, decisive success with bewildering but evanescent disaster, symbolized well his troubled career, as it superficially appears. As the helm escaped his dying hands, all seemed lost, but in truth the worst was passed. "The pilot had weathered the storm."

The death of Pitt was followed by the formation of a ministry of somewhat composite character, centring round his relative and former colleague, Lord Grenville, and his life-long rival, Fox. This held office but for fourteen months; a period long enough for it to afford Napoleon the pretext for his Berlin decree, but not sufficient to impress any radical change upon the main lines of policy laid down by Pitt. Upon its fall in March, 1807, his devoted personal friends and political followers succeeded to power. Confronted almost immediately by the threatening union between the empires of the East and West, of which the known, if concealed, purpose was to divide between France and Russia the control of the Continent, and to subdue Great Britain also by commercial exhaustion, the ministry, both necessarily and by tradition, opposed to this combination the policy transmitted to them by their great leader. Colonial enterprises were multiplied, until it could be said of colonies, as the French Directory had before sorrowfully confessed concerning shipping, that not one was left under a flag hostile to Great Britain. The navy, expanding to its greatest numerical force in 1808, was maintained in equal strength, if in somewhat diminished numbers, up to the termination of the struggle. While unable to prevent the material growth of the French navy by ship-building carried on in its ports, Great Britain continued to impede its progress and cut off its supplies by the close watch maintained over the French coast, by confining its fleets to their harbors, — and so shutting them off from the one drill ground, the sea, — and finally by frustrating Napoleon's project of increasing his own power by violently seizing the vessels of smaller continental states.

The secure tenure of the great common and highway of commerce — the sea — was thus provided for. The enemy's navy was neutralized, his bases abroad cut off, his possessions became the markets as well as the sources of British trade. It was not enough, however, for commerce, that its transit should be comparatively safe. Its operations of exchange needed both materials and markets, both producers and consumers. From these, as is known, Napoleon sought to exclude it by the Continental System, which through the co-operation of Russia he thought could be rendered effective. To this again the ministry of Perceval and Canning opposed the Orders in Council, tempered by the license system, with the double object of prolonging the resistance of Great Britain and sapping that of her enemy; measures which but reproduced, on a vaster scale, the Rule of 1756, with the modifications introduced by Pitt, in 1798, for the same ends.

The question thus resolved itself, as has before been perhaps too often said, into a conflict of endurance, — which nation could live the longest in this deadly grapple. This brings us back again face to face with the great consideration: Was the struggle which began in 1793 one to be solved by a brilliant display of generalship, shattering the organized forces of an ordinary enemy, and with it crushing the powers of resistance in the state? Or had it not rather its origin in the fury of a nation, against which all coercion except that of exhaustion is fruitless? The aims, the tendencies, the excitement of the French people had risen to a pitch, and had made demands, which defied repression by any mere machinery or organization, however skilfully framed or directed. When the movement of a nation depends upon — nay, is the simple evidence of — a profound emotion permeating each individual of the mass, the mighty impulse, from its very diffusion, has not those vital centres of power, the destruction of which paralyzes the whole. Not till the period of passion — necessarily brief, but for the time resistless — has given place to the organization to which all social movement tends, is a people found to have, as the tyrant of antiquity wished, a single neck to be severed by a blow.

The frenzy of the French nation had spent itself, the period of organization had set in, when Bonaparte appeared upon the scene; but, as the tension of popular emotion slackened, there had not been found, in the imperfect organization which sought to replace it, the power to bear the burden of the state. No longer able to depend upon a homogeneous movement of the millions, but only upon the efficient working of the ordinary machinery of civil government and armies, in her case most imperfectly developed, France now offered to the attacks of her enemies those vital points, with which, when crushed, resistance ceases. Military reverses and exhaustion by bad government brought her in 1795, and again in 1799, to her last gasp. At both epochs Bonaparte saved her.

The great captain and organizer not only brought victory with him and restored the machinery of government; he supplied also a centre around which popular enthusiasm and confidence might once more rally. He became not only the exponent of national unity, but in a very real sense the embodiment of those aspirations and aggressive tendencies, which in the first days of the Revolution had bound Frenchmen together as one man, but had afterwards evaporated and frittered away for want of that definiteness of aim and sagacious direction which only a great leader can impart. Under his skilful manipulation the lofty sentiments of the early revolutionists became catchwords, which assured his hold upon the imaginations and enthusiasm of the people, again swayed as one man to follow him in his career of aggression. Metternich well said that Bonaparte was to him simply the incarnation of the Revolution.[1]

It was with these two phases of one and the same condition that Europe had to deal between 1793 and 1814. In the one instance a people unified by a common passion and common aims, in the other the same people concentrated into a common action by submission to the will of a sovereign, apparently resistless in the council as in the field. It is true that the affections of his subjects soon ceased to follow him, except in the armies by whose power he ruled, but the result is the same. All the energies of the nation are summed up in a single overpowering impulse,— at first spontaneous, afterwards artificial, — to which during the first half of Napoleon's career was given a guidance of matchless energy and wisdom.

Such a combination is for the time irresistible, as the continent of Europe proved during long and weary years. Absolute power, concentrated force, central position, extraordinary sagacity and energy, all united to assure to Napoleon the dazzling successes which are matters of history. The duration and the permanent results of this startling career depended, however, upon the staying power of the French nation and upon the steadfastness of the resistance. Upon the Continent, the latter in its actuality ceased. Potentially it remained,— men's hearts swelled to bursting under the tyranny they endured; but before the power and the genius of the great conqueror outward rebellion shrank away. States dared not trust each other,— they could not act together; and so men went silently in the bitterness of their spirits.

There remained one small group of islands, close on the flank of the would-be ruler of the world, with a popula-

[1] Metternich's Memoirs, vol. i. p. 65.

tion numbering little more than half that of his immediate dominions, whose inhabitants deeply sympathized
with sufferings and oppression they were powerless
directly to relieve. The resistance they had offered to
the aggressive fury of the Revolution they continued to
oppose to its successor and representative; but it was not
by direct action in the field, but only by operations
aimed to abridge the resources and endurance of France,
that they could look forward to a possibility of success.
For seven years went on this final silent strife, whose
outlines have been traced in the preceding chapter of this
work. During its continuance Great Britain herself, while
escaping the political oppression and national humiliation undergone by the continental peoples, drank deep
of the cup of suffering. Her strength wasted visibly; but
the mere fact of her endurance and persistence compelled
her enemy to efforts more exhausting, to measures more
fatal, than those forced upon herself. And, while thus
subjected to a greater strain, Napoleon was by Great
Britain cut off from that greatest of all sources of
renewing vitality — the Sea.

The true function of Great Britain in this long struggle
can scarcely be recognized unless there be a clear appreciation of the fact that a really great national movement,
like the French Revolution, or a really great military
power under an incomparable general, like the French
empire under Napoleon, is not to be brought to terms
by ordinary military successes, which simply destroy the
organized force opposed.

Of the latter, the protracted and not wholly hopeless
resistance, which in 1813 and 1814 succeeded even the
great Russian catastrophe, is a signal instance; while to
subvert such a power, wielded by such a man, by any
reverse less tremendous than it then underwent, is hopeless. Two Napoleons do not co-exist. In the former case,
on the other hand, the tangible something, the decisive

point against which military effort can be directed, is wanting. Of this the struggle between the North and South in the American Civil War affords a conspicuous example. Few, probably, would now maintain that the capture of Richmond in the first year of the war, when the enthusiasm of the Southern people was at its height, their fighting force undiminished, their hopes undimmed by the bitter disappointments of a four years' struggle, would have had any decisive effect upon the high-spirited race. Positions far more important fell without a sign of such result. No man could then have put his finger here, or there, and said, "This is the key-stone of resistance;" for in the high and stern feeling of the moment resistance was not here nor there, but everywhere.

So was it in the early flush of the French Revolution. The "On to Paris" of 1793 would probably have had no more decisive results than the "On to Richmond" of 1861, had it been successful. Not till enthusiasm has waned before sorrow, and strength failed under exhaustion, does popular impulse, when deep and universal, acquiesce in the logic of war. To such exhaustion France was brought when Bonaparte took the helm. By his organizing genius he restored her military strength, the material of which still remained, economized such resources as the wastefulness of preceding governments had left, and above all secured for her a further power of endurance by drawing upon the life-blood of surrounding nations. So exhaustion was for the time postponed; but, if the course of aggression which Bonaparte had inherited from the Revolution was to continue, there were needed, not the resources of the Continent only, but of the world. There was needed also a diminution of ultimate resistance below the stored-up aggressive strength of France; otherwise, however procrastinated, the time must come when the latter should fail.

On both these points Great Britain withstood Napoleon.

She shut him off from the world, and by the same act prolonged her own powers of endurance beyond his power of
aggression. This in the retrospect of history was the
function of Great Britain in the Revolutionary and Napoleonic period; and that the successive ministries of Pitt
and his followers pursued the course best fitted, upon
the whole, to discharge that function, is their justification to posterity. It is the glory of Pitt's genius that as
he discovered the object, "Security," so likewise he
foresaw the means, Exhaustion, by which alone the
French propaganda of aggression would be brought to
pause. The eloquent derision poured upon his predictions
of failure from financial exhaustion, from expenditure of
resources, from slackening of enthusiasm, recoils from the
apprehension of the truth. He saw clearly the line of
Great Britain's action, he foresaw the direction of events,
he foretold the issue. How long the line would be, how
the course of events would be retarded, how protracted the
issue, he could not foretell, because no man could foresee
the supreme genius of Napoleon Bonaparte.

INDEX.

Britain, 71–73; exhaustion of national spirit of aggression, 74; aggressions of Bonaparte, 1801–1803, 76–97; cession of Louisiana by Spain, 77; Peace of Amiens with Great Britain, 81; renewal of war, 98; Louisiana ceded to United States, 104; maritime and financial weakness, 106–108; occupation of Hanover and heel of Italy, 109–111; preparations for invasion of England, 111–117; exactions from Spain, 133; Trafalgar campaign, 140–181; its chances of success discussed, 182–184; necessity of invading England, 184; campaign of 1805 and battle of Austerlitz, 181; naval defeat of Trafalgar, 187–195; far-reaching consequences of this battle, 196; succeeded by the Continental System, 197–200; activity of privateers, 207–210; characteristics of privateering, in Europe, 208, in Atlantic, 210, in West Indies, 212, in East Indies, 215–218; destruction of French commerce, 218–220, 375; bitterness against Great Britain and maritime neutrals, 230; anger against United States, 239; measures directed against neutral carriers, 242–248, 250–254; results of these measures, 254–258; quasi war with the United States, 258; true commercial policy of, 262–265, 280, 354; commercial measures of Napoleon, 265; Berlin Decree, 271; campaign against Russia, 273; Peace of Tilsit, 274; invasion of Portugal, 277; Milan Decree, 290; war in Spain, 292; war with Austria, 1809, 314; excessive prices in, 322; internal distress of, 333–337, 340–342, 349; want of credit, 339, 343; disputes with Russia, 344; invasion of Russia, 351; analysis of commercial measures of Napoleon, 351–357; temper and aims of leaders in French Revolution, 359–363, 367, 384, also 74; decrees of November 19, 361, and December 15, 367; effect of the maritime war upon French industry, 395; identity of spirit in the Republic, the Directory, and in Napoleon, 396–399; the struggle with Great Britain one of endurance, 406; similarity of characteristics in the external action of France from 1793–1812, 407–411;

VOL. II. — 27

continued vitality of the movement due to Bonaparte, 407, 408.

Ganteaume, French admiral, report of condition of French naval officers and seamen, 1801, i. 65; injuries received by squadron under his command, 67; commerce-destroying cruise in 1795, 202; brings Bonaparte back from Egypt to France, 323; escape from Brest in 1801, 376, ii. 61; failure to relieve Egypt, 62; maritime prefect at Toulon, 1803, 125; command of Brest fleet, 1804, and instructions from Napoleon, 131, 147; modified instructions, 149; unable to escape from Brest, 153; awaits Villeneuve outside the Goulet, 154.

Genoa, coasting trade with Southern France, i. 195, 200, ii. 7; French intrigues in, i. 201, 213; preparations in, for Egyptian Expedition, 254, 257; organized as Republic of Liguria by Bonaparte, 278, 279; Admiral Bruix reinforces, 313, ii. 5, 6; Masséna besieged in, 20–23; made a military division of France, 69, note, 85; annexed to France, 177; effect of this measure upon Austria, 177.

Gravina, Spanish admiral, commands the allied rear at the battle of Trafalgar, ii. 187, 188, 194.

Great Britain, importance of her action against France, i. 1; results to, of War of 1778, 3, 8; recovery of prosperity under second Pitt, 5; importance to, of public confidence in Pitt, 6; attitude toward Russia, 1770–1790, and interest in the Levant and Baltic, 10–17, 20–23, 25, 27; relations to Holland and the Netherlands, 15–17, 19, 21, 32; relations to Turkey, 12, 22–24; alliance with Prussia and Holland, 19, 21, 22, 25; refuses to interfere in French Revolution, 1791, 29; change of feeling in, 30; recalls her ambassador from Paris, 32; dismisses French ambassador, 34; war declared against, by France, 34; influence of, 1793–1815, 68; condition of navy in 1793, 69–75; policy of, in war of French Revolution, 81; takes possession of Toulon, 92; unpreparedness of, in 1793, 96; military and naval policy, 97·